Evil and Theodicy
in the Theology
of Karl Barth

Issues in Systematic Theology

Paul D. Molnar
General Editor

Vol. 3

PETER LANG
New York • Washington, D.C./Baltimore • Boston
Bern • Frankfurt am Main • Berlin • Vienna • Paris

R. Scott Rodin

Evil and Theodicy in the Theology of Karl Barth

PETER LANG
New York • Washington, D.C./Baltimore • Boston
Bern • Frankfurt am Main • Berlin • Vienna • Paris

Library of Congress Cataloging-in-Publication Data

Rodin, R. Scott.
Evil and theodicy in the theology of Karl Barth / R. Scott Rodin.
p. cm. — (Issues in systematic theology; v. 3)
Includes bibliographical references and index.
1. Theodicy—History of doctrines—20th century. 2. Barth, Karl, 1886–
1968—Contributions in doctrine of theodicy. I. Title. II. Series.
BT160.R57 231'.8'092—dc20 96-30661
ISBN 0-8204-3496-5
ISSN 1081-9479

Die Deutsche Bibliothek-CIP-Einheitsaufnahme

Rodin, R. Scott:
Evil and theodicy in the theology of Karl Barth / R. Scott Rodin.
– New York; Washington, D.C./Baltimore; Boston; Bern;
Frankfurt am Main; Berlin; Vienna; Paris: Lang.
(Issues in systematic theology; Vol. 3)
ISBN 0-8204-3496-5
NE: GT

Cover design by James F. Brisson.

The paper in this book meets the guidelines for permanence and durability
of the Committee on Production Guidelines for Book Longevity
of the Council of Library Resources.

This work is dedicated
to my wife

Linda

whose sacrifice, support, and encouragement
enabled me to undertake and complete this study,
and whose consistent love and spiritual strength
has made this a journey of adventure and joy.

Acknowledgements

I would like to acknowledge the help and support of Professor David Fergusson at the University of Aberdeen, Scotland, who provided sound advice and the necessary balance of criticism and encouragement in the completion of this work.

I also wish to express my gratitude and love to my children; Anthony, Ryan and Lindsay, who in their own way have sacrificed that I might realise this goal, and who have inspired and supported me as only children can.

Finally, this study owes much to my colleagues with whom I have had rich and fruitful dialogue and who always encouraged me when the going got tough. I wish to thank in particular Gary Deddo, Michael Jinkins, and Baxter Kruger for their insights and fellowship in those early days at Aberdeen. I would also especially like to thank my fellow Hay-on-Wye brothers Bruce Norquist, Sam Clark, Jon Smoot, John Yates, and Henry Brglez (the heroes of Gretna Green!) whose humour and candor made learning with them and from them a genuine pleasure. It was in the rich diversity of challenging and enriching environments from the seminar room and private study to Scott Skinners and the Potarch Inn that my own theology and faith has matured, and I am forever indebted to these men for their contribution to this part of my spiritual and professional life.

TABLE OF CONTENTS

CHAPTER I

The Place of Evil and Theodicy in Barth's Theology

Barth's Doctrine of Evil and Theodicy as a Topic of Study

In Karl Barth's long career as a prolific writer, he never wrote a separate piece of work on theodicy. Indeed the task implicit in theodicy, with its basis in apologetics, its 'defense' of a just God, its philosophical orientation and its inherent dualistic basis, all run counter to the underlying themes in Barth's theology. For the great 20th century theologian, God and evil are not two equal factors that need to be reconciled, nor for that matter are they even to be considered on the same terms. Thus Barth's often quoted statement, "As far as possible I would like to avoid mentioning God and the devil in the same breath."[1]

Barth's Christocentric theology and especially his epistemology provide the single unequivocal framework in which he is willing to discuss evil. Therefore, any discussion of evil must acknowledge the indissoluble link of evil, Satan, demons, suffering, and theodicy with the sovereignty God and His self-revelation in Jesus Christ. For this reason, Barth does not have a section which serves as his definitive word on evil, and he does not attempt a specific theodicy. However, within his vast writings, a very clear picture of his doctrine of evil and strong evidence for a resultant theodicy are clearly there to be found. Thus, to understand Barth's view of evil, one must be willing to engage the whole of Barth's theology, for his doctrine of evil is found interwoven with every major doctrine with which he deals. The enormity of this task comes immediately to the fore, yet this is the undeniable direction which a proper study must take.

In this book we will address four main issues in Barth's view of evil; 1) we will introduce four dominant motifs in Barth's theology which provide the essential insight for a proper understanding of his doctrine of evil, 2) we will trace the development and the refinement of these motifs throughout Barth's theology, 3) we will analyze each motif for its strengths and weaknesses and develop from this analysis a definition and a critique of Barth's doctrine of evil, and 4) we will construct from his doctrine of evil a 'Barthian theodicy' and assess its value for the Church, especially with regard to preaching, counseling and Christian ethics.

The question which underlies these objectives is this, "Does Barth's doctrine of evil yield a theodicy which is helpful for the Church today as it struggles with

---

[1] Karl Barth, *Die Kirchliche Dogmatik*, (Edinburgh: T & T Clark and New York: Scribner and Sons, 1956), III/3, p. VI, quoted in Eberhard Busch, *Karl Barth*, (London: SCM Press, 1975), p. 364. Footnotes throughout this book will either refer to this reference by using KD, or they will refer to the English edition, *Church Dogmatics*, Translated by T.F. Torrance and Geoffrey Bromiley, (Edinburgh: T & T Clark, 1936-1969), and will use the abbreviation CD.

the questions of suffering and evil in the time between the resurrection and the *eschaton* ?" We are first interested to discover what Barth believes about evil, its origin, its ontology, its relationship to God and creation, its activity, its power, its limits and its future. We are ultimately interested in the ways in which this doctrine may be useful and helpful to the Christian community as it faces these questions both from without and within.

We must begin by stating our belief that there is a place to talk about a 'Barthian theodicy', even given the strong warnings from Barth on the pitfalls of all theodicies. This belief is accompanied by an acknowledgement of the strong incongruity of the idea of theodicy with Barth's theological methodology as we hear from the likes of H.M. Schulweis, "For Barth, the need for theodicy is itself a symptom of man's enslavement to moral and logical criteria and norms irrelevant to the conduct of the divinely unique One,"[2] and Paul Ricoeur, "What the problem of evil calls into question is a way of thinking submitted to the requirements of logical coherence, that is, one submitted to both the rule of non-contradiction and that of systematic totalization."[3] At the heart of this incongruity is Barth's rejection of all forms of anthropocentric theologizing from which the need to 'justify God' emerges. It also flows from his insistence that God not be defined from any source other than from His own self-revelation in Jesus Christ, and that even there we are forever entrenched in a dialectic of hiddenness and revealedness in our relationship with the God who is both fully revealed and yet who remains the *Deus absconditus.*

George Hunsinger refers to what he calls Barth's particularism and actualism[4] which reject the systemization of theological knowledge. Revelation is both mysterious (particularism) and miraculous (actualism), both of which deny systemization and reject apologetics. The nature of apologetics is both neutral and defensive. Its discipline involves the taking of a neutral stance and from there providing proofs and formulae to defend a point or position. In rejecting the ability for humanity to have such a neutral stance, Barth concludes that apologetics is built upon an impossible presupposition.[5] Particularism

---

[2] H.M. Schulweis, 'Karl Barth's Job', in *The Jewish Quarterly Review*, Volume 65, January 1975, p. 157.

[3] Paul Ricoeur, 'Evil, A Challenge to Philosophy and Theology', in *Journal of the American Academy of Religion*, Volume 53, Part 4, December 1985, p. 635.

[4] George Hunsinger, *How to Read Karl Barth,* (Oxford: Oxford University Press, 1991).

[5] Barth credits Anselm for his basic rejection of apologetics as a special and distinct form of theology. "Dogmatics will always have an apologetic side. In a certain sense all dogmatics is apologetics, namely, in the sense it is setting the limits. But God's revelation defends itself. One of my most famous theological masters is Anselm of Canterbury, who tried to show the context of doctrines and to prove the necessity of reconciliation and the existence of God. The beauty of Christian truth is its *unity.* I am a pupil of Anselm. I wonder what he will say to me in heaven. Even my own brother Heinrich says I have misinterpreted him! Be that as it may; I have *learned* something from Anselm! Let the Christian truth speak for itself. If you start with an apologetic interest, you are lost." (Barth, 'Karl Barth's Table Talk', *Scottish*

demands that theological truths have their basis only and solely in God Himself. There is no independent basis of truth which can be used to defend God or prove Him. The only proof of God comes from God Himself in His acts of Self-revelation. The truth claims of Christianity are self-validating in that the truth of their claims lie solely in God. All other standards are alien standards and must be rejected.

This point shows Barth's position vis-à-vis a formal theodicy. To begin with the question, "If God is all-powerful..." is epistemologically invalid. The question is not the 'if' of God but the proper attitude that all understanding must come by faith through a personal encounter with God in Christ. This does not mean that Barth rejects all forms of apologetics,[6] but it means that in the end, "The fact remains, however, that it [the Word of God] can only speak for itself and show itself to be the basis of our statement."[7] For Barth, any acceptable apologetics must begin by "counting on the Holy Spirit as the only conclusive argument."[8]

In this way, Barth's theology leads us far closer to the need for an 'anthropodicy' than any theodicy. It is humanity[9] which needs justification, and not the God who has revealed Himself, through good and evil, as Lord! Yet we must also understand Barth's pastoral heart and his strident view that theology must serve the Church. The Bible is not closed on the subject of evil and how we are to approach God in response to suffering. Barth would seek an application of his dogmatics which would be of service to the Church and the Christian community, and that is what we offer in the idea of a 'Barthian theodicy'. Even given Barth's strong sense of mystery within the limitations of human language, and given the depth and breadth of the breach which divides the

---

Journal of Occasional Papers, (London: Oliver and Boyd, 1963), pp. 44-45) He continues later, "The best apologetic is a good dogmatics. Truth will speak for itself. You cannot convince people if you are going the wrong way. You must trust in a good way and use it. Anselm was an apologist, but he trusted in the inner strength of his own way. Anselm liked to speak of the beauty of theology - a very strong evidence, but beginning with God, not general principles. In his faith, or in his faith in the object of faith, he wrote theology. Let us trust the inner witness of the Spirit." (Ibid., p. 62)

6   Barth makes this clear in stating that the only form of acceptable apologetics is that "which is a necessary function of dogmatics to the extent that this must prepare an exact account of the presupposition, limits, meaning and basis of the statements of the Christian confession, and thus be able to give this account to any who may demand it." (CD IV/3, p. 109)

7   CD IV/3, p. 109.

8   Ibid.

9   It is our desire to use gender inclusive language wherever possible when referring to humanity, while we will use masculine pronouns for God which we feel is Scripturally required. However, Barth and most all writers up to the most recent have used the masculine 'man' as the inclusive noun to represent all humanity, and as such, when we are in dialogue with Barth, it will be necessary that we use similar language to keep the meaning of our analysis and critique clear.

non-divine creature from the Wholly Other and sovereign God, there is still a desire within Barth to say something concrete about suffering and evil which can yield for us what would be his own answer to the question of the problem of evil.

Methodology for this Study

Beginning in 1932 with the publication of CD I/1, Barth began to work through the full implications of the methodological tools he acquired in his shift to the *analogia fidei*, in conjunction with his new Christological concentration and his emerging realism. Thus it is not surprising that it is in the 9,600+ pages of Barth's *Church Dogmatics* that his handling of the issue of evil and theodicy are given their fullest and most comprehensive treatment. Barth's treatment of evil never seems to come easy and his reluctance at giving the issue more than the bare minimum attention required of a comprehensive dogmatic is the result of his rejection of any form of dualism and his view of evil within a Christocentric theology. Yet despite this reluctance Barth goes on to state that with regard to the study of evil, "This does not mean, of course, that we ought not to proceed here and everywhere with the greatest intellectual probity and with rigorous logic and objectivity."[10] Indeed the *Church Dogmatics* embraces the theme of evil and the more specific manifestations of it in sin and death throughout their entirety. John Hick commented,

> If one were to bring together the 98-page section on evil in volume III/3, paragraph 50; the 40-page exegesis of Genesis 1, 1–5 in volume III/1, paragraph 41,2; the 58-page discussion of the goodness of the created world in volume III/1, paragraph 42,3; and the 178-page treatment of sin and the fall in IV/1, paragraph 59, one would have assembled a full-scale and even massive treatise on the subject.[11]

Hick is right and yet he has only scratched the surface of Barth's presentation and discussion of the subject.[12] In fact it is surprising that Hick chose to list such a modest number of references in the *Church Dogmatics*. A

---

[10] CD IV/3.1, p. 295.

[11] John Hick, *Evil and the God of Love*, (New York: Harper and Row, 1966), pp. 132-133.

[12] We can add in support of this the words of Herbert Hartwell who, commenting on the importance of CD III/1, §42 (The Yes of God the Creator) and CD III/3, §50 (God and the Nihil) concludes, "they not only render, if viewed synoptically, Barth's view on theodicy but are of basic significance to the whole of his theology." (Hartwell, *The Theology of Karl Barth,* (London: Gerald Duckworth & Co., 1964), p. 19)

close examination of the work as a whole will show that in no less than 28 of its 73 sections, evil, sin and death are given major treatment.[13]

Because of the nature of the *Church Dogmatics,* a topical approach to this subject is inadequate.[14] Barth intended to structure his exposition in such a way as to do justice to the Subject and Object of his theology. As he develops his themes within this structure, he also develops his views of evil in its relationship to them. Being true to this Subject only, Barth utilizes a structure which is dictated by it and which it demands, and since evil is wholly dependent upon the same Object and Subject, it too is developed within this Christocentric framework.

We will look at Barth's doctrine of evil then in two different phases. First, we will trace briefly the development of the doctrine of evil in Barth's early theology up to 1932 and examine his approach to the subject of evil within a broader understanding of his theological agenda as a whole. Secondly, we will look in-depth specifically at five sections in the *Church Dogmatics* in which Barth deals most directly with the subject: the Perfections of God (CD II/1 §29–31); Doctrine of Election (CD II/2, §32–35); Doctrine of Creation and Providence (CD III/1, §41–42, and CD III/3, §48–49); Nothingness (CD III/3, §50); and The Prophetic Office of Christ (CD IV/3, §69–70). From these two studies we will conclude by looking again at the question posed by theodicy and Barth's answer, an answer which he clearly renders despite his reluctance to use theodicy as a definitive process for discerning a truly Christian and biblical understanding of evil in its relationship to God and His creation.

---

[13] This list is as follows (section numbers only) §14, §28, §29, §30, §31, §32, §33, §34, §35, §39, §41, §42, §47, §48, §49, §50, §51, §56, §57, §59, §60, §61,§64, §65, §69, §70, §72, and §73, and §78 in the *Christian Life.*

[14] In support of this choice of methodology we cite Geoffrey Bromiley, "Why is it that the selective approach is not adequate? The reason lies in Barth's theological method. Barth does not simply deal with an individual doctrine in its proper sequence and then move on to the next. For him, God himself, not the doctrines, constitutes the theme of theology... Ideally, no one should say anything about any of Barth's doctrines without first reading through the whole series at least once, and preferably more than once." (Geoffrey Bromiley, *Introduction to the Theology of Karl Barth,* (Edinburgh: T & T Clark, 1979), p. x-xi.) Imagine the decrease in the number of off-base critiques of Barth if this simple rule was followed! Hartwell states, "The *Church Dogmatics* is therefore like the painting of a vast landscape in which only the sum total of its innumerable details is capable of bringing out its full meaning and of showing how everything hangs together. Hence, if we want to do justice to the one or other aspect of Barth's theology, we shall have to take into account its other aspects as well, seeing the aspect in question in light of his whole teaching." (Hartwell, *The Theology of Karl Barth, op. cit.,* p. 17) These two statements should suffice as ample evidence of our choice of methodology in studying the doctrine of evil as it is found in the *Church Dogmatics.*

The Study of Suffering

Before turning to Barth's theology we must decide the specific way in which we will deal with suffering. The theodicy question with which we are concerned is raised from the experience of human suffering. Therefore, a key element will be our contention that the traditional process of treating suffering as a single category is inherently flawed.[15] Scripture treats suffering in a variety of forms and their internal distinction is absolutely critical if we are to stay clear of the confusion with which so many doctrines of sin and evil are burdened. Barth must also be listed with those who never made an adequate distinction of what he meant when he spoke of suffering. If we are to reach some helpful conclusions concerning his theodicy, we must first allow Scripture to help us establish the categories in which we will discuss suffering, and then we must examine how Barth's unfolding doctrine of evil enables us to develop our understanding of each.

We discuss suffering according to the following categories, and in our conclusion we will use these categories to further define Barth's own contribution to theodicy from his doctrine of evil.

1. *Suffering as the result of (wages of) sin.* In this category we will consider the forms of suffering which are the consequences of our sinful acts, as opposed to the suffering which is inherent in the world which is in a state of sin (which we will deal with in categories 4 and 5). This category includes the pain and suffering which comes upon us as the direct response and result of our own willful disobedience and rebellion against the grace of God.[16] God is passive in

---

[15] A recent example of a better and more categorical treatment of suffering is given in A. van de Beek's *Why?: On Suffering, Guilt and God*, (Grand Rapids: W.B. Eerdmans Publishing Co., 1990), in Brian Hebblethwaite's analysis in *Evil, Suffering and Religion* , (London: Sheldon Press, 1976), and in Stanley Hauerwas', *Naming the Silences*, (Grand Rapids: W.B. Eerdmans Publishing Co., 1990), where he says, "It is important that we be able to distinguish those forms of suffering that derive directly from the way of life occasioned by our faithfulness to the cross from those forms of suffering that do not... The suffering that is a consequence of our living a faithful life has a different valence than that which is not. It certainly is not less painful, but at least we can understand why it is happening." (p. 85)

[16] There is clear and ample Scriptural evidence to support this category, as sin and its consequences are a main theme in both Old and New Testaments. A few of many references will help demonstrate this form of suffering as it is promised and permitted in Scripture. The results of sin are suffering in many forms: as defeat at the hands of enemies, "Israel has sinned; they have violated my covenant, which I commanded them to keep. They have taken some of the devoted things; they have stolen, they have lied, they have put them with their own possessions. That is why the Israelites cannot stand against their enemies; they turn their backs and run because they have been made liable to destruction. I will not be with you anymore unless you destroy whatever among you is devoted to destruction." (Josh. 7:11-12); as separation from God, "But your iniquities have separated you from your God; your sins have hidden his face from you, so that he will not hear." (Isa. 59:2); as physical and psychological suffering, "All his days the wicked man suffers torment, the ruthless

this category, allowing evil in the response to specific sinful acts as He has done in the entire creation/fall scenario.

2. *Suffering as chastisement and correction from the hand of God.* God allows suffering and even actively brings suffering in order to correct us and bring us to Him and in conformity with His will. This is to be distinguished from category 1, for here God is both active and passive, both bringing the suffering Himself and using the suffering which we bring upon ourselves for a specific good purpose. Although this form of suffering results from a sinful lifestyle or a time of rebellion against Him, what distinguishes it from the suffering we bring upon ourselves is God's good and purposeful use of that which we inevitably bear as a result of our sin.[17]

---

through all the years stored up for him." (Job 15:20), "Some became fools through their rebellious ways and suffered affliction because of their iniquities." (Ps. 107:17), and "He who sows wickedness reaps trouble, and the rod of his fury will be destroyed." (Prov. 22:8); as spiritual suffering, "How much more severely do you think a man deserves to be punished who has trampled the Son of God under foot, who has treated as an unholy thing the blood of the covenant that sanctified him, and who has insulted the Spirit of grace?" (Heb. 10:29), and "But for those who are self-seeking and who reject the truth and follow evil, there will be wrath and anger. There will be trouble and distress for every human being who does evil: first for the Jew, then for the Gentile." (Rom. 2:8-9); and finally the suffering of death, "If we deliberately keep on sinning after we have received the knowledge of the truth, no sacrifice for sins is left." (Hebr. 10:26), "Do not be deceived: God cannot be mocked. A man reaps what he sows. The one who sows to please his sinful nature, from that nature will reap destruction; the one who sows to please the Spirit, from the Spirit will reap eternal life." (Gal. 6:7-8), and "For the wages of sin is death." (Romans 6:23).

[17] We find evidence for God's use of the suffering which we bring upon us and in God's sending suffering in response to our sin, both for the purpose of bringing good in the form of chastisement and correction, from an evil and rebellious action. This is demonstrated in a sampling of Old Testament passages which speak of this suffering as discipline; "Know then in your heart that as a man disciplines his son, so the Lord your God disciplines you."(Deut. 8:5), "Blessed is the man you discipline, O Lord, the man you teach from your law." (Ps. 94:12), "My son, do not despise the LORD's discipline and do not resent his rebuke, because the Lord disciplines those he loves, as a father the son he delights in." (Prov. 3:11-12), "He cuts off every branch in me that bears no fruit, while every branch that does bear fruit he prunes so that it will be even more fruitful." (John 15:2), and "When we are judged by the Lord, we are being disciplined so that we will not be condemned with the world." (1Cor. 11:32); also those which show God's wrath in sending chastisement; "If a man sins against another man, God may mediate for him; but if a man sins against the Lord, who will intercede for him? His sons, however, did not listen to their father's rebuke, for it was the LORD's will to put them to death." (1Sam. 2:25), "Now the Spirit of the Lord had departed from Saul, and an evil spirit from the Lord tormented him." (1Sam. 16:14), "But the king said, 'What do you and I have in common, you sons of Zeruiah? If he is cursing because the Lord said to him, 'Curse David', who can ask, 'Why do you do this?'" (2Sam. 16:10), "Again the anger of the Lord burned against Israel, and he incited David against them, saying, 'Go and take a census of Israel and Judah'." (2Sam. 24:1), "Finally, a spirit came forward, stood before the Lord and said, 'I will entice him'. 'By what means?' the Lord asked. 'I will go out and be a lying spirit in

3. *Suffering for the sake of testing and strengthening faith.* Scripture clearly demonstrates that God chooses to allow or bring suffering upon His people in order to test their faith and to see it strengthened. This is neither suffering as a result of sin nor is it the kind of suffering God uses to chastise and correct. Its purpose and intent is to build up and prepare us for His service. It is God in action in making us into the people He would have us be through the use of test and struggle, and as such it should be the source of blessing and praise.[18]

---

the mouths of all his prophets', he said. 'You will succeed in enticing him', said the Lord. 'Go and do it'." (1Kgs. 22:21), "So now the Lord has put a lying spirit in the mouths of all these prophets of yours. The Lord has decreed disaster for you." Then Zedekiah son of Kenaanah went up and slapped Micaiah in the face. 'Which way did the spirit from the Lord go when he went from me to speak to you?' he asked. Micaiah replied, 'You will find out on the day you go to hide in an inner room'." (1Kgs. 22:23-25), "For this reason God sends them a powerful delusion so that they will believe the lie." (2Ths. 2:11), "And if the prophet is enticed to utter a prophecy, I the Lord have enticed that prophet, and I will stretch out my hand against him and destroy him from among my people Israel." (Ezek. 14:9), "and finally there is the unequivocal evidence that in all suffering as a result of sin, God is in control and ultimately the sender of both good and this form as suffering through evil; When a trumpet sounds in a city, do not the people tremble? When disaster comes to a city, has not the Lord caused it?" (Amos 3:6), "I form the light and create darkness, I bring prosperity and create disaster; I, the Lord, do all these things." (Isa. 45:7), "'Just as I watched over them to uproot and tear down, and to overthrow, destroy and bring disaster, so I will watch over them to build and to plant', declares the Lord." (Jer. 31:28), "[The Lord said,] 'Say this to him: 'This is what the Lord says: I will overthrow what I have built and uproot what I have planted, throughout the land. Should you then seek great things for yourself? Seek them not. For I will bring disaster on all people, declares the Lord, but wherever you go I will let you escape with your life'." (Jer. 45:4-5).

[18] Two things are clear in this category of suffering in Scripture; the suffering is purposeful and directed for the good of the creature, and the suffering comes from God. This is shown in the Old Testament as a process of probing and purification; "Though you probe my heart and examine me at night, though you test me, you will find nothing; I have resolved that my mouth will not sin." (Ps. 17:3), "Many will be purified, made spotless and refined, but the wicked will continue to be wicked. None of the wicked will understand, but those who are wise will understand." (Dan. 12:10), "He will sit as a refiner and purifier of silver; he will purify the Levites and refine them like gold and silver. Then the Lord will have men who will bring offerings in righteousness." (Mal. 3:3); and also as God's direct acts and commands; "Some time later God tested Abraham. He said to him, 'Abraham!' 'Here I am', he replied. Then God said, 'Take your son, your only son, Isaac, whom you love, and go to the region of Moriah. Sacrifice him there as a burnt offering on one of the mountains I will tell you about'." (Gen. 22:1-2), and "Remember how the Lord your God led you all the way in the desert these forty years, to humble you and to test you in order to know what was in your heart, whether or not you would keep his commands." (Deut. 8:2). In the New Testament it is discussed in the form of proper preparation for trials and the perseverance when they come; "He is like a man building a house, who dug down deep and laid the foundation on rock. When a flood came, the torrent struck that house but could not shake it, because it was well built." (Luke 6:48), and "Blessed is the man

4. *Suffering as a result of our faith and faithful obedience.* The Bible also depicts suffering as that which, if we are truly followers of Christ, we will and must endure for our faith. We are commanded to take up our cross and be co-sufferers with Christ. This is the world's response (the world still under the sway of the prince of this world) to our witness. Here God is passive in allowing this suffering to take place as He allowed His own Son to suffer and die, yet He is our refuge and strength and our ever present help in time of need.[19]

5. *Suffering as a result of the sinful state of the world.* We include in this final category the idea of suffering as a result of natural evil and what is referred to as 'innocent suffering'. The world is sinful and evil is manifested in what seems at times to be random acts of violence and destruction. The suffering which has occurred as a result of the great natural disasters in history are dealt with here as the result of a sin-laden world of both humanity and creation. This

---

who perseveres under trial, because when he has stood the test, he will receive the crown of life that God has promised to those who love him." (James 1:12).

[19] Finally, we see that the Christian life brings its own sufferings as first foretold by Jesus; "If the world hates you, keep in mind that it hated me first. If you belonged to the world, it would love you as its own. As it is, you do not belong to the world, but I have chosen you out of the world. That is why the world hates you. Remember the words I spoke to you: 'No servant is greater than his master'. If they persecuted me, they will persecute you also. If they obeyed my teaching, they will obey yours also." (John 15:18-20), "A student is not above his teacher, nor a servant above his master... Anyone who loves his father or mother more than me is not worthy of me; anyone who loves his son or daughter more than me is not worthy of me; and anyone who does not take his cross and follow me is not worthy of me." (Matt. 10:24, 37-38), and we are assured from Jesus that these sufferings will also bring blessings; "Blessed are you when people insult you, persecute you and falsely say all kinds of evil against you because of me." (Matt. 5:11), and in anticipation of the work of Paul, "I will show him how much he must suffer for my name." (Acts 9:16); we then have the examples of this response to suffering in the lives of the apostles; "The apostles left the Sanhedrin, rejoicing because they had been counted worthy of suffering disgrace for the Name." (Acts 5:41), "We always carry around in our body the death of Jesus, so that the life of Jesus may also be revealed in our body." (2Cor. 4:10), "Finally, let no one cause me trouble, for I bear on my body the marks of Jesus." (Gal. 6:17), "I want to know Christ and the power of his resurrection and the fellowship of sharing in his sufferings, becoming like him in his death." (Phil. 3:10), "Now I rejoice in what was suffered for you, and I fill up in my flesh what is still lacking in regard to Christ's afflictions, for the sake of his body, which is the church." (Col. 1:24); and the command and affirmation to do likewise; "For just as the sufferings of Christ flow over into our lives, so also through Christ our comfort overflows." (2Cor. 1:5), "For it is commendable if a man bears up under the pain of unjust suffering because he is conscious of God. But how is it to your credit if you receive a beating for doing wrong and endure it? But if you suffer for doing good and you endure it, this is commendable before God. To this you were called, because Christ suffered for you, leaving you an example, that you should follow in his steps." (1Pet. 2:19-21), "But rejoice that you participate in the sufferings of Christ, so that you may be overjoyed when his glory is revealed." (1Pet. 4:13).

is the state of the post-fallen world. In addition, this category includes all suffering which cannot be attributed to the four categories above. The suffering of children, the senseless and random suffering which is often attributed to fate, the suffering which results from physical and mental diseases of all kinds (although many of these must be attributed to one of the four categories above), and the unbridled evil which has been displayed in the likes of Auschwitz and Buchenwald and all seemingly inexplicable forms of suffering are included in this final category.[20]

Our contention is that only by examining suffering according to this type of categorization can we begin to understand its place in created history and only so can we properly develop a theodicy.

---

[20] This category is dealt with so powerfully in one place in Scripture that our analysis of that instance will more than suffice for the rest. That one place is the book of Job, and Barth's understanding of Job's suffering will be dealt with in this book and will form a crucial component of our conclusion.

CHAPTER II

The Four Motifs in Barth's Doctrine of Evil and Their Development in His Early Theology

The Four Motifs in Barth's Doctrine of Evil

A thorough examination of Barth's doctrine of evil will uncover four dominant motifs which are critical to its proper understanding.[1] These motifs have a long history of development throughout the entirety of Barth's theological writings and they form the very core of his definitive teaching on evil. For this reason, the chief criticisms which emerge from Barth's doctrine of evil are also found within each of these motifs and we will develop them as the story unfolds.

The 'Necessary Antithesis'

In Barth's dialectical theology the use of contradiction was essential to the movement of theological inquiry. In this stage of his theology Barth developed the powerful concept of the 'Yes' and 'No' of God, a concept which was both modified and in many ways emboldened in the later *Church Dogmatics*. In Barth's shift from a dialectical theology, which found its starting point of the sinfulness of humanity, to the *analogia fidei* which started with the grace of the God of self-revelation, the problem of evil was taken back into the primordial time before creation. It is there in the *Church Dogmatics* that Barth will formulate the true understanding of evil in relationship to God and creation.

One conclusion we will draw is that the development of Barth's understanding of evil is not given its primary or even its most important treatment in the much celebrated §50 on *das Nichtige*, but instead this development takes on its definitive shape and form in Barth's Doctrine of God. It is there that evil emerges as the eternally rejected 'not-God' from which God has differentiated Himself and which, in a negative way, defines God. In this sense, in that its ontology lies in its role as the rejected and non-willed side of God's positive will, we find that nothingness in Barth's theology is 'necessary'.[2] From this emerges the most dominant motif in Barth's doctrine of

---

[1] We are using the term 'motif' here to describe a dominant and recurrent theme which, when understood properly, provides the reader with a more perspicacious and focused view of the doctrine as a whole and the proper context for its analysis and critique.

[2] We are using 'necessary' in terms of a factual necessity. That nothingness is defined as 'non-being' does not disqualify this term, for Barth will treat nothingness in such a way as to make this logical necessity an appropriate way of understanding the relationship of God to nothingness.

evil which we will call the 'necessary antithesis' involving evil and sin on one side and salvation and glorification on the other. The centerpiece of this motif is the view that the Fall is the 'necessary antithesis' to *Heilsgeschichte*.

This motif is supported in Barth's doctrines of election and creation in that the eternally-rejected 'not-God' becomes the *tohu wa-bohu* which God rejected in creation, but which will have its inevitable victory over the non-divine creature. This is the basis of Barth's re-worked supralapsarian view of election which is the product of a view of God who is defined in part according to His self-differentiation, and a doctrine of creation as the self-recapitulation of God. Together they give rise to the inevitable fall of humanity and thus God's eternal election of Jesus Christ becomes the ultimate justification for both creation and the Creator.

Additionally, Barth's soteriology and eschatology are heavily influenced by this motif. In the salvific work of Christ there takes place the definitive separation of evil from God as evil is defeated in space and time as it was and is eternally rejected both at the creation and in God's eternal self-differentiation. Eschatologically, humanity is now involved in the fourth separation as we move from the old-person of sin to the new creation. What we await is the revelation of evil's annihilation in the final *parousia* and the actualization of our redemption.

This motif then is the cohesive element in Barth's doctrine of evil and we must pause to look at the ideas of 'necessity' and 'antithesis' to define this motif further.

By using the term '*necessary* antithesis' we are not saying that Barth can be accused of a dualism which would give to evil any independent reality from God, nor one which would give to evil any sense of power or equality to Him. Barth is unequivocally clear that evil is eternally in absolute subjection to God. What we find throughout Barth's theology is a view of evil as a negatively willed, rejected, non-reality, and of sin as the 'impossible possibility'. As they are understood as such, in their 'peculiar ontology' and in a wholly non-dualistic way, they are the 'necessary antitheses' to grace and salvation, and as such are indispensable to the accomplishment of the eternal purposes of God for creation.

We must also clarify the 'necessary *antithesis*' in light of Barth's rejection of the idea of a Hegelian synthesis *(Aufhebung)* which results in seeing the thesis and antithesis as two forces in a sort of equilibrium. In dealing with the antithesis between the *providentia Dei* and the *confusio hominum*, Barth warns of a synthesis which, "takes the contradiction into itself, integrates the two sides and thus overcomes it."[3] The result would be that the two sides, the thesis and antithesis, could then be seen and comprehended together introducing the possibility that these two sides could have a "positive connexion between them and in this interconnexion to interpret them as the two factors or elements of one and the same reality."[4] This would have the result of divesting both of any sense of mystery and of a dissolving of their absolutely distinctive antithetical

---

[3] CD IV/3, p. 703.

[4] Ibid., p. 704.

character. This would place the *confusio hominum* in the positive will of God, giving it respectability and requiring that it be taken seriously as a true possibility.

In positing a 'necessary *antithesis*' we are neither stating that this infers a dualism of God and evil, nor that it gives an independent status to evil, nor is it meant to set evil up as the antithesis to the thesis of God in the type of Hegelian synthesis which Barth has outlined above. What we find in Barth is a view of evil which leads inevitably from his understanding of God's eternal self-distinction and of creation as the self-recapitulation of God. The result is that evil is *necessarily* ushered onto the scene of creation, and man's fall in the face of this is *inevitable*. Therefore, God self-determined to be for humanity in Jesus Christ from all eternity. In succinct terms, this is the foundation for Barth's 'necessary antithesis' in which evil, understood as necessarily a part of creation as a result of the inevitability of the Fall, is involved and used by God in creation to fulfill His good purposes for it and to bring glory to Himself. Thus evil can retain its 'peculiar ontology' of non-reality and still be seen as both 'necessary' and as a true 'antithesis' without resulting in a dissolution of its antithetical nature.

This motif gives us a view of how Barth's entire handling of evil within his theology is cast within a Christocentric frame. All of creation was made with a view to Christ, the Christ of the cross and resurrection. Thus evil, its invasion of creation, its role in salvation history, its overthrow on the cross and its ultimate annihilation are all inextricably tied not only to Christ, but to God's eternal purposes for His creation which could only be accomplished in and through Christ. Once evil is cut loose from this 'necessary antithesis', the entire structure of Barth's creation-covenant teaching falls apart. In this way we will show that the 'necessary antithesis' forms for Barth the ontic basis of evil, and it is his answer to the 'why?' question in his theodicy.

The 'Right and Left Hand of God'

In Barth's use of the 'necessary antithesis' motif, he is keen to combat all forms of dualism and to deny any sense of independence to evil. He must show that evil is wholly dependent upon God and also that God is not the Author of evil. God must be seen to both control evil and yet not to be responsible for evil. To accomplish this, Barth employs the motif of the 'right and left hand of God' which deals with the manifestation of evil as it flows from its ontic basis in the 'necessary antithesis'. God's left hand is associated with the rejecting will of God, that which negates in its non-willing of nothingness. In the providence of God we will see that it is also from the left hand of God that evil is given its power, its limits and its peculiar ontological reality as that which is both controlled by God and yet which is also inimical towards Him. In this way the 'right and left hand of God' motif can be seen to answer the 'how?' question in Barth's theodicy.

Part of this motif is developed from Barth's understanding of the relationship between the love of God and the freedom of God, both of which must be demonstrated in the activity of the left hand as well as the right hand of God. Barth keeps the categories of the 'Yes' and 'No' of God from dialectical theology but gives them a distinctively Christological flavour where the 'No' of God must be seen in its relationship to His eternal 'Yes' in His incarnation. Both 'Yes' and 'No' are efficacious as two sides of God's will, and so the problem of evil is taken up into God in Barth's theology.

Finally, given the present evil in the world, Barth seeks to hold together the seemingly contradictory ideas that evil was completely and utterly destroyed on Calvary, and that it is still a menacing force today, at battle with not only creation, but still in a very real way with God Himself. Barth uses this left hand of God to demonstrate this balance by restoring the older Reformed doctrine of the *voluntas permittens*. Thus evil is permitted by God under His sovereign providence to serve His own purposes, yet as evil it continues to be a threat if it is seen outside of its true status in relationship to Christ, that of brokenness and impotence. This motif then is essential in understanding how Barth seeks to combat all sense of dualism while at the same time preserving the absolute sovereignty of God, all without making God responsible for evil.

Barth's 'Noetic Eschatology'

The third motif necessarily follows from the first two and Barth's soteriology which sees the completed work of salvation in the earthly work of Christ. We use the term 'noetic eschatology' for this motif to describe the fact that in Barth's theology the *eschaton* will be an unveiling of what we already are, and thus is to be wholly 'noetic' (as opposed to 'ontic' or 'salvific'). We recognize that Barth's soteriology includes a crucial role for the human response to grace. For our purposes, we are drawing on the distinction which he maintains between the ontic and noetic because it is critical to Barth's understanding of the role of evil after the cross. Evil exists in the shadow of the cross and the ontic union of all humanity in Christ, and therefore it can only have its peculiar 'being' under the control of the left hand of God. In this scenario, Barth discusses illness, war, suffering and death and he works out his theodicy with the view not towards evil *per se*, but towards the actuality of the eschatological hope of the community.

The tension that exists for Barth is between his most strident declarations of the utter destruction of evil in the historical work of Christ in the cross and resurrection, and the continuing presence and role of evil in this protracted time before the final *parousia*. Because the final *parousia* is wholly revelatory in nature, and in it there is to be expected no ontological alteration to our status as 'in Christ', then the 'permission' of evil and even the continuation of creation after the resurrection is problematic.

Barth's 'Revelatory Positivism'

When we speak about revelation we are confronted by the divine act itself... Revelation in fact does not differ from the person of Jesus Christ nor from the reconciliation accomplished in Him. To say revelation is to say 'The Word became flesh'.[5]

For Barth, divine revelation and the divine Revealer are not separate, for in revelation, "*God* reveals Himself. He reveals Himself *through Himself*. He reveals *Himself*."[6] Therefore the role of the theologian is one of a faithful witness to this divine revelation and so Barth rejects the idea that humanity can conceptualize God in some metaphysical construct or 'systematic theology'.[7] Instead, theology is controlled by its Object, and this 'positivism'[8] is, "the objective fact of a reality outside of man which is neither of man's making nor at his disposal but, on the other hand, inescapably affects him and determines his destiny."[9]

We have termed this motif Barth's 'revelatory positivism' to represent his view that theological language concerning evil and sin is by nature imperfect.[10]

---

[5] CD I/1, pp. 117, 119.

[6] Ibid., p. 296.

[7] Jürgen Moltmann, '*Gottesoffenbarung und Wahrheitsfrage* ', in *Parrhesia* , (Zürich: EVZ-Verlag, 1966), p. 160.· Thus Moltmann writes, *Das Wort Gottes reicht die Wirklichkeit dar, die es ansagt: nämlich Gottes Gottheit und Herrschaft. Von Gott kann man also nur wahrhaftig und begründet reden auf dem Grunde seiner Selbstoffenbarung in seinem Worte. Gotteserkenntnis ist nur auf dem Grunde der Selbstoffenbarung Gottes und des von ihm Erkanntseins möglich. Gott zu denken meint ein Nachdenken seines eigenen Selbstdenkens und des von ihm Gedachtwordenseins. Die Frage nach der Gottheit Gottes kann darum nicht aus Erfahrungen von Welt oder Existenz recht gestellt werden, sondern nur als Rückfrage nach seinem Sein aus dem Hören seines offenbaren Namens.* ("The Word of God proffers the reality which it announces: namely God's deity and power. One can only speak of God truthfully therefore based on the foundation of His self-revelation in His word. Recognition of God is possible only on the basis of God's self-revelation and the being recognized by Him. Thinking of God means reflection on His own self-thinking, being thought-of-by-him. The question or the deity of God cannot be put properly from experiences of the world or existence, but can only be a question about His Being from the hearing of His revealed name.")

[8] "There is in Barth's thought a note of positivism. He is always the champion of the concrete against, for instance, the abstract or merely possible..." (D. MacKinnon, 'Philosophy and Christology', in *Essays in Christology for Karl Barth*, ed. T.H.L. Parker, (London: 1956), p. 283, quoted in David Ford, *Barth and God's Story, op. cit.,* p. 48)

[9] Hartwell, *The Theology of Karl Barth: An Introduction, op. cit.,* p. 27.

[10] We must be clear here to distinguish our use of this term from the famous critique of Dietrich Bonhoeffer and his followers. (Bonhoeffer, *Letters and Papers from Prison*, (London: SCM Press, 1967), see pp. 153, 156f, and 181; and see also Regin

Fundamental for Barth is the distance between God and humanity as a result of sin. In his use and reinterpretation of Anselm, Barth sees that language can be filled up by God to provide a medium of revelation as God reveals Himself in it to us. Yet because the Object of the revelation is ultimately incomprehensible, this mediated revelation can only take the form of analogy. As such, it is always broken and incomplete while at the same time being also adequate as far as our need to know is concerned.

Hunsinger refers to this as Barth's realism which does not equate language with the Subject, yet it assumes that language can be filled out by God in such a way that He can be genuinely known.[11] In this way Barth can say that revelation is neither absolute nor relative but sufficient. It is to be interpreted as a narrative witness and as such it is an appropriate analogical witness with a strictly kerygmatic purpose. In the shift from dialectical theology to the *analogia fidei*, Barth's realism emerges along with the new Christocentric emphasis of his theology. Recasting his theology from Christ's perspective

---

Prenter, *'Dietrich Bonhoeffer und Karl Barth's Offenbarungspositivismus'*, in *Die mündige Welt,* III, 1960, pp. 11f; Martin Storch, 'On the Meaning of 'Revelational Positivism', in *Exegesen und Meditationen zu Karl Barth's Kirklicher Dogmatik,* 1964; Heinrich Ott, *Reality and Faith: The Theological Legacy of Dietrich Bonhoeffer,* (Philadelphia: Fortress Press, 1972), especially pp. 120-146; and in Barth's defense, Helmut Gollwitzer, *'Begegnung mit Dietrich Bonhoeffer'*, in *Ein Almanach,* 1965, p. 112). In his prison letters Bonhoeffer challenged Barth's move from a criticism of religion (which Bonhoeffer wholly embraced) to a 'revelational positivism'. Bonhoeffer saw this shift as creating a 'law of faith' where all revelation is to be accepted on equal footing and one is left to 'Eat bird, or die'. However, Bonhoeffer's strongest critique was the impact of this 'positivist doctrine of revelation' on the incarnation, believing that it 'tears away what is a gift for us' by not treating the incarnation with methodological seriousness. Bonhoeffer saw this as the negative opposite of his own preferred non-religious or existential interpretation. Our use of 'revelatory positivism' is in no way meant to be associated with Bonhoeffer's interpretation or critique. We believe that there is in Barth's theology more than adequate balances against such an interpretation which were either unknown to or unacknowledged by Bonhoeffer. This view has been taken up by Simon Fisher who finds problems in the fragmentary nature of Bonhoeffer's criticisms as well as continuity errors which he believes, "renders questionable any attempts to extend Bonhoeffer's criticism into a wholesale condemnation of Barth's opus." (Fisher, *Revelatory Positivism?,* (Oxford: Oxford University Press, 1988), p. 312) The fact that Fisher finds this theme in the early 'liberal' Barth as well as the mature Barth is further evidence for our use. (This is supported as well by Bruce McCormack in his review of Fisher's book in *Scottish Journal of Theology,* Volume 43, Number 4, 1990, pp. 504-508). Therefore, we are using the term because Barth's doctrine of evil is developed according to his unique doctrine of revelation which can be described as 'revelatory positivism' in a way which overcomes Bonhoeffer's criticism.

[11] Hunsinger, *How to Read Karl Barth , op. cit.,* see especially pp. 43-49.

gave Barth a new understanding of creation and the creature in its relationship to the Creator which impacted upon his understanding of evil and sin in creation.[12]

In a similar way, Ingolf Dalferth called Barth an 'unabashed realist',[13] describing how ontologically, semantically and epistemologically, Barth keeps the reality of the self-revelation of the Subject of Christian faith as the constant imperative in his theology. Commenting on Dalferth's article, Trevor Hart says, "The ontic rationality of the object has priority over and determines the noetic rationality of our understanding of it. In other words, we can and do know

---

[12] Von Balthasar sees several facets to this transition which impact upon Barth's view of sin and evil in its relationship to creation. He finds already in Volume I Barth's understanding that man has no "innate, natural, *a priori* disposition that favours his acceptance of faith; it is a gift of God." This gift is in the form of action and because it is God's action towards man, it can only be described through the process of analogy. This is spelled out later in the *Church Dogmatics* as requisite because "the relationship between God and creation can never be one of equality... Thus the relationship can only be described as some *middle road between* the two above extremes, and this middle road is analogy." According to von Balthasar, this leads in volume three to the fact that Barth "must posit a creation that is good in itself even though it is not God. For the first time he has to give serious attention to the notion of *creature* ... Now Barth can say that creation itself is blameless in its freedom, its self-awareness, and its position *vis-à-vis* God." (*The Theology of Karl Barth, op. cit.*, pp. 94-97)

[13] Ingolf U. Dalferth, 'Karl Barth's Eschatological Realism', in S. W. Sykes (ed.) *Karl Barth: Centenary Essays*, (Cambridge: Cambridge University Press, 1989), p. 14. Dalferth develops this realism in three categories. *Ontologically*, he says Barth holds that there is a reality which is wholly independent of human thought and logic, and which is also independent of the tools of language and words which we use in an attempt to reproduce that reality. Thus the Subject and Object of theology can only be "a reality which precedes everything we say about it and which cannot be exhausted by anything we can say about it." (p. 17) *Semantically*, following from the ontological independence of this truth and reality, it also stands independent of the verifiability of it. What we say of this reality may be true, and under the guidance of the Holy Spirit is often true, but those assertions and statements regarding the truth are not demonstrable. The ontological reality is not reduced to verifiability. The key here is that the truth of theological statement and utterances about the reality to which they bear witness can only occur within a relationship with that ontological reality. Here is the role of *fides*. Therefore truth is not bound up with the statements themselves, but with their relationship to reality (the true Reality - Jesus Christ). This is the critical distinction and connection between 'truth of statement' and 'truth of being'. Barth believes that theological statements can faithfully depict this reality, but they cannot do so exhaustively or completely. The reality is not fully comprehensible, and therefore it is not controllable by man (Barth's objectivism). It cannot be contained in the tools of language and thought, but instead, as these are employed in the relationship with that reality, they become 'referentially transparent'. *Epistemologically*, this independent ontological reality may be know by us in some way as it really is. We do have real knowledge of this reality in the relationship we have to it and in it. Yet the object of our faith, this independent and revealed reality determines the relationship and the knowledge we have of it.

God, and we do so in accordance with who and what he really is, by virtue of an attitude of trust in the veracity of his self-disclosure."[14]

This realism, or what we have termed 'revelatory positivism' forms the basis for Barth's understanding of theology as a task never at rest at a point of conclusion, but in a never-ending search for knowledge with regards to this revealed truth. Theological statements are therefore constantly in need of demolition and reconstruction as they seek to speak about God. Jacob Taubes makes the point that for Barth, "Theological language is born out of the dualism between the ideal standard and the status quo of man's situation."[15] Thus Barth's theological methodology can accommodate and actually invites paradox and contradiction.[16] Far from apologising or working to extricate himself from such, Barth reminds us again that such dilemmas are to be expected when dealing with this issue.

In this way, Barth's intention, which springs from the heart of this methodology, is to describe and not explain. If that description leads to paradox or contradiction, the tension of the paradox must be allowed to stand rather than to revert to flawed human reason and logic to 'solve' the paradox according to some philosophical or metaphysical construct. Hans Frei is correct in seeing that in Barth, "Theology, then, is by and large an exploration of the meaning of first-level Christian assertion. It is an exploration not usually of their truth, but of their meaning; it is their *re-description* in technical concepts rather than their *explanation*."[17]

A classic example is found in his dealing with the concept of evil as he concludes, "it is of a piece with the nature of evil that if we could explain how it

---

[14]   Trevor Hart, 'Dalferth on Barth's Eschatological Realism', (University of Aberdeen post-graduate seminar paper; Department of Systematic Theology, June 1990), p. 2.

[15]   Jacob Taubes, 'Theodicy and Theology: A Philosophical Analysis of Karl Barth's Dialectical Theology', in *The Journal of Religion*, Volume 34, Number 4, October 1954, p. 231.

[16]   In reacting to H. Scholz, *"Wie ist eine evangelische Theologie als Wissenschaft möglich?"* Barth rejects the attempt to impose science's concept of the impossibility of contradiction onto theology, "Even the minimum postulate of freedom from contradiction is acceptable to theology only when it is given a particular interpretation which the scientific theorist can hardly tolerate, namely, that theology does not affirm in principle that the 'contradictions' which it makes cannot be resolved. But the statements in which it maintains their resolution will be statements concerning the free activity of God and not therefore statements which 'dismiss contradictions from the world'." (CD I/1, p. 9)

[17]   Hans Frei, *Types of Christian Theology*, (New Haven: Yale University Press, 1992), p. 81. (emphasis mine) He continues later, "Barth was about the business of conceptual description: He took the classic themes of communal Christian language molded by the Bible, tradition and constant usage in worship, practice, instruction and controversy, and he restated or redescribed them, rather than evolving arguments on their behalf." (p. 158)

may have reality it would not be evil."[18] Jüngel commented, *"In diesem Sinn hat Barth die unbestreitbare Faktizität des Bösen in der Welt zurückgeführt auf eine nur mythologisch beschreibbare Größe."*[19] Such is the nature of Barth's 'revelatory positivism' which views theological language as, by nature, an imperfect and broken medium. He employs this motif throughout in critical places where he is faced with a final position which is illogical, inconsistent or contradictory, and he unashamedly finds great value in the fact that his theology produces such problems, for they occur only when we are attempting honestly to witness to the truth.[20]

   This motif is given a most succinct development in Barth's excursus on the book of Job in CD IV/3.1. Here Barth deals with Job within his section on the 'Falsehood of Man', and in a pre-critical reading of the book, Barth locates Job's struggle not with his antagonisors, nor his 'friends' nor with Satan who was 'allowed' to reign the torment upon him. Job's struggle is with his God, and it is not doubt that torments Job, but faithfulness. "He does not doubt for a moment that he has to do with this God. But it almost drives him mad that he encounters him in a form which is absolutely alien."[21] It is only in the very midst of the suffering brought by God that Job finds wisdom, and through it comes not only the revelation of the injustice done to Job but, "the justice in its injustice."[22] God is justified not in the 'happy ending' but in the midst of His alien wrath and seeming injustice. "God would not be God if He were not free both to give and to take away," and in line with his doctrine of *creatio ex nihilo*, Barth continues, "Job would not be Job if he were not free to receive both evil and good from God."[23]

   How do we respond to this seeming great contradiction, this paradox that God should manifest Himself in this alien form, as though He were our tormentor and enemy rather than our Saviour and friend? In the clearest of all forms of the motif of 'revelatory positivism' Barth concludes that God, "does not ask for his [man's] understanding, agreement or applause. On the contrary, he simply asks that he should be *content not to know why* and to what extent he exists, and does so in this way and not another. He simply asks that he should

---

18 CD IV/3.1, p. 177.

19 Eberhard Jüngel, *'Die Offenbarung der Verborgenheit Gottes'*, in *Wertlose Wahreit*, (München: Christian Kaiser Verlag, 1990), p. 177. "In this sense Barth reduced the indisputable fact of evil in the world to a size which can only be described mythologically."

20 Taubes continues, "In Barth's theology the reconciliation of the contradiction is never developed 'out' of the contradiction themselves, but is interpreted as the absolute sovereignty of divine freedom", therefore Barth "is aware of the dilemma and faces it squarely, that a dogmatic of the church must at some point become 'inconsistent'. For 'consistency' may be a virtue of reason, but surely not of a divine mystery." (Taubes, 'Theodicy and Theology', *op. cit.,* p. 241)

21 CD IV/3.1, p. 402.

22 Ibid., p. 426.

23 Ibid., pp. 387-388.

admit that it is not he who plans and controls."[24] This call to faith and acceptance rather than reason and solution is at the heart of Barth's theology and, when coupled with the idea of the broken nature of all theological language which he developed from Anselm, his 'revelatory positivism' becomes an important part of his theological method.

The Development of the Four Motifs in Barth's Early Theology

The Historical Setting for Barth's Early Theology

Throughout history the Church's view of evil has been tied to its theories of atonement, and as such evil took on a form which distinguished it from the likes of Zoroastrianism which posited a strict dualism between two separate and distinct spirits, one a God creating all that is good, and the other an evil being creating all evil. Zoroaster built this doctrine on the grounds that God could not be obviated of all of the evils in the world, and therefore their source must come from outside of Him. In a way curiously similar to the Sufism which challenged Zoroastrianism[25], the early Christian church developed an understanding of evil in a seemingly dualistic sense, with the one great caveat that the dualism is not of the metaphysical sense but "in the sense in which the idea constantly occurs in Scripture, of the opposition between God and that which in His own created world resists His will."[26] In this way the Church posited a radical but not absolute dualism, and it is in this radical sense that they developed their doctrine(s) of atonement with regard to the defeat of evil and Satan in the victory of Christ.[27]

---

[24] CD IV/3.1, p. 431. (emphasis mine) This contentment with ignorance is to be maintained even when God, in an exercise of His freedom, "encounters, confronts and opposes man in a way which is sinister, strange, disquieting and even terrifying." (Ibid.)

[25] "To the Sufi, darkness does not truly exist; it is merely the negation of the light. 'God desireth to be known', says the Sufi, 'things are known only through their opposites; God is good; therefore he can only be known by the appearance of evil. The mystery of evil is therefore identical with the mystery of creation'... God is Absolute Being as well as Absolute Good; therefore evil is Not-Being as well as Not-Good." (Whyte, *The Natural History of Evil* , (London: Watts & Co., 1920), p. 13) It is interesting how Moltmann's idea of God's revelation in His opposite and Augustine's *privatio boni* can both be found here.

[26] Gutav Aulén, *Christus Victor* , (London: SPCK, 1931), p. 21n.

[27] In this understanding of the term dualism, we can agree with F.M. Young's statement, "the early Church presupposed some form of dualism in its presentation of Atonement. From the New Testament to the Cappadocians, the Christian felt himself to be involved in the warfare between God and the devil, good and evil, light and darkness, life and death, righteousness and sin." (F.M. Young, 'Insight or

Origen and the Greek Fathers, along with Tertullian and the Latin Fathers, developed their atonement theories generally within this Christianized dualistic understanding. Christ's work conquers the opposing powers, and although the Greek Fathers held more to the concepts of ransom (Origen)[28], sacrifice (Gregory of Nazianzen), recapitulation (Irenaeus), debt (Athanasius) or deception (Gregory of Nyssa) which focused on the rights (granted or usurped) of the devil over humanity, while the Latin Fathers took the lead from Tertullian in holding more to the ideas of merit and satisfaction with relationship to God, Gustav Aulén still concludes that, "the classic idea of the Atonement is the dominant view of the Western and Eastern Fathers."[29] This 'classic view' speaks of the victory of Christ over Satan and the evil powers of the world which hold humanity in bondage, and thus of the reconciliation of the world to God.

Yet the atonement theories of the Greek Fathers seem at times to be intensely dualistic which calls into question whether they actually made a sharp enough distinction between metaphysical dualism and a Christianized dualism. Certainly the idea of the ransom paid to the devil, made famous by Gregory of Nyssa's divine 'fish-hook', and the talk of propitiation to a 'hostile and angry God' in the atonement theory of John Chrysostom tend strongly in this direction.[30] In holding in some form to the right of the devil over humanity, the Greek Fathers were forced to a separation between theodicy and the preaching of redemption. On the metaphysical side, evil exists and is powerful and must be explained in a world created and controlled by God. On the other, God has defeated evil and redeemed fallen humanity, and here evil is given the unique role of that which is necessary for such a redemption.

When the Fathers were forced to define better the dualism in their theology by the emergence of the absolute dualisms of the Gnostics and Manichaeans, they introduced theodicy on the metaphysical level without necessarily reconciling it with their doctrine of redemption. The key distinction to be made is that the Greek Fathers saw that evil was both defeated and that it was the instrument God used for that defeat. This distinction has found its way into Barth's doctrine of evil as he deals with the metaphysical question of evil under the motif of the 'necessary antithesis' while he discusses the existential reality of evil in its defeated state and subservient role according to the work of the 'right and left hand of God'. In preserving this distinction, Barth, too, will find difficulty in bringing the discussion on these two levels together with consistency.

Incoherence? The Greek Father on God and Evil', in *Journal of Ecclesiastical History*, Number 2, April 1973, p. 113)

[28] Yet Origen held that evil was not a positive force, and therefore Satan and the demons could be restored. (See W.H.C. Frend, *The Rise of Christianity*, (Philadelphia: Fortress Press, 1984), pp. 373-381).

[29] Aulén, *Christus Victor, op. cit.*, p. 55.

[30] See Young, 'Insight or Incoherence? The Greek Fathers on God and Evil', *op. cit.*, pp. 114-118.

Augustine added what was to become the critical clarification of this view in his description of evil as 'non-being', *privatio boni*, which was already enmeshed within the Christian Platonists from Clement of Alexandria onwards. Evil was extracted from the two polar positions of being either absolutely distinct from God (against the Manichees–or the 'second God' of the Marcionites) or a characteristic of the nature of God. Although Augustine rejected the Platonic equating of evil with matter (for all of God's creation is good) he did adopt the teaching of Plotinus in which evil as non-being has both the power to be the inimical foe yet is always totally dependent upon and under the control of God.[31] As non-being, evil could be denied an *ousia* without dissolving into non-existence. This view of evil as non-being dominated the writings of the Cappadocian Fathers and the early Greek and Latin views of atonement and theodicy.[32]

Augustine placed evil as 'non-being' outside of God's primary and essential good creation, giving it an alien and parasitic character. As the *nihilo* from which all was created, Augustine developed his doctrine of evil in the same metaphysical sphere as Plotinus' *ouk on* adding to the split between what may be termed metaphysical and empirical evil. This distinction, combined with the view of evil as parasitic and inimical, forms the basis for both the Church's consequent doctrine of evil and the problems inherent in orthodox theodicy. The theodicy question emerges again with regard to the paradox of the responsibility of sin which falls on the one hand to humanity, created with a free will, and on the other hand to God in the providence and predestination of His sovereign will.

Augustine started with the angels and moved to the fall of humanity and in both he affirmed this dilemma–namely, holding that the acting agent is wholly responsible because evil willing is a self-originating act *(prima causa)* and yet positing that the Fall and sin were predestined according to the eternal will of the sovereign God.[33] With regards to Adam's fall, by being finite and created *ex nihilo*, the free will in Adam was a corrupt will, and thus "there would have been no evil work, but there was an evil will before it."[34] The justification of God in this intense predestination comes solely from the idea that since all creation is *ex nihilo*, we owe all good to God and deserve all the evil we experience.

We will see Barth's use and reinterpretation of the *privatio boni* in his description of evil as *das Nichtige*, and more importantly, Barth's attempt to

---

[31] See Plotinus, *The Enneads*, translated by Stephen MacKenna, (London: Faber and Faber, 1956), Eighth Tractate, I.3.

[32] It can be credited to Athanasius that he offered one of the earliest systematic presentations of redemption which, in seeing evil as non-being, rejects the heavy demonological language of the time and focuses on the work of Christ and the defeat of evil. In this way, Athanasius is a forerunner of the doctrine of evil and theodicy which emerged later, and which influenced Barth in his own handling of evil as *das Nichtige*.

[33] "the angelic darkness though it had been ordained, was not yet approved." (Augustine, *City of God*, (London: J.M. Dent and Sons, 1945), Volume I, p. 20)

[34] Augustine, *City of God*, Volume II, p. 43.

hold together both humanity's responsibility for sin and a form of divine sovereignty which is, if anything, more strident than Augustine's.[35] Barth will also borrow from Augustine's aesthetic view of creation's dark side and thus Augustine's idea that 'the universe even with its sinister aspects is perfect' is developed into Barth's *Schattenseite* of creation. Finally, Barth's motif of the 'necessary antithesis' is a strong reflection of Augustine's view that "God judged it better to bring good out of evil, than to suffer no evil at all."[36] Thus even in God's foreknowledge of the extent and depth of evil, the good which He produces from it is His own justification, and evil becomes a 'necessary' element in the process.

Barth's doctrine of sin is also influenced by Anselm in his rejection of all ideas of ransom, debt and deception on the basis that the devil has no rights, either given or usurped, over humanity. Anselm broke with the idea of a Christianized dualism and developed his atonement theory on purely judicial grounds. God is 'satisfied' in the death of Christ, the judicial balance has been restored (although not in a truly 'just' way). Anselm locates the plan and execution of atonement in the will of God–the justice of God requires satisfaction–and in the atonement God receives the compensation for sinful humanity. That Christ's death is also a victory over the devil is a side issue for Anselm who takes evil out of the center, replacing it with the will of God and divine justice. We will see how Barth, in adopting this idea in part from Anselm, also sought to relegate evil to a minor role, placing the eternal will of God in election instead at the heart of his soteriology.

Thomas Aquinas built upon the Augustinian theme and yet his formulation of evil is one which is consistently rejected by Barth. Aquinas saw God's role in the fall of Adam as passive permission in the view that 'what can fail sometimes will'.[37] The finitude of humanity opens up the possibility of this 'can fail', and when the inevitable happens, God permits it, for "*Ordo autem universi requirit... quod quædam sint quæ deficere possint, et interdum deficiant.*"[38] Aquinas sought to explain evil and predestination all under the umbrella of God's providence, where predestination is only one aspect of God's purposeful and directed providence. The locus of humanity's 'ability' to fail lies in its multiplicity as distinct from the perfect simplicity of God. Thus finitude and multiplicity necessarily produce the state of 'able to fail'. God does not direct the Fall, but when the inevitable occurs, He permits it and moves in His

---

[35] For an interesting discussion of how vestiges of Augustinian-Lutheran dualism still remained in Barth, see T.F. Torrance, *Karl Barth, op. cit.,* especially pp. 138-141.

[36] Augustine, *Confessions and Enchiridion*, (London: SCM Press, 1955), xxvii.

[37] Aquinas, *Summa Theologiae*, (London: Blackfriars, 1963), II, Question 18, Article 5.

[38] Aquinas, *Summa Theologiae, op. cit.,* VIII, Question 49, Article 2. "This requires... that there should be some things that can, and sometimes do fall away."

providence to overcome its consequences by transforming evil into good.[39] Barth reacted harshly to Aquinas' passive view of God's permission of humanity's inevitable Fall. Barth's doctrine of evil breaks with Aquinas' subordination of predestination to preservation (reversing them according to his dominant doctrine of election) and of the passive character of Aquinas' *aeterna Dei praedestinatio*, replacing it with the election of Jesus Christ as both the electing God and the Elect Man.[40]

Yet Aquinas does provide Barth with a critical distinction in Augustine's *privatio boni* when he speaks of both 'privation' and 'negation' in such a way that only the former can be called evil, allowing the latter to become the explanation for the dark side of creation without making evil a necessary (and equal, as was the problem in Leibniz) component in God's good creation.[41] Hence Aquinas can say, *"Unde malum quod in defectu actionis consistit vel quod ex defectu agentis causatur non reducitur in Deum sicut in causa,"* and follow it immediately with *"Sed malum quod in corruptione rerum aliquarum consistit reducitur in Deum sicut in causam."*[42] Barth's *Schattenseite* certainly benefitted from Aquinas' distinction as Barth could develop his shadowy side of creation while also rejecting and refuting all senses of an equilibrium of good and evil in God's creation. This distinction will also be carried over into the critical tension in Barth between the impossibility of sin (negation in creation does not make humanity 'able to sin') and the inevitability of sin (finite creation is inherently vulnerable to the impossibility of sin–yet the Fall occurs not by God's permission, but according to His eternal decision of election and reconciliation).

---

[39] Charles Journet provided an even stronger apophatic definition to Augustine's *privatio boni* by viewing evil not only as the privation of good, but by a loss of good that should otherwise have been present. Therefore the force of evil is both in its absolute badness, and in the loss of the goodness which it has usurped. In addition, in seeing that there is more than one possible outcome to every action, Journet viewed suffering as the 'unavoidable secondary effect' of the moral acts of humanity. In this way he posited that God's control of evil is that of an 'accidental willing' and not a direct act. Finally, Journet viewed evil as 'inseparably connected with good', taking Augustine's teachings to their logical conclusion. (Charles Journet, *Le Mal*, English translation by Michael Barry, *The Meaning of Evil*, London: Geoffrey Chapman, 1963, p. 77)

[40] See for example, CD II/2, pp. 107 where Barth concludes, "If we say only what Thomas would say, then we have knowledge only of the election of the man Jesus as such, and not the election and personal electing of the Son of God which precedes this election... In face of it [this error by Thomas] we can only attempt to create the necessary knowledge by constructing a *dectretum absolutum.*"

[41] See for example Aquinas, *Summa Theologiae, op. cit.,* Ia, Question 48, Articles 2, 3, 5.

[42] Aquinas, *Summa Theologiae, op. cit.,* Ia, Question 49, Article 2. "Hence the evil which lies in a defective activity or which is caused by a defective agent does not flow from God as its cause" and "Nevertheless that evil which consists in a decay of some things is traced back to God as its cause."

In the Reformation, Luther's view of evil cut across a number of previous constructions, and it is difficult to isolate one view which is sufficiently representative. Clearly Luther returned to the Christianized dualism of the early Fathers using the most graphic descriptions for the deceit of the devil in the work of Christ.[43] While holding to the Augustinian idea of the *privatio boni*, Luther saw Satan in a personal sense as the embodiment of all that is evil, and as such Satan took on a very dualistic form.[44] Satan is one of the great enemies of humanity, and he is combined with 'the world' and 'our flesh' throughout Luther's writings as that which must be renounced and overcome. In this way Satan is the great accuser whose accusations are rejected in the work of Christ. In strictly Augustinian terms, Luther sees the origin of Satan as a created angel (with the *imago Dei* !) who fell away, and thus it is by both the devil and human disobedience that sin entered into the world.[45]

Yet Luther also sees the wrath of God as a tyrant and enemy of humanity, so much so that its overcoming in the atonement is given primary treatment. In a vestige of Barth's near internal dualism in the use of his 'right and left hand of God' motif, Luther opposes the wrath of God to His Divine Love, seeing both as His good will yet also describing God's wrath as the 'worst of all tyrants'. It is God's own victory in which the Divine Love wins out over the curse of the wrath of God. Luther also developed his view of the *Deus absconditus* from this idea of the two sides of the nature of God, and again we see here early signs of what Barth will seize upon in his view of revelation in which God is both wholly revealed and wholly concealed in His self-revelation to humanity.

---

[43] Two examples will suffice here. In speaking of the deceit of the devil at the time of death Luther writes, "Here the devil practices his ultimate, greatest and most cunning art and power... he sets man above God... the devil is determined to blast God's love from a man's mind and to arouse thoughts of God's wrath. The more docilely man follows the devil and accepts these thoughts, the more imperiled his position is." (Luther, 'A Sermon on Preparing to Die', in *Luther's Works*, Volume 42, ed. Martin O. Dietrich, General eds. Jaroslav Pelikan and Helmut T. Lehmann, (Philadelphia: Fortress Press, 1969), pp. 102-103) In discussing God's 'giving up' from Romans 1:24, Luther writes, "Then the devil, who is constantly waiting for such an occasion, receives, or thinks he has received, God's authority and command... It is certainly not correct to accuse God of ordering man to do evil; but He deserts him so that he is no longer able to resist the devil." (Luther, 'Lectures on Romans', in *Luther's Works,* Volume 25, ed. H.C. Oswald, p. 161)

[44] Despite this tendency, we do not agree with N.P. Williams' statement, "It is difficult to avoid the conclusion that Luther has plunged headlong into the abyss of Manichaeism." (N.P. Williams, *The Ideas of the Fall and Original Sin*, Bampton Lectures, (London: Longmans, Green and Co., 1927), p. 429) This is an overstatement of Luther's position and one which takes an unbalanced view of his theology as a whole.

[45] Thus in the *Small Catechism*, Luther writes, "Sin was brought into the world by the *devil*, who was once a holy angel but fell away from God, and by *man*, who of his own free will yielded to the temptation of the devil." (Luther, *Small Catechism* , (St. Louis: Concordia Press, 1943), p. 86)

Finally, Luther's doctrine of God held to an absolute sense of sovereignty and as such he rejected the speculations of theodicy which emerged most frequently with regard to his teaching of predestination. By His *creatio ex nihilo* God shows how He makes good out of that which is evil, and because He is God, Luther can also affirm, "whatever is something precious, honorable, blessed, and living, He makes to be nothing, worthless, despised, wretched and dying."[46] Therefore, God sends trials to test us while at the same time holding back the evil that may befall us and overwhelm us.[47] If we ask why God sends evils, and why He allows some to be hardened and perish eternally, Luther's stinging reply is reminiscent of Calvin and Barth,

> Let, therefore, his [God's] goodwill be acceptable unto thee, oh, man, and speculate not with thy devilish queries, thy whys and thy wherefores, touching on God's words and works. For God, who is creator of all creatures, and orders all things according to his unsearchable will and wisdom, is not pleased with such questionings.[48]

Calvin takes these ideas further in the construction of his supralapsarian system with regard to election and atonement. He modifies Aquinas' view of God's permitting of the Fall by placing the Fall in the positive and direct willing and action of God. Therefore, in his strict, eternal distinction between the elect and reprobate, Calvin sees a wholly different role of Satan, and of God, with respect to both classes of humanity. To the elect, Satan is allowed only to 'exercise' believers so as to strengthen them, but he is never allowed to conquer them—which he could do if God had not kept him from it.[49] To unbelievers, however, Satan is allowed full sway to blind them and make them his own.

Calvin held, with the early Fathers, that Satan has "undisputed possession of this world until he is dispossessed by Christ,"[50] and it is only as the kingdom of Christ rises that the kingdom of Satan falls. Calvin holds to the sovereign Lordship of God over evil, for while we are commanded to be in "perpetual contest with the devil", we are reminded that in this entire contest,

---

[46] Martin Luther, 'The Magnificat', in *Luther's Works*, *op. cit.*, Volume III, p. 127.

[47] "Hence, He suffers us now and then to be assailed by some slight malady or other ill... and yet at the same time preventing the many evils that threaten us on every side from bursting in upon us all together." (Luther, 'The Fourteen Consolations', in *Luther's Works*, *op. cit.*, Volume I, p. 124f.)

[48] Martin Luther, *Table Talk*, (London: H.G. Bonn, 1857), pp. 29-30. He continues, "though misfortune, misery, and trouble be upon us, we must have this sure confidence in him, that he will not suffer us to be destroyed either in body or soul, but will so deal with us, that all things, be they good or evil, shall redound to our advantage." (p. 30)

[49] John Calvin, *Institutes of the Christian Religion*, Translated by Henry Beveridge, (Grand Rapids: W.B. Eerdmans Co., 1983), Volume I, pp. 153.

[50] Calvin, *Institutes of the Christian Religion*, pp. 154-155.

"Satan cannot possibly do anything against the will and consent of God."[51] As in Luther, Calvin finds the answer to the question of the justice of God's election solely within this idea of sovereignty. Thus Calvin can admit, "that God often acts in the reprobate by interposing the agency of Satan; but in such a manner, that Satan himself performs his part, just as he is impelled, and succeeds only insofar as he is permitted." He concludes, "since the will of God is said to be the cause of all things, all the counsels and actions of men must be governed by his providence; so that he not only exerts his power in the elect... but also forces the reprobate to do him service."[52] Barth's view of the sovereignty of God and the instrumental role of evil within it are seen here, as well as the desire to coordinate such a view with a sense of real value in the 'perpetual contest with evil'.

Again, with Luther and the entire Augustinian tradition, the justification of God (to whatever extent that one can even speak of such things!) lies solely in the *creatio ex nihilo* in which God becomes the preserver of creation against nothingness. Coupled with humanity's responsibility for the Fall, we then can see all good coming from God, and all evil as the result of our own sinfulness. It is clear, however, that this Augustinian picture produces a myriad of problems for theodicy which cannot all be set aside as paradox due to the absolute distinction between the finite and infinite, for they demand greater clarification and perhaps an entire restructuring of the Augustinian doctrine. In a sense, we will see Barth attempt to do both. In addition, the great divide will occur when Barth seeks to construct a doctrine of election-predestination-reconciliation which is not *pars providentiae*. Barth will fundamentally re-structure Calvin's supralapsarianism and directly reject the *decretum absolutum* in favor of his own formulation of Jesus Christ as the Electing God and the Elect Man.

Post-Reformation Theodices

What of the dominant theodicies since the Reformation? Theodicies can be classified in general under one of three categories which correspond to the three axioms of the Christian faith which constitute the problem of evil. J.S. Whale has described these as, "the absolute sovereignty of God... [the fact that] He is love, in all its goodness and holiness... [and] the indubitable reality of evil in God's world."[53] The Augustinian tradition sought to hold to all three while those who have desired a more logical, systematic or accessible and explanatory theodicy have developed their answers by way of the diminution of one of these axioms; the 'Dualists' diminish the sovereignty of God, the 'Pessimists' diminish the love of God which, for some, leads to the question of His very existence, and the 'Optimists' diminish the reality of evil.

---

[51] Ibid., pp. 151, 153.

[52] Ibid., p. 201.

[53] J.S. Whale, *The Problem of Evil*, (London: SCM Press, 1936), p. 11.

The 'Dualists' do not necessarily follow a Manichaean line, but they all have in common the diminution of the orthodox understanding of God's sovereignty and providence in order to alleviate God of all charges of being responsible for evil, sin and death. To keep Him from being responsible, they make Him more or less impotent. Nicholas Berdyaev and Wilfred Monod are representative of this genre of late 19th and early 20th century philosophical theologians. Berdyaev, taking one principle idea from Kant, sees the origin of evil in freedom, and not the God-given freedom of the Christian tradition but an *irrational, uncreated* freedom which emerges as part of the nothingness from which the world was created.

Yet even in his objectifying of freedom and creating a dualism between nothingness and God ("God is all-powerful with respect to being, but not with respect to nothingness, to freedom–that is why evil exists"[54]) Berdyaev still seeks a middle ground between an Augustinian monism and Manichaean dualism.[55] This is found in the irrational freedom which is before creation and outwith the control of God. Berdyaev has been called the "expert on abysses"[56] and yet he sees a positive end in the eternal relationship between good and evil, "In the beginning was the Word, but in the beginning also there was freedom. This latter is not opposed to the Word, for without it the meaning of the world does not exist. Without darkness there is no light. Good is revealed and triumphs through the ordeal of evil."[57] In this way Berdyaev uses freedom, in its two forms of good and evil, as the 'necessary antithesis' to the meaning of creation. It is not surprising that he credits Jacob Boehme and the *Ungrund* for the basis of this idea. We will see how Barth's dialectic reflects much the same idea in the 'Yes' and 'No' of God.

Wilfred Monod, a contemporary of Barth's, took the dualistic idea further in seeing that God's omnipotence must be redefined with regard to His relationship with the world. In Monod we have many of the roots of modern theodicies which limit God's sovereignty and attempt to tie together God's future with that of creation. God creates humanity as totally independent from Himself, and as such God is not able to control them nor the evil which their decisions unleash upon them. Instead, God works in and with creation, He 'does his best' but is not always successful. The justification of God is couched in utilitarian terms where the sum total of good is greater than evil as God works to transform the latter into the former. Thus when Monod says that "God tries but does not

---

54 Nicholas Berdyaev, *Freedom and the Spirit*, (London: The Centenary Press, 1935), p. 160.
55 "The source of evil is not in God, nor in a being existing positively side by side with Him, but in the unfathomable irrationality of freedom, in pure possibility, in the forces concealed within that dark void which precedes all positive determination of being." (Berdyaev, *Freedom and the Spirit*, p. 165)
56 Henri Blocher, 'Christian Thought and the Problem of Evil', in *Churchman: A Journal of Anglican Theology*, Volume 99, Part 2, 1985, p. 103.
57 Berdyaev, *Freedom and the Spirit, op. cit.*, pp. 165-166.

always succeed,"[58] when he builds his eschatology upon the idea of God's *becoming* omnipotent in the final *parousia*, and when he speaks of divinity in terms of moral exigency, we have early signs of process theology and the theodicies of the likes of David Griffin[59], John Hick[60] and Jürgen Moltmann.[61]

These modern theodicies can be seen as embracing the necessity for the diminution of the orthodox understanding of God's sovereignty, and a granting to humanity of an increased sense of independence (as in Hick's 'epistemic distance'), a strict limitation on God's ability to control evil (as in Griffin's theodicy), and a near panentheism (as in Moltmann's use of the *Shekinah*, his employ of Isaac Luria's *zimzum* and his collapsing–as in Karl Rahner–of the distinction between the economic and the immanent Trinity). What will be clear from Barth's doctrine of evil will be his unequivocal rejection of this entire train of thought, although he will use the idea of a 'necessary antithesis' between evil and God's good purposes in creation and he will, consequently, work hard to differentiate this idea from its roots in the dualistic camp.

The 'Pessimists' are not found generally within Christian theology but comprise primarily existentialist thinkers who pose the philosophical challenge to the theistic view of evil. Thus, here we may cite the writings of Bertrand Russell, John Mill, Jean-Paul Sartre, Albert Camus, Fyodor Dostoyevski, David Hume and C.E.M. Joad, and the list could be considerably extended. What ties the participants together in this category is the protest against the Augustinian answer to the problem of evil, and to that extent it is an attack upon the central element of that view, namely Christian faith. Theistic faith cannot, for these writers, accomplish the justification of God from whom evil must finally be seen to proceed, whether by permission or direct action. Dostoyevski's attack on the justification of suffering and evil in *The Brothers Karamozov*[62] and Camus' critique of a God of love in *The Plague*[63] are indicative of this genre of protest literature. This objection is heard in the renunciation of Christianity in Russell[64], the bitter attacks of Joad[65], and in the more measured challenge in Mill[66], and in Hume's *Dialogues Concerning Natural Religion*.[67]

---

[58] C. Werner, *Le problém du mal*, Paris, 1944, in Blocher, 'Christian Thought and the Problem of Evil', in *Churchman: A Journal of Anglican Theology, op. cit.*, p. 103.

[59] See, for instance, *Encountering Evil: Live Options in Theodicy*, Stephen Davis, editor, (Atlanta: John Knox Press, 1981), pp. 101-136.

[60] See John Hick, *Evil and the God of Love* , *op. cit.*

[61] See among others, Jürgen Moltmann, *The Crucified God*, (London: SCM Press, 1973), and *The Trinity and the Kingdom of God*, (London: SCM Press, 1981).

[62] Fyodor Dostoyevski, *The Brothers Karamozov*, (London: Penguin Books, 1958), see Book Five, chapters 4 and 5.

[63] Albert Camus, *The Plague*, translated by Stuart Gilbert, (New York: Random House, 1948).

[64] See for instance Russell's 'Why I am not a Christian', in *The Basic Writings of Bertrand Russell*, eds. R.E. Egner and L.E. Denonn, (London: George Allen and Unwin, 1961).

In these writings God simply ceases to be believable in light of evil. If He is not omnipotent, or if He is not benevolent–and the existence of evil proves that either or both must be true!–then He is not worthy of worship, and perhaps not even of belief. The existential encounter with evil will not yield to a metaphysical construct on the one hand, nor to a call to faith on the other. All that is left is the pessimism of unbelief or, at least, a rejection of any recognition and worship of such a Deity. This is the birth-place of the 'death of God school' and of the world-view of the meaninglessness of life. In one sense Barth's early writings fall into this category as he seeks to destroy all sense of human worth outwith humanity's relationship to God, and there only to find its worth in its total impotence and depravity. Yet Barth's theology in whole is a stinging indictment of this category, even while Barth's theodicy will, in the end, be based solely upon an absolute and total faith in the sovereign God of providence. We may also place the mainstream of post-holocaust writings here, especially that of Elie Wiesel whom we will consider in more detail later. This literature is the result of the cataclysmic collision between impregnable faith and devastating evil. Yet the protest here is on a fundamentally different level than those mentioned above–for this is the protest of faith crying to its God in whom it can only see as the sender of the torment. It is perhaps the place where the only true theistic theodicy can be attempted, where faith in God and the reality of evil are both suffocatingly real and unequivocal.

The 'Optimists' found their answer to the problem of evil in an incorporation of evil into the created, good structure of the world. Taking their lead from earlier Stoic writings, this genre seeks to place evil within God's creation, and therefore it remains under His sovereign control and within the purview of His benevolence. Because of the utilitarian and instrumental view of evil, it can be incorporated into creation as a created and necessary element of the 'best of all possible worlds'. Here we have the comprehensive work of G.W. Leibniz[68] and we can list as well the likes of F.D.E. Schleiermacher[69], Pierre Teilhard de Chardin[70], the great pantheist Benedict de Spinoza, and modern day Christian Science (through Mary Baker Eddy). Optimism embraces the sovereignty of God in such a way that He is justified by the balance of good over evil in a world which is designed by Him to contain both in a process in which evil is either transformed into good or outweighed by it.

---

[65] C.E.M. Joad, *God and Evil*, (London: Faber and Faber, 1918).

[66] See especially Mill's third essay on Theism in, 'Three Essays on Religion', in *Essays on Ethics, Religion and Society*, ed. J.M. Robinson, (Toronto: University of Toronto Press, 1969).

[67] David Hume, *Dialogues Concerning Natural Religion*, (New York: Bobbs-Merrill Co, Inc., 1970).

[68] G.W. Leibniz, *Theodicy: Essays on the Goodness of God, the Freedom of Man and the Origin of Evil*, (London: Routledge & Kegan Paul Ltd., 1951).

[69] F.D.E. Schleiermacher, *The Christian Faith* , (Edinburgh: T & T Clark, 1956).

[70] See especially Pierre Teilhard de Chardin, *Le Milieu Divin*, (London: Collins Fontana, 1927); and *The Phenomenon of Man*, (London: Collins, 1959).

What distinguishes the optimists from the dualists is that God is directly responsible for evil and it is under His control as is all the rest of His creation. The optimists are unabashedly direct about God as the author of evil and of the necessity of evil in the world. Either that or evil is seen as illusory, not real and only experienced when faith is abandoned. In either sense, the radicalness of evil and the inimical role it plays in relation to God and creation is either diminished or lost entirely. In this way optimism is vulnerable to the reality of radical evil (as was seen when the optimism of Leibniz was devastated by the Lisbon earthquake and the ridicule of Voltaire's *Candide*). Barth's doctrine of evil is certainly sympathetic to much of the optimists agenda for it coincides with his all-embracing sovereignty of God and it gives a central role to the transformation of evil into good in God's activity in and for His creation. Yet he also presents a thoroughgoing rejection of optimism and its creation of an equilibrium between good and evil such that evil becomes the positively-willed creation of God. In seeing God's self-revelation in Jesus Christ, and that revelation centering on the cross, Barth finds the optimists domestication of evil to be reprehensible. This diminution of sin and evil in relation to God is the heart of Barth's comprehensive and sometimes bitter critique of the great work of Schleiermacher.

A final word can now be said of 'dialectical theology' which was born in the *Ungrund* of Jacob Boehme and which emerged in the theology of Søren Kierkegaard in his rejection of Hegel's optimism and idea of the *Aufhebung*. Dialectical theology was poised against the philosophical challenge of Kant and much of the reaction of the Enlightenment to Augustinian and Reformed formulations of the relationship of God and evil to the developing anthropocentric view of the world. The influence which these writers had on Barth is substantial as we will see, and his use of and remodification of many of their central themes is critical for a proper understanding of Barth's own doctrine of evil and its distinction from others in the 'dialectic' school. Therefore, we will follow the development of the main themes of Barth's doctrine of evil as they emerged in his early theology.

As with all of Barth's theology, his doctrine of evil emerged in dialogue with and in a reaction against the prevailing views of evil both from orthodoxy and from the philosophy and literature of the late 19th and early 20th century. In his work in both Reformed and Lutheran traditions, Barth was to incorporate and wholly restructure Augustinian theology, and in no greater place than his doctrine of evil.

Barth's Break with His Theological Roots

In 1909, when Karl Barth left his studies in Marburg to enter pastoral work in Geneva he claimed himself to be "second to none among my contemporaries in credulous approval of the 'modern' theology of the time."[71] As a student of

---

[71] Busch, *Karl Barth, op cit.*, p. 51.

Adolf von Harnack, Martin Rade, and most notably, Wilhelm Herrmann, Barth espoused the positivism and advancing Idealism of the late 19th century theological school which had reduced theology to the philosophy of the history of the Christian religion.[72] He was especially influenced by Herrmann and his amalgamation of Kant and Schleiermacher, and his view of revelation as the "event which confronts us with the reality of God."[73] Marburg was steeped in the 'modern' teaching which Barth later described as "religionistic, anthropocentric, and in this sense humanistic."[74]

For Barth, the outbreak of the First World War in 1914 brought the shocking and complete collapse of the ethics of Liberal Protestantism when ninety-three German intellectuals issued a 'terrible manifesto' in support of the war policy of Wilhelm II. "Among these intellectuals I discovered to my horror almost all of my theological teachers whom I had greatly venerated."[75] Barth saw this act as a 'twilight of the gods' in which "religion and scholarship could be changed completely into intellectual 42cm cannons."[76] This 'ethical failure' led Barth to a severe rejection of the theology of his teachers. "In despair over what this indicated about the signs of the time I suddenly realized that I could no longer follow either their ethics and dogmatics or their understanding of the Bible and of history. For me at least, 19th-century theology no longer held any future."[77]

To fill the theological void left by this rejection, Barth turned in two seemingly opposite directions; to the theology of the two Blumhardt's on the one hand, and to the radical critique of Franz Overbeck on the other. Barth found a starting point for a new direction for his theology in Blumhardt's connection between the knowledge of God and the Christian's hope for the future and in his understanding of the "reality contained in the word and concept of the 'Kingdom of God',[78] as it stood under the banner of 'Jesus is Victor'."[79] In the

---

[72] From von Harnack and Herrmann Barth states that he learned "Faith and Revelation are possible only with the presupposition of an absolute relation to an absolute history." (Karl Barth, *'Der christliche Glaube und die Geschichte'*, *Schweizerische theologische Zeitschrift* 29, 1912, p. 4)

[73] Karl Barth, 'Principles of Dogmatics According to Wilhelm Herrmann' in *Theology and Church*, (London: SCM Press, 1928), p. 248.

[74] Karl Barth, *The Humanity of God*, (London: Collins, 1961), p. 35.

[75] Karl Barth, *Evangelical Theology in the Nineteenth Century*, (London: Collins, 1961), pp. 12-13.

[76] Busch, *Karl Barth, op. cit.*, p. 81.

[77] Barth, *Evangelical Theology in the Nineteenth Century, op. cit.*, p. 13.

[78] Karl Barth, *Das Christliche Leben*, p. 443, as quoted in Eberhard Jüngel, *Karl Barth: A Theological Legacy, op. cit.*, p. 63.

[79] Barth was greatly moved by the story told by the elder Blumhardt of the exorcism of a demon from a little girl at which the demon cried out these words - Jesus is Victor. Barth saw that "the entire story of the Blumhardts stood under this sign: 'Jesus is Victor!'" (CD IV/3.1, p. 169)

Blumhardts, Barth saw a living and dynamic Christianity whose theology centred on a proclamation of the Kingdom of God in the power of the resurrection.[80]

In Overbeck, Barth found a fresh critique of modern theology and he employed (although in a way certainly not intended by Overbeck) as a key statement Overbeck's remark, "Theology can no longer be established through anything but audacity."[81] Thus in Overbeck, "Barth apparently found the scholar who made it possible for him to radicalize what he had learned from the theology of the two Blumhardts."[82] Also influenced by Friedrich Zündel and his emphasis on the Wholly Other breaking in on our time; by Søren Kierkegaard's ideas in his treatise *Either/Or* where he opposed Hegel's 'mediation of contradiction', and in his teaching of the eternal 'Moment'; and by Fyodor Dostoyevski's challenge to orthodox Christianity,[83] Barth had made a substantive break from his past and was now in a transition to an entirely new theological frame. In this new frame Barth would develop an eschatological theology under the banner 'Jesus is Victor' (from the elder Blumhardt) emphasizing the 'infinite qualitative distinction' between God and humanity (from Kierkegaard) and employing the idea of the contradiction between a real necessity and a factual impossibility (from Overbeck). This was the theology which was to explode "the axiom of an immanent continuity between man and God."[84] With it, Barth sought to contest the immanentism, reductionism and anthropocentricism of neo-Protestantism and to free it from its 'procrustean bed' of false ideologies. Here were the roots of dialectical theology with its particular importance to Barth's doctrine of evil. In these roots already there can be seen Barth's emphasis on the Otherness and sovereignty of God, his dialectical basis for his use of the 'Yes' and 'No' of God, and his eschatology which will encapsulate all human history under the heading 'Jesus is Victor'. Therefore, these early influences on Barth at the time of his conversion from liberal Protestantism are foundational for an understanding of the development of his later doctrine of evil.

---

[80] For an excellent example of Barth's indebtedness to Christoph Blumhardt, see Karl Barth, *Action in Waiting*, (Rifton, New York: Plough Publishing Company, 1969). In this little book Barth responds to Blumhardt's article 'Joy in the Lord' and traces of all four of our motifs emerge both in Blumhardt's article and in Barth's enthusiastic critique.

[81] Karl Barth, 'Unsettled Questions for Theology Today', in *Theology and Church*, (London: SCM Press, 1928), p. 72.

[82] Jüngel, *Karl Barth: A Theological Legacy, op. cit.,* p. 65.

[83] For a helpful discussion of Dostoyevski's impact on Barth's dialectical theology, see Erich Bryner, '*Die Bedeutung Dostojewskis für die Anfänge der dialektischen Theologie* ', in *Theologische Zeitschrift*, Volume 38, May-June 1982, pp. 147-167.

[84] Torrance, *Karl Barth: An Introduction to His Early Theology 1910 - 1931, op. cit.,* p. 84.

The Foundations for a New Theology

In 1916, Barth gave two addresses in which he set out the basic tenets of his emerging theology. In 'The Righteousness of God' Barth described the current modern theology as the new 'Tower of Babel'. Into humanity's self-secure realm comes the righteousness of God through its consciousness, confronting humanity as something that is without, coming to it "now as an obstruction opposing against you an inexorable No."[85] Barth develops here the idea that the sinful human will is 'impossible' and that there is another will which is the true and real will.[86] Rather than seeking longingly after this radically new will, we recede into religious self-righteousness and build our own Tower of Babel.

It is precisely here where Barth attacks the ethical failure of liberal Protestant theology by asking a version of the theodicy question, "If God were righteous, could he then 'permit' all that is now happening in the world?"[87] This for Barth must be a pointless question if we are to begin with the understanding of the righteousness of God. It is only if we question God's righteousness that we can ask 'if', and because we do ask this question, the Tower of Babel crumbles in the presence of the impotent idol to which it was erected. In the dust of this collapse comes the re-creation of our will in response to the true and righteous God who confronts us as one who is Wholly Other and who can only be embraced by faith.

Barth's second address, 'The Strange New World Within the Bible' came nine months later and in it Barth turned his attack on the historification of Biblical studies and liberal theology's rejection of the sovereignty of the Wholly Other God. Barth proclaimed that studying the Bible is a daring proposition one can only undertake with faith, for in it there is a history which on its own is 'stark nonsense' but which can be understood if it is seen in its true light as God's history. Here are the roots of Barth's later development of his doctrine of time. Our history is only understandable in its relationship to God's history which, as opposed to our own, is "a history with its own distinct grounds, possibilities, and hypotheses."[88] This new world of God's history takes us beyond what we would call history and this 'going beyond' is an act of faith. As we take this step of faith we are lead inevitably to a critical decision "where one must decide to accept or reject the sovereignty of God. This is the new world within the Bible."[89]

---

85 Karl Barth, 'The Righteousness of God', in *The Word of God and the Word of Man,* (London: Hodder and Stoughton, 1928), p. 10.

86 "There is above this warped and weakened will of yours and mine, above this absurd and senseless will of the world, another which is straight and pure, and which, when it once prevails, must have other, wholly other, issues than these we see today." (Ibid., p. 13)

87 Ibid., p. 21

88 Karl Barth, 'The Strange New World in the Bible', in *The Word of God and the Word of Man, op. cit,* p. 37.

89 Ibid., p. 41.

In these two addresses, Barth seeks to establish a clear break with the theology of his time in four critical areas; 1) in the supplanting of the human will from its central place and consigning it to the status of 'impossible' by virtue of humanity's rejection of the true righteousness of God, 2) by assigning to God's righteousness a confrontational role as the Wholly Other which is outside our control and which destroys our attempts to internalize or historicize it, 3) by rejecting any historification which does not find its origin in the act of God in history (and by reinterpreting our history accordingly)[90] and in an acknowledgement of His sovereignty, and 4) by re-establishing faith as the basis for all theological enquiry.

All four of these early positions are indicators of how Barth will develop his doctrine of evil within the creation-reconciliation-redemption frame in which his theology moves. In the first area, the title 'impossible' will shift to the sin of humanity in the face of the grace of the Creator, yet the direction will remain the same. In the second, Barth will build the 'No' of God the Creator in the face of this confrontation and the grace of the 'Yes' which will overwhelm the 'No' in the salvation of his creation. In the third, Barth will focus his reinterpretation of all human history, and all human reality, in light of the one true history and reality in Jesus Christ. This is a critical strand in Barth's theology which will be discussed in much detail, especially with regards to the critics of Barth who have misinterpreted this idea. Fourthly, Barth will continue to move faith to the forefront and, in the end, it will be his answer to the theodicy question. Here then we see emerging the early signs of all four of our motifs.

The Epistle to the Romans –1919

In the *Epistle to the Romans* in 1919, Barth developed his dynamic eschatological basis for theology and he also made his strongest attack on what he saw to be the dissolving of true theology into the history of religions.[91]

---

[90] Here we can see the continuing impact of Overbeck. In his work on Overbeck's critique of modern theology Barth states, "two points, which are at once gateways and ends, determine and characterize, according to Overbeck, the being of man and of humanity. With the term 'Super-History' *(Urgeschichte)* or creation-history he designates the one, with the term 'death', the other." (Karl Barth, 'Unsettled Questions for Theology Today', in *Theology and Church*, (London: SCM Press, 1928), p. 58) This idea of 'super-history' or *Urgeschichte* will play an important role in Barth's understanding of the relationship between worldly history and salvation history.

[91] Herbert Hartwell says that it was "an uncompromising attack on a theology which had confused theology with psychology (religious experience) and philosophy (speculative rationalism) and faith with piety, and on a Christianity which had exchanged the Gospel of God's sovereign and free gracious dealing with man in Jesus Christ for a religion in which God was treated as a mere object which man imagined he had at his disposal, and which he felt to be beneficial to his moral, cultural and religious life." (Hartwell, *The Theology of Karl Barth, op. cit.*, p. 9)

Barth and Thurneysen interpreted Romans using a hermeneutic of simultaneity which outraged the likes of von Harnack and Jülicher who saw it as an outright denial of history. In this new, anti-historical hermeneutic, all understanding must take place in the context of the presupposition that the interpreter can 'stand in objective partnership with Paul' and as such, history as we know it, history as it was viewed by the liberal theologians of his day, must go through a radical reinterpretation.

An important development in this first edition for our purposes is Barth's idea of sin and time. Sin is viewed as humanity's desire to establish our independence from God,[92] and Barth sees the emergence of this sin as the cause of the emergence of time; as the result of the splitting up of the divine and the temporal, the world as the sphere of the flesh split from its original divine Spirit resulting in a state of *katastasis*. Thus our time, the time of this world, is not the ultimate reality, but is under the determination of the 'No' of God in His rejection of this time of sin.

The reconciliation of this time and of the creation bound by it is the unfolding 'revolution in God'.[93] This 'revolution' is seen in a number of paradoxes which give way to a unity in God.[94] It is the movement of God toward the accomplishment of His goal of the establishment of the Kingdom of God, and therefore it is a strictly eschatological revolution. In Barth's use of the unity of opposites we begin to see the emergence of the central ideas of dialectical theology. Certainly there is a Hegelian influence here although it will continually be pointed out that Barth's use of synthesis is constantly redefined and reconstructed throughout his theology to serve his own purposes, often differing completely from anything Hegel himself ever had in mind.[95]

---

[92] In answering the question 'what constitutes the fall?' in Barth's theology, von Balthasar replies, "There is only one sin: man's desire to establish his independence *vis-à-vis* God." (Hans Urs von Balthasar, *The Theology of Karl Barth*, *op. cit.*, p. 50)

[93] The development of this line of thought in Barth is important as we look at modern critiques of Barth's doctrine of time and the charges that are brought concerning the connection of God's actions with our 'real world and time'. Here it should be noted that time is reinterpreted according to God's perfect time and in itself it has no reality. It is the desire of humanity to have a reality distinct from God which brought sin and the emergence of this time. Thus, this time does not have some independent status of reality in relationship to God and His creature.

[94] Barth says of the gospel that is it "nothing new, but the oldest; nothing particular, but the most universal; nothing historical, but the presupposition of all history... not an old acquaintance, but a new one; not universal, but particular; not a mere presupposition, but history itself." (Karl Barth, *Der Römerbrief*, (1st Edition), pp. 7f., and p. 387)

[95] For instance, Barth sees the goal of dialectical theology not as the acquisition of final truths but the engaging in the endless movement from accepted positions to new understandings. It is a process of moving between the two contradictory stances in order to move above and beyond them. What then is achieved as a new stance, the new synthesis beyond thesis and antithesis, becomes yet a new thesis for which a

'The Christian's Place in Society'

This use of synthesis is seen in Barth's revolutionary Tambach lecture entitled 'The Christian's Place in Society'. Barth set out here the two-fold nature of the Christian's response to the events of the world. Since the world was created by God, the Christian is resigned to affirm the world that God has created even if it requires naïvete. That is the thesis of Christian action. The antithesis is the active rejection of the world in its current form and the struggle to right it where it is wrong. This is the tension of the Christian life, but it is a tension which stands not under a future synthesis towards which thesis and antithesis move, but a completed *a priori* synthesis from which all things move.

The key for Barth's use of this Hegelian terminology is that it is *from* the synthesis *(Aufhebung)* that the thesis and antithesis move. The antithesis is not even a reaction to the thesis, but only a reaction to the synthesis which has already taken place. The synthesis is *before* the thesis and antithesis and is in fact their source. As the Christian struggles between the 'Yes' of affirmation and the 'No' of rejection he is aware that there is something higher, a *totaliter aliter* which is awaited and hoped for, a movement from God which is anticipated in the movements of humanity.

I mean a movement from above, a movement from a third dimension, so to speak, which transcends and yet penetrates all these movements and gives them their inner meaning and motive; a movement which has neither its origin nor its aim in space, in time, or in the contingency of things, and yet is not a movement apart from others: I mean the movement of God in history.[96]

This movement of God in history is characterized by nothing less than total victory, "God in history is *a priori* victory in history. This is the banner under

---

new antithesis must be sought. In this way, Barth parts with Hegelianism in that the *via eminentiae* is not a true synthesis *(Aufhebung)*, but is instead a new openness to further examination. Speaking on this point, von Balthasar says, "Theological dialectic continually calls out for further completion. It is essentially a stance of openness, a web of incomplete thoughts and sentences that points beyond itself to the inexpressible fulness of the divine message." (von Balthasar, *The Theology of Karl Barth, op. cit.,* p. 65) This means that theological doctrines are essentially contingent as they do not contain the truth themselves, but they are pointers and indicators, directing the interpreter beyond themselves to the Truth in Jesus Christ. T.F. Torrance states that in the face of the false syntheses of Neo-Protestantism, Barth's synthesis of grace and revelation "could only take on the radically dialectical form of *diastasis*." (Torrance, *Karl Barth: An Introduction to His Early Theology, op. cit.,* p. 83)

[96] Barth, 'The Christian's Place in Society', in *The Word of God and the Word of Man, op. cit.,* p. 283.

which we march. This is the presupposition of our being here."[97] Barth has expanded on the understanding of how our ideas of reality, space and time must be reinterpreted in light of the one true reality of the sovereign God. Refusing to give ground on the 'infinite qualitative distinction' between God and humanity, Barth builds a sense of confrontation between this sinful world and the movement of God from above. Yet in doing so, he gives ground for an understanding of God who, although Wholly Other and transcendent, can and is also immediate and involved, 'penetrating' our movements and forming the very motivation for them. Thus in speaking of the 'need of Christian preaching', Barth raises the dilemma of the preacher,

> I sought to find my way between the problem of human life on the one hand and the content of the Bible on the other. As a minister I wanted to speak to the *people* in the infinite contradiction of their life, but to speak the no less infinite message of the *Bible*, which was as much a riddle as life. Often enough these two magnitudes, life and the Bible, have risen before me (and still rise) like Scylla and Charybdis; if *these* are the whence and whither of Christian preaching, who shall, who can, be a minister and preach?[98]

Barth's later doctrine of the sovereignty of God as seen in the freedom of God owes much to this early position which refused to let the emphasis on the transcendence of God overwhelm any possibilities of God's immanence and involvement.[99] By 1920, Barth had laid the groundwork for an eschatological theology which could both preserve the distance required of the Wholly Other and yet not lose the immanence required of the incarnation. Over all humanity stood the great synthesis that is before all thesis and antithesis–the victory of Jesus Christ.

Here again we see the foundation for Barth's developing view of sin and evil. A central feature of that view is that the freedom of God will preserve God's sovereignty over evil, while allowing Him ample room to engage the enemy on the field of battle on behalf of and in the form of His beloved creature. Thus evil can be both under the control of and yet seemingly inimical towards God in this newly discovered freedom. In addition, in the face of the

---

[97] Barth, 'The Christian's Place in Society', p. 297.

[98] Barth, 'The Need of Christian Preaching', in *The Word of God and the Word of Man, op. cit.* , p. 100.

[99] Having said this we understand and agree with some of the criticisms that see in Barth's early theology an overemphasis on the transcendence of God and the deity of Christ; an overemphasis to which Barth himself admits. Yet here we must see that there is room for the understanding of the immanence of God but only if it is seen in its relation to His sovereignty - exactly the tack Barth takes in rejecting *Kenoticism* in his explanation of the humiliation of God in the incarnation and in positing what he considered to be a more immanent immanentism than even panentheism itself which is possible only in the freedom of God.

contradictions in the time of the Church the believer can now see that although he or she struggles with the 'Yes' and 'No' of God, this thesis and antithesis are not looking for some future synthesis either on earth or in heaven, but instead they look back to the eternal and *a priori* synthesis which is already accomplished in Jesus Christ. For that reason they look forward not to a new synthesis, but to Christ in His victorious return. Barth's realism, his doctrine of the perfections of God, his dichotomy of the 'Yes' and 'No' of God and his views of the relationship between God and *das Nichtige* can all be seen in their early forms in his work in this period. In the 1920's they were to receive a thorough development in his dialectical theology.

The Birth of Dialectical Theology

From 1920 to 1922, Barth orchestrated the *Wendung* which he saw as necessary to topple the 'idol' of modern theology. He later described liberal theology as a ship that was running aground, "the moment was at hand to turn the rudder an angle of exactly 180 degrees."[100] In 1920, Barth presented an address entitled "Unsettled Questions for Theology Today" which he based upon Overbeck's *Christentum und Kultur* and in which he called the theological community to take cognisance of Overbeck's critiques and warnings about the current confusion and misdirection of liberal theology.[101] Barth seized upon Overbeck's rejection of a Christianity subjected and bound to time and history. "If Christianity, then not history; if history, then not Christianity... History is precisely the basis upon which Christianity can *not* be established."[102] Again we see the foundations for Barth's development of the reinterpretation of time and history in the tension of the ideal and the real. Our history, our time is not the reality, but it is taken up and reinterpreted by what is true reality, the time and history of God in Christ for humanity.

A second and most important theme Barth acquired from Overbeck was that of paradox, of the 'impossible possibility'. Barth developed Overbeck's idea (based upon Matthew 18:3) that "Christians must be children, but they cannot."[103] Speaking in 1922 to a meeting of the *Freunde der Christlichen*

---

[100] Barth, *Humanity of God, op. cit.,* p. 38.

[101] In a well-phrased statement Jüngel notes, "Overbeck has such great significance for Barth's theology because he made the aporia of the theology of his day exceptionally clear. In Overbeck, Barth found that which he himself had at first only sensed and then had tried to articulate ever more clearly: the profound impotence of 'modern theology', hidden only too well behind the fig leaf of culture-Protestantism." (Jüngel, *Karl Barth: A Theological Legacy, op. cit.,* p. 56)

[102] Barth, 'Unsettled Questions for Theology Today', *op. cit.,* p. 61.

[103] Franz Overbeck, *Christentum und Kultur,* (Basel: Benno Schwabe & Co., 1919), p. 64. Barth said of this statement by Overbeck, "The challenge of Matthew 18:3 ['Unless you turn and become like children, you will not enter the Kingdom of heaven'] by itself either eliminates Christianity or unhinges the church." (Barth, 'Unsettled Questions for Theology Today', *op. cit.,* p. 63)

Welt, Barth says, "As ministers we ought to speak of God. We are human, however, and so we cannot speak of God. We ought therefore to recognize both our obligation and our inability and by that very recognition give God the glory. This is our perplexity. The rest of our task fades into insignificance in comparison."[104] This is the great dialectic statement in which Barth juxtaposes two antithetical statements but does not look to a human synthesis beyond which we can move. From Overbeck, Barth had concluded a rejection of all synthesis between God and humanity, revelation and history, Christianity and the world, faith and world history.

Barth described the characteristic feature of this process of dialectic as "its question about the superior, new element which limits and determines any human self-understanding."[105] By using contradiction between real necessity ('we ought to speak of God') and factual impossibility ('we cannot speak of God') Barth sees theology as an 'impossible possibility'.

An important point here is how Barth viewed this idea of the 'impossible possibility' of theology. He is not saying that theology is ultimately impossible, but that its sole possibility lies in that which is Wholly Other and distinct from the theologian. Theology is possible only because of the miracle of God's coming to humanity in the divine moment, which is not an earthly reality. Here Barth ties together strands from Kierkegaard (the 'moment') and Schleiermacher (the 'eternal in a moment'), but he is mostly reliant upon his use of Plato. From Plato Barth was able to envisage a moment which was in a transition between rest and motion and which occupied no space nor required any time, and as such a moment which had no before or after. Therefore within the limits of earthly reality, this moment is impossible. For Barth, *finitum non capax infiniti*. This then is how God comes to us, this is how theology is possible, but only possible as the breaking in of the eternal upon the temporal, as this moment which has no before or after. Only when conceived as a human and earthly impossibility can the possibility of theology be considered. This is the basis for the dialectic of the 'impossible possibility'. It is also helpful when we see Barth shift this term later to the reality of sin.

Later in the same address Barth says, "Man is a riddle and nothing else, and his universe, be it ever so vividly seen and felt, is a question. God stands in contrast to humanity as the *impossible* in contrast to the possible, as *death* in contrast to life, as *eternity* in contrast to time."[106] The solution to this thesis and antithesis is not a coordination or a compromise or a synthesis in Hegelian terms. The solution is "the absolutely new event" which makes the impossible possible, death life, eternity time and God human.[107] Under the banner of 'dialectical theology' God and humanity can be considered in their relationship, however not independently, but only in relation to their mutual presupposition

---

104   Barth, 'The Task of the Ministry' in *The Word of God and the Word of Man, op. cit.,* p. 186.
105   Busch, *Karl Barth, op. cit.,* p. 144.
106   Barth, 'The Task of the Ministry', *op. cit.,* p. 197.
107   Ibid., p. 197.

in God's becoming human, only of God *and* His creature in Jesus Christ. Only from this presupposition, only from this 'living truth' can theology become possible, can the creature speak of God, for it is this living truth and it alone which is the "determining content of any real utterance concerning God."[108] The synthesis is Jesus Christ, but He is the synthesis which does not result from thesis and antithesis but which is above and before them. The relationship between God and humanity, the real and the impossible, is made possible by the action of God in becoming human, in bridging the gap and bringing humanity to God. Only in and from this *a priori* synthesis is theology possible, but from there it is possible and necessary.[109]

For Barth at this stage of his thinking, dialectical theology was necessary precisely because the reality of God *and* humanity is found in the person of Jesus Christ. The *and* is indispensable, and it renders theological language wholly incapable of articulating or apprehending this mystery of God's revelation. Revelation for Barth is the event in which God gives the definitive Word about Himself. Rather than being in our control, this revelation confronts us in such a way that we are rendered unable to do anything but hear and respond. Because revelation is God Himself in the mystery of the incarnation, the interpreter does not possess this object, but is afforded only fragmentary glimpses of it. Thus theological language, unable to apprehend its subject, must undergo constant critique, revision, negation and reconstruction in order to move beyond accepted statements and towards that which is ultimately inexpressible. In attempting to express this mystery, thesis gives rise to antithesis in an endless modification and re-assembly of theological truths. In addition, for the object itself, the more it is known the more unknowable it becomes, and the dialectic process continues. In this process, the object is also subject, and as such the monologue of interpreter to object necessarily becomes a dialogue and interpretation becomes self-involving.

Dialectical Theology and the Four Motifs

From Overbeck, Barth began to work out his distinctive ideas of the 'Yes' and 'No' of God within this understanding of thesis and antithesis. In 1920 Barth gave an address which directly confronted his former teachers, especially

---

[108] Ibid., p. 206.

[109] "This possibility, described with the most paradoxical expression 'impossible possibility', is conceived as something foreign to the reality of the world, an alien power whose potency can in no way derive from the energy (as the Greeks called reality) of the world; it is indeed impossible within the context of the world. Within the reality of the world, this possibility *must* appear as a paradox. For this reason 'the impossible possibility of the faithfulness of God' reveals itself for Barth 'in the paradox of faith'. Yet 'the faithfulness of God in the paradox of faith' is sufficient. 'It suffices for us because with it we stand on sure ground and can walk a sure path'." (Jüngel, *Karl Barth: A Theological Legacy, op. cit.,* p. 66; quoting Barth, *Epistle to the Romans*, (2nd Edition), p. 113)

von Harnack and the historical-critical school of theology. Entitled 'Biblical Questions, Insights and Vistas' the address was a thoroughgoing renunciation of the historical critical method in favour of the crisis of the revelation of God in Scripture. The knowledge of God is not a possibility we may employ or reject in our search for truth, but it is the presupposition for all such searching. Barth's simple statement that 'we are not outside but inside' was the epistemological break with his former teachers. For him the knowledge of God is antithetical to all other kinds of knowledge and he rejected the system of 'double-entry bookkeeping' which requires that the word of God be kept separate from a world view. Instead, we stand in the tension between a 'Yes' and 'No' as we are confronted by Scripture, and in this confrontation both 'Yes' and 'No' have a simultaneity, "There is never so decisive a 'Yes' that it does not harbor the possibility of the 'No': there is never so decisive a 'No' that it is not liable to be toppled over into the 'Yes'."[110] We must then stand and work within this tension, for there is no neutral place. True religion finds its truth in its other-worldliness and its non-historicity.

It is here where the answer to the 'Yes' and 'No' of dialectic is to be found. The truth is not in the 'Yes' or 'No' but "in the knowledge of the beginning from which the 'Yes' and 'No' arise."[111] Here again Barth points to the synthesis *(Aufhebung)* which is above and before the thesis and antithesis.[112] The truth lies not in this world but in the non-historical, other-worldliness of the *a priori* synthesis of God and humanity in Jesus Christ.[113] The Bible in its other-worldliness has but one theme and that is God Himself, the 'real God', who as the Wholly Other is not one thing among other things just as Christianity is not one religion among other religions.

This God is incomparable, sovereign and He rules, requiring our total obedience. By nature "He must rule. He must himself grasp, seize, manage, use... He is not in another world over against this one; he *submerges all of this* in the other."[114] In this way the dialectic of 'Yes' and 'No' is critical for our

---

110   Barth, 'Biblical Questions, Insights and Vistas', in *The Word of God and the Word of Man, op. cit.,* p. 59.

111   Ibid., p. 73.

112   Ricoeur uses Hegel and Barth as, "two exemplary exponents of such dialectic thinking; Hegel being the paradigm of a conclusive dialectic, Barth the paradigm of an inconclusive, even broken dialectic. With Hegel we try to think more, with Barth to think differently... for Barth the dialectic deepens the gap between the wholly other and the world of creatures." Ricoeur goes on to call the product of this 'broken dialectic' a 'productive failure' and Barth's teachings on *das Nichtige* as a 'broken theology'." (Paul Ricoeur, 'Evil, A Challenge to Philosophy and Theology', in *Journal of the American Academy of Religion* , Volume 53, Part 4, December 1985, pp. 642-643)

113   We can say this here although the Christocentric nature of Barth's theology did not emerge as the central theme of his theology for some 12 years.

114   Barth, 'Biblical Questions, Insights and Vistas', *op. cit.,* p. 74. (emphasis mine)

knowledge of God, for Barth will go on to say that the only way to understand the New Testament is to see that the 'Yes' is contained in the 'No'. It is only from the 'No' that the 'Yes' comes, "Life comes from *death!* Death is the source of all."[115] From this statement Barth continues in a remarkable fashion to show that it is from death (thence comes!) which everything in our knowledge of God flows. The theme of the Bible is the Easter message that this death is swallowed up in victory. It is a victory that follows death in such a way that Barth concludes, "The divine first is on the further side of the human last."[116] This Easter message, this theme of the Bible means nothing less than the sovereignty of God, the *'Totaliter aliter!'* Thus the resurrection means the new world, eternity, a new corporeality, and it is, in the end, the 'one experience of man'.

Perhaps the single most powerful impact of dialectical theology was made by the 2nd edition (1922) of Barth's *Commentary on the Epistle to the Romans*. In it Barth was able fully to build upon the foundation he had laid in his break with liberal Protestantism. Here Barth uses the idea of *krisis* to the full in expounding upon the creature's position before the true God. The *krisis* of humanity is that it has lost its original identity through sin and now stands confronted by the 'No' of God. The result of sin is the unbridgeable abyss which places humanity at an intolerable distance to God.[117] Barth employed his interpretation of parts of Plato and Kant, and he sought fiercely to maintain Kierkegaard's 'infinite qualitative distinction' *(den 'unendlichen qualitativen Unterschied')* between time and eternity, and between God and humanity.[118] Christian revelation is, according to Barth, radically distinguished from all other forms of revelation in the dialectic of the pure actuality and holiness of God's revelation and the alienated and totally sinful state of humanity headed for damnation.

The basis for the hermeneutic in this second edition was Barth's axiom that 'God is God' and because interpretation must conform to its subject matter there is created a hermeneutical circle including that which is understood and that which is to be understood.[119] Fundamental for Barth is the fact that God is in heaven and His creature is on earth for "the relation between such a God and such

---

[115]   Ibid., p. 80.

[116]   Ibid., p. 87.

[117]   Taubes commented, "If the dialectic of the first edition of the *Roemerbrief* can be interpreted in the light of religious Hegelianism, the second edition reveals the influence of Kierkegaard's negative dialectic on every page. Man in his totality takes on demonic features and functions only as an antithesis in the divine drama of redemption." (Taubes, 'Theodicy and Theology', *op. cit.,* p. 237)

[118]   Thus in the preface to the Second Edition Barth states, "If I have a system, it is limited to a recognition of what Kierkegaard called the 'infinite qualitative distinction' between time and eternity, and to my regarding this as possessing negative as well as positive significance." (Barth, *Epistle to the Romans, op. cit.,* p. 10)

[119]   See Jüngel, *Karl Barth: A Theological Legacy, op cit.,* p. 77.

a man, and the relation between such a man and such a God is for me the theme of the Bible and the essence of philosophy."[120] This qualitative distinction means that revelation can only be manifested to humanity under the 'No' of God (the negative significance of the 'infinite qualitative distinction'), which is the judgement and condemnation of God towards sinful humanity. It is directed at the creature who would attempt of its own effort to cross this dividing line, to bring itself up to God or God down to itself. This was the goal of the neo-Protestant theologies which Barth rejected. This attempt by humanity was the sin of humanity, and that sin put it under the judgement of God. In this state of judgement, under the 'No' of God, the revelation of God could only be a crisis for God's creature. "The crisis consists in this, that man in *all* his endeavours stands under the condemnation of the radical 'No' of the true and living God, the 'No' of His holy judgement in the presence of which man cannot live, but can only *die*."[121]

Barth sees the 'No' of God as a response to the sin of humanity as the natural and ever-present state of humanity. The creature is not known other than as the person of sin, for sin is the "characteristic mark of human nature," and the Fall, rather than an event, is that "which occurred with the emergence of human life."[122] Thus God can only come to humanity as a crisis, as the holy fire in the rubble of dark human existence. This is Barth's dialectic crisis which forms the basis for so much of his early theology.

Yet this crisis is misunderstood if it is reckoned as only negative and judgmental. The key to the crisis is that the overwhelming 'No' is itself overwhelmed by the pervasiveness of the 'Yes' of the grace of God. The 'No' is necessary so that the 'Yes' may have its full and saving effect. The two are inseparable.[123] Here again we see the indissoluble link Barth sees between the 'Yes' and the 'No', giving the 'No' a *necessary* role in its relationship to the 'Yes'. So Barth can say, "Grace is not grace, if he that receives it is not under judgement. Righteousness is not righteousness, if it be not reckoned to the sinner. Life is not life, if it be not the life from death. And God is not God, if he be not the End of men."[124]

Speaking of this crisis in its form as death Barth states, "It is judgement and betterment, barrier and exit, end and beginning, 'No' and 'Yes', the sign of the

---

[120] Karl Barth, *The Epistle to the Romans, op. cit.,* p. 10.

[121] G.C. Berkouwer, *The Triumph of Grace in the Theology of Karl Barth., op. cit.,* p. 27.

[122] Barth, *The Epistle to the Romans, op. cit.,* p. 173. Later Barth will develop this idea that the first Adam was immediately the first sinner, and from such will come the evidence for our positing the inevitability of the Fall, even of a pre-destined Fall which is further support for our motif of the 'necessary antithesis' developed in Barth's doctrine of evil.

[123] "Those who take upon them the divine 'No' shall themselves be borne by the greater divine 'Yes'." (Barth, *The Epistle to the Romans*, p. 41)

[124] Barth, *The Epistle to the Romans*, p. 187.

wrath of God and the signal of His immanent salvation."[125] The 'Yes' of God is the great miracle of God which comes to humanity exclusively from God in the form of the crisis of faith, grace and salvation. There is a 'breaking down' *(Aufhebung)* and 'building up' *(Begründung)* that is a dominant theme in this second edition. It can be seen with regards to the Gospel of which Barth says, "the whole concrete world is dissolved and established."[126] Barth is again using his own unique interpretation of the Hegelian term *Aufhebung* which enables him to speak of *krisis* as confrontation but not in the direct oppositional way in which it was developed by Hegel.[127] Thus Barth can say that "God conducts men down into Hell, and there releases them."[128]

The relationship between the 'Yes' and the 'No' is crucial for understanding this teaching in Barth. The 'Yes' and the 'No' stand in a dialectical tension with one another, yet they are in tension solely for the sake of the 'Yes'.[129] The 'No' is both necessary and necessarily transitory. It is in and through the judgement of God that the grace of God shines out, for until humanity stands under the judgement and condemnation of God, it cannot know His grace and mercy, His salvation and reconciliation. It is the 'No' which is the necessary prelude to the 'Yes'. As the two stand together in a dialectic of crisis, there is a clear and decisive movement in one direction and one direction only. The dualism of the 'Yes' and the 'No' moves in the direction of dissolving itself as the 'Yes' overcomes the 'No'.

Within this dualism, Barth talks at length about the role of human suffering. The determining factor in this discussion is the phrase 'by faith only'. It is only in faith that we can see how,

> in the peace of God there is sighing and murmuring and weakness... there is suffering and sinking, a being lost and a being rent asunder in the peace of God... in the peace of God there is room also for what the

---

[125] Ibid., p. 169.

[126] Ibid., p. 35.

[127] This is pointed out in a helpful article by W. Lowe where he writes, "Whatever one is to make of the migration of this cardinal term from Hegel [*Aufhebung*] to Barth, it is safe to assume that it does *not* denote a flat, oppositional negation. Barth says as much by coupling *Aufhebung* and *Begründung*. The resultant phrase, translated as 'dissolved and established', recurs so frequently as to constitute a fundamental trope of the Barthian argument." (W. Lowe, 'Barth as a Critic of Dualism: Re-reading the *Römerbrief*, in *Scottish Journal of Theology*, Volume 41, 1988, pp. 384-385)

[128] Barth, *The Epistle to the Romans, op. cit.,* p. 393.

[129] "The Yes and the No do not limit or compensate each other, but they are *interdependent* in such a manner that the No that is pronounced over all human righteousness points, as *God's* No, to the righteousness of God *with a view to salvation.*" (Berkouwer, *The Triumph of Grace, op. cit.,* p. 25)

world calls unbelief: *My God, my God, why have you forsaken me?* This is the onslaught of death and of hell.[130]

Unsurprisingly, it is in the midst of this suffering that redemption occurs, the 'Yes' is manifest in the midst of the 'No'. The Christian can persevere because of faith for faith "believes in the midst of tribulation and persecution." Thus endurance of the 'No' is possible because we know of the 'Yes', "because we know... No! we do not know it. We know our ignorance. But God knows it; and we believe, and dare to know what God knows."[131] All people suffer, but to the unbeliever it is only a 'No'. Despite the evil of our world in all of its cruelty and bitterness, behind the great contradiction of life, the believer sees the 'Yes', and this 'Yes' in the 'No' is the risen Christ in the crucified One, and thus "we are able to behold at the barrier the place of exit, and in the judgement the Coming Day of Salvation. We, as believers, stand in the negation of the negation of the suffering of Christ."[132] Thus we have a new premise for our tribulation, and what seems as only senseless human suffering becomes an actual positive action of God. "The obstacle to our life becomes the stepping stone to the victory of life."[133] Finally, in our brokenness, it is not some alien 'not-God' who is at its roots, but God Himself. Thus Barth concludes,

> When we recognize that in suffering and brokenness it is God whom we encounter, that we have been cast up against Him and bound to Him, that we have been dissolved *(Aufhebung)* by Him and uplifted by Him, then tribulation worketh *probation* of faith, and faith discovers God to be the Originator of all things, and awaits all from Him.[134]

Again we see clearly how the 'Yes' and 'No' of God are not separate from Him and so the sufferings and tribulations which are manifested from the left hand of God, from His 'No', must not be given some independent status nor can they be assigned to an independent power. It must be seen here that early in Barth, as will be rigourously maintained in the *Church Dogmatics*, both the 'Yes' and the 'No' have their origin and purpose in God. The 'No' of condemnation and the 'Yes' of grace stand equally under the control and command of God. Therefore, "whether a man stands 'fallen' in Adam or 'under grace' in Christ, he is what he is in God, in God Himself, and only in God."[135]

Barth seems quite happy here to locate the origin and responsibility for the 'No' in God, but only as a result of human sin. However, when this is coupled with Barth's statements on the sinfulness of humanity from creation, there

---

130 Barth, *The Epistle to the Romans, op. cit.,* p. 155.
131 Ibid., p. 155.
132 Ibid., p. 156.
133 Ibid., p. 156.
134 Ibid., p. 157.
135 Ibid., p. 177.

emerges the very basis for the problem Barth will face in the *Church Dogmatics* and which is the evidence for our motif of the 'necessary antithesis' of evil to the eternal plans of God. It also is evidence for our second motif of the 'right and left hand of God' and already we see emerging the problems Barth faces in holding together the two ideas of the absolute sovereignty of God and the responsibility for evil from the sin of humanity.

There is also support here for our third motif concerning Barth's 'noetic eschatology'. In line with what Barth has said about suffering above, in the *Römerbrief*, Barth calls into question the reality of this world. What we see, the 'No' of God in the world around us is not the real, final reality, but only points to the 'Yes' which is seen in the eyes of faith. Thus Barth is building upon his commentary on 1 Corinthians 15 and supporting his later development of a thoroughly noetic *parousia*.

Finally, we also have evidence for our fourth motif in Barth's use of Kierkegaard's denial of immediacy of God to humanity. This denial is in part Barth's rejection of the *analogia entis* and can be seen in his quoting of Kierkegaard, "to be known directly is the characteristic mark of the idol."[136] Thus our knowledge of God is by His special self-revelation and it is mediated. Barth raises here the role of faith in the person of Abraham to show that the focus of faith must be on the Object of faith. Thus Barth says of the dialectic of 'Yes' and 'No',

> *Das ist die Unmöglichkeit der Erkenntnis, die Unmöglichkeit der Auferstehung, die Unmöglichkeit Gottes... Eben die Beziehung auf diese Unmöglichkeit ist Abrahams Glaube, der... in völliger Unanschaulichkeit am Rande der Genesishistorie auftaucht... wie es (das Unmöglich) auch am Rande der Philosophie Platos, am Rande der Kunst Grünewalds und Dostojewskis, am Rande der Religion Luthers audgetaucht ist.* [137]

This is the basis for the limitation of our knowledge of God and it is later developed in Barth's interpretation of Anselm. From it comes the understanding of the basic brokenness of theological language in Barth's 'revelatory positivism'.

All four of the motifs in Barth's doctrine of evil are clearly evidenced here, and the development of each has taken a significant step in this critical dialectical period in the early 1920's. Barth's combination of the transcendent Wholly-Otherness of God, the sovereignty of God, the dialectic of 'Yes' and 'No', the

---

[136] Ibid., p. 38.

[137] Barth, *Der Römerbrief, op. cit.,* p. 118. "That is the impossibility of cognition, the impossibility of the resurrection, the impossibility of God... Abraham's faith which appears in complete abstract form on the edge of the history of Genesis is the very reference to this impossibility, just as (the impossible) has appeared marginally in Plato's philosophy, in the art of Grünewald and Dostoyevski and in the religion of Luther."

theme of 'Jesus is Victor' and the pre-historic understanding of the God-humanity 'synthesis' which is the presupposition for all 'possible' theology, all point the way to how his understanding of evil will develop.

This development can be seen at several levels. First, Barth will highlight the sovereignty of God in his doctrine of the Perfections of God in CD II/1, with a special emphasis on how the Wholly Other can, in his freedom and according to his love, become immediate and involved with his creation.

Secondly, Barth will shift his use of the 'Yes' and 'No' from the God-humanity relationship of dialectic theology–which makes the sin of humanity the starting point–to his understanding of the God-nothingness relationship under the influence of the *analogia fidei* of his later theology which found its starting point in the grace of God.[138] It is important here to see, however, that the critical link between the 'Yes' and the 'No', and especially the invaluable contribution made by the 'No' on behalf of the 'Yes', will be maintained. This will form the basis for our first motif that for Barth the 'No', the rejected *das Nichtige*, even in its peculiar ontology, plays a similar 'necessary' role in its relation to the 'Yes' as we have seen here in Barth's early dialectical use of the terms.[139]

---

[138] Although Barth can be said to have "given up the whole conceptual framework of his early (dialectical) work" he still built upon this work and preserved from it a number of critical ideas which were only amended or slightly altered by his later christological emphasis. Thus von Balthasar can conclude, "we should not forget that his early dialectics has not spent its force. When we interpret his *Dogmatics*, we must remember that Barth has never abandoned that first flash of insight, his desire to create a theology, not of being but of 'happening'." (von Balthasar, *The Theology of Karl Barth, op. cit.,* p. 45 and 47)

[139] A point needs to be made here about the source of this 'Yes'-'No' language and of dialectic itself, for it is helpful for the building of our case for our first and second motif. 300 years before Barth, the philosopher and theologian Jacob Boehme saw a shaft of light shine in the darkness of his workshop and he proceeded to build a philosophy which depicted light as dependent upon the opposition of darkness. He developed the idea of the *Ungrund* positing that the No was the very necessary and indispensable partner to the Yes. "All things exist by yes and no, be they divine, diabolical, terrestrial or whatever one likes. The 'one' as yes is power and love, the truth of God and God in person. But it cannot be recognized as such without the no and without the no there would be neither joy nor grandeur nor sensibility." (From E. Bloch, *La philosophie de la Renaissance,* Paris, 1974, p. 79; quoted in Henri Blocher, 'Christian Thought and the Problem of Evil', in *Churchman: Journal of Anglican Theology,* Volume 99, Part 2, 1985, p. 115) Ernst Bloch built on Boehme's idea and concluded that there was evil and good in the heart of God. This idea is clearly unacceptable to Christian theology, but strands of it seem alive in the dialectical theology as we have shown. Barth's use of the 'Yes' and 'No' of God lean strongly in this direction with the very important distinction that the 'No' is not an independently negative (and certainly not a diabolical) element, but the justifiable wrath of God in response to the rebellion of His creation. Still we must not be too blind by this to see the remnants of Boehme's ideas at work. Along these lines we see the continuing influence of Hegel and his ideas of the necessity of evil, and we

Thirdly, the combination of the sovereignty of God, the *Christus Victor*, and the 'Yes' and 'No' terminology will provide Barth with the tools to show how God can be sovereign over evil (and thus reject dualism) and yet allow evil to be inimical towards God and His creation. By employing the 'right and left hand of God' motif as His 'Yes' and 'No', His accepting, positive will and His rejecting negative will, Barth finds his answer to the central criticism posed by the theodicy question–is God willing (His 'Yes'), and is God able (His sovereignty), whence then is evil (His 'No')? Our criticism arises already at this point in our questioning whether this 'Yes'-'No' dichotomy, which works well here to understand the holy God and the sinful world, and which works equally well to understand the holy God and the rejected nothingness, can really be employed to understand the relationship between two 'wills' in God Himself?

This brings us to the problem of evil in Barth's earlier writings. Barth faces the accusation that if the 'No' is in God, then God is the Author of evil. If the 'No' is *necessary* to the 'Yes' being spoken, if the state of humanity which is the nature of humanity demands this crisis for the 'Yes' of God to be heard, then isn't God simply the Originator of evil in order that he may manifest His grace? Barth answers this accusation by stating that God is justified as the Author and Originator of the 'No' purely because of the 'Yes'! The 'No' is only a mystery for those who have never heard the 'Yes'. Judgement, condemnation, sin, suffering and death are an enigma only to those who have not seen that it is only through judgement that we can have forgiveness, it is only in our state of condemnation as a result of sin that we can know salvation through God's miraculous grace. It is only in suffering and death that we can come to Christ in the wholeness of His presence.

The miracle which is the self-justification of God lies in our adoption as the children of God. As a result of this adoption as the ultimate sign of grace and

---

can see also Fichte's idea of the 'positive necessity of the negative'. So too we need to raise initially here the theology of Paul Tillich with regards to his use of the Boehmian terms *Urgrund* and *Ungrund*. Tillich states that "being is essentially bound to non-being." (Paul Tillich, *Systematic Theology I*, (Chicago: University of Chicago Press, 1951), p. 235) Being is by nature both itself and non-being, and therefore God "is the eternal process in which separation occurs and reunion surmounts it." What must be overcome is "the demonical, the anti-divine principle which nevertheless participates in the power of the divine." (p. 242) In *The Courage to Be*, Tillich makes this all-important conclusive remark, "it is non-being which turns God into a living God. Without the No which he in himself and in his creature must surmount, the Yes which God says to himself would be without life." (P. Tillich, *The Courage to Be*, (London: Nibet and Co. Ltd., 1952), p. 176) Thus God is only God as he rejects the non-being and works with creation to surmount it. Again we see vestiges of Tillich in Barth but with some strong modifications. Barth will see the rejection of the 'not-God' as the eternal and effortless work of God. This Barth will call God's 'eternal self-differentiation' and this idea will be critical for our thesis. We will treat it at length but here want only to point out its basis in a line from Boehme, Bloch, Fichte and Hegel and embraced by Tillich. We will also see this theme as a major player in the theology of Moltmann which will also be taken up in some detail in the following chapters.

love, Barth says, "God has justified Himself in our presence and us in His presence. The theodicy has occurred, beside which all our endeavours to justify God are merely taunting ridicule. Speaking with His own voice, and encircled by the glory of His brightness, God has done once for all the existential deed–He has received men as His children."[140]

There are two themes here which will be present in a modified form in the *Church Dogmatics*. First, Barth will not allow for anything to be given an independent status outside of God. Whether positively under the 'Yes' of God or negatively under His 'No', everything has its origin and preservation in God. Barth will be careful to show that evil can only be said to originate in God as it finds its existence in God's rejection of it. Nonetheless he will make it clear that evil has no independent status and in the end is wholly dependent upon God.

Secondly, and closely related, Barth argues that God's actions under the administration of His 'left hand' (or His 'No') are justified because of the work of his 'right hand' (or His 'Yes'). Barth already uses this argument here, and he will expand on this in the development of his doctrines of election, and especially of creation where he will insist that the creation is never to be severed from the covenant, for without it there is no justification of creation, nor of the Creator. The concern that arises in connection with this idea will be seen in our criticism of the justification of the time *post Christum* where we find in Barth that the work of the right hand of God is complete, but the work of His left hand, even under the supposedly more passive *voluntas permittens*, increases to the point of intolerability.

The final point concerns revelation and our ability to have knowledge of God. The motif of Barth's 'revelatory positivism' and the brokenness of theological language emerged mostly from Barth's work and reinterpretation of Anselm's *Fides Quaerens Intellectum*, although there were clear signs of this shift earlier, especially in Barth's Göttingen lectures. Additionally, there is already the groundwork here for such an idea. The sovereignty of God means that even though theology is made possible in the God-man Jesus Christ, that which is finite will never be able to comprehend the infinite (from Plato). Even though this impossibility is overcome in the great possibility of God with humanity, Barth confronts us continually with the fact that 'we need to recognize both our obligation and our inability'. This is for Barth an acceptance of knowledge of God as *aporetic* knowledge, knowledge enfolded in a sense of doubt and perplexity.[141] Later Anselm will give Barth the theological validation for this idea which plays so prominently in his doctrine of evil in the *Church Dogmatics*. In summary, we have located the foundation for all four of our motifs in the early development of Barth's theology within his dialectic frame.

---

[140] Barth, *The Epistle to the Romans, op. cit.,* p. 300.

[141] Jüngel comments that the ideas of perplexity and doubt had no place in Barth's earlier theological studies. Thus aporia was a vital key which allowed Barth to further sever the ties with the Liberal Protestantism of his day. Jüngel concludes, "with this aporetic knowledge, his [Barth's] theological beginnings came to an end." (Jüngel, *Karl Barth: A Theological Legacy, op. cit.,* p. 69).

Barth's Dialectic Eschatology

The fourth motif, that of Barth's 'noetic eschatology', receives further treatment in Barth's early work in his commentary on 1 Corinthians 15 published in 1924 entitled 'The Resurrection of the Dead'. Here Barth affirms that the creature has not found God but God has found His creature and has "set him on his path, took him captive, entrusted him with his stewardship, without making any covenant with him, without making him promises for his person, simply as the Lord who can command."[142] In this confrontation,[143] God allows Himself to be known by humanity and as humanity knows God and recognizes Him in His absolute sovereignty, humanity sees that it is separated from its goal by "an unbridgeable chasm."[144] As we stare across this chasm we live in crisis, in the dichotomy between this life and the true reality.[145] Our hope lies in our waiting for the full revelation of the sovereignty of God, and this hope is based on the understanding that the God who is the end is also the God who is the beginning in a continuing *parousia*. On our side of the chasm, life is lived out under the sign of death, which is the "peak of all that is contrary to God in the world, the last enemy."[146] For us the Kingdom of God is still coming when God will be all in all, "That God is all in all is not true, but must become true... if it is to be genuine, it must only be comprehended now as Christian dualism, as the tension between promise and fulfillment, between 'not yet' and 'one day'."[147] So in this world Barth can see Christ as "striding from struggle to struggle and finally approaching the inconceivable supreme victory."[148] Barth concludes that the meaning of the Kingdom of Christ, "is

---

[142] Karl Barth, *The Resurrection of the Dead*, (London: Hodder Stoughton, 1933), pp. 53-54.

[143] Barth says of the resurrection, "The great answer which, by reason of the fact that it is exactly given *there*, first awakens all of questions of life, comprehends in a single question, can only confront mankind as the question of all questions, and in this disguise as question can only be grasped as answer also." (Ibid., p. 107)

[144] Ibid., p. 87.

[145] "The dead: that is what we are. The risen: that is what we are not. But precisely for this reason the resurrection of the dead involves that that which we are not is equivalent with that which we are: the dead living, time eternity, the being truth, things real." (Ibid., p. 114) He continues in this real-unreal dichotomy, "the life that we dead are living here and now is not *this* life, of which we can only ever say that we are not yet living it." (p. 115) Here we see the sharp distinction between what we call 'reality' and what is the true reality. This is Barth's emerging realism and it is key to his development of his doctrine of time and his eschatology.

[146] Ibid., p. 178.

[147] Ibid., p. 179.

[148] Ibid., p. 178.

never exhausted in what is present and given."[149] So we live in faith and hope that what lies beyond the chasm is our future and will overcome that which we know now as daily life and the struggle under the shadow of death.

Here we see the seeds of Barth's later eschatology with his wholly noetic *parousia* and his realism which sees the stark difference between what we see and experience as *Wirklichkeit* and the true reality in Christ. Barth's talk here of the striding of the Lord from struggle to struggle is a point which seems to have been forgotten by Barth until much later in his *Church Dogmatics*, for it is not until the end of IV/3 in his writings on the Prophetic Office of Christ under the title 'Jesus Christ, the True Witness' that we see him develop this idea of the battle between the Lord and the nothingness in the time of the community. In his stress on the completed work of Christ and the transcendence of God's time, as well as the continued defense of the absolute sovereignty of God in relationship to evil, Barth loses this sense of a continued battle in the world. As we will see, even when he does take it up in CD IV/3, he is unable to give the battle any real legitimacy.[150]

Part of this entire eschatological dilemma for Barth arises with his doctrine of time and history, and here we see the foundation for so much of what he will develop in CD I/2. Here in 1924, in his rejection of the historification of *Heilsgeschichte*, Barth posits a concept of time which, although for us is like a ribbon which is "unwound endlessly," is instead for God "rolled up into a ball, a thousand years as a day. Together he calls Abraham and us and our children's children."[151] That time is like a ribbon rolled up in a ball is the precursor for Barth's idea of 'contingent contemporaneity' in his doctrine of time. This accounts for Barth's understanding of creation-reconciliation-redemption as one act of the *parousia*. Since God's time is without past, present or future, this one

---

[149] Ibid., p. 180.

[150] Here the battle with evil is given its full force as seen in this important excerpt: "The error of the Corinthians may be understood in this wise: they comprehended what had happened in Christ in the world as something finished and satisfying in itself. In reality it is only a beginning, in fact only an indication; Christ is come to deliver the Kingdom to the Father, after he has taken their force away from the powers warring against God, and has undermined the world, so to speak (Zündel). The hostile powers are all independent beginnings and forces, whose relationship to God is not yet clear. We must see Christ in *conflict* with all that is in this sense obscure, not at peace with it. The Christian monism of the Corinthians, who regarded the Kingdom of God as already established, is a pious godlessness. No, the Kingdom of God is in course of coming, and *that* is characteristic for our situation in Christ." (Ibid., p. 177) There are some shocking features to this statement given what Barth will develop in his *Church Dogmatics*. The uncompleted work of Christ and the independence of the hostile powers with regards to God are striking here, for they will be either greatly modified or completely dropped in Barth's later eschatology. We have said that the idea of the ongoing conflict of Christ also undergoes great revision and only emerges with any force at the very end of the *Church Dogmatics*.

[151] Ibid., p. 218.

parousia (what Barth will call the 'time of revelation' or 'God's time for us') stands in a dialectic relationship to our 'lost time'.[152]

The primary problem here is the criticism we have leveled–namely, that this eschatology makes a justification for the time of the community *post Christum* difficult at best, and in doing so, it leaves Barth open for a direct attack on the question of theodicy. Nowhere in the *Church Dogmatics* does Barth's dilemma come more to the fore than in his attempt to deal with the issue of evil in the time between the resurrection and the final *parousia*. The roots of this dilemma are seen here already in Barth's understanding of God's time and of the one simultaneous *parousia*. We must remember that although he can talk here of a struggle in which the Lord is engaged in this present time, it is a struggle in the tension between a thesis and an antithesis which flow *from* an *a priori* synthesis–namely, the completed work of Christ, the eternal *parousia*. We also have here a glimpse of the basis for Barth's doctrine of election from which the charge of universalism is raised, not that Barth affirms such but that his theology leaves no room for a viable alternative. This glimpse is seen in the following statement,

'In Adam all die',is the account of every human life ruled off; 'in Christ shall all be made alive'. Note the antithesis of present and future. The former indicates our condition with which we have to reckon; the later is the promise in which we may hope. Observe also, the 'all', obvious from the start, the later following 'who belong to Christ' (Christ's), to be understood not as exclusively, but as representative. The resurrection, like death, concerns *all*.[153]

Thus we find the early foundation for Barth's eschatology which will undergo great modification as it re-appears in the *Church Dogmatics* as our motif of Barth's 'noetic eschatology'.

---

[152]   Here we have a major indication of Barth's intention with regards to the differentiation of salvation time and our time. He writes, "We thus stand in the connexion of *salvation history*, which is a real history: the perishing of an old, the becoming of a new, a path and a step on this path, no mere relationship, but history which is not enacted in time, but between time and eternity-*the* history, in which the creation, the resurrection of Christ, and the End, as verse 48 indicates, are one day." (Ibid., pp. 211-212) Far from being detached from our history, as some critics have stated, salvation history is the connexion of our time with God's time, and it gives a true reality to our time. To claim a detachment of God's reality to ours is to put imperative before indicative, and it is to reverse the direction of the traversing of the abyss which stands between God and us.

[153]   Ibid., p. 175.

Barth's Göttingen Dogmatics, 1924–1925

In what D.L. Migliore calls the first of three cycles of dogmatics in Barth's career,[154] Barth developed his view of evil during a series of lectures given in Göttingen in which he addressed the problem of evil as an aspect of God's creation and under His providence.[155] Again we find here more than just vestiges of these motifs, but their development into themes which Barth will return to time and again in the cycles of lectures which follow in his career. His doctrine of evil in the *Church Dogmatics* can be anticipated here as these motifs are given further definition and refinement.

In §19 entitled '*Die Schöpfung*' Barth seeks to distinguish between the *valde bonum* of creation and the existence of *Übel, Sünde und Tod*. Starting with sin and death Barth affirms,

> We have spoken about the perfection of God's creation. In what I have done I have intentionally not mentioned two words: the words sin and death. And for the reason that they do not belong. Sin and death have nothing to do with God's creation.[156]

---

[154] The following two cycles were Barth's lectures in Münster and the publication of *Die Christliche Dogmatik im Entwurf, 1. Die Lehre vom Worte Gottes, Prologomena zur Christlichen Dogmatik*; and Barth's lectures in Bonn which are contained in the *Church Dogmatics*. (Daniel L. Migliore, 'Karl Barth's First Lectures in Dogmatics: *Instructions in the Christian Religion*', in *The Göttingen Dogmatics,* ed. by Hannelotte Reiffen and translated by Geoffrey Bromiley, (Grand Rapids: W.B. Eerdmans Publishing Company, 1990), pp. xv-xvii)   We find that in both the *Göttingen Dogmatics* and supremely in the *Church Dogmatics* Barth refines and develops his understanding of evil. Yet the same cannot be said for his treatment of evil in *Die Christliche Dogmatik im Entwurf,* which is sketchy and which adds nothing distinct to the development of this doctrine in his early theology. For this reason we do not have a section on *Die Christliche Dogmatik im Entwurf.*

[155] It should be pointed out here the impact which Heinrich Heppe's *Dogmatics* has on Barth at this point.   Barth credits Heppe's work for helping him to find a way to 'do' dogmatics, "I found a dogmatics which had both form and substance, which was oriented on the central themes of witnesses to the revelation given in the Bible, and which could also explore their individual details with an astonishing wealth of insights." (Barth, *Introduction to Heppe's Dogmatics*, (Allen & Unwin, 1950), p. 5, quoted in Busch, *Karl Barth, op. cit.,* p. 154)   Heppe's influence was part of the reason Barth could later write a *Church 'Dogmatics'* and, consequently, that we can in fact talk about a 'doctrine' of evil in Barth's theology.

[156] Karl Barth, *Unterricht in der Christlichen Religion*, Volume II, (Zürich: Theologischer Verlag, 1990), p. 242. "*Von der Vollkommenheit der Schöpfung Gottes sprachen wir. Ich habe zwei Worte im Bisherigen absichlich nicht ausgesprochen: die Worte Sünde und Tod. Und zwar darum nicht, weil sie nicht hierher gehören. Sünde und Tod haben mit der Schöpfung Gottes nicht zu tun.*" (translation mine)

He picks up evil soon after, *"Als Übel ist die Welt, ist das, was wir so heißen an der Weltwirklichkeit, nicht von Gottes geschaffen."*[157] Thus none of what Barth calls *dieser dreinen Größen* (*Übel, Sünde und Tod*) can be attributed to the positively-willed creation nor can they be associated with the *Vollkommenheit der Schöpfung Gottes* nor with creation as *valde bonum*. To understand the place of these three matters, Barth reintroduces the dialectical of the 'Yes' and 'No' of God, and the corresponding *Nachtseite* and *Lichtseite* which both must be seen in the *Vollkommenheit der Schöpfung Gottes*. Therefore, *"Die Nachtseite des Daseins, die Gerichtsseite des göttlichen Wortes hat für uns ein mächtiges Übergewicht gewonnen. Wir stehen teifer im Nein als im Ja."*[158] In this way the dark side of creation is part of the goodness of creation in that it is suited to be part of God's revelation to His creation; a self-revelation which consists in both revealedness and hiddenness. *"Die Nachtseite des Daseins eignet sich besser zum Träger und Medium auch des göttlichenWortes selbst als seine Lichtseite."*[159] Here we see more evidence of a growing dependence upon the 'Yes' and 'No' of God, which is a part of His nature and which is therefore a part of His self-revelation in creation. When this is shifted to the 'right and left hand of God' in the *Church Dogmatics* we have the basis for Barth's attempt to reject all dualism while exonerating God of the charge of *auctor peccati*.

Barth also moves the whole discussion of evil in creation into the realm of ultimate mystery, and in an early sign of his understanding of the brokenness of theological language under the motif of his 'revelatory positivism', Barth refers the problem of evil, sin and death in creation as *'dreifache Rätsel '*.

In §20 entitled *'Die Vorsehung '* evil receives its most direct treatment and here again Barth is faced with the dilemma of God's lordship over creation and the presence of evil as a part of its existence. Barth makes the point that the *Vollkommenheit der Schöpfung Gottes* lies in its 'createdness' for perfection is manifested in its light and dark side. Barth describes this as a *"doppeltes Reden [ist], ein Fragen und Antworten, ein Sich-Verhüllen und Sich-Enthüllen."*[160] This is important for Barth for it allows him to set up the all-important tension in his theology between the ability of His creation to fall (because of their non-divinity displayed in this dark side) and the impossibility of their fall (in the goodness of creation on both the light and dark side). This tension is seen in that while Barth insists that God's good and perfect creation does give rise to sin, evil and death, *"Das bedeutet nicht, daß das Übel notwendig zur Welt*

---

[157] Ibid. p. 243. "Then evil in the world, as the so called created world reality, is not from God."

[158] Ibid. p. 244. "The dark side of existence, the judgement side of the divine Word has gained for us one powerful emphasis. We stand deeply (profoundly) in the 'No' as in the 'Yes'."

[159] Ibid. p. 244. "The dark side of existence is better suited to be a bearer and medium, as the divine Word is itself suited to the light side."

[160] Ibid. p. 293. "a double communion, a questioning and answering, a concealing of Himself and a revealing of Himself."

gehört,"[161] yet he admits that, "*die Welt als unsere Menschenwelt ist ganz und gar die Welt der Sünde und des Übels und des Todes.*"[162] The distinction is found in Barth's rejection of Schleiermacher's view of evil as a '*Lebenshemmungen*', for this would make evil a necessary part of God's good creation. We remember that in the 'necessary antithesis' motif we are not affirming anything like Schleiermacher's *Lebenshemmungen*, for in this motif nothingness is never seen as part of the positively-willed creation. It is, however, an inevitable aspect of God's creation as His self-recapitulation of His eternal state of self-differentiation.

When Barth speaks of God's working good from evil, he seeks to distinguish this from the conclusion that God created the evil that He may bring the good from it, and thus that God needed the evil for the sake of the good. However, we believe that the distinction between Schleiermacher's *Lebenshemmungen* and Barth's view of the role of evil to God's eternal will for creation is fundamental. The distinction lies in that Barth will never say that God created evil that good may come. What he does say is that God created knowing that evil would be temporarily victorious, and thus chose through election to work good from what was, to His perfect and yet non-divine creation, both impossible and inevitable. The roots of this impossibility-inevitability tension are seen here,

> It is very difficult, it must be admitted, to put into words the sharp distinction between the created and the fallen world. It is not only because the world in question is one and the same, not only because we know no other world than the fallen one, but especially because the difference between the created and fallen world (and between created and fallen man at its centre), although this difference seems as wide as a chasm, is but a hair's breath. It would be better to state it bluntly than to think about it because with every word one says, one runs into the danger (to be avoided at all costs) of justifying the Fall, the disobedience, the destruction of the world with the thought that God wanted the world in this form and still wants it so. One runs the danger of justifying God (which is also to be avoided) because of the connection *which must exist* between God's creation and the possibility (not however reality!) of the Fall, the disobedience and the destruction of the world created by Him. (emphasis mine)[163]

---

161 Ibid. p. 293. "This does not mean that evil is necessarily part of the world."
162 Ibid. p. 288. "this world as our world of man is entirely a world of sin, evil and death."
163 Ibid. p. 291. "*Es ist sehr schwar, das ist vorweg zuzugeben, jenen scharfen Schnitt zwischen der geschaffenen und der gefallenen Welt auch nur einigermaßen einleuchtend in Worte zu bringen, und zwar nicht nur darum, weil es sich ja um eine und dieselbe Welt handelt, nicht nur darum, weil wir keine andere Welt kennen als die gefallene, sondern vor Allem darum, weil der Unterschied zwischen der geschaffenen und der gefallenen Welt und in ihrem Mittelpunkt zwischen dem geschaffenen und dem*

Here Barth introduces one of the many tensions which run throughout his doctrine of evil for he affirms that if we deny the connection between God's creation and the possibility of the Fall, we deny God's providence, for 'divine providence is providence of the fallen world'. There is in creation, as the *Vollkommenheit der Schöpfung Gottes*, the possibility of the Fall. This point is crucial, for Barth is led here to admit, "*Wir wenden in unserer Lehre vom Menschen mehr davon zu reden haben. In unserem Zusammenhang genügt der Nachweis: Es leigt im Begriff des Menschen als Geschöpf, daß er sündigen kann.*"[164] This capability of sin, which Barth thoroughly rejects in the *Church Dogmatics*, comes about through the combination of humanity's non-divinity and its created free-will. Therefore Barth maintains, against the Hegelian idea of the upward fall and the Kantian view that sinfulness is part of the created nature, that humanity is not by nature sinful.

> First of all we have to speak of man. He is not a sinner, not even from the point of view of predestination... man becomes a sinner through the free decision of his will. Without this freedom he would not be what he is, a creature wanted and placed in the world by God.[165]

Although it is through our misuse of this God-given freedom that we sin, this misuse does not have the strong negative character which Barth develops later as the '*unmöglichen Möglichkeit*' in the *Church Dogmatics*, for here it is simply an 'inversion *(Umkehrung)*' of the positive use of our freedom. Barth says the same for death, for,

> Death exists in God's world as the last enemy (1 Corinthians 15: 26). But indeed it is a possibility for which there is room in His world, a

---

gefallenen Menschen, obwohl er einen Abgrund bedeutet, doch so haarscharf fein ist, daß man ihn vielleicht besser bloß behaupten als irgendwie zu denken versuchen würde, weil man dabei mit jedem Wort, das man sagt, Gefahr läuft, entweder (ws hier vor Allem zu vermeiden ist!) den Abfall, die Empörung, die Zerrüttung der Welt zu rechtfertigen durch den Gedanken, daß Gott die Welt nun einmal so, in dieser Verfassung gewollt habe und noch wolle, oder aber (was hier auch zu vermeiden ist!) Gott zu rechtfertigen unter Übergehen des Zusammenhangs, der zwischen Gottes Schöpfung und (nicht der Wirklichkeit!, aber) der Möglichkeit des Abfalls, der Empörung, der Zerrüttung der von ihm geschaffen Welt bestehen muß" (translation mine)

[164] Ibid. p. 292. "In our teaching on man we shall have more to say of this. Within our context there is sufficient proof that it lies within the concept of man as God's creature, that he is capable of sin."

[165] Ibid. p. 292. "*Vom Menschen ist hier zunächts zu reden. Er ist nicht Sünder, auch nicht unter dem Gesichtspunkt der ewigen doppelten Prädestination... er wird es durch freie Entscheidung seines Willens. Ohne diese Freiheit wäre er nicht, was er ist, vor Gott als wirklich gewolltes und gesetztes Geschöpf.*" (translation mine)

hostility to God based on His relationship to creation, as the world's overthrow and destruction, a possibility that might not be impossible if the freedom of the creature were to be taken into consideration.[166]

It is through this misuse of freedom by the creature that evil becomes a reality in the created world. *"Tut er es, ist damit eine Wirklichkeit in die Welt getreten, die Gott nicht geschaffen, nicht gewollte hat, so gewiß sie ohne ihn nicht wäre, indem sie in seiner Welt ist und kraft der Freiheit seines Geschöpfs."*[167] Thus evil remains both under the lordship of God and the sole responsibility (at least for its entrance into creation) of the creature. This is the point Barth will make again and again, yet in a different form later in the *Church Dogmatics*. The three axioms of the lordship of God over evil, evil's character as distinct from God but not independent of God, and humanity's responsibility for evil in the world, are all held together in Barth's doctrine of evil and the structure and tensions of this doctrine can be seen here in fragmentary form. Clearly Barth is aware of the potential dangers here, for if evil is too closely aligned with God's will according to an absolute sovereignty, then evil loses its inimical character and we end up siding with Schleiermacher. If, however, the enmity between God and evil is overemphasized, it is difficult not to grant some sense of independence to evil which Barth believes must not be done, *"denn die stärkste Betonung der gottwidrigen Wirklichkeit des Bösen darf nichts bis zur Aufrichtung eines metaphysischen Dualismus gehen."*[168]

To keep from this *metaphysischen Dualismus*, Barth develops his thinking on evil according to three distinct themes throughout his doctrine of evil which can be evidenced here. First, he subsumes evil, sin and death under God's providence, depriving it of any independent status. This is again an early sign of the 'right and left hand of God' motif,

> Here too one can speak of the God-willed possibility of evil... It is just the same with evil and death, let us add. When all is said and done, how could they be other than a means in God's hand, indeed tools (here

---

[166] Ibid. p. 295. *"Als der letzte Feind steht er mitten in Gottes Welt (I Kor. 15,26). Aber freilich eine Möglichkeit, die in seiner Welt Raum finden konnte, eine Gottwidrigkeit auf dem Boden seiner Beziehung zum Geschöpf, als ihre Umkehrung und Zerstörung, eine Möglichkeit, die nicht zum vornherein unmöglich sein konnte, wenn die Freiheit des Geschöpfs in dieser Beziehung wirklich gesetzt sein sollte."* (translation mine)

[167] Ibid. p. 292. "If man does sin, a reality has entered the world which God did not create, did not want, and this is as certain as the fact that without Him this reality would not have been, although it is in His world only by virtue of the freedom of His creature."

[168] Ibid. p. 296. "for the strongest emphasis of the God-hating relationship of evil may not go so far as to establish a metaphysical dualism."

the expression is now suitable) with which He creates what He wishes?[169]

Secondly, Barth holds to both positions that God foreknew evil and the Fall, but humanity is responsible for it. In creating His creatures 'free', God knew they would fall. This is the unequivocal result of Barth's 'necessary antithesis' where that from which God has eternally differentiated Himself is able to win victory over His non-divine creation. Two thoughts are at work here. One is that humanity's freedom must be true freedom, and again here there is less talk of the impossibility of sin, for

> With regard to His free creature God does nothing contrary to His will. To express it differently He does not compel. What He does not owe man he denies him, an irresistible grace. In this freedom of man lies the reality of sin.[170]

Thirdly, God's decision to create even with this foreknowledge must be vindicated, and here is the centrality of Barth's doctrine of election to the justification of the Creator within the context of his doctrine of evil.[171] Barth does not develop this idea here with any force, and even when he is compelled to think of this justification, he points more toward the third theme in his understanding of evil, namely, his 'revelatory positivism'.

This third theme is given much attention in the Göttingen lectures.[172] For instance, in articulating the 'Scripture Principle' Barth admits, "*Es wäre vergebliche Mühe, sich die Augen verschließen zu wollen vor der nicht aufzulösenden, sondern nur als solche einzusehenden Paradoxie der These, daß die*

---

[169] Ibid. p. 297. "*Auch von hier aus kann man von der gottgewollten Möglichkeit des Bösen reden... Ebenso im Übel und im Tode, werden wir hinzufügen. Was sollten sie in ihrem letzten Effekt Anderes sein als Mittel in Gottes Hand, freilich als Werkzeuge (hier dürfte der Ausdruck nun passend sein), mit denen er schafft, was er will!*" This view of sovereignty and the inevitable instrumentalism which results is indicative of the 'right and left hand of God' motif.

[170] Ibid. p. 298. "*Gott tut etwas nicht, was er seinem freien Geschöpf gegenüber auch nicht tun will, er zwingt es nämlich nicht, anders ausgedrückt: er versagt ihm, was er ihm auch nicht schuldig ist, eine unwiderstehliche Gnade. In dieser Freiheit des Menschen ist die Sünde Wirklichkeit.*"

[171] We will show the inviolable link which Barth must maintain between God's eternal self-differentiation-election-creation-covenant-reconciliation; for in this linkage lies the justification of creation and the Creator which Barth's doctrine of evil demands.

[172] See especially §15 *Die Erkennbarkeit Gottes*. Here Barth confirms this motif in such statements as, "*Daß der Mensch ihrer fähig ist, das wird behauptet, daß er fähig ist jener Teilnahme an Gottes Selbsterkenntnis, jenes Stehens im Offenbarungsverhältnis, jener indirekten Gotteserkenntnis.*" (Barth, *Unterricht in der Christlichen Religion*, p. 32)

Schrift das Worte Gottes ist."[173] Later in his Göttingen lectures, God's sovereign use of evil is subsumed under the general heading of *permissio* and yet Barth is not comfortable with this, especially when it is translated as 'permission'. Instead, when we try and describe evil,

> We stand at a point in which we can think of God as neither participating (active) nor non-participating (passive) if we are not to arrive at dualism. God in His mystery is inscrutable.[174]

Barth affirms the mystery of this relationship and calls on all expositors on providence to begin their task with faith, for only as such can it be discussed and examined.[175] Perhaps we have here an early sign of Barth's shift from a dialectical methodology to the *analogia fidei* which took full form in his reinterpretation of Anselm's *Fides Quaerens Intellectum*. Certainly Barth saw that speaking of evil required a different form of speech than other excursus on providence, and this speech could only be broken and incomplete, requiring the use of something along the lines of the analogy of faith,

> When one touches on the whole area designated by the words sin, evil, death, one must realise above all in (the) connection with the teaching about Providence, that we stand here before a mystery, which if it is to be included at all, must be considered differently in our thinking on Providence.[176]

It is his understanding of evil, sin and death as the *'dreifache Rätsel'* that leads Barth continually to revert to this mystery in the face of the dilemmas which inevitably arise when these three axioms are held together.

---

[173] Barth, *Unterricht in der Christlichen Religion*, p. 262. "It would be fruitless to try to close our eyes to a paradox that can only be perceived and not resolved, namely, that of the thesis that scripture is God's Word." (Barth, *The Göttingen Dogmatics, op. cit.,* p. 215)

[174] Ibid. p. 298. *"Das ist es ja, daß wir hier vor dem Punkt stehen, wo wir uns Gott weder aktiv noch passiv beteiligt und doch auch, wenn es keinem Dualismus kommen soll, nicht unbeteiligt denken können. Gott in seiner Verhüllen ist eben unbegreiflich. "*

[175] *"Alles Nachdenken darüber, wie Gott sich offenbaren kann, ist wirklich nur ein Nach-Denken der Tatsache, daß Gott sich offenbart hat."* (Ibid. p. 185)

[176] Ibid. p. 290. *"Wenn man den ganzen durch die Worte Sünde, Übel, Tod bezeichneten Kreis berührt, muß [man] doch (man denke doch nur einem Augenblick an die durch sie bezeichneten Realitäten!!) auch im Zusammenhang der Lehre von der Vorsehung vor Allem anerkennen, daß wir hier vor einem Geheimnis stehen, das, wenn überhaupt, jedenfalls anders in den Vorsehungsgedanken ein zubeziechen ist. "*

In these ways it can be seen how the motifs of the 'necessary antithesis', the 'right and left hand of God', and Barth's 'revelatory positivism' were further developed in Barth's Göttingen lectures.[177]

Faith and Anselm's *Fides Quaerens Intellectum*

Barth refers to the 1920's as his "years of apprenticeship."[178] In the late 1920's, as the proponents of dialectic theology were moving in different directions, it was clear that the future of theology for Barth needed yet a further basis upon which to build. His conflicts with Rudolf Bultmann and Emil Brunner led Barth to a rejection of existentialism and natural theology, and his own aborted effort at constructing a dogmatic in his *Christliche Dogmatik im Entwurf* impressed upon Barth the need for a new direction. "I simply could not hold to the theoretical and practical *diastasis* between God and man on which I had insisted at the time of the *Romans*... I had to understand Jesus Christ and bring him from the periphery of my thought into the centre."[179]

In 1931 Barth's discovery of Anselm revolutionized his entire theological method, so much so that he was to completely revise the already published first volume of the *Church Dogmatics*.[180] Prior to doing so Barth published his book on Anselm, *Fides Quaerens Intellectum*, in which Barth discovers the tools which were already emerging in his 1927 work *Die Christliche Dogmatik im Entwurf*, and which he subsequently employed in the rewriting of the first volume and the subsequent writing of the entire rest of the *Church Dogmatics*. This discovery had, according to Barth, freed his thought in a new way of the "last remnants of a philosophical or anthropological... justification and explanation of the Christian doctrine."[181] Von Balthasar comments that after Barth's conversion from liberalism to radical Christianity, which was displayed in his commentary on the Epistle to the Romans, Barth's second great turning point, "was his emancipation from the shackles of philosophy and his quest for a genuine theology that could stand on its own feet. This latter process lasted

---

[177] Although it is incorrect to say that Barth ignores eschatology in his Göttingen lectures, we found here no exceptional treatment of the 'noetic eschatology' motif to merit its mentioning.

[178] Busch, *Karl Barth, op. cit,* p. 193.

[179] Ibid. p. 173.

[180] "In this book on Anselm I am working with a vital key, if not the key, to an understanding of that whole process of thought that has impressed me more and more in my *Church Dogmatics* as the only one proper to theology." (Karl Barth, *Anselm: Fides Quaerens Intellectum,* (Richmond: SCM Press and John Knox Press, 1960, p. 11)

[181] Busch, *Karl Barth, op. cit.,* p. 206.

about ten years; it found expression in his little book on the Anselmian proofs for God's existence."[182]

The Relationship of Fides and Intellectere

In Anselm's ontological proof of God, Barth interpreted the key saying *quo maius cogitari nequit* as ascribing to God a name which is so above all anthropological conception that we can only stand before the bearer of that name as the creature before the Creator.[183] As this Creator then reveals Himself to us, we are made able to talk and speak of Him but only in faith, the faith in that which is beyond our human conception, and therefore in faith which seeks understanding. "In this relationship which is actualised by virtue of God's revelation, as he thinks of God he knows that he is under this prohibition; he can conceive of nothing greater, to be precise, 'better', beyond God without lapsing into the absurdity, excluded by faith, of placing himself above God in attempting to conceive of this greater."[184] Thus Barth's interpretation of Anselm's *fides quaerens intellectum* became the fundamental model for his theological epistemology.

For Barth, *quarere intellectum* is immanent in *fides*. Faith does not require proof, but "Anselm wants 'proof' and 'joy' because he wants *intellegere* and he wants *intellegere* because he believes."[185] Faith is the "knowledge and

---

[182] von Balthasar, *The Theology of Karl Barth, op. cit.*, p. 80. The strict division in the progression of Barth's theological development as found in von Balthasar, which puts the change from dialectic theology to the *analogia fidei* solely as the product of Barth's work on Anselm, has been challenged by Bruce McCormack in his doctoral dissertation, 'A Scholastic of a Higher Order: The Development of Karl Barth's Theology, 1921-1931', Princeton Theological Seminary, 1989, where McCormack provides evidence that this shift ocurred earlier, particularly in Barth's work in Göttingen.

[183] "We are dealing with a concept of strict noetic content which Anselm describes here as a concept of God. It does not say that God is, nor what he is, but rather, in the form of a prohibition that man can understand, who he is. It is *one définition purement conceptuelle*." (Barth, *Anselm: Fides Quaerens Intellectum, op. cit.*, p. 75) For Barth it is not a content of thought only with which we are dealing, but a true content filled up with God Himself. Thus E. Gilson is incorrect when he maintains that Anselm's name for God expresses only a content of thought or an essence. (Gilson, *'Sens et nature de l'argument se saint Anselme'*, in *Archives d'histoire doctrinale et littèraire du Moyen Age 9,* (1934) as quoted in G. Watson 'Karl Barth and St. Anselm's Theological Programme', in *Scottish Journal of Theology*, Volume 30, Number 1, 1977, p. 31n.) There is ontological reality behind the noetic content of the name of God, and that ontic actuality fills up the noetic with a distinct richness of content far beyond the idea of essence or thought.

[184] Karl Barth, 'Anselm: Fides quaerens intellectum', (Richmond: SCM Press and John Knox Press, 1960), in C. Green's (ed.) *Karl Barth: Theologian of Freedom*, (London: Collins, 1989), p. 146.

[185] Barth, *Anselm: Fides Quaerens Intellectum, op. cit.*, pp. 16-17.

affirmation of the Word of Christ," understanding is "reflecting on what has been said and affirmed beforehand by the creed," and this understanding involves a searching and seeking to articulate the truth of the God who has revealed Himself.[186]

Barth has now found a relationship between God and human knowledge of God which clarifies and keeps well in place the ontological objectivity and transcendence of the former over the latter, even in God's self-revelation.[187] Thus Barth affirms, "on no account can the givenness or non-givenness of the results of *intellegere* involve for faith the question of its existence."[188] Here is a direct indication of Barth's ever growing realism. Gordon Watson writes, "the truth of any noetic *ratio* is dependent upon its correspondence to the ontic *ratio* for the establishment of the veracity of its concepts and propositions; under no circumstances can it be conceived as creative."[189] If it is true that there is no relationship between the result of our search for knowledge and the legitimacy of our faith, it is equally true that our faith itself demands this search.

Faith is a 'movement of the will' in which a rational creature will seek after knowledge as a result of faith. This faith is not an anthropocentric or existential phenomenon, but keeping to his roots in Kierkegaard and Zündel, Barth describes faith as "something new encountering us and happening to us from the outside... and that it comes to us and that we have the *rectitudo volendi* to receive it, is grace."[190] As we receive faith in grace it moves us in a search for greater a understanding of its object. Yet despite the grace in faith, there is a limit to the *intellegere* which is achievable by humanity, and so the hunger for *intellegere* is a continuing one carried out in the faith that the "God in whom we believe is the

---

[186] Busch, *Karl Barth, op. cit.,* p. 206.

[187] We can see here Barth's break with Kant who separated the idea of dogmatic faith from the more preferable 'pure rational faith'. Only the latter can be a true source of knowledge for only the results of pure rational faith can result in an idea whose objects can be adopted into one's maxims of thought and knowledge. Therefore Kant refers to dogmatic faith as "dishonest or presumptuous." (Kant, *Religion Within the Limits of Reason Alone*, (New York: Harper and Brothers, 1934), p. 48)

[188] Barth, *Anselm: Fides Quaerens Intellectum, op. cit.,* p. 17.

[189] He continues by quoting Barth, "Fundamentally, the *ratio* either as ontic or noetic is never higher than the Truth but Truth itself is the master of all *rationes* beyond the contrast between ontic and noetic, deciding for itself, now here, now there, what is *vere ratio*." (Barth, *Anselm: Fides Quaerens Intellectum*, p. 47) He concludes that "Because Truth disposes of all *rationes* the revelation of Truth must be in the form of authority. The human capacity for reason itself becomes a *vere ratio* when it conforms to this something that is dictated. This is not to be understood as a sacrifice of intellectual integrity, but the only possible and ultimately rational attitude one can assume before the authority of the believed but hidden *ratio* of the Object of faith." (Watson, 'Karl Barth and St. Anselm's Theological Programme', *op. cit.,* p. 32)

[190] Barth, *Anselm: Fides Quaerens Intellectum*, p. 19.

causa veritatis in cognitatione."[191] For these reasons, theology is a necessary response, a hunger for understanding in response to faith.

Conditions of Theology as Fides Quaerens Intellectum

Barth finds within Anselm eight conditions of theology[192], of which three stand out for our consideration. The first (number 3 in Barth's list) is the idea that "every theological statement is an inadequate expression of its object... it is only God himself who has a conception of God" because "God shatters every syllogism."[193] From this Barth builds upon his *analogia fidei* by stating that "it is possible for expressions which are really appropriate only to objects that are not identical to God, to be true expressions... even when these expressions are applied to the God who can never be expressed."[194] Therefore there is both a brokenness to all theological language about God and yet, through the analogy of faith, God can be known according to these 'true expressions' of the inexpressible. The tension established here between the inadequacy of our ability to conceive of God and the ability of God to be expressed by analogy, is expressed in our motif of 'revelatory positivism'.

This is heightened in the second condition (number 5 in Barth's list) in which he states that there are both those *maiores et plures rationes* which are ultimately inaccessible to us and those *rationes* which are only temporarily hidden but which are "intrinsically accessible and have still to be laid bare in the future."[195] It is God who allows this progress to occur from time to time when these theological insights are allowed to flourish. We have here also the basis for Barth's particularism which emerges within his *Church Dogmatics*. There we will find in Barth a remarkable tolerance for mystery and a rejection of all temptations to explain away contradictions which arise in order to posit some sort of solution, and we will be critical of this approach in selected places. We have here its roots in Barth's indissoluble union of God with His revelation, and its consequent impact upon language and its incapacity to apprehend and explain that revelation.

Our question is how we are to know if a given theological insight is a 'laying bare' of those *rationes* which are only temporarily hidden or if it is a heretical leap into the beyond and an abandonment of faith? Barth lays out the conditions for validity of theological statements (number 6 on Barth's list) which prove little help. Although the ultimate criterion is Scripture–all theological statements must not conflict with Scripture–the very nature of theology makes this criterion of only very limited use. Theology begins where clear biblical evidence ends and so there is an inherent vulnerability to all

---

191 Ibid. p. 21.
192 Ibid. pp. 26 - 40.
193 Ibid. p. 29.
194 Ibid. pp. 30-31.
195 Ibid. p. 32.

theology which can find its approval only in the human sphere of the author and his listeners. The final approval has no appellate court which is normative.

From these conditions of theology we find the roots of Barth's understanding that theological statements can be both valid and invalid, that in their essential brokenness they can, from time to time and via certain vehicles of analogy, express the inexpressible and give us sure information and knowledge of God. When this cautious view is coupled with Barth's understanding of the status of the theologian with regards to the subject of evil and sin, the brokenness of theological language regarding evil takes on its full force. Yet in the midst of this there is also the twin teachings that God can be known, indeed that he makes himself known in the *analogia fidei* and that those seemingly inexpressible areas of knowledge are made accessible to us by faith in the power of the interpreting Spirit. All of this brings us to wonder to what extent Barth can use the brokenness of theological language as a refuge for theological paradoxes with regard to his doctrine of evil. If there is only a limited justification for the tolerance of such paradoxes, then we find the heart of our criticism of our fourth motif here in the centre of Barth's all-important work on Anselm.

Continuing in his interpretation of Anselm, Barth considers the manner of theology done according to the necessity, possibility and conditions laid out above. In an important statement for our motif, Barth says that the inner and outer texts of revelation are "wrapped in mystery and we can grasp them only by a special effort of understanding that goes beyond mere reading."[196] Here Barth places theology in a position beyond the Biblical text by its very nature, where its statements cannot be validated by an appeal to Scripture. Theology is a continual process of building, tearing down *(Aufhebung)* and rebuilding *(Beständigung)* without the final hope that the process can end. The product is not a final synthesis, but a transitory one which will give rise to yet another antithesis and so on.

The Rising Conflict of Theodicy with Barth's Emerging Theological Methodology

It is clear at this early stage how the whole basis of theodicy conflicts with Barth's theology. At the very place where theodicy seeks a definitive answer, a final synthesis from the thesis and antithesis which form its 'problem', Barth seeks only new understandings which will themselves undergo additional negation and reconstruction. In addition, we already see Barth's understanding of revelation as inseparable from God Himself. As such, the object of inquiry of theodicy cannot be put under the microscope, but it is itself the Confronter. Far from needing to justify God, the interpreter stands in need of His justification, and the language used to accuse God is utterly transcended by Him, ultimately shifting the problem from 'theodicy' to 'anthropodicy'. From the very outset,

---

[196] Ibid. p. 42.

the ability to justify God is beyond us as we stand in relation to God. It is also beyond the ability of language which is in need of God's grace to be able to speak authoritatively about Him. The very nature of the theological task makes justification of God both impossible and unthinkable,

> *Beides ist wahr, und beides hat seinen Grund darin, dass die Theologie ihre eigene Existenz, ihre Notwendigkeit und ihre Möglichkeit, ihre Arbeit und ihre Ergebnisse nicht selbst zu rechtfertigen braucht, nicht selbst rechtfertigen kann und auch nicht selbst rechtfertigen wollen darf.*[197]

Although Barth will move away from dialectical theology as his main methodological tool, he never abandons either its high view of revelation or its rejection of any and all final and absolute syntheses in theology. Barth time and again refers to the 'brokenness of all theological language' in his use of the 'revelatory positivism' motif in his attempts to expound upon sin and evil.[198] In using this motif, Barth believes he is free to draw conclusions from his work which at times bring the charge of speculation and conjecture. Yet Barth here has laid the groundwork for an understanding of theology as building upon Scripture but going beyond the confines of 'It is written' as the basis for every theological statement. This also goes hand in hand with Barth's realism which sees the Truth as a living and dynamic Lordship which is involved in the theological work of the Church. Barth will not let theology be tied to 'proof-texting' but sees it as an expression of the relationship between a living Church and a living Lord, and as such it must be given this dynamic of validation and progression.

Necessitatis and Rationes

In this same section, Barth produces a long and involved argument involving *necessitatis* and *rationes*. The end product is the position that *necessitatis* must precede *rationes* [199] and therefore,

---

[197] Link, '*Fides quaerens intellectum: Die Bewegung der Theologie Karl Barth's*', *op. cit.*, p. 279. "Both [theology's richness and difficulty] are true and both have their origin in the fact that theology does not need to justify its own existence, its necessity and its possibility, its work and its results; theology cannot justify them and is not allowed to want to justify them."

[198] "We soberly acknowledge that we have here an extraordinarily clear demonstration of the necessary brokenness of all theological thought and utterance... it is broken thought and utterance to the extent that it can progress only in isolated thoughts and statements directed from different angles to the one object. It can never form a system." (CD III/3, p. 293)

[199] This is the result of the twofold conclusion that ontic necessity precedes noetic rationality and ontic rationality precedes noetic necessity.

'rational' knowledge of the object of faith is derived from the object of faith and not *vice versa* ... His [Anselm's] starting point is therefore not to seek 'what can be' but to seek 'what is' and in fact to seek 'what cannot fail to be'. It is precisely as 'what cannot fail to be' that he tries to conceive 'what is'. Corresponding to the basis in faith there has to be a reason in knowledge; to the ontic a corresponding noetic necessity.[200]

This will be the pattern for the development of Barth's theology–from the ontic to the noetic; from the object of faith to the knowledge of the object of faith; from indicatives to imperatives, and never the other way around. The attainment of the *intellectum fidei* comes about by one's being mastered by the object of faith, and then moving to a true ontic *ratio*.

The Aim of Theology

A final word needs to be said in conjunction with the aim of theology, for here we see the seeds of Barth's ontological union of all humanity on Christ. Barth believes that Anselm had no apologetic intent in his 'proofs' but instead presupposed faith on the part of all of his readers. Indeed the lack of faith seemed almost an impossibility for Anselm, therefore he is not seeking to 'prove' God as though one could apprehend such proofs from a state of unbelief, but he is attempting *intelligere* from the basis of faith. This is seen in Barth's view that in Anselm the *ratio veritatis*, "is at no point the subject of discussion but on the contrary it forms the self-evident basis for discussion."[201] Barth concludes by querying whether Anselm knew of no other way of addressing people other than as believers, Christians, non-sinners. In this way the proofs are not an attempt to stand on one side of the gulf between believer and non-believer, but in these proofs Anselm crossed the gulf, "though on this occasion not in search of a truce as has been said of him and has often happened, but–here reminiscences of the days of the Crusaders could come to fore–as conqueror whose weapon was the fact that he met the unbelievers as one of them and accepted them as equal."[202]

As Barth discusses this idea in Anselm one can begin to sense the growing understanding of the true impossibility of unbelief, the impossibility of humanity turning from God, the ontological impossibility of sin.[203] Here are

---

[200] Barth, *Anselm: Fides Quaerens Intellectum*, *op. cit.*, p. 52.

[201] Ibid. p. 60.

[202] Ibid. p. 71.

[203] It is only the 'fool' who fails to achieve understanding, and this fool is akin to the sinful man who would attempt to justify himself before a holy and righteous God. Commenting on this Watson writes, "The fool is one who cannot appreciate at the decisive point, the inexpressible freedom of God in His movement toward the creature: by this fact he is simply revealed to be a fool." (Watson, 'Karl Barth and St Anselm's Theological Programme', *op. cit.*, p. 38.) Yet the fool and the believer are

the roots of Barth's shift of the 'Yes' and 'No' of dialectical theology away from the God-humanity relationship to the God-evil relationship. With the emphasis turning from sinful humanity (as in dialectical theology) to the God of grace (as in the analogy of faith), the inimical relationship ceased to be between Creator and creation and was shifted to Creator and non-created, to the positively willed and the negatively willed, and ultimately (although not for some years to come) to the work of the right hand of God and the work of His left hand.

Summary of Barth's Interpretation of Anselm

In summary, Barth's discovery of Anselm and his unique interpretation of his ontological proof of God has given him the methodological justification for affirming faith as the final answer to all questions of theodicy. In seeking to understand God in the mystery of His revelation in Jesus Christ, our words can only be incomplete and formative in the continuing theological (and ecclesiastical!) process of understanding the 'vision of God'.[204] This is the influence of Barth's emerging realism.

When, in addition, we are dealing with the very special area of evil, sin and nothingness, this understanding is even more fragmentary and the conclusions drawn from it even more difficult and paradoxical. For here we must not only try to talk about the hidden and revealed God but we must attempt to articulate the nothingness which stands over and against us and with which we still must battle daily.[205] Thus we are still in the field of contradiction, incompleteness and discord and in such we can only respond with faith in the truth and reality which is always above and outwith this contradiction. Yet because the reality of revelation is truly 'The Reality', we can do so with confidence and joy in spite

---

in the same ontological position. The believer must believe from the same position in which the fool rejects, and therefore Watson can conclude "the epistemological implications of the freedom of God's election of man in Jesus Christ has this effect for both the fool and the believer." (pp. 38-39)

[204] This mystery involves what Watson calls a "structural hiddenness of revelation" which is inseparable from his revealedness. Thus, "it is precisely because God is the revealed God that he is the veiled and incomprehensible God; the whole point of the proof is to raise this incomprehensibility of God from being an article of faith to the level of understanding its necessity in terms of the Object of theological knowledge." (Watson, 'Karl Barth and St Anselm's Theological Programme', p. 35)

[205] This nothingness Barth will define as *das Nichtige* and here in Anselm, in Barth's interpretation of the *Proslogion III*, there is a movement in this direction. Of it Watson writes, "the nerve of the proof is seen to consist in what it denies rather than what it asserts. By what this revealed Name forbids, God is distinguished from all things whose existence can possibly be conceived as non-existent." (Watson, 'Karl Barth and St Anselm's Theological Programme', p. 37) From here Barth will go on in the *Church Dogmatics* to say that God is the eternally Self-differentiating God in His eternal rejection of the 'not-God'. It will also be in His rejection of what He does not will (and therefore as that which is by definition non-existence) that the origin of evil will be found.

of and even in response to the existential encounters with the manifestations of evil.[206] Faith is not determined by this existential encounter, but by the ontological reality which it knows and believes in that existential encounter.[207]

In Barth's interpretation of Anselm we find the basis for our third and fourth motif. We find the continued emergence of the 'real-unreal' dichotomy which is so important for Barth's eschatology and which will feature in his defense of the time of the Church. We also find the entire structural basis for Barth's idea of the brokenness of theological statements within his 'revelatory positivism' and his corresponding justification of paradox and mystery.

---

[206] Important for Barth's entire theological methodology is the idea that God's Self-revelation is always in act. The conclusion of *Proslogion II* is that God cannot exist in the understanding alone but in act, *in re*, and in this way *in intellectu*. From this in part Barth will derive his understanding of God's being in act according to his intense actualism. Accordingly we can reject the idea of Henri Bouillard of a 'common rational structure' which applies to believer and unbeliever in favour of the fact that the rationality of the creature is determined exclusively "within the context of the event of revelation and the nature of the God who is there revealed. Since in revelation we have to do with an act and not a state of revealedness, speech about God cannot be separated from that event in which the revealed God's nature and existence coincide. Therefore the 'man outside the church, the man who is without revelation and faith, knows nothing in actual practice of him who bears the Name'." (Watson, 'Karl Barth and St Anselm's Theological Programme', pp. 41-42.) We have reason to ask of Watson's article from which we have quoted just how this idea of the inexorable link between the freedom of the creature to know God's being and the freedom of God to reveal Himself constitutes what Watson calls "a characteristic systematic weakness in Barth's own theological project." (p. 31) We have benefitted from Watson's analysis of Barth's interpretation of Anselm, but we cannot agree with his conclusion.

[207] This is a place where we can see the critical distinction between Barth and existentialist theologies, and here is one of the roots of the disagreements Barth has with Schleiermacher.

CHAPTER III

Evil and the Perfections of God

One of the most important treatments of the relationship of God to evil in the *Church Dogmatics* is Barth's excursus on the perfections of God (CD II/1; pp. 257–677). Here Barth lays the foundation for the motif of the 'necessary antithesis' in his understanding of the nature of God and His electing will. This forms Barth's answer to the 'why?' of evil from which he develops the second motif of the 'right and left hand of God' in answer to the question of the 'how?' of the operation of evil. Since Barth's foundation for evil's 'peculiar ontology' (the 'why?') and for its noetic 'existence' (the 'how?') are formulated here, this section requires careful study.[1] In addition, a number of critical definitions are given here including God's immutability, omnipotence and omniscience ('If God is all-powerful..?'), and their relationship to the proper understanding of God's love, grace and mercy ('If God is all-loving..?'); and God's relationship to creation in the debate of proximity *(Nähe)* (and its impact upon panentheism, process theology and liberation theology) vs. remoteness *(Ferne)* (and its impact upon theism, protest atheism and the preservation of the freedom and grace of God vis-à-vis His creation).

The Relationship of God's Freedom and Love

For Barth, God's being must be understood as 'being in person' *(Sein in Person)* consisting in God's act, His *actus purus*, or self-moved act.[2] To detach God's essence from His act is to have "substituted for the Biblical idea of God an idea which is easily recognizable as the highest idea conceivable to man."[3] Barth terms the reality *(Wirklichkeit)* of God as that which holds together God's being and act, and only in this reality can we understand Barth's idea of the freedom of God. Because God is in His very being a 'being in freedom' *(Sein in der Freiheit)*, He is the determiner of His own being and of all existence.[4] The negative aspect of the freedom of God–His freedom from external compulsion–so

---

[1] It is strange that most commentators all but ignore this section in their critiques of Barth's view of evil, for neither in Hick's *Evil and the God of Love*, nor in Berkouwer's *The Triumph of Grace in the Theology of Karl Barth*, nor in Moltmann's *The Crucified God* is this section dealt with in any detail. In the numerous articles and even other theses written on this topic there is almost a complete vacuum of information or analysis of Barth's perfections of God, missing the important role it plays in an understanding of his doctrine of evil and his eschatology.

[2] CD II/1, p. 268.

[3] Ibid. p. 303.

[4] Barth can say of God that He is, "*der freie Schöpfer, der freie Versöhner, der freie Erlöser*" and therefore, "*der freie Herrschaft.*" (KD II/1, p. 339)

emphasized in classical Reformed dogmatics, can only be properly understood against the background of the truth of the positive aspect of the freedom of God–that the very being of God *ad intra* is a *Sein in Person*. Therefore, all of God's acts are free acts as He is free in Himself, and His being is a being in action.

On this understanding of God's freedom, Barth develops His doctrine of the condescension of the Son in the incarnation in direct opposition to *kenoticism*. God is free to be passible, mutable and contingent not by a setting aside of His deity and freedom, but as the very demonstration of the fulness of His deity and freedom. Here lies the heart of a critical difference between Barth's theology and many modern day writers on the *theologia crucis* and theodicy.

For Barth, God in His freedom can be passible and contingent, opening the way for an understanding of the suffering and pain of God within an undiluted doctrine of God's sovereignty. This aspect is missing in a whole host of process and liberation theologians who locate suffering and pain in God's eternal essence. For them, God is eternally a sufferer, a God in pain, a God at the mercy of creation for the accomplishment of His own internal history. By rejecting the distinction in the immanent/economic Trinity and the two aspects of God's will–freedom and love–these theologies tend toward a panentheism, and even pantheism, where God's mutability dissolves into vulnerability at the expense of His sovereignty. Barth is able to embrace the best intentions of process and liberation theology without sacrificing God's sovereignty; in his theology the categories of God's co-suffering with humanity, His proximity to His creation, and His identification with the poor and oppressed all find their fullest possible expression within God's freedom as motivated by God's love, and not at the expense of His sovereignty. This distinction must be understood. Barth rejects mutability, passibility and contingency as being part of the essence of God. Instead they are manifestations of the freedom of God under the motivation of God's love for His creation.

Barth's 'freedom of God' operates then within a strong dialectical understanding of the transcendence/immanence of God vis-à-vis His creation, and within the deity/humanity of God in the incarnation. This dialectical tension is characterised in the perfections of God's freedom (transcendence, hiddenness, righteousness, holiness, etc.) and His love (immanence, revealedness, grace, mercy, etc.). This is the foundation for the 'Yes' and 'No' of God from which Barth derives the motif of the work of the 'right and left hand of God'.

Much criticism of Barth is due to a misunderstanding of His doctrine of the freedom of God as when he is accused of allowing the transcendence of God to overpower His immanence, or of a latent docetism where the divinity of Christ swallows up His humanity. Barth's critics fail to see the important tension which Barth seeks to maintain with regards to the freedom and love of God. To avoid the same mistake we must reconize this tension and never allow either side to be over-stressed.[5]

---

[5] We acknowledge, as does Barth, that in his earlier writings he tended to over-stress the freedom of God over the love of God and His deity over His humanity. This was due in part to his strong rejection of liberal Protestantism and his desire to 'clear the

Since God's perfections describe God as He really is and not merely God's characteristics, there is no hidden God behind the revealed perfections nor is God limited by them. Multiplicity and simplicity are both in God. As with the Trinity there is a unity and distinction of perfections which are seen in Barth's categories of love and freedom. This understanding is important for Barth's later discussions concerning evil and creation, for Barth associates the perfections of divine freedom with the transcendence of God and those of the divine love with the self-giving of God. This sets up Barth's thematic epistemological realism where the noetic order always runs from the love of God, God's being 'for us', to the freedom of God, God's being 'in Himself'.[6] The latter is the ontic reality behind the former and the movement must always be from the revelation of the one to the understanding of the reality of the other.[7] Behind the concrete

---

decks' of the anthropocentric theology of the day. It is clear to the careful and thorough reader of Barth that he makes the necessary correction in his later writings and in the latter sections of the *Church Dogmatics*. It is quite telling that when Barth wished to do so, he was able to develop a comprehensive doctrine of the humanity of God and the intense historicity of the work of Christ *from the very heart of his theology as a whole.* The humanity of Christ and the historicity of His work of reconciliation are present everywhere in the *Church Dogmatics*, if not everywhere stressed. Therefore Barth was able to incorporate critiques of his early docetic tendencies and make the necessary corrections simply by showing that it was a matter of emphasis and not a basic flaw in his theology. (see Barth, *The Humanity of God, op. cit.,* pp. 43-64) Here we see how both sides are given full measure at the very outset with regards to the perfections of God, and we reject as shortsighted the interpretations which miss this key point.

[6] Here is one example why Barth was such a critic of Schleiermacher. Writing on epistemology, Schleiermacher said, "we can arrive at ideas of divine attributes only by combining the content of our self-consciousness with the absolute divine causality that corresponds to our feelings of absolute dependence." (F.D.E. Schleiermacher, *The Christian Faith, op. cit.,* p. 325)

[7] Robert Brown attacks Barth's idea that there is a necessity to the noetic absoluteness of revelation. He insists that Barth has not shown that noetic absoluteness must by necessity follow from ontic absoluteness and calls Barth's derivation of noetic from ontic absoluteness a "defective philosophical thesis." (R. Brown, 'On God's Ontic and Noetic Absoluteness', in *Scottish Journal of Theology*, Vol. 33, 1980, p. 540.) Brown's inability to understand Barth here springs from two errors of interpretation with regards to knowledge of God. First, Brown fails to see that Barth is speaking of *fallen* humanity which is unable to know God because of sin which leads Brown to make false conclusions about humanity's ability to know God outside of special revelation. Having no anthropology, Brown misses the critical point that it is the dichotomy of the holy absoluteness of God to the fallen creation which makes noetic absoluteness necessary. Secondly, Brown makes the traditional mistake of seeing a distinction between a general knowledge of God and 'saving' knowledge of God, indicating just how far he is from understanding Barth's theological frame. Brown assumes that humanity can have general, factual knowledge or information of God apart from the noetic absoluteness of special revelation. We would ask Brown what knowledge is there of the true God that is not saving knowledge of God? To 'know' God is to find oneself as a sinner before the

revelation of God in his loving self-condescension to humanity lies the ontological reality of the God who is free in Himself to be and do what He is and does in His loving relationship with humanity.[8] Thus God is fully revealed and fully concealed to us in His self-revelation. Keeping to a dialectical balance, the love and freedom of God are inseparable and yet they have an inner distinction that must also be recognized.[9]

The motifs of the 'necessary antithesis' and the 'right and left hand of God' operate within this ontic-noetic relationship corresponding respectively to the freedom and love of God. Barth's ultimate answer to the 'why?' of evil (the ontic ground of evil) is the basis upon which Barth develops the 'how?' of evil (the noetic manifestation of evil) through the use of the metaphor of the 'right and left hand of God'. The motif of the 'necessary antithesis' is developed within the freedom of God as the ontic basis of Barth's doctrine of evil. The 'right and left hand' motif in the love of God is the manifestation of this ontic 'reality'.

The Origin of Evil

Barth contends that God is both unique and simple *(einzig und einfach)*; He is unique in that there is none other like Him and He is simple in that He is indivisible. Working in the Reformed tradition of Calvin and Anselm and their dependence upon Tertullian, Irenaeus, Augustine and Aquinas these two ideas form the basis for the rest of Barth's expositions on the perfections of the divine freedom, as well as for his attack on panentheism and his understanding of creation and its relationship to the glory of God.

---

holy and righteous God. It is to be confronted by the eternal and transcendent God and to be found lost and in need of mercy and grace. To 'know' God is to flee for refuge to His infinite mercy, or it is not knowledge of the one true God. Brown's God of whom he can obtain factual information apart from special revelation is the deistic God who is at man's disposal to be known and treated at man's discretion. Barth's epistemology leaves no room for such a God, nor for some neutral stance which man can take in the face of a 'general' knowledge of God. It is not surprising that Brown concludes that for dogmaticians to enter into a 'fruitful and meaningful' dialogue on this issue requires "the laying aside of a confessional posture." (p. 548) With faith out of the way and human reason at the helm, all syntheses of philosophy and theology are possible! We reject Brown's critiques and use him as an example of the inability of much of philosophy to interpret Barth's theology, failing from the start to respect the theological frame in which he operates.

[8] "In this manner Scripture invites us to serious and true faith in God Himself and not merely to committal to the economy or sport of a great Unknown, even though he may be called the One who loves in freedom. To attest and expound this biblical unity of the Lord and His glory is the business of the doctrine of the divine perfections." (CD II/1, p. 325)

[9] Although Barth maintains that there is no contradiction between two, and insists upon their unity, it is in their distinction that we find Barth struggling to be true to both.

God's simplicity means that in His omnipresence God is distinct from all that is other and outside Himself. This distinction involves both remoteness *(Ferne)* and proximity *(Nähe)* as aspects of His omnipresence. God is both distant and near, both intimately bound and wholly independent of creation *in one and the same being*. He is Lord over all that is outside Himself, and Lord over remoteness and proximity itself.[10] Because these stand in an antithesis to each other he can conclude, *"Darum is Gott der Herr über diesen Gegensätzen."* (God is the Lord of this antithesis).[11] This is the basis of Barth's interpretation of the sovereignty of God.[12] Omnipresence in relationship to another is possible only because of the love of God which sought after and created fellowship with another in creation. Because it has done so, all of the perfections of the divine love can really be seen as perfections of the divine omnipresence, as God is now proximate to that which He has lovingly created. The perfections of grace, mercy and patience only take form outside of God in that God has created a world and is proximate to it. Because God has these attributes, when He creates in love and seeks fellowship in His omnipresence, He is at once gracious and merciful in the relationship He has with His creation. This is how Barth sees these perfections working together. Therefore unity and omnipresence cannot be separated from the love of God.[13]

For God's omnipresence to be directed outwards, the creation of space was necessary as a quality of creation, and space entails time, finititude and temporality. All of this is in distinction to God and is only possible in that God creates in love and is present in His freedom. God is present to His creation in the same way He is present within Himself; there is a similarity between the unity (proximity) and distinction (remoteness) of the three modes of being in the Trinity and God's relationship with His creation. Barth is trying here to produce an idea of omnipresence that steers clear of an identification of God with creation.[14] Barth is keen to keep the glory of God distinct from creation and to keep God independent from and Lord over all that He has brought into existence.

---

[10] Here we see Barth's use of *Aufhebung* developed during his dialectical period, where thesis (proximity) and antithesis (remoteness) all flow from the *a priori* synthesis-namely, Jesus Christ, who is over all thesis and antithesis taking them up into Himself.

[11] KD II/1, p. 519.

[12] See CD II/1, p. 462.

[13] However, God would still be omnipresent even if there were no creation. All of the perfections of God are necessarily a part of God as He is in Himself and are operating in their perfection in the Godhead. Thus God is omnipresent in Himself before He is outwardly towards us, and the same can and must be said for all of the perfections of God as Barth has developed them.

[14] There are vestiges of Aquinas here who sought to show that all existence was in God and yet that God was distinct from creation. Having refuted Gregory's idea that 'God exists by presence in everything', he concludes with the careful qualifier, *"secundum scientiam et voluntatem magis res sunt in Deo quam Deus in rebus."* (and so, by his knowledge and will, things exist in God rather than God in things) (Aquinas, *Summa Theologia,* Volume 2, *op. cit.,* pp. 119-121)

This idea emerges earlier in the *Credo* where Barth builds this two-fold idea of the transcendence and immanence of God in creation saying first that "Heaven and earth are *not themselves God*, are not anything in the nature of a divine generation or emanation... the world must not be understood as eternal."[15] Thus creation is not a movement of God in Himself but a free *opus ad extra* as an operation of the love of God. Yet this does not cast any doubt upon God's sovereignty or self-sufficiency. Therefore, "the world cannot exist without God, but if God were not love (as such inconceivable!), He could exist very well without the world."[16] In bringing the two ideas together, and making his epistemological point in the process, Barth concludes,

> in standing over against the world that He has made, God is *present* to it—not only far, but also *near*, not only free in relation to it, but *bound* to it, not only transcendent, but also *immanent*. Here there can be no question of any conception of transcendence to be defined by logic. We are concerned with the transcendence of God the Creator. The knowledge of that compels the recognition of His immanence also.[17]

This understanding of God's immanence allows Barth to articulate a rich understanding of the closeness and intimate involvement of God with His creation without at the same time losing God in creation. This way Barth can talk of God with His creation with all of the closeness of panentheism (even closer, according to him), and of the involvement of God with the history of His creation with all of the fervour of process theology and liberation theology, without sacrificing the sovereignty of God as is necessary in these other views of God and creation.[18] It also allows Barth to fill out a picture of the complete vicariousness of Christ's humanity while rejecting *kenosis*.

---

[15] Barth, *Credo, op. cit.,* p. 31.

[16] Ibid. p. 32.

[17] Ibid. p. 34.

[18] Moltmann clearly advocates a break with the traditional distinction between immanent and economic Trinity replacing it with his view of the proximity of God in His indwelling *(Shekinah)* of His creation. Moltmann was unafraid of the implications of a panentheistic stance because of his understanding of sovereignty as he saw it derived from the cross. Without an absolute sovereignty to defend, Moltmann was free to see God indwelling His creation, working with it and through it to bring about His own purposes and will in creation. (Cf. *God in Creation, op. cit.,* pp. 13-16, 94-98; *The Church in the Power of the Spirit,* (New York: Harper and Row, 1975), pp. 50-65, for examples). Barth sought to keep the distinction between the immanent and economic Trinity alive to protect the sovereignty of God as he interprets it from the God of love and freedom who reveals Himself as Lord. Paul Fiddes sees this as the "driving of a wedge between God in his essence and his works" which results in Barth's desire to retain a sense of impassibility in the immanent Trinity while allowing God to truly suffer in His economic acts. (Fiddes, *The Creative Suffering of God,* (Oxford: Clarendon Press, 1988), pp. 121-122) We believe Fiddes

This view of God's relationship to creation is critical for Barth's doctrine of evil, and here we have early evidence of his ideas concerning its origin. Since in His freedom God can be both finite and spatial, Barth insists that the space made available for creation could come from nowhere else (a difficult spatial idea in itself) but from He who has space for Himself. Space for creation is "given out of the fulness of God" *(der ihm aus der Fülle Gottes gegehene Raum).*[19] This bears a resemblance to Moltmann's discussion of the *zimzum,*[20] where the creating of space by God for creation necessarily allows for the possibility and the 'reality' of nothingness *(das Nichtige).* If God is everywhere present prior to creation, then He in a sense 'created space' by vacating it to make room for creation, and that space can only be defined as nothingness–that which is 'not-God'. This lends credibility to Barth's identification of the *tohu wa-bohu*[21] in Genesis 1:2 with *das Nichtige.* Barth contends there that there were chaotic possibilities which God rejected in His process of creation. He concludes, as does Moltmann, that evil and nothingness were the necessary by-product of this creating of space by God. The origin of evil is thus affirmed not as a creation of God, but as a necessary result of God's loving choice to create.

Barth posits that even this space which God made for creation is in God Himself, "Everything which exists is in space and therefore in His space, too, and therefore also in Himself as well, so that it cannot be withdrawn from Him in the spatiality proper to Him."[22] That evil cannot be 'in' God gives rise to this necessity of the chaos from which the world was separated at creation. In addition, since evil also cannot be independent of God, it must exist under his sovereign control even while it is not 'in' Him. Here then are the seeds of the 'necessary antithesis' as the motif for understanding the existence of evil, and the 'right and left hand of God' as the motif for understanding the function of evil as it exists under the control of God.

---

is correct in seeing too great a distinction here which contradicts Barth's strong excursus on the unity of the *ad intra/ad extra* of God's acts.

[19] CD II/1, p. 474.

[20] Moltmann derived this idea from Isaac Luria. "In order to create the world 'outside' himself, the infinite God must have made room beforehand for a finitude in himself. It is only a withdrawal by God into himself that can free the space into which God can act creatively. The *nihil* for his *creatio ex nihilo* only comes into being because-and in so far as-the omnipotent and omnipresent God withdraws his presence and restricts his power." *(God in Creation, op. cit.,* pp. 86-87) Creation takes place in the space made by an 'inversion of God into himself'. (Moltmann, *Trinity and the Kingdom of God, op. cit.,* p. 108)

[21] *tohu wa-bohu,* "formless and empty" (NIV)

[22] CD II/1, p. 476.

Constancy, Omnipotence and the Necessity of Evil

We have now arrived at the core of one of the most important discussions in the early *Church Dogmatics* for demonstrating the development of the motifs. Here Barth discusses his critical understanding of the omnipotence of God and what he terms His 'constancy' *(Beständigkeit)*, both of which are foundational for his doctrine of evil.

By *Beständigkeit* Barth posits a pseudo-necessity in God where God acts "with the necessity in virtue of which He cannot cease to be Himself, the One who loves in freedom."[23] Therefore, Barth can say that in this constancy God is 'immutable' *(unveränderlich)* employing his actualism which demands that the predicate is conditioned by the subject, and that the subject is understood in His self-revelation in Jesus Christ. Thus 'immutability' *(Unveränderlichkeit)* is conditioned by the God who has revealed Himself in His condescension, powerlessness and death; the predicate is never arbitrary and never conditions the subject, but is completely subjected to it and conditioned by it.[24] In this way Barth posits an immutability in God without being forced to take on the philosophical baggage of an abstract, Aristotelian sense of immutability *per se*, nor of an equating of immutable with the concept of 'immobility' from the Greeks.[25] Instead God's immutability is the assurance that He can never turn against Himself and be what He is not,[26] and therefore, "what He does in virtue

---

[23]　Ibid. p. 492.

[24]　Hunsinger makes this point by using 1 John 4:8, 'God is love' stating, "Barth's actualistic mode enables him to explain why it is a mistake to reverse the biblical dictum that 'God is love'...so that instead it would say 'Love is God' - as though God could be equated with an abstract concept of love in general... The statement cannot be reversed, because 'God' refers to an acting subject, and 'love' to the quality of God's activity." (Hunsinger, *How to Read Karl Barth* , *op. cit.,* pp. 31-32)

[25]　We find vestiges of Aquinas here in his three reasons why God is 'altogether unchangeable'. 1) To change means to have some unrealized potential, which God cannot, 2) God is simple and things that change are composite (persisting and passing away), and 3) God cannot acquire anything (as required by change) but is already all things. In similar ways Barth sees God as having no potential that is unrealized and he sees him as being simple and one. Also for Barth, in God's choice to be for man in Jesus Christ, in the humiliation that He undertakes in the incarnation, He is not undertaking anything new, but he is for us in Christ from all eternity. In advocating the *logos ensarkos* and rejecting the *logos asarkos* Barth is also in line with this third idea of Aquinas.

[26]　In an article defending classical theism's idea of immutability, R. Muller sees Barth as basically a proponent of the classical theistic idea of immutability, as opposed to C. Pinnock and J. Moltmann who, according to Muller, hold to the Hegelian 'ontology of becoming'. Muller disagrees with Jüngel and sees that for Barth God's entrance into history does not constitute an alteration of being. In this he is right and it is a helpful distinction between Barth and the more process-type theologies as we have pointed out. Muller's unfortunate criticism of Barth's rejection of the term 'immobility' is purely a semantic misinterpretation of Barth's point and

of His freedom for the sake of His love will never be the surrender but always at every point the self-affirmation of His freedom and His love, a fresh demonstration of His life."[27]

God's Freedom in Creation

From this basis constancy must mean that creation was an act which corresponds perfectly with God's being and will and nature, and that it was a free act which was not done under any sense of internal or external compulsion. That God created a reality distinct from Himself is a confirmation and full expression of His nature as the God who loves in freedom, of grace and mercy, of righteousness and holiness. Yet it was not a necessary act, and God's choice not to create would have been no less an expression of His nature and will as the God who loves in freedom. Barth rejects Hegel's idea that God needed the world as an 'other' to realize Himself as God.[28] This is where Moltmann breaks with Barth in contending along Hegelian lines that the creation of another reality outside of Himself was the only thing God could do in acting according to His own nature. God is by nature the Creator (seen in His eternal begetting of the Son) and creation is the only possible product of the God who is internally fellowship and love.[29] Barth will not allow any basis for a necessity in God that is counter to his being in love and freedom.

---

it should not color the rest of what Muller has to say. (Richard Muller, 'Incarnation, Immutability, and the Case for Classical Theism', in *Westminster Journal of Theology*, Volume 45, 1983, pp. 22-40)

[27] CD II/1, p. 494.

[28] Barth again is in line with the thought of Aquinas here who wrote, "[God] is not disposed towards some extrinsic goal, but is himself the ultimate goal of all other things." (Aquinas, *Summa Theologia*, Volume II, *op. cit.,* p. 89)

[29] It has been historically argued that the distinction of the immanent and economic Trinity was necessary to protect God's liberty and grace, for grace is only grace if God could have freely chosen otherwise, and God can only have true liberty if He can choose without compulsion. Moltmann has countered that if God's nature is by definition *love*, He is not inwardly compelled to act not in contradiction to who He is, and so He must always act lovingly. His will and His nature must coincide and his liberty can only be *His* liberty if it is the liberty to act lovingly. (On God's compulsion in His nature as love, see *God in Creation, op. cit.,* pp. 75-85; *Trinity and the Kingdom of God, op. cit.,* pp. 57-60. On God's nature as love as defined by the cross, see *The Way of Jesus Christ, op. cit.,* p. 175) Moltmann refutes Barth's insistence that God did not have to create and the idea that God could have been eternally happy without creation in the inner-trinitarian circle. Instead he sees God doing what only the Father, in relationship to the Son in the Spirit could do if he is truly a God of love, for the reason for the Father's creation through the Son and by the Spirit is to be found in the heart of the Father-Son relationship itself. "It is in his love for the Son that the Father determines to be the Creator of the world. It is because he loves the Son that he becomes the Creator... So creation does not only respond to God's will, it corresponds to his eternal love as well." (*Trinity and the Kingdom of God,* pp. 111-112) Therefore we should, "view the eternal divine life as

God is not bound to the world. He binds Himself! The covenant is His eternal will, but His *free* will. Even in the ontological realm there is an *extra nos*. In the sense that we are not God, that God is God and we are only His creatures, God is *extra nos*. But as such He is not only free to do without us, but He is loving in His freedom. In His love He will not remain *extra nos* ![30]

Insofar as Barth seeks to show that God's choice to create was a true and pure choice of love, we agree with this understanding of freedom in relation to creation.[31] We are critical of Moltmann who makes creation a necessary act of God, unnecessarily subordinating the freedom of God to His love, therefore

---

a life of eternal, infinite love, which in the creative process issues in its overflowing rapture from its trinitarian perfection and completeness, and comes to itself in the eternal rest of the sabbath." (*God in Creation,* p. 84) If he is the Creator God, as the eternal begetting of the Son surely demonstrates, then creation in love is who God is. Yet Moltmann goes to such great lengths to make this point that he is forced to conclude "in this sense, God 'needs' man." (pp. 57-60) This is one of the great weaknesses in Moltmann's theology.

[30] Barth, 'Karl Barth's Table Talk', *op. cit.*, p. 14.

[31] G. Hendry sees a latent Hegelianism operating in Barth with regards to God's free choice in creation. He cites Barth's use of Hegel's *Übergriff* as an indication of his indebtedness to Hegel and as the basis for his understanding of creation as an 'over-reaching' *(Übergriff)* of God's glory. To keep such a notion of creation from making creation requisite for God, Hendry cites Barth's use of the freedom of God and His choice to create, concluding that Barth reduced the relation between the inner process of the triune life of God and the external work of creation "from a logical to an analogical one." By doing so, Hendry posits that Barth sought to "preserve Hegel's conclusion while rejecting his premise." (G. Hendry, 'The Freedom of God in the Theology of Karl Barth', in *Scottish Journal of Theology*, Volume 31, Number 3, 1978, pp. 229-244) Barth wishes to find a link between the internal relationship of Father, Son and Spirit with the relationship between Creator and creation without positing a logical link which would make creation necessary. It can be seen here how Moltmann sought both the premise and the conclusion of Hegel. Hendry concludes that Barth is unsuccessful in doing so because of the systematic nature of his doctrine of the freedom of God and because of a lack of any true coherence between inter-trinitarian relations and the Creator-creation relationship. Part of this conclusion stems from Hendry's own interpretation of Barth's idea of freedom which is certainly debatable as it is based on the acceptance of the idea that Barth's doctrine is built solely upon a transcendental methodology. The other critique requires us to accept that the link between 'God and His Word' and 'God and His creature' is merely esthetic and nothing more. Barth has already refuted such a notion at length and we believe his arguments are sound. For both of these reasons we believe while Hendry's article is at times illuminating, his conclusions clearly miss the mark.

raising the question as to whether then God can ever cease to create and still be God.[32]

Barth is correct to keep the love of God independent of any contingency to create, for God is neither the monistic God whose very essence is tied up with the created world, nor is God immutable *in abstracto* so that in His eternal remoteness He has no relation to the mutable world. Both ideas fail to see that it is the love of God that is the basis of creation. Because this choice was made both in the freedom and love of God, God is free to show His love by dwelling alongside His creation without being absorbed into it or destroying it. He does so in His freedom and He chooses to do so in His love without sacrificing either, but actually affirming both in this one act of creation.

The critical point can now be made; if evil is the necessary by-product of creation and God in His freedom chose freely to create, then God's free choice included the choice of allowing evil and giving it access to His created world. This is what S. Gottschalk referred to in describing nothingness as "a structural necessity within his [Barth's] doctrine of creation."[33] As Barth continues the development of his doctrine of evil, he will build upon these two ideas that evil in creation was possible because of the nature of God's act of creation, and that God's choice to create was a free choice. This sets up the necessity of the justification of creation in Barth's soteriology and the annihilation of evil in his eschatology.

Constancy and Evil

We find two further points which are foundational for the rest of what Barth will say in the *Church Dogmatics* concerning creation and evil. First, in the salvific work of God on behalf of rebellious humanity there is never in any sense a conflict created within God Himself. Barth's words here are very important.

It is a mark of the divine nature as distinct from that of the creature that in it a conflict with Himself is not merely ruled out, but is inherently impossible. If this were not so, if there did not exist perfect, original and ultimate peace between the Father and the Son and the Holy Spirit, God would not be God. Any God in conflict with Himself is bound to be a false God *(ein falscher Gott)*.[34]

---

[32] This point in Moltmann's theology is the consequence of his entire theological frame, the analysis of which is outside the scope of this book. It will suffice to say that throughout his theology Moltmann seeks to emphasize the proximity of the suffering God to His creation and to link the two with a mutual destiny (from this idea Moltmann is able to build his strong idea of Christo-praxis). Thus creation is a necessity in Moltmann's system (and here we have to think about Hegel's influence) and it cannot be conceived as a 'choice' by God in the exercise of His freedom.

[33] Stephen Gottschalk, 'Theodicy After Auschwitz and the Reality of God', in *Union Seminary Quarterly Review*, Volume 41, Part 3-4, 1987, p. 81.

[34] CD II/1, p. 503.

This point must be considered both in relation to Barth's idea of the 'right and left hand of God', and in view of Moltmann's idea of the divisive, if only momentary, act of Christ on the cross as he (Moltmann) investigates what the cross means for God Himself.[35] Moltmann holds up the death cry of Jesus 'My God, My God, why have you forsaken me', and asks if this does not show a conflict in the Godhead?[36]

In the same way K. Kitamori states that since both love and justice are combined in one essence in the same God, the result is nothing less than the eternal pain of God, and this is seen as God against God on Golgotha.[37] Barth contends that God is never more fully God in complete keeping with His nature of love and freedom than when He is on the cross crying out these words,[38] that in response to humanity's opposition God poses His own opposition to

---

[35] This theme runs throughout the whole of Moltmann's major works but is most prevalent in *The Crucified God*.

[36] If the Trinity is to be maintained, there is on the cross an abandonment of God by God! Moltmann calls this abandonment by God the "torment of his torments." (*The Crucified God, op. cit.,* p. 149) There is a split in the relationships of the persons of the Trinity. For the Father did not just distance himself from the Son, he abandoned him, made him to be 'sin for us' (2 Corinthians 5:21) and therefore caused a true separation, if only temporarily, in the persons of the Trinity. There is a dialectic going on here between the separation of the Father and the Son in the midst of the cohesion, perhaps the ultimate cohesion of their will. Moltmann states that they are both so "widely separated" so as to make it a purely "Godless death", yet they also simultaneously "present a single surrendering movement." (*The Way of Jesus Christ, op. cit.,* p. 174) Yet he goes even further than this. The Father passed judgement upon the Son. God judged God and found him guilty. God took guilt upon himself, judged that guilt and condemned himself to die for that guilt. The result could only be that a change took place in God. "In the action of the Father in delivering up his Son to the suffering and to a godless death, God is acting in himself. He is acting in himself in this manner of suffering and dying in order to open up in himself freedom and life for sinners... God overcomes himself, God passes judgement on himself, God takes the judgement of the sin of man upon himself. He assigns to himself the fate that men should by rights endure. The cross of Jesus, understood as the cross of the Son of God, therefore reveals a change in God, a *stasis* within the Godhead: 'God is other.' And this event in God is the event of the cross." (*The Crucified God*, pp. 192-193)

[37] Kitamori, *The Theology of the Pain of God, op. cit.,* p. 21.

[38] This view must be maintained even when Barth seems to lean towards Moltmann's view, such as in his prison sermon given on Easter Day in 1961 where Barth said of the death cry of Jesus, "At that moment he [Jesus] literally could not help saying to himself and hearing: I, God, have abandoned you, Jesus, for a brief moment. In this moment of wrath I have hid my face from you, my dear child. What God did there was indeed terrible: this abandoning, this hiding of his face in the moment of wrath-not from some evil-doer, but from the only really pure, holy and faithful man-his own dear son." (Karl Barth, *Call for God: New Sermons from Basel Prison*, (London: SCM Press, 1965), p. 52)

overcome it. This act is in total keeping with the nature of God who "cannot cease to act as the Creator and Lord of the world."[39] In God's response there is never a conflict within Himself.[40] His entire work of salvation and reconciliation, as well as His future work of redemption are all in keeping with His divine nature, the being of God who loves in freedom.

The second point concerns the relationship in its distinction between Creator and creation. Because these two are dissimilar (as opposed to the complete unity of the Godhead) conflict can arise and (here we are anticipating what Barth will develop more fully later) actually must arise. There *must* be the possibility of this conflict within creation if God is truly to create another outside of and in distinction to Himself, for without this possibility of defection, creation would not be distinct from God and therefore 'not really His creation'. Negatively then, a creature, created by God in His love and freedom, must *necessarily* be open to the possibility of sin and rebellion, even if this means the creature's own destruction. Positively, this means that the creature is ever and always dependent upon God's preserving grace, and it is upon this idea, along with those we have cited above, that Barth will build his doctrine of the providence of God.

Here we must raise the question as to whether God could have created a world in which humanity's disobedience would be impossible? Could not God have created humanity with a nature that would always choose the right? Must creation necessarily include the possibility of rebellion? Barth answers,

> A creature freed from the possibility of falling away would not really be living as a creature. It could only be a second God–and as no second God exists, it could only be God Himself.[41]

Since the distinction is maintained between Creator and creature, the possibility of sin is a requisite part of that distinction. At this point several questions arise. Does this throw into question either the power or the goodness of the Creator? Is He at some level responsible for sin and evil if He is bound

---

[39] CD II/1, p. 504.

[40] Jüngel points out, "*Die Möglichkeit eines Widerspruches zwischen Gott und Gott, die Möglichkeit eines gegensatzes zwischen einam dann allerdings nicht im Lichte, sondern im Dunkel verborgenen deus nudus bzw. deus absolutus einerseits und dem in Jesus Christus offenbaren Gott andererseits kommt bei Barth nicht einmal ansatzweise in Betracht.*" Jüngel, 'Die Offenbarung der Verborgenheit Gottes', *op. cit* p. 177. "The possibility of a contradiction between God and God, the possibility of a contrast between a *deus nudus* hidden, not in the light, but in the dark, or a *deus absolutus* on the one hand and God revealed to us in Jesus Christ is not even considered as a possibility by Barth." Fiddes also comments, "Karl Barth resisted any view of a division within God himself; he was willing to speak of God's enduring his own contradiction (i.e. judgement) of sinful humanity on the stage of human history, but not of God as contradicting himself within his own inner being." (Fiddes, *The Creative Suffering of God, op. cit.,* p. 202)

[41] CD II/1, p. 503.

by these rules in His creation? If His good creation carries with it such a basic flaw, does this reflect upon the perfection of the Creator? Barth answers,

> Sin is when the creature avails itself of this impossible possibility *(unmöglichen Möglichkeit)* in opposition to God and to the meaning of its own existence. But the fault is that of the creature and not of God. In no sense does it follow necessarily from what God is in Himself. Nor does it follow from the nature of creation itself. It follows inevitably only from the incomprehensible fact *(unbegreiflichen Faktum)* that the creature rejects the preserving grace of God.[42]

Barth's line of reasoning here is tenuous. However given what he has presented thus far it does remain intact. Since humanity has the possibility to fall away we must conclude, for there to be integrity in Barth's argument here, that it also has the possibility of being forever obedient. If we change humanity's 'possibility' for sin to its 'inevitability' to sin, then Barth's position is greatly weakened. We see emerge here what we will develop as the 'inevitability-impossibility' tension in Barth's doctrine of the Fall. This tension is a direct result of the 'necessary antithesis' and the 'right and left hand of God' motifs and it will be a major theme in the development of evil in Barth's doctrine of creation. What is as stake is the ultimate responsibility for evil and suffering, for if suffering is seen as a direct result of sin, as Barth has already stated, then potentially we have the classic accusation against God fully intact. If the Fall was inevitable, God must bear the responsibility for sin, and subsequently for suffering and evil. This is what is at stake in this critical understanding of humanity's status as created by God in relationship to sin.

Constancy, *Heilsgeschichte* and the Necessity of the Fall

Barth's epistemological agenda has been concerned to show that we can only know God the Creator from the work of God the Reconciler. It is only in Christ that we have revealed the Father, the will of God and the purposes for His creation. To understand Genesis 1–3 we must see its Author as the God revealed to us in Jesus Christ. Christology is normative even and perhaps especially for our understanding of creation.

This is not to say that creation and reconciliation are one and the same event. Indeed quite the opposite is true. The work of reconciliation is a new and separate event from that of creation. In it God has *turned more intimately* to His

---

[42] Ibid. pp. 503-504. Here we see how the idea of the *unmöglichen Möglichkeit* has moved from the God-man relationship of Barth's earlier dialectical period, to the God-evil relationship here in the *Church Dogmatics*.

creation and "something other and greater than mere creation has taken place."[43] This 'greater' is the key for what will now follow. The work of reconciliation far surpasses the work of creation and must not be equated with it. This relationship and distinction between God's work of creation and reconciliation is absolutely essential for understanding the whole of Barth's theology.

With absolute clarity Barth posits that there was a *positive benefit* that came from the Fall. As a result of the confrontation that arose from Genesis 3, *'man is now taken seriously' (der Menschen jetzt ernst genommen)*.[44] As humanity has sought the pseudo-divinity of the knowledge of good and evil, it has at once imprisoned itself in its own sin and set itself on the road to its own destruction. Yet it has also done another extraordinary thing. In this new, corrupt and fallen state, humanity receives from God a new and special blessing, and it is only in this new relationship between *fallen* humanity and God that God confirms Himself as truly great![45] Speaking of post-Fall humanity, Barth asks, "Is it not the case that now *for the first time* the reality of the creature emerges as a reality distinct from God and the preserving grace of God as grace that as such waits for gratitude and can only be really received in gratitude?"[46]

The newness and strength of the relationship of God with fallen humanity over and against the one He had previously with unfallen humanity gives the former a sense of priority and importance and stature over the latter. Barth unhesitantly embraces the idea of *felix culpa* in the comparison of "the regularity of man's unfallen existence before God in Paradise with the fire of being loved and being able to respond in love that now burns in the hearts of His children as the basis of this selection."[47] Barth is actually saying that the state of fallen humanity is greater than that of pre-fallen humanity because of God's gracious act towards His fallen creation in the reconciliation of the cross and

---

[43] Ibid. p. 507. Barth continues, "It is so much greater that the dangerous saying is forced to our lips: *felix culpa, quae talem et tantum meruit redemptorem.*" (Ibid.)

[44] "It is He, as Creator the only and perfect Lord of men, who now enters into a confrontation of this kind. And it is in the freedom which he [man] has snatched on his own authority, in the pseudo-divinity in which he knows good from evil, that man is now taken seriously." Ibid. p. 507.

[45] This theme is echoed throughout Barth's writings. We will cite two additional quotes as evidence. In Barth's Gifford Lectures given in 1937 and 1938, he said, "Man's salvation is his deliverance, but it is more than that. It is his restoration, but it is more than that. It is his translation to a *higher status* than the one which he had occupied by virtue of his creation and within the original dispensation. Salvation means therefore not merely that man is saved from certain very serious consequences of his sin, or merely that his original relation to God is restored. Beyond all this, salvation means that man becomes a new man." (Barth, *The Knowledge of God and the Service of God*, op. cit., p. 81) And further, "When God gives man the Holy Spirit, we become *more* than man was before the Fall. This elevation of man is the 'new birth'." (Barth, 'Table Talk', op. cit., p. 57)

[46] CD II/1, p. 508. (emphasis mine)

[47] Ibid. p. 508.

resurrection, and this theme will emerge again in his doctrine of creation and reconciliation.

Clearly here Barth is ascribing a necessary place to the Fall. Evidence for this grows as Barth follows this discussion with a look to the future of reconciled humanity and finds its *eschaton* in the coming of God Himself in whom are found redemption and eternal intimate participation in and with God. What would have been the eschatological hope of pre-fallen humanity? It would not have been this glorious hope, for "this perspective does not belong of necessity to the essence and conception of creation as such."[48] In fact, had there been no Fall, even the promise of everlasting life would be in question, "He does not reply to human rebellion simply with a *restitutio ad integrum*, but with the revelation of a perfection concealed even in the original creation in its integrity. He does not only make the sick whole, but gives him a share in the hope of everlasting life."[49] Barth anticipates the critical questions that arise from this line of reasoning, for he has certainly stated that the restoration made under the threat of death and eternal punishment far exceeds that which would have been possible if sin and its consequences had never been a factor in the relationship of Creator and creation. This implies that the eternal will of God was to save His creature from its sin through His acts of reconciliation, and that the Fall was pre-destined as a part of creation so that 'such great a salvation' could take place.[50]

---

[48] Ibid. p. 510.

[49] Ibid. p. 510.

[50] In 'The Homecoming of the Son' (CD IV/2 §64), Barth points out that the incarnation as the humiliation of the Son in the assumption of the corrupt human essence, was for that essence its exaltation. The incarnation occurs so that man may come to God in this exaltation in the Son of Man. Barth goes on to say that this exaltation in the incarnation, 'is the content of the eternal will and decree of God. As it takes place, there takes place the reconciliation of the world with God'. Was God's purpose in creation, as it was created with a view to Jesus Christ, to unite the human essence in the divine essence in the act of the incarnation and thus bring man to God in the exaltation of the Son of Man? If this is the sole purpose, could this have been done, and indeed was it originally envisaged to be done in a world that was not fallen, where there was no sin and corruption which required atonement, where there was no judgement of God that demanded it be borne? The key question is whether God's will and goal for His creation *could* have been accomplished without the Fall, sin and the cross, and if it was God's plan that it be accomplished in this way? Barth talked of the atonement as a reaction of God to sin and of the atoning work of Christ as both reconciliation and the fulfillment of the covenant. Can we separate the atonement for sin, reconciliation and the defeat of nothingness on the cross with the incarnation and the exaltation of the human essence? If we can, then our criticism of Barth as positing a necessary antithesis is invalid, for clearly the Fall was not necessary for God to come to man in the Son of God in the incarnation, to assume human essence and exalt it, bringing it back to God in the Son of Man. The cross is not required in this scenario. For Barth, the reconciliation which takes place in the incarnation is described as the assumption by the Son of God of the created antithesis including both the good and the shadowy side of creation, and as such it does not require the Fall and sin. The eternal purpose of God in creation is seemingly fulfilled as is the

We have here the strongest evidence yet of a 'necessary antithesis' which is the central motif in Barth's doctrine of evil. He assigns to evil a critical role to play in the execution of the eternal will of God, the will not just in seeking to create fellowship with another distinct from Himself, but a will to save that creation and bring it up into Himself in His Son for their glory and His own. We recognize that Barth wants to deny to evil any positive role and yet he employs this 'necessary antithesis' throughout his handling of the problem of evil. It begins with the fundamental understanding of God's purposes in creation not to have fellowship *per se*, but to grant to His creation a special status and participation which is only available to it through the act of reconciliation and devotion to which God is committed prior to the first moment of creation. Salvation and redemption and all they mean for the eternal fellowship of God with His creation are the meaning and goal of creation. How can there be salvation without the Fall? What is to be restored or reconciled without rebellion and the separation it brings? Two final quotes will suffice to prove our point on this issue in this section. "The meaning and secret of the creation and preservation of the world is revealed in the history of *salvation*."[51] "We can say

---

covenant apart from the Fall. All of this can be said if there is allowed the idea of an incarnation and Ascension without the cross and atonement. John Thompson asks this same question as he queries if the incarnation only has meaning in relation to man's *felix culpa* ? He admits that Barth does seem in a very few instances to affirm that such is his position and indeed it would be "fully consistent with Barth's basically supralapsarian exposition of election." (John Thompson, *Christ in Perspective in the Theology of Karl Barth, op. cit.,* p. 23) However he concludes, "Rather must we say that the New Testament knows of no other God-man but the crucified Lord Jesus. It would have been better had Barth at this point combined the absolute and relative bases of the incarnation." (p. 24) This would have meant that God's eternal sovereign choice to be 'for' man would always be related to the salvation of that man from sin. Thompson is right in pointing out that Barth is seeking here to maintain a two-fold truth that 1) God's is eternally 'for' man in His election which implies the incarnation, and 2) that sin is never to be coordinated with grace. In a telling concluding remark Thompson says, "for Barth the two aspects, God's primary will and his reaction to sin, are in fact one and the same." (p. 24) Therefore we agree with Thompson and maintain that to hold to the possibility of such a distinction between incarnation and atonement, between the assuming of human essence and the assuming of sinful humanity, is to misread Barth's intentions. Barth never sees God as envisaging a creation which would be fulfilled by incarnation alone. We must remember the statement from Barth we quoted earlier, "Since everything is created for Jesus Christ *and His death and resurrection,* from the very outset everything must stand under this twofold and contradictory determination." (CD IV/2, p. 45) Always and from the beginning, in the eternal decree and act of God on our behalf, in His election and self-determination to be for us in Jesus Christ, the exaltation of the creature and the fulfillment of the covenant were going to require the cross and resurrection. That the "Word became flesh" is the manifestation of the eternal will of God in time and space." (p. 45)

[51] CD II/1, p. 512. Barth goes on to say a few pages later that God's perfect self-revelation could only take place in the God-man Jesus Christ. The incarnation means the revelation in its perfection of the immutable divine nature. The revelation of God

already that the reason why God created the world and set up in it the *office of reconciliation*, is because He is able, willing and ready to be one with the creature in Jesus Christ and because He did in fact do this."[52] Salvation history is the goal of creation, and therefore the Fall is fundamentally important to the execution and completion of that goal. *O' felix culpa* !

The 'Power of God' and His Recapitulation

Within his all-embracing understanding of the freedom of God, Barth gives full expression to the idea of the 'necessary antithesis' in his view of God's omnipotence. As God stands over His creation, He is its Lord and thus He preserves and sustains it. He does this in the freedom of His power, His omnipotence. Barth is careful to define the term 'power' *(Vermag)* according to the actualistic mode of his thought where the critical direction of subject to predicate must be maintained and never reversed. Thus it is God, the God who loves in freedom, who is omnipotent. Power in and of itself is evil.[53] Real power is conditioned and defined by the One who is powerful.[54] Just as the goodness of God and the righteousness of God consist in the fact that in them God is Himself, so the power of omnipotence is proper to God and in its exercise He is true to Himself.

From this understanding of God's omnipotence, Barth makes the important case that God can exist eternally in Himself and in Himself God 'recapitulates' *(wiederholt)* Himself. Barth is saying that all of God's works *ad extra* are *extensions of this internal recapitulation.* "The reason why God created the world and man was to be the scene and instrument and servant of His self-manifestation *(Selbstbetätigung)*."[55] This is evidenced in his doctrine of the Trinity where the eternal fellowship of the modes of being in their *perichoretic* relationship sought to create this fellowship in another outside of themselves. Thus our relationship with God in Christ is pre-figured in the eternal Trinitarian

---

in this perfect way was solely dependent upon the incarnation to which God was committed from the foundation of the world. But not just the incarnation of the Son, but of *Jesus Christ as the Reconciler and Redeemer.* This again is clear evidence that for Barth, the Fall is of central importance for the successful completion of God's eternal will for His creation. (pp. 515-516)

[52] Ibid. p. 515. (emphasis mine)

[53] See CD II/1, p. 524.

[54] Barth makes strong qualifications for his use of the term *vermag* in referring to the omnipotence of God. In *Dogmatics in Outline* he asserts that "power in itself is nothingness!" *(Dogmatics in Outline, op. cit.,* p. 48) In stark contrast, God's power under the perfection of omnipotence is power under the control of God's love, "this power, God, is the power of His free love in Jesus Christ, activated and revealed in Him." (p. 49) For this reason omnipotence is a strictly Trinitarian term, "What distinguishes God's power from impotence is that He is the triune God." (p. 49)

[55] CD II/1, p. 532.

relationships in the Godhead, and in this way creation is the self-manifestation of God.

Barth's point is that in God there exists an eternal self-distinction in which He distinguishes Himself from that which is not-God.[56] As Barth develops this idea he ties to it the 'Yes' and 'No' of God's saving work. As seen here, God's goal in creation is the self-manifestation of His own inner being in which this eternal self-distinction takes place. For God, the maintenance of this self-distinction is effortless and never in doubt.[57] In creation God wills that humanity be confronted by that which God has rejected in Himself from all eternity.

In essence, God creates in space and time what He is eternally in Himself, and that necessarily means that He creates a world where humanity is confronted by the nothingness, the 'not-God' which God has eternally faced and rejected in his eternal self-distinction. Barth states this quite clearly, "In God Himself there is a simple and immediate victory of light over darkness, with the issue never for one moment in doubt. In the creaturely sphere and for man–as man is to be the witness to the divine glory–this victory *must take on historical form*, thus becoming an event in time."[58] Barth concludes with the dramatic statement, "He [God] wills the confrontation of man by the power of evil."[59] Thus God, although not willing that humanity should fall, does will (positively) that the creature should be confronted by the power of evil.

This is a further step from what was stated above where Barth merely contended that God could not create humanity in such a way that it would be impossible for His creature to fall away. Here we have a direct purpose in God to create humanity purposely in confrontation with evil. This is necessary if creation is to be the *Selbstbetätigung* of God, and if God is eternally self-differentiating. Thus what has happened eternally in the internal conflict of God (not with Himself, which Barth has already maintained is impossible, but with the 'not-God') must be played out on the stage of creation with the outcome of victory already assured.

Barth will go on in his doctrine of creation to call creation, in agreement with Calvin, the 'theatre of the glory of God'. This view places the origin of evil in the internal eternal conflict in God which is then played out in the creaturely sphere. Thus we have both the 'Yes' and the 'No' of God, His willing

---

[56] Berkouwer makes the point that the rejected and excluded possibility which God does not will and will never will is "a negative reality over which God has *from eternity* pronounced judgement." (*Triumph of Grace, op. cit.*, p. 70) Berkouwer rightly interprets Barth as seeing God in an eternal rejection of the 'not-God', which is the basis for the origin of evil in creation according to the idea of creation being the recapitulation of God.

[57] See CD II/2, p. 141.

[58] CD II/2, p. 141. (emphasis mine) Barth continues, "it was necessary that this man should really be confronted with what God Himself repudiates, even as God Himself is confronted with it in that self-differentiation, in that disavowal of what He is not, and does not will."

[59] Ibid. p. 141.

and His non-willing, and we his creatures will bear witness to both. Berkouwer concludes, "*He wills man as sinful man*, as man who is confronted with that which God has rejected, in the same way in which God is confronted with it in His eternal self-distinction."[60]

Three points must be made here. The first is that clearly Barth is setting up a 'necessary antithesis' between evil and God's plan for creation. In the eternity of God there has always been the need for the self-distinction of God from that which is 'not-God'. Thus Paul Fiddes is not correct in commenting of this non-willed 'existence', "*Das Nichtige* exists because God does *not* want it to exist."[61] Instead, *das Nichtige* exists because God exists as the eternally self-differentiating God and as none other. Barth holds this position in an attempt to steer clear of all forms of dualism, and yet the two do not seem to be mutually exclusive. Evil can have a necessary role to play and yet be subject to the power of God. Barth could have dealt with evil more directly as that which is the necessary backdrop for all of God's work *ad extra*,[62] although we affirm Barth's intention to focus away from evil and solely on Christ.

The second point follows on from this. If there is a 'necessary antithesis' that can be affirmed without necessitating a dualism, then we also wonder how Barth can affirm later that nothingness has no perpetuity? If God has eternally been the self-differentiating God, and if good is even in part defined by the absence of (differentiation from) evil, then how can we suddenly escape the necessity of evil in the second coming? It could be argued that the salvific work of Christ does away with all evil once and for all. But then we must ask if creation was necessary to accomplish something that was not possible in God Himself? If evil can be annihilated, God must have been able to do this in and of Himself apart from creation or the entire category of the perfections of the divine freedom are in jeopardy. We will take this up in more detail later.

Thirdly, those seeking a post-modern theodicy must acknowledge and build upon Barth's contribution towards a better understanding of the origin of evil and eschatology. Reminiscent of Jacob Boehme, Barth has courageously articulated

---

[60] Berkouwer, *The Triumph of Grace, op. cit.,* p. 220. (emphasis mine)

[61] Fiddes, *The Creative Suffering of God , op. cit.,* p. 218. This is one small mis-statement in an otherwise very helpful book. Fiddes sees in Barth a tacit approval and a useful correction of "Hegels' scheme of a self-negating God," for Barth has understood God's self-differentiation as Father and Son as a "description of his opening up of himself to non-being." (p. 239) As such, God's eternal self-differentiation is the negative ontological basis for nothingness.

[62] Berkouwer raises H. van Oyen's point that Barth's triumph of grace "does not radically exclude the shadow of dualism between the works of God on the *right hand* and those on the *left hand*. The very *components* of the triumph reveal the characteristics of dualism. Creation and preservation can, in Barth's theology, be understood only in terms of *salvation*." (*Triumph of Grace, op. cit.,* p. 247) This is a restatement of a part of our motif of the 'necessary antithesis' which so dominates Barth's doctrine of evil. Berkouwer would have done better to help the reader see, however, how this 'Barthian' dualism differs fundamentally from the classical ideas of dualism as we have attempted to do.

a key element in our understanding of evil and its relationship in eternity to God and, conversely, to creation–namely, that absolute good cannot exist in a vacuum. Good cannot exist without evil, even if evil exists only as non-existence, as nothingness and that which is non-willed. Good is defined in part by the absence of and its differentiation from evil. This is what Fiddes called the 'dialectic of Being and non-being', and in such, "we can only conceive of Being in dialectic with non-being."[63] God is defined in His self-revelation in Jesus Christ, and in Jesus Christ we see the true depth of sin, evil and death which is rejected in God's eternal self-differentiation. In addition, it is *Jesus* Christ in which God is self-revealed; the eternally Rejected and Judged, the *homo labilis* and the *Logos ensarkos*.

The result is that "God's self-differentiation as Father, Son and Spirit in his inner life is bound up with an experience of negativity."[64] Therefore, if God is the eternally self-differentiating God, then there can be no talk of the creation of a world in which there is only good and no evil. That world is impossible. The best of all possible worlds is one in which the inevitable evil is defeated and humanity is brought into direct fellowship with God. That is precisely the world that God has created.[65] We must be bold in asserting the necessity of evil, and Barth's understanding of the eternal self-differentiation in God is the basis for that assertion.

God's 'Yes' and 'No'

Under God's sovereign lordship the alien powers of evil and nothingness are tolerated and brought into God's service by the exercise of His divine omnipotent knowledge and will. God's power is the power of His personality as One who knows and wills. Since God's omnipotence is that of His will, God has the power according to His will also to not-will, and God's non-willing is effectual! This is not the bringing into existence something that has an equal footing in some negative way to that which is willed, but a complete rejection and non-willing, a denial of existence, power and status to that which is rejected. Therefore any power or existence that is found in the non-willing of God is that which has been given to it by God and is thus that which is always under His control.

It is critical here to understand that the divine knowledge and will are seen as the knowledge and will of the divine omnipotence. These aspects of the nature of God are interchangeable in that what God knows He wills and what He wills He knows. Barth is careful to point out that God knows that which He has

---

[63] Fiddes, *The Creative Suffering of God, op. cit.,* p. 262.

[64] Ibid. p. 263.

[65] There are clearly vestiges of a Leibnizian optimism here, and it would not be far off the mark to see Barth's cosmology as a Leibnizian theodicy re-built on a Christological foundation.

rejected, but this does not mean that He wills it, rather He wills its rejection, and in so doing He limits and controls it.[66]

> Within the limit of being imposed by God Himself, God knows everything. Again, this includes even non-being, even the merely possible and the impossible, even death and hell, all things in their own way–but still all things. Non-being also exists in its own way, not as something infinite, but as something finite, conditioned by the fact that God knows it.[67]

God knows everything, for there is no self-concealment against God. Thus we can never escape the knowledge, and therefore the grace and judgement of God, not even in the depths of hell.

In the same respect under God's 'omnivolence' *(Allwillen)* everything is willed by God, thus with regards to nothingness, "it is only by God's rejecting will, His aversion, that it can have its particular form of actuality and possibility."[68] This 'rejecting will' *(verwerfenden Willen)* of God is synonymous with the work of the 'left hand' of God. Under this left hand lies the existence of nothingness as dependent upon and in submission to God alone, and we see how it emerges by necessity from God's eternal self-differentiation. The key question is, does evil exist by the rejecting will of God or does God eternally will to reject it in its existence?[69] The answer provides an important distinction between Barth and those forms of theodicy which posit some form of dualism. There is here the struggle between the locating of the necessity, form and origin of evil in God, and an outright dualism. Barth tends towards the former, and to support this assertion let's pause here and pull together what he has said thus far.

---

[66] CD II/1, p. 552. This includes what Barth terms the 'impossible' *(unmöglichen)*. "He knows also the impossible, that which from Him and by Him is not possible. He knows it as that which He has rejected, excluded and denied: sin as sin; death as death; the devil as the devil. And He also wills it to be this, to be what it is in virtue of His rejection of it, in the way which belongs to it as the impossible." (Ibid.)

[67] Ibid. p. 553.

[68] Ibid. p. 556.

[69] Barth may have sought to steer clear of Schleiermacher's conclusions that sin must be a part of the divine will since it continues, for if the divine will so desired it, sin "of necessity would vanish altogether and at once." (Schleiermacher, *The Christian Faith, op. cit.,* p. 327) He goes on to say that if sin and evil are ordained by God (even if only to be done away with through redemption) then there must be divine attributes which include their ordination. (See p. 341) Barth is seeking to say both that God wills all things and that God is not the Author of evil. Thus he must stay clear of Schleiermacher's conclusions without sacrificing the sovereignty of God. This is the tension in which Barth operates in the 'right and left hand of God' motif.

Barth asserts that God is eternally self-differentiating, therefore giving a primordial 'existence' (even if its existence is a non-existence in rejection) to evil as that from which God is differentiated. God is not dependent upon creation for anything, and therefore God can, at any time, bring about the annihilation of evil in the sphere of creation. That God chooses not to do so means that He continues to give to evil its power, place and role in creation. That God could destroy evil and does not, that He continues to give it its power and place in creation, that its very existence is dependent upon God under the administration of His 'left hand', and that it does indeed continue to exist here can only lead us to the conclusion that evil exists because God wills (even if we are to accept the idea of His rejecting will) for evil to exist in its current form. This whole line of reasoning will be fully supported by Barth in various sections which are to follow, especially in his understanding of providence and the divine permission.

In the knowing and willing of God's omnipotence nothing exists outside God which does not exist first and eternally in Himself, in His knowledge. Therefore the existence of evil as that which is rejected is the reflection of God's eternal knowledge of evil in His eternal self-distinction. This is Barth's answer to foreknowledge, not that He knows all things that are and will be, but that all things are and will be because He knows them. God does foreknow evil, however not as an effect from a cause, as is true for all that which is positively known and foreknown by God, but as the limits of that which is known. Thus God is the Lord and source of being, but "only the Lord and not the source of non-being."[70] Yet, we must also say that if He is not its source He is certainly its Sustainer, Enabler and Empowerer as it 'exists' under His 'left hand'. Here again we see the vestiges of Barth's dialectical theology. By saying that God is not the source of non-being, Barth is not also inferring that God is not responsible for non-being. These two are not the same. For non-being, according to Barth, is destructible, and destructible by God, yet it continues to receive that which it requires from God for its existence, even as the rejected and non-willed. This is Barth's dilemma in his continued protection of the absolute sovereignty of God, his denial of dualism, and the problem of the origin of evil.

The Love of God as Acceptance and Opposition

This 'right and left hand of God' motif is developed within the tension of acceptance and opposition as found in the perfections of the divine loving. With regards to grace and holiness, Barth describes grace as "an inner mode of being in God himself" which seeks and creates fellowship without regard to the worthiness and unconditioned by any merit on the part of the beloved.[71] In this mode God not only seeks and creates such fellowship, but when unworthiness and even opposition are encountered in it, God in his love overcomes them both. Therefore grace means condescension. Barth makes a clear break with the Roman Catholic understanding of grace as a gift from God that is external to

---

[70] Ibid. p. 560.
[71] Ibid. p. 353.

God Himself. Grace is not a commodity to be packaged and then imputed through the means of grace, but grace is God Himself. His gracious acts are His very being and there can never be a separation between the two.

This understanding of grace lies at the heart of Barth's doctrine of the sacraments.[72] It also underlines Barth's concept of the radicalness of the forgiveness of sins. When God answers the depth and seriousness of our sins with his own grace, He is giving nothing less than Himself for the defeat of sin. God gives us no external commodity but "God was reconciling the world to himself in Christ" (2 Cor 5:19). In grace God distinguishes himself from his creation, and His divinity consists and confirms itself in grace. It is in grace that God is *ad extra* that which he is eternally *ad intra*.

Keeping to the dialectical tension of grace (love) and holiness (freedom) God's love is holy love, and as such it is properly distinct from any and all other love. In seeking and creating fellowship God never ceases to be the Lord, therefore His own will will be distinguished and maintained such that "He condemns, excludes and annihilates all contradiction and resistance to it."[73] Barth is concerned to emphasize the transcendence of God in both; in grace we see He who condescends in His grace to save us, and in holiness we see that in His freedom He comes to us as the Lord, who is and always remains true to Himself and whose will prevails.

The same can be seen with regards to our opposition to God. In His grace He perseveres and does not cut us off, but in His holiness He overcomes and destroys that which opposes Him. Therefore grace is manifested in the forgiveness of sins and holiness in the judgement upon sins. For Barth these two may be distinguished but they cannot be separated, for together they constitute a proper understanding of the Lord of the covenant.[74] There is a 'relationship in tension' that is established here between the forgiveness of sins and the judgement upon sin which Barth maintains is good and necessary.[75] We

---

[72]   I have wrestled with Barth's doctrine of baptism in my M. Th. thesis, not disagreeing with his understanding of grace but with his understanding of the nature and purpose of baptism itself. Barth has given us the tools in a marvelous way to gain a whole new and rich understanding of the sacraments and he has employed those tools himself in his view of the Eucharist. However, for numerous reasons stated in the thesis, he fails to do the same when it comes to baptism. (See my thesis "A Comparative Study of the Doctrine of Baptism in the Theologies of Martin Luther, John Calvin and Karl Barth," M.Th. Thesis, University of Aberdeen, 1990)

[73]   CD II/1, p. 359.

[74]   This is one of many places where Barth borrows from the Chalcedonian formula in order to explain a relationship. His use follows the Chalcedonian idea of the tension between distinction and unity. (For more on Barth's use of the Chalcedonian formula, see Hunsinger, *How to Read Karl Barth* , *op. cit.*, pp. 185-188)

[75]   In Romans 5, Barth sees a similar duality in the relationship between Adam and Christ, "Even under the lordship of *sin* and *death* his [man's] nature is still human nature and so is the image and likeness of what it will be under the lordship of *grace* and *life*. That is how the essential disparity between Adam and Christ is contained

live in a relationship with God that includes both opposition and acceptance; acceptance only in the context of opposition. There must be an awareness and, more pointedly, a bowing to this opposition if we are to experience his grace.[76] "If He is not present to us in this tension, He is not present to us at all."[77] Therefore judgement and forgiveness, though seemingly self-contradictory, are in fact unified and inseparable and together they define holiness.[78]

We see the dialectic of the 'Yes' and 'No' of God at work here. It is in the very nature of God that we have both the opposition and the acceptance, and most importantly, we must face this 'No', this opposition, if we are to experience the 'Yes', the grace and acceptance of God. The 'No' is no external factor but it is, in the form of His holiness, *a constitutive element in the nature of God*. To see it as an adjunct, a temporary appendage or something foreign or alien in God is to misinterpret Barth at this crucial stage. The 'Yes'-'No' dichotomy (which is the same as the 'Right Hand'-'Left Hand' dichotomy) is a description of the very essence of God in Barth's discussion of God's perfections.

This theme is continued in the mercy and righteousness of God, where mercy is implied in grace. We His creatures are in distress and in His grace God moves to us in mercy. Just as God's being is grace, so His being is mercy which lies in His will "springing up from the depths of His nature."[79] This mercy is directed towards humanity which has brought upon itself suffering and misery. In an important statement Barth contends, "in concrete the mercy of God means therefore *His compassion at the sight of the suffering which man brings upon himself*, His concern to remove it, His will to console man in his pain and to help him to overcome it."[80]

Barth builds a picture of a God who by His very nature of grace and mercy is truly moved by the plight of humanity. God then responds in His mercy, condescending to humanity in grace, hating and rebuking sin according to His righteousness, and saving His creature in the power of His holiness. Barth demonstrates this powerfully when he says of Christ, "He took our place because He was God's eternal Son, because it was manifest in Him that God's eternal being is mercy, because there is nothing more real and true behind and beyond this substitution, because *this substitution is the very essence of God's own*

---

within their formal identity. Our relationship to Adam is a subordinate relationship, because the guilt and punishment we incur in Adam have no independent reality of their own but are *only the dark shadows of the grace and life we find in Christ*." (Barth, 'Christ and Adam: Man and Humanity in Romans 5' *op. cit.*, pp. 10-11)

[76] Barth made this point in his commentary on Romans, "Grace is not grace, if he that receives it is not under judgement. Righteousness is not righteousness, if it be not reckoned to a sinner. Life is not life, if it be not life from death. And God is not God, if he be not the End of men." (Barth, *The Epistle to the Romans, op. cit* , p. 187)

[77] CD II/1, p. 362.

[78] "God is holy because His grace judges and His judgement is gracious." (Ibid. p. 363)

[79] Ibid. p. 369.

[80] Ibid. p. 371-372. (emphasis mine)

being, of His divinity (diese Stelbvertretung das Innerste und Eigentlichste in Gott selber, das Wesen seiner Gottheit ist)."[81] Again 'the Being of God in act' is identical with His being in eternity, a being whose very nature is grace and mercy.[82]

As grace preceded holiness, so mercy must precede its counterpart in the freedom of God, namely righteousness, for "the righteousness of God is a determination of the love, and therefore of the grace and mercy of God."[83] Stating that the mercy of God can only be the mercy of *God* because it is the mercy of the *righteous* God, Barth seeks to preserve a unity between mercy and righteousness, for in the work accomplished according to His very nature as the former there is involved necessarily a work which maintains the worth of God in Himself.[84] God can and must be seen both as the Judge whose activity is wholly the execution of the Law, and as the righteous Judge who cannot affirm Himself more strongly than in the exercise of His grace in the forgiveness of sins. Thus grace is the proof of the existence of the righteous God, and just as we are to cleave to the opposition of God's holiness to find comfort in His

---

[81] Ibid. p. 375. (emphasis mine)

[82] In stark contradiction to this idea, Schleiermacher rejects the traditional understanding of the mercy of God to the point of concluding that "mercy is not a dogmatic term." (*The Christian Faith, op. cit.,* pp. 353-354)

[83] CD II/1, p. 376.

[84] Ibid. p. 377. Barth sees a weakness in the Protestant orthodoxy with regards to their understanding of the relationship between mercy and righteousness. He cites Quenstedt as an example of the danger of seeing in God a righteousness that is wholly demanding of man and which merits out rewards to the obedient and punishment to the sinners. Barth also includes here a typical swipe at Schleiermacher for his definition of the righteousness of God as the 'divine causality'. Against Quenstedt directly and Schleiermacher indirectly Barth finds in Luther how God's righteousness is known and seen in and by His mercy. Barth also sees in Polanus a misunderstanding of the vital linkage between righteousness and the will of God. There is not the necessary determination of righteousness by the mercy and grace of God to keep the righteous God from taking on a arbitrary air. Therefore the two cannot be maintained here either. Barth uses Anselm to correct Polanus as an example of a move from the righteousness of God to His mercy. God's mercy flows from the *altissimum et secretissimum bonitatis tuae* and in this way He is righteous in the very act of showing Himself to be merciful to the wicked. He can only do this from the stance of being righteous in Himself. Therefore if He has mercy on the unjust He does so rightly because He is in his very nature righteous. What God wills is just because He wills that which is worthy of Himself as true righteousness. Barth concludes, "From Luther on one side and Anselm on the other we have to learn that there is no righteousness of God which is not also mercy and no mercy of God which is not also righteousness. If this is the case, it is clear that no progress is possible if there is a fluctuation between God's mercy and righteousness, a hesitant and alternating consideration and underlining now of the one and now of the other." (p. 380) It is essential here to see how Barth seeks to hold the two together and yet how he allows the mercy of God to precede the righteousness of God as he allows the grace of God to precede His holiness.

grace, so too we must have faith in his righteousness which binds us to His mercy.[85]

Here we have not only the furtherance of the 'Yes'-'No' dichotomy but a growing emphasis on the order of 'No' before the 'Yes'. Although it is implied that the 'Yes' has the final priority, the 'No' is a *necessary* and *requisite* component to the functionality of the 'Yes', and in building his doctrine of evil from this point Barth sees that in the same way the work of left hand of God is a *necessary* and *requisite* component to the functionality of the work of the right hand of God. When Barth locates evil under the left hand of God–there being both rejected and also sustained and given its possibility for 'being'–he provides further evidence for both the centrality of the 'right and left hand' motif and for the 'necessary antithesis' from which it emerges.

Barth's 'Noetic Eschatology' and the Justification of God

The Victory of the 'Yes' and the Justification of Evil

If this 'No' is spoken wholly on behalf of the 'Yes', the justification of the 'No' is utterly dependent upon the victory of the 'Yes'. Barth places the revelation of this justification in the coming glory of God in the post-temporality of time. Barth defines eternity not as that which has no distinctions between past, present and future, but as that which has all of these dimensions in God who has all time and eternity in Himself, and in whom these distinctions are *simul*.[86] "The fact that the Word became flesh undoubtedly means that, without ceasing to be eternity, in its very power as eternity, eternity became time."[87] In this way God becomes temporal, taking time into Himself by revealing Himself in Jesus Christ, in a man in time and space.

Barth describes this temporality of eternity as pre-temporal, supra-temporal and post-temporal; God precedes creation, accompanies it in its duration and will continue to exist after its end. The whole of salvation history depends upon this idea of the readiness of eternity for time, for without it this history would be nothing more than myth or fable. It is the readiness for time that is the concrete expression of God's love for humanity and His turning towards it in grace and mercy. God's pre-temporality is described in the same way as His other perfections, as complete and whole in Himself, immutable and non-contingent.

---

85 CD II/1, p. 383.

86 Aquinas says of eternity that it is constituted both by its being unending and that it "exists as an *instantaneous whole* lacking successiveness." (*Summa Theologia, op. cit.,* Volume II, p. 137) He goes on to say that eternity belongs to God and that God, "is in his own invariable existence, and so is identical with his own eternity just as he is identical with his own nature." (Ibid) Barth holds, with Aquinas, that eternity is an instantaneous whole and that it belongs to God. He will not allow, however, that eternity is identical with God.

87 CD II/1, p. 616.

In His supra-temporality God accompanies us in eternity as we move towards our goal in eternity. Our future hope is based upon the newness of the supra-temporal eternity as over and against the continuing process of our temporal time. God is post-temporal in the same way which He is pre-temporal and with Him in this post-temporality we who are here and now reconciled in Christ will then and there be redeemed. This is our future, the goal of our life, towards which we can only move, for to move away from it is to move towards nothingness.[88]

What will this end bring? In the accounting of the time given to humanity, in this post-temporal time when God will be 'all in all' (1 Corinthians 15:28) "all that has been will have been to Him as it was from Him and by Him, and *will have fulfilled its purpose in being in its own place and way*, and to that extent will *have been vindicated in some sense according to the plan and order of God*."[89] The end of time will bring the justification of everything which God has incorporated into His plan, resulting in our praise to God for His wisdom and mercy. This is the hope given to us in God's self-revelation in Jesus Christ, and "God's revelation stands before us as the goal and end of time."[90]

Barth must be interpreted here as saying that struggle and hardship, suffering and pain, and even sin and death in this life will be shown to be a part of God's plan of salvation. Thus they will be vindicated according to the role they played in bringing everything to its desired and pre-determined goal. We must remember that evil and nothingness are incorporated in the 'plan and order of God' *(Sinn und der Ordnung Gottes)*. We find here the future justification of evil at the time of its final defeat and destruction, which serves as the vindication of God and His permission of evil. This is also Barth's basis for the idea that the justification of creation is found in the covenant, and it is echoed in Barth's exposition of the glory of God. We see yet again God's purposes in creation inextricably tied to the coming of the Son.

> The whole point of creation is that God should have a reflection in which He reflects Himself and in which the image of God as the Creator is revealed, so that through it God is attested, confirmed and proclaimed... *It was in order that there should be this reflection that the Son became flesh.*[91]

Suffering Under the Righteousness and Patience of God

Before we conclude let's shift away momentarily and look at Barth's understanding of suffering in anticipation of his final theodicy. Barth forbids us

---

88   Ibid. p. 629.
89   Ibid. p. 630. (emphasis mine)
90   Ibid. p. 630.
91   Ibid. p. 673. (emphasis mine)

to cling to the understanding of righteousness in Jesus Christ that would bring us comfort only, in lieu of a righteousness that brings with it the rewards and punishments of a true righteousness.[92] As such God in His righteousness exhibits wrath, anger and condemnation towards the sin that separates us from Him, taking upon Himself our sin in order to destroy its domination of us. This is the place where the love and grace and mercy of God is most brilliantly seen! Clearly for Barth the divine 'No' of Calvary is presupposed in the divine 'Yes' of Easter Day, and the two are inseparable. Without the divine 'No', without the death of Jesus Christ on the cross, the divine 'Yes' of Easter Day is not the "Yes of God's vindicating and rewarding righteousness."[93] We can never see the one without the other. In seeing the 'No' of Good Friday as the ultimate 'No' of God's all-consuming judgement, Barth provides a key to his understanding of suffering as judgement for sin in our relationship with God,

> This event [Good Friday] is the judgement which reduces to insignificance the seriousness of all the other judgements which from the beginning of the world have been seen to sweep over peoples and individuals–from the great catastrophes of nature and history which have and will come upon thousands and even millions, to that which we all have sooner or later to bear in the deprivation of health, wealth and opportunities in consequence of our own and other's folly or wickedness, and finally in the unique form of our death.[94]

In real terms for Barth, the "infinite weight and meaning of suffering and death has been borne *(unendliche Gewicht des Schmerzes, des Todes getragen worden ist)*."[95] Our own sufferings will be forgotten, but this one ultimate

---

[92] Here Barth identifies suffering with judgement of sin, which we will place under the first category of suffering as outlined in Chapter I. As sinners before the holy and righteous God, our sins cannot go unpunished, yet Barth will maintain that even our punishment for sins can never again have the flavour of enduring the wrath of God, since that was done once for all on Calvary.

[93] CD II/1, p. 394. Barth's answer to suffering can be found in part in his statement, "The New Testament answer to the problem of suffering - and it alone is the answer to the sharply put query of the Old Testament - is to the effect that One has died for all." (CD I/2, p. 109) Looking back to the Old Testament and specifically the persons of Job and the Psalmist, Barth believes that their suffering protests are answered in their fullest in Christ. Simply put, they have ceased to be a problem. As for the New Testament, suffering now comes as a result of the fact that we are and continue to be sinners, yet we are constantly saved by the cross under whose shadow we live. When we take upon ourselves to be our own master we are found guilty in our sin, and punishment for sin results. Again this is the understanding of suffering according to our first category. We will show how Barth defines some suffering distinctly differently from any idea of a punishment for sin and it is there that we will see the importance of the distinction in our categories of suffering.

[94] Ibid. p. 395.

[95] Ibid. p. 395; and KD II/1, p. 444.

suffering on the cross of God's own Son stands as the watershed event to which all human suffering can now only bear witness. Barth does not mean here to down-play the reality of suffering in the world, but instead we have here an excellent example of Barth's realism, for he is showing that the depth of suffering and the radicalness of the sin which permeates it is only truly seen in its horrible reality in the passion of Jesus. The great threats and judgements of the Old Testament were carried out in their fullest in the crucifixion. Calvary is the place of the real and true judgement of God, for the holiness and righteousness of God as the divine anger towards sin and sinners is seen in its fullest here and only here .

This means we no longer face the prospect of enduring the wrath of God which would annihilate us. What are we then to make of the sufferings and trials of this life? If they are not the judgements of God, the wrath of God, what are they? Barth offers the somewhat opaque answer that our current sufferings are *Zeichen und Schatten, Ankündigungen und um die Nachwehen,* (signs and shadows, announcements and echoes)[96] of this one great suffering, and they are therefore only *Zeichen des göttlichen Gerichtes* (signs of divine judgement).[97] He has previously laid the groundwork for the basing of a theodicy in the idea of representative suffering. Barth's exposition here must be understood as an expression of his realism and the resultant dichotomy between our personal experience and the ontological reality of the Truth of our existence.

According to this realism, our experiences of suffering have their true reality in their union with the ultimate reality of God's Word, the one great suffering of Christ. As we are ingrafted into a union with that suffering, our sufferings take on a form of reality in their 'reflection and foreshadowing' of that to which they are united.[98] This is the way which Barth understands 'the fellowship of Christ's sufferings', and it corresponds to our fourth category–suffering as a result of our faith and obedient walk with Christ. It is important here to see that these sufferings are not a punishment for sin, and the fact that Barth does not make

---

[96] *Nachwehen* is translated here as 'echoes' which is not as strong as the word would imply. The better translation would be 'after-pains'. (CD II/1, p. 406)

[97] Suffering for our faith too is a "faint but not obscure reflection of His [suffering]." (CD IV/1, p. 44)

[98] This is an important example of the way in which Barth sees the dichotomy between the ontic reality of the work of Christ for us-which includes His suffering-and the noetic pseudo-reality of our existence. Thus our suffering finds its real correspondence in union with the true sufferings of Christ. Far from down-playing the reality of our suffering, this idea is helpful for an understanding of suffering for the both the Christian and the non-Christian. For the Christian there is healing in the union of our suffering with Christ. For the non-Christian, suffering in isolation is a vestige of hell itself and because it denies union with Christ, it is a source of nothingness or evil. Thus there is in the Christian faith an overcoming of the true evilness in suffering in the union of our sufferings with the redemptive sufferings of Christ.

this important distinction when using the term 'suffering' here points out the need to distinguish between these categories of suffering as we have done.

This is seen clearly in Barth's view of an "inner, essential connexion between the one passion of the Son of God and the many sufferings which we see afflicting Israel, the Church, the world and ourselves."[99] Here he follows a very important line of reasoning in his dealing with the reality of the divine intervention for sinful humanity which has taken place in Jesus Christ. This real intervention becomes effective for us only as we are taken up to participate in His life, through our union in Christ. If we are truly to participate in this life, if we are really united with Christ for this purpose, does this not presuppose that we too will see, feel and experience the suffering of the judgement of God?[100] Barth assures us that these sufferings are only *Ankündigungen und um die Nachwehen der Wirklichkeit des göttlichen Gerichte*, yet they are real sufferings nonetheless.[101] It is part of taking up our cross where our cross, our sufferings and even our death are alongside His. This judgement is not the one we need to fear, for it is finished judgement, fulfilled judgement, vanquished judgement, yet because we live under the shadow of the cross, it is judgement we must bear. Why, we may ask, must we still bear it? How do we know we are to understand suffering in this way? Barth contends that this is a matter of faith. In a direct answer to the theodicy question he concludes,

> We do not believe if we do not live in the neighborhood of Golgotha. And we cannot live in the neighborhood of Golgotha without being affected by the shadow of divine judgement, without allowing this shadow to fall on us. In this shadow Israel suffered. In this shadow the Church suffers. That it suffers in this way is the Church's answer to the world on the question of a 'theodicy'–the question of the justice of God in the sufferings inflicted on us in the world.[102]

---

[99] CD II/1, p. 405.

[100] In bearing our own cross our suffering "involves hardship, anguish, grief, pain and finally death." (CD IV/2, p. 602), and thus the suffering Christian "exists only in the echo of His sentence, the shadow of His judgement, the after-pains of His rejection. In their cross they have only a small subsequent taste of what the world and they themselves deserved at the hand of God." (p. 604)

[101] KD II/1, p. 456. "We are not only permitted but commanded to regard all human suffering which we have only briefly sketched as a suffering with Him, in His fellowship, and therefore to understand the irruption of this suffering into the life of the Christian as the sign of this fellowship, and thus *the manifestation of the supreme dignity of the Christian... * we must think of the suffering which... arises in all its terror from the fact that the Christian too, in spite of what he already is, still stands under the law of sin and is still afflicted with the burden of the flesh." (CD IV/2, pp. 611-612)

[102] CD II/1, p. 406.

Barth's realism and his dialectic style allow him this rich understanding of our ability to participate in the sufferings of Christ, and to see through the unreality of our present trials to the One reality to which they point and into which they are ingrafted. He does all of this without either denying the reality of the evil we experience or giving to it too lofty a status as a true *Wirklichkeit*. However, just how seriously we can take evil in the time *post Christum* is a problem in Barth's doctrine of evil which we will continue to explore.

A final aspect of suffering is found in God's patience. God's perfections include His patience in which He gives us space and time and accompanies us along our way. Barth finds God's patience with Israel running throughout the Old Testament depicted in His self-restraint in the non-execution of the full judgement upon His chosen people and centred in His resolve to save them. Similarly we have certainly merited destruction, but God, in a full demonstration of his righteousness and holiness, sees to it that this is not to be our actual end. "Our preservation is meaningful and necessary. It is necessary because *God has linked His life with ours*, and has sacrificed Himself for us so that *as truly as God Himself lives we cannot perish*."[103]

Therefore although Israel's sufferings were punishments from God for disobedience, they were only "temporary and as such *symbolic judgements and punishments (zeichenhafte Gerichte und Strafen)*."[104] They are included under the patience of God which is both righteous and merciful, gracious and holy. This is a helpful understanding of this distinct form of suffering. Under the patient and gracious will of God His people will suffer *as a result of sin*, but this is not the great suffering which would certainly annihilate them. That suffering has been reserved for God alone in Jesus Christ. This will need further articulation as we critique the idea of 'innocent suffering' under the connection of sin to suffering. We agree here with Barth that as we are still in a fallen world we will bear the consequences of that sin in the form of suffering.

We conclude this section by looking briefly at suffering in the time of the Church *post Christum*. Barth's view of this suffering in part affirms an idea which is central to Moltmann's whole theological agenda concerning theodicy, namely that we suffer in our relationship with Jesus Christ. Ours is a shadow of His suffering, our cross a shadow of His cross and our death a shadow or reflection of His own death. In this way there is a participation in the sufferings of Christ quite distinctly spelled out by Paul and echoed in Barth. Now Barth, again in a similar way as Moltmann, believes that this relationship provides a key for understanding the Christian's response to personal suffering, "The relationship with Jesus Christ in which we must suffer is sufficient to overrule our suffering and the gift of the whole of our life for good (Romans 8:28)."[105]

---

[103] Ibid. p. 419. (emphasis mine) Here again we see the God whose portrait Barth painted so magnificently in his understanding of the grace, mercy and love of God in their properly balanced relationship and inseparable unity with His righteousness and holiness as known in His self-revelation in Jesus Christ.

[104] Ibid. p. 420.

[105] Ibid. p. 421.

The very fact that it is in this relationship that we suffer is the answer to how we can endure it. Because the unbearable components in suffering are its isolation, hopelessness and seeming meaninglessness, they are all overcome in this idea of God's co-suffering (and pre-suffering) for us and with us. We do not suffer alone, but have a sure and confident hope in our suffering, for we know that it is inexorably tied to His suffering for us. In addition, we know that all things, even the deepest grief and sorrow, can and will work together for good as we are called to suffer in this relationship with Jesus Christ.[106] In all of this Barth concludes that we can suffer in patience as we wait for our redemption to be revealed in the final *parousia* of Jesus Christ.[107] Here Barth has provided a helpful understanding of how we can bear our present suffering under this particular category of suffering. How this applies to other categories of suffering is yet to be seen. In addition, this presupposes that Barth's theology can accommodate suffering in any form in the time *post Christum*, and this will be a difficulty in his emerging doctrine of evil.

The Inter-Relationship of the Four Motifs and Barth's Theodicy

In considering theodicy with respect to his doctrine of God, Barth shows how these motifs are inter-twined; mutually supporting and clarifying each other. This point is emphasized in Barth's understanding of God's will as 'pure will'.[108] As pure will there is nothing that is outside it, and therefore nothingness owes its being and existence wholly and totally to this will. The result of this absolute and pure will corresponding to the absolute and pure sovereignty of God is seen in the following statement which is of such importance we are quoting it at length.

> If we ask why creation or each of us or everything has to be as it is, the only answer is that it must be so by God's free will. If we ask further why being is limited by non-being or why creation has to be obstructed or contradicted by sin and death and the devil, again the only answer we can give is that by the same free will of God by which it was created creation has to have this limitation by what is not created, by non-being, and *even non-being must also have this definite place and therefore its particular place.* If we ask the further question why there must be reconciliation, why the decision in which God shows Himself

---

[106] This is a point where Barth's theology is in direct opposition to Moltmann. While Barth is happy to see a future justification to human suffering, Moltmann rejects all such justifications outright.

[107] The term 'final *parousia*' is used here to keep in line with Barth's understanding of the three-fold *parousia*, which are really all one and the same. The *parousia* encompasses the 40 days of Easter, the coming of the Holy Spirit at Pentecost and the final coming of the Son in glory.

[108] *"Und dieser sein Wille is reiner."* (KD II/1, p. 631)

as Lord and Victor in His creation by saying Yes at this place and No at that, here accepting and there rejecting; and if we ask further why for this reconciliation and this decision there has to take place what does take place, why God Himself must become man, Himself enduring this limitation of His creation by sin and death and the devil in all of its fearful totality, and in this way conquer–the only answer we can finally give is *that this is how God has known it from eternity, and this is also how He has willed it from eternity*, in His divine freedom.[109]

What we have only hinted at Barth has here stated openly and overtly using all four motifs; the problem of evil is found in the will of God. The existence of evil, the proliferation of evil, the power of evil and the effect of evil are all carried out and sustained by, in and through the will of God, the *eternal* will of God. Barth would have us take every question unearthed in the theodicy debate and find its answer in the will of God. Yet at the same time Barth maintains that God is totally in the right, free of all responsibility for evil which instead rests firmly on our shoulders as we stand before Him as the rebel, the defiant sinner, the lost and damned creation. He is able to do so by returning us again and again to the freedom and love of God and concluding that all of this is "in some way God Himself, and God is free to be God in this way both in Himself and therefore also for us."[110] The key words here are 'in some way' *(so oder so)*, for they belie the mystery of how the God revealed in Jesus Christ can really be this God. Are we to accept this 'some way' by faith that the loving and gracious God we see in Christ really is worthy of love and trust and devotion even if He is also the Author, or at least the Permitter 'in some way' of all of the evil and pain and suffering we experience? We must remember also that this is not just God's will with regards to creation, but it is the *eternal will* of God. Before creation God willed all of this!

This brings us to back to a previous discussion. If God created humanity necessarily able to sin, we stated that this could only exonerate God's creation if He also created humanity as wholly able to not sin. Now we see that this is clearly not the case, for we have Barth affirming the very opposite.[111] From all eternity humanity was a fallen humanity in need of reconciliation and redemption. God's becoming man, enduring the limitations of creation and taking sin and death upon Himself to save His creation was part and parcel of His eternal will. Humanity was created as fallen humanity, and evil is allowed to operate that God's eternal will for humanity may be executed.

This is the heart of the 'necessary antithesis' motif. God is in control of it all; His will, the role of evil, humanity's necessary rejection, salvation history,

---

109 CD II/1, p. 561. (emphasis mine)

110 Ibid. p. 561.

111 This is also strongly implied in Barth's later statement, "There was never a golden age. There is no point in looking back to one. The first man was *immediately* the first sinner." (CD IV/1, p. 508)

humanity's future redemption and the final destruction of evil. All of this is in the script with the world created as the stage upon which this great drama is to be played out. This we have shown as the motif of the 'right and left hand of God'. The whole of the drama is determined ahead of time, for the Knower knows it all and the Willer must will it all or it will not occur. When we add to this Barth's strong inclination toward *apocatastasis* under the motif of his 'noetic eschatology', we complete this highly deterministic picture. And yet this sovereign God is the God of love, His purposes for us are gracious and merciful, His goal for us is eternal fellowship with Him which He has made possible through His own condescension and death in His Son. He will destroy sin, He will gather His creation victoriously up to Himself and reign for eternity. Given all of this, can we rightly accuse this gracious picture Barth has painted for us? Barth's justification of God is found totally within his understanding that the Christian God is the God of Calvary. Only in this way can we properly understand the relationship between the determinism of God's sovereignty and humanity's freedom.

Finally, Barth again raises the question of theodicy under an exposition of the *voluntas efficiens* and the *voluntas permittens*. This is really the culmination of what Barth wants to say in building this foundation for his doctrine of evil. Here Barth contends along similar lines to orthodox theology, that God does not cause evil but *permits* it to operate under His control (omnipotence) and according to His will and its two aspects where God wills to *schaffen, verusachen, und hervorbringen* under the right hand of God, and yet never without *Negieren, Richten, Verurteilen, und Überwinden* under the left hand of God.[112] God is free to cause what He will and permit what He will and no accusation can be brought to bear upon Him because He is acting according to His loving nature. In fact God would not be God if He were not the God who causes and, equally, the God who permits and forebears. So for Barth this permitting is *a necessary aspect of a divine will* ! "It is not a free will which wills only to act and not also to refrain from action. And it is not a divine but a demonic, satanic will which so wants its own way–even if this way is the divine holiness and righteousness–that it can only assert and enforce and not also make concessions."[113]

How should we interpret this idea of God's 'making concessions'? To whom is Barth referring in these concessions? It cannot be concessions to His creation, for we would certainly wish that no concessions be made and that evil be destroyed from the beginning. It seems that there can be no room for concessions to evil, for that would compromise the immutability of God as Barth has developed it in relation to that which God has rejected. That only leaves an internal concession to the eternal will of God which would permit evil a place and role as a means to an end. Barth gives strong evidence for this interpretation in the same section when he says of God's mighty not-willing of the evil counterparts to His own holiness, righteousness and wisdom, "To this

---

[112] KD II/1, p. 671.
[113] CD II/1, p. 596.

extent and in this way there is a mighty permission of them to go their own way. It is, of course, only permission, a restricted toleration, the forbearance of God *which aims at a goal and has therefore an end.*"[114] God's concession is an internal concession to Himself, in the permission of evil as a means to an end. God is able to do this, not being influenced by another but being true to Himself in making concessions to His own will. Evil has a purpose in the will, goal and plan of God and for such it is maintained, supported and given a limited power. Yet even in the awfulness of the manifestation of the full extent of this power, because it is operating only within the will of God, it is an act of the goodness and love of God towards His creation. It is Barth's realism that enables him to hold together all of these ideas with consistency and integrity.

> There must not be at any point a diminution either of the character of evil as evil, of the unconditional goodness of the divine creative will, of the omnipotence of the divine will as that of the Lord over the evil which He has not created, or of the goodness of this will of the Lord which is identical with His will as Creator. Nor must there be a diminution of the unity of the divine will as the willing of what is good even as it works through the evil that is rejected and nevertheless permitted by it.[115]

All of this must be accepted by faith which is the cornerstone of Barth's theodicy. There can be no question of giving in on either the love or the sovereignty of God. Both are total and absolute. All seeming contradictions, questions, protest cries and despair which occur in the realm of humanity must embrace this ontological truth that God is the God who loves in freedom. The unity of love, grace and mercy with holiness, righteousness and absolute sovereignty give us all of the comfort we need to accept our lot in life with faith in the eternal goodness and love of God. "If God is greater in the very fact that He is the God who forgives and saves from death, we have no right to complain but must praise Him that His will also includes a permitting of sin and death."[116] Therefore we are called upon always to affirm that the "*voluntas permittens* are fully and wholly the *voluntas divina.*"[117]

This holds true as well for the relationship between permitted evil and creation, for the supreme and best and truest good for creation is revealed in its salvation from the edge of the abyss.[118] As we live on the frontier of nothingness we are constantly reminded that we were created *ex nihilo*, and that we were separated from and brought out of the chaos which was the totality of

---

114 Ibid. p. 596. (emphasis mine)
115 Ibid. p. 595.
116 Ibid. p. 595.
117 Ibid. p. 595.
118 Ibid. p. 595.

what has been eternally rejected by God. Grace and salvation take on their full meaning in contrast to the ever threatening kingdom of darkness. Because of grace, we can accept the divine *voluntas permittens* and, when viewed from the vista of grace in Jesus Christ, we have no accusation to bring against God for its existence. Barth does not defend God's honour in lieu of the the *voluntas permittens*, but to the contrary he proves God's righteousness and holiness by the very fact that He is both *efficit* and *permittit*.

Clearly here we have evil being given a quite necessary role for the understanding of God's goodness and the salvation of humanity. The abyss is necessary to show us from where we came and from what we have been saved.[119] Yet there is a parallel here to the role of the Law and Gospel in traditional Protestant theology, and we must let Barth's correction of the latter also come to bear on our discussion. Barth breaks with Reformed Protestant theology by locating the true knowledge of the Law in the Gospel, where the Gospel allows us to see the sin (the Law) to which we were bound and from which we have been saved.[120] In a similar way, we can only see and understand the abyss from the safe haven of the salvation won for us. Therefore, if here Barth is showing signs of his dependence upon evil to bring about the eternal purposes of God under the 'necessary antithesis' motif, we must also say that he maintains the order that evil serves to show us from where we have come and not as a necessary motivator to move us to where we need to be. The 'No', as the 'left hand of God', is permitted solely for the sake of the 'Yes' or the 'right hand of God'. We are all already in Christ. To those to whom this incredible grace has been revealed, evil becomes the abyss not that we strive to escape, but to which we look back, having been rescued from it in Christ. Thus we have the justification of God *via* His salvation for creation where His eternal self-determination is a co-component of His eternal self-differentiation.

If the evil that continues to inflict us under the *voluntas permittens* serves to keep us ever mindful of that fact, then according to Barth's 'noetic eschatology', they may indeed play a positive role in the life of the Christian. This can only be so, it must be said, when such suffering and its meaningfulness for Christians is seen in the eyes of faith upon which Barth's 'revelatory positivism' is built and his entire theodicy depends.

---

[119] Hauerwas comments of the necessary connection between suffering and redemption that, "There is no problem of suffering in general; rather the question of suffering can be raised only in the context of a *God who creates to redeem*." (Hauerwas, *Naming the Silences, op. cit.,* p. 79, emphasis mine)

[120] In a similar statement Barth says, "Because we know Christ the Conqueror, we can know Christ the Crucified. Because we know Adam and ourselves as men who are pardoned and men who are going to share God's glory, we can also know Adam and ourselves as sinners who were once condemned to die. Now we live in the full and direct light of the truth of Christ." ('Christ and Adam: Man and Humanity in Romans 5', *op. cit.,* p. 23)

CHAPTER IV

Evil and Barth's Doctrine of Election

The Eternal Decision of God

The unusual placing of election for Barth–prior to the doctrines of creation and reconciliation–gives immediate indication of how he views the connection between creation and the Fall. In keeping with his development of the omnipotence of God, Barth sees all existence as pre-ordained in the grace of God. All movements of God towards humanity, because they are free and unmerited, are truly acts of grace. In God's primal decision He chose Himself for humanity and in so doing He chose humanity for Himself. This two-fold determination is wholly contained in the election of Jesus Christ, for Jesus Christ is the electing God and the elected man, and "everything else that we have to say about it [election] must consist in the development and application of what is said in these two statements taken together."[1]

This primal self-determination is at the heart of Barth's doctrine of election. It does not find its goal in creation, in the establishment of the external basis of the covenant, but in the fact that God determines Himself from eternity to be God for humanity solely in Jesus Christ. "It defines grace as the starting point for all reflection and utterance, the common denominator which should never be omitted in any statements which follow."[2] Thus God's self-determination skips over any idea of a possible eternal paradisal community and immediately ties God's determination to seek and create fellowship with the revelation of that determination in the life, death and resurrection of Jesus Christ. This is supported by Barth's affirmation of the *logos ensarkos* and consequent rejection of the idea of an abstract or detached *logos asarkos*.[3]

To augment this idea Barth states that all the works of God, according to both His positive will and His negative will, are foreordained as a part of this definitive movement of God to humanity in His primal self-determination. This puts Barth in the unique position of seeing sin, death, hell and the devil as a part of God's gracious movement towards humanity. Barth makes this point quite clear. Having identified sin, death, the devil and hell as the 'enemies of God', Barth says,

---

[1] CD II/2, p. 145.

[2] Ibid. p. 93.

[3] "In the *eternal decree* of God, Christ is God and man. Do not ever think of the second Person of the Trinity as only *Logos*. That is the mistake of Emil Brunner. There is no *Logos asarkos*, but only *ensarkos*." (Barth, 'Table Talk', *op. cit.*, p. 49) While Barth does not reject the *logos asarkos* outright (see, for example, CD III/1, p. 54, and CD I/2, p. 168ff), he does reject a detached view which would either give way to a 'Christ principle' in abstraction from the incarnate Jesus, or a twofold Christ, thus undermining the Chalcedonian formulation.

Even the enemies of God are the servants of God and the servants of His grace. Thus God and the enemies of God cannot be known at all unless both they and their negative character and whole work of negation are *known in the service which they render as instruments of the eternal, free and immutable grace of God.* [4]

Here we have a further unveiling of Barth's instrumental understanding of evil as it operates solely under the sovereign lordship of God. Evil is a servant of God and it has a distinctive role to play in the execution and completion of God's will in creation.[5] That goal is the salvation of the creature from nothingness bringing it up in the Son into the fellowship of the Father and the Son in the Spirit. Because of this connection, many interpreters of Barth have rightly concluded that the electing action of God is the 'ontological context of nothingness'.[6] It is in the very electing activity of God that nothingness is given its 'peculiar ontology' of existence-in-rejection. Yet Barth still rejects an eternally enduring chaos as the correlate to the eternal election in Christ. The very nature of nothingness as the reverse side of election means that while election is eternal, nothingness is only a *"passing* reality."[7]

Two things must be clarified here concerning the 'necessary antithesis'. First, the 'No', while not eternal, is still what Berkouwer calls "the *unavoidable*

---

[4] CD II/2, p. 92. (emphasis mine)

[5] This position is taken by Nicolas Berdyaev who concluded that evil must have a positive role if its existence (even as non-being, another idea he shared with Barth) was not to make the creation of the world a failure. "The paradox of evil lies in this, that evil is meaningless, a falling away from Meaning [God], a mockery of meaning, and at the same time evil must have some positive meaning, if the final word in being belongs to Meaning, that is to God... We must recognize both the fact that evil is meaningless and the fact that it has a meaning... If evil is pure senselessness, a violation and mockery of the world's Meaning, and if it is crowned with eternal hell, then the hellish meaninglessness is part of God's plan, and the creation of the world was a failure." (Berdyaev, *The Destiny of Man,* (London: Centenary Press, 1931), pp. 317-318). Berdyaev's conclusions concerning the role of evil in a creation which has meaning and purpose include necessarily for him the idea of *apocatastasis.* If hell exists, then evil has destroyed God's plan for creation. This idea that the justification of evil can only be found when linked to universalism is echoed by Moltmann, and vestiges of this underlying connection are found in Barth as well.

[6] This view is held by Berkouwer, "The electing Yes of God implies His wrathful No, and *by reason of* this wrathful judgement the chaos, sin, *exists* ... It cannot be denied that the chaos appears on the horizon of Barth's theology at the point where he speaks of election." (*Triumph of Grace, op. cit.,* p 219) It is also held by Walter Whitehouse, "Its [nothingness'] ontological context is the *electing action* wherein God is who He is." (W.A. Whitehouse, *The Authority of Grace: Essays in Response to Karl Barth,* (Edinburgh: T & T Clark, 1981), p. 45)

[7] Berkouwer, *Theology of Karl Barth, op. cit,* p. 219.

reverse side of election."[8] To understand this we must remember Barth's line of thought concerning the eternal self-distinction of God from 'not God', and creation as the self-recapitulation of God in this self-distinction. This must be stressed both as a consistent theme in Barth's theology and as central to his doctrine of evil! Creation then is a witness and testimony to this self-distinction in God, and as such it must witness to both the 'Yes' and 'No'.[9] Because this is the truth of the Creator, the creature bears witness to this two-fold truth, and thus it must be confronted by sin "even as God Himself is confronted with it in that self-differentiation *(Selbstunterscheidung)*, in that disavowal of what He is not, and does not will."[10] Therefore, just as God exists in an eternal self-differentiation, so creation *must* exist in confrontation with the nothingness which God has eternally rejected.

When Barth adds to this that creation could not for a single moment stand firm in the face of this confrontation with nothingness, we must conclude that the manifestation of evil in creation is a pre-destined situation which corresponds to the eternal election of all humanity in Jesus Christ. *The tie between eternal self-differentiation, creation as the self-recapitulation of God, and the eternal decision of God to be 'for us' in the Elect man Jesus Christ must never be forgotten.* In this context we re-assert our motif of a 'necessary antithesis' as that unavoidable 'No' which must, in creation, accompany the divine 'Yes'. This is so simply because God is who He is! Thus even if the 'No' is not eternal, an idea we will challenge later, the absolute exigency of the 'No' for the witness of creation and the accomplishment of the eternal purposes of God must be seen here to have been forcefully demonstrated. In addition, Barth stated clearly in his excursus in the perfections of God that the blessing of the salvation of the creature would not be possible if humanity had remained in the pre-fallen state in which it was created.

This special blessing could only come to humanity if it was first the enemy of God and thus stood on the brink of the abyss. God's grace was most fully grace when He reached down not just to that which was other than God, but to that which rebelled against God in the impossible possibility of sin. That supreme act of grace, the perfect revelation of God in His Son, the achievement of the eternal goal of God and the completion of the purpose of creation all were wholly and completely dependent upon the fallen state of humanity! We see the continuing influence of Barth's dialectical theology, for it was already in Romans that he stated, "this fallen state is a consequence of no single historical

---

[8]   Ibid. p. 220.

[9]   Barth makes the point that God does not will at random. He wills the man who would be a reflection of Himself, and therefore the man who would "testify to His glory and thus reveal and confirm and verify both positively what He is and will, and negatively what He is not and does not will." (CD II/2, p. 141.) This 'No', this negative witness "forms the boundary of the Yes: so assuredly is God God and not not God: so assuredly does He live in eternal self-differentiation from all that is not God and is not willed by God." (p. 141)

[10]   CD II/2, p. 141.

act: it is the *unavoidable pre-supposition of all human history.*"[11] This is the first point which is unequivocal given what Barth has stated thus far.

Secondly, both Berkouwer[12] and Whitehouse[13] caution us that Barth is not here attempting to construct some extreme logical dialectic. Both remind us that Barth rejects any notion that the thesis (the 'Yes') and the antithesis (the 'No') will move beyond to some form of synthesis. Again the 'necessary *antithesis* ' may come in for criticism at this point. However both Berkouwer and Whitehouse are using the term 'synthesis' in its Hegelian form. For Barth, thesis and antithesis can exist without the necessity of the movement in which both are dissolved into the higher synthesis *(Aufhebung)* of Hegelian thought. For as we have seen, Barth sees the synthesis as the *a priori* from which both thesis and antithesis flow—namely, Jesus Christ Himself. Barth repeatedly makes the point that Christ takes both the thesis and the antithesis up into Himself, and as such they both owe their existence to Him alone, as in the strong statement, "He is the God who gives man a share of the divine 'Yes', and for the sake of the 'Yes', in the divine 'No'. He is the God who puts man in this antithesis and Himself overcomes it."[14] They do not move beyond and above Him, but they flow from Him and He is eternally above them. So we can posit the idea of an antithesis, the 'No' of God, to the thesis of the 'Yes' of God without requiring the Hegelian type of synthesis of which we are warned by Berkouwer and Whitehouse. In these two ways, our motif of a 'necessary antithesis' is further strengthened early in the development of Barth's doctrine of election.

The Inevitability of the Fall

A second point is emerging which will be given its fullest expression in Barth's doctrine of creation, namely, that because so much depended upon the Fall, humanity was not created just so that the Fall was possible, but was destined to fall. When faced with that which was by definition greater than itself, the creature of God in its distinction from God was powerless against sin and was doomed to fall. Doomed to fall? We can and must say pre-destined to fall according to the eternal will of God and His purposes and goal of creation.[15]

---

11 Barth, *The Epistle to the Romans, op. cit.* p. 181. (emphasis mine)

12 Berkouwer, *Triumph of Grace, op. cit.,* p. 219.

13 Whitehouse, *Authority of Grace, op. cit.,* p. 45.

14 CD II/2, p. 142.

15 Barth is trying to be faithful to the understanding that God in His omniscience must have foreknown the Fall of creation. This has been shown repeatedly in Barth's ideas of the eternal self-differentiation of God and of creation being the self-recapitulation of God. Neither the Fall of man nor the election of Jesus Christ to save the creature was a surprise to God, but both were contained in His eternal foreknowledge and therefore in His eternal will. Barth here is following Augustine who wrote, "For man's sin could not disturb God's decree, nor force Him to change

God did not positively will the Fall of the creature, but in His eternal election of Jesus Christ as *homo labilis*, the Fall is fully assumed as the state of humanity and thus is 'pre-determined', yet not by the positive will of God, but under the permission of the left hand of God.

We see this clearly in Barth's doctrine of election where he indicates that the wrath of God, the sentence of guilt for sin, the execution of His judgement on humanity's rebellion and the full rejection of sinful humanity which was all suffered and taken up in Jesus Christ was determined from all eternity.[16] "The elected man Jesus was foreordained to suffer and to die... the election of the man Jesus means, then, that a wrath is kindled, a sentence pronounced and finally executed, a rejection actualised. It has been determined thus from all eternity."[17] *From all eternity* there would be sin and rebellion, and evil would necessarily have this temporary victory. There is with the election of humanity in Jesus Christ both the positive and good creation and its necessary counterpart in that which is of the negative or non-will of God.

> [But] this involves necessarily the rejection of Satan, the rebel angel who is the very sum and substance of the possibility which is not chosen by God... Satan is the shadow which accompanies the light of the creation of Jesus Christ. And *in the divine counsel the shadow itself is necessary as the object of rejection (Gegenstand der Verwerfung)*. To the reality of its existence and might and activity (only, of course, in the power of the divine negation, but to that extent grounded in the divine will and counsel) *testimony is given by the fall of man*, in which man appropriates to himself the satanic desire. When confronted by Satan and his kingdom, man in himself and as such has in his creaturely freedom *no power to reject that which in His divine freedom God rejects.* [18]

His purpose. God foreknew and anticipated both, that is, how bad man (whom He had created) should become, and what good He meant to derive from him, for all his badness." (*The City of God* - Volume II, (London: J.M. Dent & Sons, 1945), p. 40) In defending the providence of God he writes later, "Why then might not God that knew this [the fall of man] beforehand permit him to be tempted by the malicious wicked spirit, not being ignorant that he would fall, but knowing withal, how doubly the devil would be overthrown by those that His grace should select out of man's posterity." (p. 58)

[16] In his commentary on Romans, Barth clearly saw the Fall not as one act in history but as a state of man in which the historical act of Adam was the first manifestation of that state. The fallen state was part of the Supralapsarian election by God prior to creation. Therefore, "according to it, predestination unto rejection precedes the 'historical' fall. Only insofar as Adam first did what we all do, is it legitimate for us to call and define by his name the shadow in which we all stand." (*Romans, op. cit.,* pp. 172-173)

[17] CD II/2, p. 122.

[18] Ibid. p. 122. (emphasis mine)

There are three themes here which call for further treatment, two explicitly and one implicitly. First, there is a necessary role for Satan, evil and sin in God's purposes in creation which come from the divine counsel and will of God. This is not the will of God for evil to exist, but the will of God to create in His own image and to bestow the blessing which can only come to one who is standing on the edge of the abyss.[19] Thus we agree with David Ford when he says of evil, "its function is to occasion the cross."[20]

Second, humanity could not have withstood the temptation to sin and thus the Fall was the inevitable product, and we may now say a pre-determined and necessary product, of God's gracious movement to humanity in creation. This is the essence of what Barth means by election when he says "from all eternity He sees us in His Son as sinners to whom He is gracious."[21]

Third, it is implied that God's primal self-determination was necessitated by His eternal self-differentiation. Self-differentiation and self-determination are the necessary correlates of grace! God's gracious and primal self-determination was not to seek and create a relationship with another distinct from Himself for eternal fellowship *per se*, but was, instead, to be 'for' this creation in the form of the suffering and death of His Son to atone for the *inevitable* sin of His creation.

In all of this talk of the 'inevitability' of sin we must return to the question of a latent dualism in Barth's theology. As we have shown, the classic idea of dualism between good and evil, or between God and Satan does not exist in Barth, and he must be credited for constructing a doctrine of evil devoid of such a concept. Yet what he does allow (although he does not always admit it) is the idea of a duality, and the force of the duality is its necessity for his entire theology. The negative side of the duality–nothingness–is a required player in the plan of creation, yet it is never an independent reality and therefore it never occupies the place required of the foe of a Manichaeistic type of dualism. The role that it does play is that of the 'necessary foe' to God and His good purposes, and to creation as created by the loving Creator, all while being under the control of God. This gives to evil the distinct role of the 'necessary antithesis' in Barth's doctrine of evil. This must connote that the temporary victory of the enemies of God in His creation was the necessary and only possible outcome (and the best, according to Barth) given that this creation must be confronted by that which God has eternally rejected in his self-distinction of God from 'not-God'. For that which God has eternally rejected His creation could not possibly reject because of its non-divinity, even though creation is the product of the positive will of God.[22]

---

[19] Barth offers an important qualifier which is thematic in his theology, "This whole realm that we call evil-death, sin, the Devil and hell-is *not* God's creation, but rather what was excluded by God's creation, to that which God said 'No'... We must not look for darkness in God Himself." (*Dogmatics in Outline, op. cit.,* p. 57).

[20] Ford, *Barth and God's Story, op. cit,* p. 75.

[21] CD II/2, p. 124.

[22] This raises the question of how Barth can put the responsibility for sin on the shoulders of humanity? It is not because we had some Pelagian form of freedom which

We can follow this line of thought in one short section of CD II/2.[23] Barth begins by stating, "Because there is no darkness in God, there can be no darkness in what He chooses and wills." He continues that "God willed man and elected man with the promise of eternal life." However, "Man was willed by and chosen by God with his limitation... The danger-point of man's susceptibility to temptation, and the zero-point of his fall, were thus *included in the divine decree. In their own way they were even the object of the divine will and choice*." Therefore in creation, the good which is willed by God, "stands out from what He does not will, the evil, where *by the very existence of good* there is conceded to evil and created for it a kind of possibility and reality of existence, where it can and does enter in as a kind of autonomous power, as Satan." This is not an accident or an unplanned event, but it is the necessary and inevitable product of the creation of the non-divine creature, for "without evil 'permitted' in this sense there can be no universe or man." It was this unavoidable presence and victory of evil which was foreseen and overcome already in the eternal self-determination

---

would have granted an arbitrary sense of choice in which to reject or submit to the temptation to sin. No, since humanity's fall is pre-ordained, so its bearing of the wrath of God is just and proper only because this bearing of the judgement against sin is "according to the will and counsel of God." (CD II/2, p. 122) Here we must return again to Barth's understanding of the relationship between Law and Gospel. As Barth has asserted that a man can only see his sin, his lostness and the judgement under which he stands from the vista of the Gospel in which he finds grace and forgiveness, so that same man can only be understood to rightfully stand under the condemnation for that which he was powerless but to do if he sees that the counsel that so decrees such a sentence is the counsel of the One who has elected all humanity in Jesus Christ from all eternity. It is only in the light of grace, and therefore only in faith, that we can see and accept the judgement that stands over us as the judgement that was borne by another and, therefore, as the love of God. Barth shows how, in the case of Israel's handing over of Jesus, this idea of necessary sin and blame hold together. It was necessary in that "Nothing else could have happened. It was inevitable... because it was only by rejecting Christ that Israel could serve the gracious purposes of God." (p. 34) However "if grace was to abound, if sin and death were to be removed from the world, Christ *had* to be condemned as a sinner and He *had* to die." (Ibid.) The Jews, in their rejection and condemnation of Jesus were "carrying out the good, righteous and merciful will of God. They did it as *completely blameworthy instruments*." (p. 35, emphasis mine) How could they be held blameworthy for doing what was both inevitable and according to the good will of God? Barth answers, "The accusation against the Jews over their rejection of Christ is in the last resort invalid because either it is completely null and void or it falls upon God Himself. In doing as they did they were acquitted from the guilt and punishment their action deserved by God's action in bearing their guilt and punishment on their behalf." (p. 36) Thus the results of their sinful actions saved them. Yet the fact that they had to sin in order to be saved in this way does not make them less blameworthy for that sin. In a direct restatement of the idea of the *O' felix culpa*, Barth concludes, "If they had not acted as they did, God would not have borne their guilt and punishment and they would not have been acquitted at all. For what they did to Christ the Jews cannot be excused, but neither can they be accused or condemned." (p. 36)

[23] CD II/2, pp. 169-170. (emphasis mine)

of God in the election of Jesus Christ. Only in this way can we understand Barth when he says of the foreordination of humanity for God's glory, "this foreordination cannot be fulfilled except on the brink of the abyss of foreordination to evil."[24]

Evil in Barth's Re-Structured Supralapsarianism

Barth's doctrine of evil is indelibly shaped by his re-modification of the Reformed doctrine of Supralapsarianism. It is critical here to understand what Barth rejected of the Reformed position. According to Barth, the role of evil in the Supralapsarian position is "an element in that [God's] original plan," and for this reason, "the Fall had inevitably to take place, not apart from but in accordance with the will of God."[25] This was so in order that the mercy and justice of God could be manifest in His creation, with election and reprobation corresponding to creation and Fall.[26] In a key interpretation Barth concludes,

> He [the Supralapsarian] knows, in fact, that for the sake of His own glory God from all eternity predestined each individual man either to the one alternative or the other, either to election or to reprobation. And he knows that God created man, and each individual man, and allowed him to sin in the person of Adam, in order that he might fulfil either the one destiny or the other, and therefore be a means to the revelation of God's glory, whether of His mercy or of His justice.[27]

With regards to evil, then, the Supralapsarian position has two important aspects: 1) it provides an understanding of why God has allowed evil its place in creation–for the necessary 'No' of God's justice as the limit of His 'Yes' of mercy, and 2) it does not keep evil and sin from being truly evil and sinful. Therefore the Supralapsarian position can incorporate evil, in all of its evilness, into the plan of God as a tool which He uses to bring about the ultimate goal of creation–namely, His own glorification. We must quote Barth at length, to see what he chooses to modify, *and what he accepts without modification* from the Supralapsarian position.

---

24 Ibid. p. 171.

25 Ibid. p. 129.

26 Here the Reformed position owed much to Augustine whose writings are full of the manifestations of the mercy and justice of God. One striking example will prove the point, "if all had tasted of the punishments of justice, the grace and mercy of the Redeemer had had no place in any: and again, if all had been redeemed from death, there had been no object left for the manifestation of God's justice." (*City of God, op. cit.,* p. 335)

27 CD II/2, p. 128.

According to him [the Supralapsarian], we cannot say simply that God created man to allow him to fall into sin. Nor can we say that He allowed him to fall into sin in order to damn him, or in His mercy to save some. Rather, all these individual *media* combine to form one single *medium*. And to know that *medium* as such, and the basis and meaning of all individual *media*, we must see them in the light of their ultimate purpose: that God created the universe and man, that He allowed the fall of man, that He allowed the general condemnation of sin to follow, and that in mercy He delivered some men from the general condemnation, in order that in and through this whole process He Himself might be glorified as the God of mercy and justice.[28]

In contrast to this, Barth poses and refutes the Infralapsarian position and proposes a re-definition of the Supra-position.[29] Berkouwer presents the most succinct summary of Barth's interpretation when he writes, "[for Barth] supra recognizes and indicates the danger of dualism; infra the danger of monism."[30] Barth's distaste for the Infra-position is consistent with his entire theological agenda which seeks to hold together creation and redemption, and to center both in Jesus Christ. The Infra-position undermines the inseparable connection between creation and *Heilsgeschichte* by assigning the work of Christ on behalf of the elect to a subordinate, post-creation place in the plans of God. At the root of the rejection of the Infra-position are the two critical points that it 1) closed all doors for a movement in the direction of seeing Christ as the one Elect (both the electing God and the *homo labilis*) by holding to two decrees in God, and 2) it is motivated not by faith but by logic and morality.[31] It is not surprising

---

[28] Ibid. p. 129.

[29] A chief concern of the Infralapsarian was that the Supra-position, in the end, made God the Author of evil. Thus the Infra-position sought to dislocate the election of fallen humanity from the eternal decree of creation, and thus to dislocate God's perfect plan for creation from the subsequent disobedience of the creature. The Infra-position was primarily determined to protect the doctrine of election from what it saw as the monistic bent of the Supra-position, and what it believed to be the resultant watering down of the true evilness of evil. Barth refers to this attempt as 'logico-empirical objections' which were at least in part responsible for the "later cleavage between natural and revealed theology." (CD II/2, p. 136) For a refutation of this interpretation, see Berkouwer, *Divine Election, op. cit.,* pp. 271-276.

[30] Berkouwer, *Divine Election,* p. 271.

[31] One wonders here if Barth did not hearken back to his profound understanding of Kant and his view of election as mystery. Kant was unable to find any logic that could account for a grace that saved some and damned others and he concluded, "this [double predestination] again yields no concept of a divine justice but must refer to a wisdom whose rule is for us an absolute mystery. As to these mysteries, so far as they touch the moral life-history of every man, of this God has revealed to us nothing and can reveal nothing since we would not *understand* it." (Kant, *Religion Within the Limits of Reason Alone, op. cit.,* pp. 134-135) For Barth, election is not hidden in secret and unknowable decrees, but is revealed to us in Jesus Christ.

that Barth opted for a modification of the Supra-view given his stress on the sovereignty of God, his ideas of providence and his desire to defend against dualism and to emphasize the coherence between creation and covenant.

In creating a "purified Supralapsarianism" which needed to be "drastically corrected and supplemented,"[32]　Barth stripped away its mistaken presuppositions in order to render the required purified doctrine. We must be certain to understand these presuppositions for they are the core of Barth's rejection.

First, the Supra view holds incorrectly that the *obiectum praedestionis* is the individual abstractly understood and not humanity *in concreto* (and even more importantly, not the man Jesus Christ). Secondly, it holds incorrectly that there is a balance between election and reprobation within the fixed system of the decrees of God and as such that the Fall and evil are part of the *positive will* of God to bring about both destinies. Third, it is incorrect to build from this that God's glory consists in the preordaining of some to heaven and some to eternal torment. Finally, it is incorrect to conclude that for this purpose God created the world.

Thus Barth's modifications of the Supra-view are as follows:

1. It is not for God's own glory *per se* that He created but, "the primal and basic purpose of this God in relation to the world is to impart and reveal Himself, and with Himself His glory, He Himself being the very essence of His glory."[33] Here Barth builds upon the idea that the perfections of God are not to be separated from God. Thus to impart His glory is, for God, to impart and reveal Himself.[34]

2. Barth replaces the idea of an abstract election of humanity with the election of humanity *in concreto*, and not any individual but the One person who would obey Him and in whom God's witness would be known in both its positive and negative forms. The clear and decisive point in Barth's doctrine of election is that God's eternal will is the election of Jesus Christ as that man. This elected man testifies to the glory of God and therefore both to what He has willed and what He has not willed, to the 'Yes' and the 'No' of God. Therefore the elected man is both the man of grace and, from eternity, *homo labilis*. *Homo labilis* is the state of humanity as elected by God in Jesus Christ; *homo lapsus* is the sin of humanity in its rejection of the grace of God. The critical distinction for Barth here is that God willed *homo labilis*, but He did not will *homo lapsus*! Humanity is responsible for the guilt associated with the sinfulness of the world, yet the election to save humanity, the election of humanity in Jesus Christ from eternity means that God positively willed to be for humanity, for *this* humanity, for fallen humanity, and thus the elect man, Jesus Christ, is from eternity *homo labilis*. Here we can see that there is no pre-

---

[32]　CD II/2, p. 143.

[33]　Ibid. p. 140.

[34]　Barth sees glory here in the same way he viewed grace, not as a commodity packaged and separate from God but part of God Himself.

Fall/post-Fall aspect at this point in Barth's theology, but humanity was elected as *homo labilis* from eternity. The *lapsus* of humanity is a contemporary event as the creature chooses the impossibility of sin over grace.

The Fall of humanity was not a single historical event but an indicator of the state of humanity as *homo labilis*. Yet the idea of humanity's rejection, of the Fall of humanity is fundamental for Barth's theology and it must not be subsumed under a seeming determinism here. Humanity sinned against the grace of God and the title *homo lapsus* is accurate and well-deserved. However the Infra-view in which the election of humanity was the election of *homo lapsus* is rejected because it cannot apprehend the idea of Jesus Christ the *Logos ensarkos,* as the eternally Elect sinful man. Barth's doctrine of election is an attempt to locate the election of humanity in the eternal decree of God without being bound by the dualistic and deterministic system of the Supralapsarian. His answer lies in this distinction of the election of humanity as *homo labilis* and the rejection of humanity as *homo lapsus*.[35]

Here is a critical point in Barth's understanding of the relationship between election and evil. God willed elected humanity as sinful humanity, that is, elected humanity must necessarily be confronted by that which eternally confronts God and is rejected by Him, and humanity's inevitable fall in the face of this confrontation opens up the way for the defeat of nothingness, for "this victory must take on historical form, thus becoming an event in time."[36] In this way Barth seeks to preserve the idea of our responsibility for sin *(homo lapsus)* and to keep God from the accusation of *peccator Originare.*

3. Barth rejects the Supra view that God's glory is attained in the two-fold determination of election and reprobation. Instead, Jesus Christ, as the elect man, witnesses to both the 'Yes' and the 'No' according to God's purpose in creation and in doing so He is confronted by evil. By allowing evil to overcome Him on the cross He establishes the final victory over nothingness and its

---

[35] Barth clarifies this connection, "We cannot hold it against God that He did not prevent but permitted the fall of man, i.e., his succumbing to the temptation of the devil and his incurring of actual guilt. In God's eternal decree these things did not involve any injustice to the creature, for by this same decree God decided that the risk which He allowed to threaten the creature and the plight into which He allowed it to plunge itself should be His own risk and His own plight. God created man. In that sense He exposed him to the risk. Yet from all eternity God did not let Him fall, but He upheld him even when Satan's temptation and his own culpability resulted in a fall into sin. Thus even when we think of man in this negative determination, we still think of him as the one whom God loved from all eternity in His Son, as the one to whom He gave Himself from all eternity in His Son, gave Himself that He might represent him, gave Himself that He might bear and suffer on His behalf what man himself had to suffer. We must insist upon man's responsibility for this failure to do on that frontier what he ought to have done as the creature of God and hearer of the Word of God. But much more, we must insist upon the responsibility which God Himself shouldered when He created man and permitted him to fall." (CD II/2, pp. 165-166)

[36] Ibid. p. 141.

ultimate rejection at the resurrection. Thus in Christ, that which is the eternal state of evil vis-á-vis God, namely rejection, finds its historical correlate in the time and history of creation. As such, humanity can be lifted up in Christ for fellowship with God and His corresponding glorification–which is the goal of creation. This is the glory of the Creator, not that His mercy and justice would be fulfilled in some self-centred display of glorification, but that He would give Himself to His creature, and through its salvation, through the fellowship that would be made possible, God would be glorified.

4. Finally, Barth sees the goal of creation as centred in this desire for God's glorification through His self-revelation in the election of Jesus Christ. In this way election and creation are as inseparable as creation and covenant, for the covenant is the covenant unto election. As we will see in the next chapter, the justification of creation lies solely in the covenant, which in turns has its basis in election.

Clearly the inevitability of the *homo lapsus* (although not the product of the divine will) is the basis of the election of humanity in Jesus Christ as *homo labilis*. The great and eternal 'for us' in Barth's doctrine of election corresponds to the 'against us' which was the inevitable situation of God before humanity and humanity before God in the face of the Fall. This Fall was the eternally determined situation of humanity due to the process of creation which demanded that God's creature be tempted by the eternally rejected chaos and which knew that the creature would succumb. This is the unavoidable result of the combination of the 'necessary antithesis' motif and the understanding of creation as the self-recapitulation of God. Thus it is correct to say that in Barth's theology God did not 'will' the Fall, but the Fall was assumed in the decrees of election and creation. Election and creation were decreed and carried out under the cloud of man's inability to resist the evil which must befall him, and yet the cross turns the negative into a positive by locating the victory of Christ over evil in the space-time history of humanity on the behalf of the fallen creation. All of this was part and parcel of the eternal plan of God, that the eternally rejected nothingness would become the temporally defeated nothingness and would, as a result, cease to 'exist'.

In supporting this amended version of Supralapsarianism Barth also rejected the traditional doctrine of the double decree in which God makes the choice to reject some in a demonstration of His righteousness and holiness. Although Barth has no argument with the right of God to make such a determination,[37] he delineates his own position from the orthodox view in the use of the term 'double'. In accusing the older dogmaticians of seeing 'double' as meaning 'dual', in which God can decree both good and evil with a sense of equilibrium

---

[37] "What right have we to tell God that in His love, which is certainly quite different from ours, He cannot equally seriously, and from the very beginning, from all eternity, condemn as well as acquit, kill as well as make alive, reject as well as elect? Even to-day we must defend the still older doctrine against this type of objection." (CD II/2, p. 171) These words must be kept in mind and differentiated from the part of the classical Supralapsarian position which Barth has opposed.

and equality, Barth protests that the double decree does not establish a balance between evil and good as decreed from God. "The concept which so hampered the traditional doctrine was that of an equilibrium or balance in which blessedness was ordained and declared on the right hand and perdition on the left. This concept we must oppose with all the emphasis of which we are capable."[38] Barth's distinction between 'double' and 'dual' is important for any understanding of his view of evil, and it can be traced through a series of steps as follows:

1. Humankind is the product of God's overflowing glory and God willed humanity for eternal life in his eternal decree to be 'for' His creation.

2. Humanity was therefore willed and chosen by God but with its natural limitations–the creature was able, in the abuse of its freedom, to do harm to God–and thus the risk of the Fall was included in the divine decree.

3. In creation, then, God's unopposable glory (in His eternal self-distinction) enters the sphere where there exists both light and darkness in contradiction and confrontation.

4. God cannot create another outside of Himself without also creating it in this contradiction, without also creating for the creature its shadow, and consequently giving to that shadow a sense of existence. As such, creation is the manifestation of the eternal self-differentiation of God.

5. The existence given to evil is wholly different from the existence given to God's creature–evil exists only as that which contradicts, it exists not from any autonomous or proper place in God but only as that which yields and flees and will be ultimately defeated.[39]

6. God then permits and wills evil only because of His desire to create humanity in the outpouring of His own glory–and the former is a necessary co-product of the latter.

7. There is a radical disproportionality between creation and evil where the former is that of the positive will and action of God, and the latter is permitted only as that which has its basis and meaning in confrontation and opposition to the former.

8. God did not foreordain humanity to evil and its consequences, but His foreordination could only be fulfilled in humanity as it stood at the brink of the abyss[40] of the foreordination of evil.[41]

---

[38] Ibid. p. 171.

[39] Barth may have been seeking to distinguish his views from Schleiermacher who held that although God was not the author of sin "in the same sense" as He is the author of redemption, nonetheless, "the existence of sin alongside of grace is ordained for us by God." (*The Christian Faith, op. cit.,* p. 326)

[40] This idea is found in one of Barth's sermons given in Basel prison in 1959, "There can be no question that essentially we all live at the edge of an abyss, where the fall into evil, folly and malice in thought word and deed is at all times terribly close to us." The result of this situation is, "we can and may believe only that God is for us." (*Call for God: Sermons from Basel Prison, op. cit.,* p. 17) The location of humanity on the edge of the abyss of nothingness constitutes an existential crisis in

9. In God's 'Yes' the negation is wholly overcome and shown to be what it truly is, only the shadow with no independent basis of reality.

10. It is only in this way, as the shadow, the necessary by-product, in its radical disproportionality and in its defeat in the 'Yes' of God in Jesus Christ that we can understand and accept the placing of the existence of evil in the decree and will (the negative will) of God.

Hence for Barth, God can be said to have ordained a double decree without ascribing to evil any sense of dualism. As Barth showed in his exegesis of Paul's use of the phrase 'how much more' in relating God's grace to sin, here too he puts the 'No', the shadow, in complete subordination to the 'Yes', the positive will of God. Thus both can result from the will of God and be called 'good'. The key is not that humanity was somehow created with the goal of never sinning, but that even in its inevitable fall, God from all eternity would never allow a foreordination to evil to stand. So in His self-determination God took on Himself the results of the Fall and saved His creation, giving to it its goal of eternal life and the bearing of the *imago Dei*.[42]

This supports the idea of a 'necessary antithesis' where this antithesis does not imply in any sense a dualism or equilibrium of the two forces, nor does it imply a 'dual' decree. It simply maintains that the accomplishment of the goal of the one is dependent upon the completion of the role assigned to the other. There is not a balance, but there is a dependence. God's decree, for it to be truly His own, had to contain this permission of evil and the inevitability of the Fall, sin and the threat of eternal damnation. "Without evil as 'permitted' in this sense there can be no universe or man, and without the inclusion of this 'permission' God's decree would be something other than it actually is."[43] We conclude of this motif that although Barth cannot be accused of adopting this idea of a 'necessary antithesis' as an *a priori* axiom, nonetheless this motif constitutes a central theme which runs the length and breadth of his theology.[44] It is therefore a factual and not a logical necessity as Barth seeks to describe and not explain the nature and existence of evil.

Barth's theology which is requisite for our understanding of the depth of the love of God for us.

[41] Again here Barth's view is to be distinguished from Schleiermacher's as the latter wrote that although God is not the author of sin, "it [sin] is ordained by God as that which makes redemption necessary." (*The Christian Faith, op. cit.,* p. 335) Barth rejects the idea that sin is ordained by God.

[42] CD II/2, p. 173.

[43] Ibid. p. 170.

[44] Berkouwer makes this point most forcibly when he looks at the relationship of sin and grace and concludes by seeing in Barth's theology the overwhelming necessity of the echo of sin to the manifestation of God's grace, saying, "because sin is this *echo*, the triumph of grace is the center of Barth's theology." (*Triumph of Grace, op. cit.,* p. 381)

The Elect and the Rejected in the 'Necessary Antithesis'

This idea is developed further with regard to the determination of the elect and the rejected. Barth holds that although all are elect in Jesus Christ, there is a difference between those who are called and those who are determined as witnesses. In the case of the Church, Israel assumes the role as the witness to the world to what the Church was and would be without the grace of God. This is the necessary role of the rejected Israel. Yet it must and will inevitably fail because it is impossible to go back behind and before the cross and claim that which has been finally and totally dealt with in Christ. The future of all humanity is in the covenant of grace and it is that which is witnessed to in the role of the rejected Israel in its relationship to the elect Church. Similarly the elect individual is called by God to see and witness who they are in Jesus Christ. The rejected individual is the one who, although seeing, does the impossible and continues to reject his or her election. "This, then, is how the elect and others differ from one another: the former by witnessing in their lives to the truth, the latter by lying against the same truth."[45]

Both the elect and the rejected have a necessary and positive role to play, for Christ, The Rejected, is Lord over them both and they, in their own distinctive ways, are His witnesses.[46] Yet even though we have a clear distinction between the two classes of humanity, it is only in Jesus Christ that we see purely what an elect person is and also what a rejected person is, for He is the only one and true Elect and the only one and true Rejected. "He is the Rejected, as and because He is the Elect. In view of His election, there is no other rejected but Himself."[47]

There is then a determination of the elect and the rejected in Jesus Christ. The elect has been called into the blessedness of union and communion with God in Christ which is not deserved but which must be responded to with praise and thanksgiving. In the mystery of God's election, the elect has been called into this grace in the determination of the elect in Jesus Christ (according to Barth's objectivism). The only possible response is a life which bears witness to this election, and thus which bears witness to Jesus Christ. In doing so, in the power of the Holy Spirit, the circle of grace and reconciliation in which the elect participates widens to all humanity as the Gospel is preached and God's election is witnessed to in the lives of the elect.

In contrast to the elect, "A 'rejected' man is one who isolates himself from God by resisting his election as it has taken place in Jesus Christ."[48] This is

---

[45] CD II/2, p. 346.

[46] Ibid. p. 347. Barth's words are important here to our idea of a necessary antithesis, "Thus not only the former (elect) but *no less indispensably, in their own place and after their own totally different fashion, the latter, are His own representatives*, just as originally and properly He is theirs." (emphasis mine)

[47] CD II/2, p. 353.

[48] Ibid. p. 449.

not a statement as to the subjective response of humanity in its reaction to the grace of God, for the rejected are 'determined'.[49] There is in the divine pre-determination a determination of the rejected. Yet the two determinations are not the same, just as the positive willing and the negative non-willing of God are not on the same level. In the one covenant of God with humanity, the covenant of grace, God has destroyed the rule of Satan over humanity, rejecting the rejection in which humanity stands before Him. The rejected person is that person with whom Jesus Christ stood in solidarity on the cross, overcoming his and her non-willed rejection with God's supremely willed rejection in Jesus Christ. Thus the rejected person is the one who is not-willed by God. His or her rejection is 'impossible' in that it cannot accomplish its purpose, for there is only One Rejected.

Consistently, the 'No' exists only for the sake of the 'Yes', and thus the rejected person provides a clear picture to the elect of what they were and what they would still be without the grace of God, they are witnesses to the grace and election of humanity in Jesus Christ. It is precisely in this role that some are determined to be the rejected. We must remember that Barth sees the rejected as those who have rejected the grace and freedom that is theirs in Jesus Christ, and he ties this rejection to the divine pre-determination of God. Therefore again we see Barth using the non-willing of God in His divine decree as the 'necessary antithesis' for the positive willing; the rejected provides the dark background which gives the necessary relief to the brightness of the elect. The two determinations are not equivalent, but they are *mutually necessary* for God's good purposes in creation to be achieved. Therefore the rejected give proper and necessary relief as those who are denied by the Gospel. In so doing, the rejected have something very important to say and a role which is critical to the determination of the elect. "He has a part in the determination of the elect. He is not, therefore, without a divine determination. And his *ex profundis*–even if they are the *profunda* of hell–becomes *Gloria Deo ex profundis. What would become of the determination of the elect if the rejected were not with him with his own distinctive determination?*"[50]

Finally, the determination of the rejected is to manifest the purpose of the Gospel and therefore this determination is the beginning of the determination of the elect. Therefore the rejected have no future outside of the covenant of grace, meaning that their final determination is to hear the gospel and come to faith.[51]

---

[49] *"Der eine Wille Gottes, der beide bestimmt, ist hier das allmächtige, heilige und barmherzige Nicht-Wollen Gottes."* (KD II/2, p. 499)

[50] CD II/2, p. 457. (emphasis mine)

[51] This understanding of the true status of the rejected, as those whose final determination is to come to faith, forms the basis for Barth's view of missions and evangelism. The history of this view stems partly from what we saw in Barth's interpretation of Anselm's *Fides Quaerens Intellectum* where he surmised that, "perhaps Anselm did not know any other way of speaking of the Christian *Credo* except by addressing the sinner as one who had not sinned, the non-Christian as a Christian, the unbeliever as believer, on the basis of the great 'as if' which is really

Thus the ultimate *telos* of the rejected is not that of indirect witness, but the becoming of the direct witness as one of the elect.[52]

The necessary role of evil is shown yet again in Barth's point that God in His divine decree from all eternity did what Judas did in the temporality of his act in Gethsemane. Jesus was 'handed-over' three times; in the eternal decision in God in the sending of the Son by the Father, in the obedience to the Father by the Son, and in the work of Judas. Thus Jesus was handed-over and delivered up from all eternity, both by the Father and by Himself, and even Judas' great sin was nothing more than the work of the will of God. And his work was critical, for the whole apostolic tradition would not exist had not Judas' act of handing-over been carried out! Here again God uses evil for the accomplishment of His own will. However here it is not a matter of God's working the best possible outcome from inevitable human sin (as we would find in the Infralapsarian position), but of God using sin and evil as an instrument specifically with the pre-determined purpose of bringing His goals to their fulfillment. When Barth ties this idea to the purpose of God in creation we see again the necessity of the existence of evil, of sin, and the inevitably of the Fall, to the fulfillment of the eternal will of God.

> We cannot understand the positive divine *paradounia*, which is the basis of all others and in the light of which even Judas ultimately stands, unless we hold to the original and authentic *paradounia*. And to know this we cannot begin at a lower level than that of the decree of God's eternal love, in which the Father sent the Son and the Son obeyed the Father, by which the will of God turned towards man even before he was created–His creation itself being dependent upon this decree–with the inconceivably merciful intention of enabling him, and all creation through him and in him, to participate in fellowship with Him and

---

not an 'as if' at all, but which at all times has been the final and decisive means whereby the believer could speak to the unbeliever." (*Fides Quaerens Intellectum, op. cit.,* p. 71) Elsewhere, Barth returns to the same point, "Missionaries must tell people the truth about themselves. Missionaries must believe that Christ died *for them*: Indians, Chinese, Africans and so on. The missionary approaches not an ontologically different kind of human being, but beings who are, not in the Body, but in the realm of Christ, in the power of His sovereignty... You cannot say more than 'they are sinners'. However, we should not approach them as sinners, but as virtual brothers. Remember the degree to which we are all only virtual brothers! If we understand our own situation, then we will understand those *extra muros*." ('Table Talk', *op. cit.,* pp. 15-16)

[52] Here Berkouwer rightly concludes, "Rejection [in Barth's theology] is now no longer an independent shadow and menace, but the accepted and therefore withstood rejection, namely, in and through Christ. This rejection is thus transmitted-as the rejection of Christ-into the *kerygma* and there becomes the essence of glad tidings." (*Divine Election, op. cit.,* p. 229)

eternal life, by giving Himself to be his Covenant-partner. The kingdom of God is fulfilled in this decree.[53]

Thus creation was established upon the decree that the Son would come and suffer and die for the sins of all humanity so that the eternal purpose of fellowship and participation, which means eternal life, may be achieved. The coming of the kingdom of God was only possible in the coming of the crucified and risen Son of the Father. Without the cross, the eternal purposes of creation could not be fulfilled nor the kingdom of God manifested in this ultimate and predetermined way. Such is the centrality of election, grace and the cross to Barth's entire theology. As such, we see again the key role the Fall plays in the completion of the will of God. Barth has no place anywhere in his theology for the idea of an eternal pre-fallen state. All of the purposes of God are set against the necessary backdrop of the Fall and its consequences for His creation.

Universalism in Barth's 'Noetic Eschatology'

The question is now raised; if the final determination of the rejected is to hear the gospel and believe, does this denote a sense of *apocatastasis*? A credible question to ask here is whether Barth's theology has room for the idea of true and lasting unbelief? This question is critical to our criticism of Barth's 'noetic eschatology' where he attempts to find a justification for the time of the community.

Like sin, Barth calls unbelief 'impossible'. By this he does not mean that it cannot occur, but that it is incomprehensible that it in fact does occur, for it cannot accomplish its purpose even in its shadowy existence. Humanity's 'No' cannot overrule God's 'Yes' which was spoken against the great 'No' on behalf of all humanity. Here too, we see that even those who are determined for rejection have contained in that determination a second determination to faith. Humanity's choice to reject God to its own perdition, meaning that it would have to bear the wrath of God and be rejected before Him, is an impossible choice in Barth's theology. If we ask then how Barth can reject universalism, we come against an interesting point made by Berkouwer. He posits that Barth has moved the problem and uncertainty which lay in the heart of the decrees of God in the orthodox Reformed system, to the place of the problem of subjectivity in his own system. Where the Reformed view struggles to justify the 'why?' of God's eternal double decree, Barth faces the dilemma of justifying the contradiction of the impossibility of unbelief and the outright rejection of *apocatastasis*.[54] Barth does recognize this dilemma and he seeks to build a doctrine of human response and its role in his soteriology, but as we will see he is not wholly successful in overcoming this objection.

---

[53] CD II/2, p. 491.

[54] Berkouwer, *Triumph of Grace, op. cit.,* p. 287. For his discussion on the 'impossibility of unbelief' in Barth's theology, see also pp. 265-266.

Judas and *Apocatastasis*

Barth provides some clarity to his view of universalism in his view that Judas, who was a true disciple and therefore among the elect, was at the same time rejected as the one who betrayed Jesus. Therefore, "Judas is the great sinner of the New Testament."[55] In his attitude and actions Judas represents the Jews who are in their own way, as those who are at once closest to the coming Messiah, also the rejected in their betrayal of Him. Judas' sin brought upon him the curse of the rejected, the threat of perdition and the lostness of one to whom there could be no promise of grace extended and from whom no genuine penitence was possible. The horror with which the whole of the New Testament treated the betrayal of Judas is justified, for Judas had himself become a devil. Thus Judas is the witness as the rejected to the One who has come as the Elect.

Yet in the midst of the 'for' of Jesus and the 'against' of Judas, there can be posited neither the sure perdition of Judas as a sign of the coming perdition of rejected men, nor a limitation on the grace of God to save even Judas, nor the reliance on a sure doctrine of universalism. This situation between Judas and Jesus can only be described as the 'open situation of proclamation' *(die offene Situation der Verkündigung),* and here we see Barth's rejection of a logical system which would produce reasoned answers or solutions to this seeming dilemma. This is a demonstration of his 'revelatory positivism' where Barth seeks to be a faithful witness rather than a systematic metaphysician. As such he understands the nature of theological language to be incomplete and broken in character, especially when, like here, we are dealing with the nature of sin. In the use of this motif, Barth seeks not an explanation or solution to this dilemma, but simply a description of what has been revealed and then a call to live by faith with the resulting paradox. This paradox is clear in Barth's position on *apocatastasis,*

> The church will not then preach an *apokatastasis,* nor will it preach a powerless grace of Jesus Christ or a wickedness of men which is too powerful for it. But without any weakening of the contrast, and also without any arbitrary dualism, it will preach the overwhelming power of grace and the weakness of human wickedness in the face of it.[56]

Barth can neither claim a universal salvation, nor claim that any form of human wickedness can stand in the face of the almighty fire of the grace of God, but he is ever determined that we take grace more seriously than sin! That all humanity can be saved is certain, that it will be saved is hoped for; this is the simplest form of Barth's position on *apocatastasis.* Yet in the end he seems to leave little doubt that he sees universal salvation as the only conceivable end of

---

[55] CD II/2, p. 461.
[56] Ibid. p. 477.

humanity,[57] as in the statement, "we must not minimize the fact that we know of only one certain triumph of hell, the handing-over of Jesus, and that this triumph of hell took place in order that it *would never again be able to triumph over anyone.*"[58]

God has made Himself the Rejected in Christ, and therefore rejection can no longer be borne by anyone in its fullest.[59] Hell has no power to triumph and no person can be rejected in the place of the One eternally Rejected. This opens up for Barth *die eschatologische Möglichkeit einer Grenze jener Zornesüberlieferung* (the eschatological possibility of a limit to this delivery of

---

[57] It seems that when Barth is directly addressing the issue of *apocatastasis* he speaks of it only in terms of that which is to be hoped for and prayed for, but not something we can be assured of or count upon. Yet throughout the *Church Dogmatics*, Barth gives ample evidence to show that universal salvation is the only possible conclusion to which his theology leads. We will treat this in more detail in Chapter VII, however we cite as one example the succinct statement in III/2 concerning creation and death, "God does nothing in vain. What He willed and created cannot disintegrate into nothingness." (p. 537) Yet he has defined hell and eternal damnation as the creature sinking into the nothingness from which he, by God's grace, is saved and preserved. This one instance is indicative of how Barth's theology leads in the direction of *apocatastasis*. What other option is there if nothing which He willed or created can ever "disintegrate into nothingness"?

[58] CD II/2, p. 496. (emphasis mine)

[59] There can be no question that Barth is seeking a balance here in the understanding of the all-inclusive humanity in Christ-which sees all humanity ontologically 'in Christ' and never able to be rejected-and the continuing real threat of eternal perdition. This balance (or perhaps continuing contradiction) is illustrated in Barth's Gifford Lectures where he makes the expected statement that, "In God's decision and man's election and in the death and resurrection of Jesus Christ it has already been decided that in ourselves and by ourselves we are *all* sinners, but that through the complete incarnation of the Son we are *all* righteous." (*The Knowledge of God and the Service of God, op. cit.,* pp. 98-99) Yet by being 'all righteous' it does not take away from the necessity of faith, for he goes on immediately to say, "If I lack faith, and have sought my salvation elsewhere than in Jesus Christ... how can my lie be disclosed and judged as anything but a continuing in sin and therefore in the darkness of eternal death?" (p. 99) True faith has nothing to fear, but false faith will "cause man to lose fellowship with his Saviour and to fall back into sin and under its curse." (p. 101) In the end, however, Barth returns to the ontological oneness we have in Christ, "this [eternal death] can only be mentioned as a warning, an indication of what man might be if left to himself and thus lost, but what in Jesus Christ he cannot be, a reminder of the fact that outside of the Word of God there is no life but only temporal and eternal torment. If we adhere to the Word of God, we can and shall think of this torment, of which the Confession speaks, only as something that has fallen into oblivion for time and eternity." (p. 243) Thus we see this tension in Barth to preserve the full extent of the completed work of Christ on behalf of all humanity while not giving in to an antinomianism nor a universalism. Whether this tension can rightly be maintained will continue to be a question which we will pursue under our fourth motif.

wrath).[60] Barth is careful to maintain that the perdition of the rejected is sure and certain as they have rejected the free grace of God.[61] Yet their hope is that there is a limit, an *eschaton* to the wrath of God beyond which they will come face to face not only with the Judge, but with the Judge who was Judged in their place. "For He has done it for them, in order that they should not suffer the judgement which accompanies the cleansing of the world's sin, and therefore should not be lost."[62] This does not mean we can know for certain what will happen to the rejected. It does give us a solid reason for hope in the eschatological reality of Jesus Christ in the place of sinners.

In all of this we must question, along with Berkouwer,[63] and von Balthasar,[64] and others, why Barth so strongly denies universalism when his entire doctrine of election seems to lead him inextricably in this direction. Berkouwer gives us a clue found in Barth's response to the question of universalism "grace which would in the end automatically have to reach and embrace everyone and anyone would certainly not be sovereign, would not be divine grace."[65] Do we see here a conflict in Barth's understanding of the relationship between the work of the 'right and left hand of God'? *Apocatastasis* would mean that the love of God would extend to all humanity 'automatically',

---

[60] KD II/2, p. 551.

[61] This tension continues in Barth as he seeks to preserve the true awfulness of the state of the rejected. He tries to maintain this balance in a key section in *Dogmatics in Outline* where he writes, "That which is not of God's grace and right cannot exist. Infinitely much human as well as Christian 'greatness' perhaps plunges there into the outermost darkness. That there is such a divine No is indeed included in this *judicare*. But the moment we grant this we must revert to the truth that the Judge who puts some on the left and others on the right, is in fact He who has yielded Himself to the judgement of God *for me* and has taken away all malediction from me. It is He who died on the cross and rose at Easter... There is a decision and a division, but by Him who has interceded for us." (*Dogmatics in Outline, op. cit.,* pp. 135-136)

[62] CD II/2, p. 496.

[63] Berkouwer asks quite pointedly how we can read Barth's doctrine of election and conclude anything other than an *apocatastasis*? "Considered from the viewpoint of Barth's doctrine of election, it is far from plain what right of existence the rejection of the *apokatastasis* can have... It remains obscure, however, why the *apokatastasis* is not included *in* the *decretum concretum* of the revelation of Christ." (*Triumph of Grace, op. cit.,* pp. 112-122, 116)

[64] "Yet, it is clear from Barth's presentation of the doctrine of election that universal salvation is not only possible but inevitable... While Barth tries to avoid talking about universal redemption, it is clearly built into the very groundwork of his doctrine on creation." (von Balthasar, *Theology of Karl Barth, op. cit.,* p. 163)

[65] Karl Barth, *Die Botschaft von der freien Gnade Gottes,* 1947, p. 7, quoted in G.C. Berkouwer, *The Triumph of Grace in the Theology of Karl Barth, op. cit.,* p. 115. Berkouwer even more strongly states elsewhere, "with Barth Christ is not so much the mirror of election as the manifestation of the election of God, a universal manifestation which may be disregarded in unbelief, but which cannot be undone." (*Divine Election, op. cit.,* p. 161)

that it would 'have to reach and embrace everyone'. This idea, although wholly in line with the love of God and the eternal will and self-determination of God as revealed in His Son, and wholly consistent with the divine election of all humanity in Christ, would contradict Barth's understanding of the freedom of God.

We have seen how Barth sought to defend and protect the grace of God by not allowing any 'claim' to universal salvation. Distinction must be maintained here between what we can claim dogmatically to be the truth (especially in view of the limitations of theological language) and what God can do. The dangers of the universalist position which Barth understands is that it makes the sinner the claimant for that which is only his or hers by an act of incredible grace. The danger is that a dogmatic universalism may undermine the true grace of God. Yet does the fact that this very real danger exists necessarily render the universalist position in error? This was Barth's point concerning the inherent dangers of the orthodox Supralapsarian view. The real question is, however, not whether universalism is right or wrong *per se*, but whether Barth can continue to reject it as the logical result of his own theology by continuing to state these dangers as reasons for its rejection?

Freed from the inherent dangers of this position, Barth surely would embrace the idea that even the rejected will in the end face only the One Rejected for them. In that confrontation, the rejected become the ones who see and embrace the One who bore what they could not. Berkouwer concluded quite rightly, "There is no alternative to concluding that Barth's refusal to accept the *apokatastasis* cannot be harmonized with the fundamental structure of his doctrine of election."[66] In the end we must not miss the importance of Barth's warning concerning the dangers inherent in offering a claim on God for His salvation of all. Yet we must also not let Barth use this to shrink back from the logical conclusion of his theology, a conclusion which will have profound impact on his doctrine of evil and his answer to theodicy.

---

[66] Berkouwer, *Triumph of Grace, op. cit.,* p. 116.

CHAPTER V

Evil and Creation

The 'Creation-Chaos' Conflict

From the foundations Barth laid in the perfections of God and election where the ontic basis for evil emerged from the 'necessary antithesis' and the manifestation of evil was assigned to the 'left hand of God', Barth now demonstrates the centrality of his doctrine of evil to the whole of his theology as he develops his doctrine of creation and providence within a 'creation-chaos' dichotomy.[1]

Although Barth's exposition of *das Nichtige* in §50 is important, his understanding of evil as the rejected chaos is a theme which is consistently developed throughout the entirety of his doctrine of creation. Berkouwer correctly commented, "The line which Barth draws in the doctrine of creation is continued in the doctrine of providence and particularly in connection with his conception of chaos."[2] Rosemary Radford Ruether believed it was possible to read Barth's whole theology "out of his view of the basic struggle between creation and chaos, and to exhibit all the parts of his theology as working out of this basic conflict which runs through and underlies every doctrine."[3] Therefore, Barth's theme of *das Nichtige* is integrated into his doctrine of creation from the very outset, colouring all that he is to say concerning God's creative and providential work. It is this whole picture which forms what Barth called the "backbone of all Christian doctrine."[4]

---

[1] If Barth's doctrine of election forms the heart of his theology, his four volumes on the doctrine of creation form its centrepiece. Within its four volumes there are six sections which bear most directly upon the development of his doctrine of evil. Although use will be made of all sections, our focus will be on §41-Creation and Covenant; §42-The Yes of God the Creator; §48-The Doctrine of Providence; §49-God the Father as Lord of His Creature; §50-God and Nothingness; and §51-The Kingdom of Heaven, the Ambassadors of Heaven and Their Opponents.

[2] Berkouwer, *Triumph of Grace, op. cit.,* p. 63.

[3] Rosemary Radford Ruether, 'The Left Hand of God in the Theology of Karl Barth; Karl Barth as a Mythopoeic Theologian' in *Journal of Religious Thought*, Volume 25, Number 1, 1968-1969, p. 4. Unfortunately, in Ruether's article the important development of Barth's view of evil in his doctrine of election, which preceded his doctrine of creation, and upon which the latter is built, is overlooked, and thus some misguided conclusions result in what is an otherwise very helpful article.

[4] Barth, *The Heidelberg Catechism for Today, op. cit.,* p. 57.

The Creation-Fall Relationship and the 'Necessary Antithesis'

The entire interpretation of Barth's doctrine of creation with regards to the doctrine of evil is dependent upon a prior understanding of two critical points; 1) Barth's view of the creation story in Genesis as 'saga', and 2) Barth's view of the relationship between creation and the Fall.

Genesis 1–3 as 'Saga' and the 'Non-Chronological' Relationship of Creation and Reconciliation

Barth views Genesis 1–3 not as 'historical' *(historische)* but "a legitimate 'non-historical' *(unhistorische)* and 'pre-historical' *(praehistorische)* view of history, and its 'non-historical' and 'pre-historical' depiction in the form of saga."[5] This forms a crucial hermeneutical point for he says, "In what follows I am using saga in the sense of an intuitive and poetic picture of a pre-historical reality of history which is enacted once for all within the confines of space and time."[6]

It is important here for us to understand that Barth, in interpreting 'saga' as 'creation history', does not interpret the creation stories in a chronological, time-ordered fashion, but as a witness to the state of creation and the root causes of the Fall of humanity. Therefore, Barth can take the content of the creation sagas with all seriousness because of their *kerygmatic* intent and their divine inspiration[7], while rejecting the idea of a chronology which would require a pre-fallen state and a place for the Fall in human history. When we read Barth on the the purpose of the tree of the knowledge of good and evil, and when we hear him referring frequently to the Fall, we must remember at the outset that Barth is not thinking of a time sequence in history, but of a single pre-historical event which sets the scene for the true history *(Geschichte)* of creation within the covenant.[8]

---

[5] CD III/1, p. 81.

[6] Ibid. p. 81. "*...ein divinatorisch-dichterisch entworfenes Bild einer... praehistorischen Geschichtswirklichkeit.* " (KD III/1, p. 88)

[7] Lest we be led to think that Barth reduces the strength of the Biblical witness by using the term 'saga', we quote him from this section, "The biblical writers are never more than ministering witnesses, and for the confirmation of their witness the self-witness of the divine reality by the *testimonium Spiritus sancti* is everywhere indispensable. And this is the case here too where they speak non-historically and pre-historically." (CD III/1, p. 93) Barth goes on to call the written witness to this pre-historical history '*Geschichtsschreibung*'.

[8] The tension which exists at this point has caused confusion with Barth's critics. While we must affirm that Barth has no time for speculation on the idea of a perpetual, pre-fallen creation, it is also a mistake to think that Barth rejects all notions of a pre-fallen paradisal state. What he is rejecting is the notion that a pre-fallen state was the eternal purpose of God which later went wrong due to some exercise of freedom on the

Thus Adam and the Fall story are meant to depict all humanity, 'it is the name Adam the transgressor which God gives to world-history as a whole'. Human history continually re-enacts the Garden of Eden fall, and its state from the conception of its history is one of fallenness. Thus Barth concludes, "There never was a golden age. There is no point in looking back to one. The first man was immediately the first sinner."[9] This is the reason why election is so critical to Barth's entire theology. It also illuminates what is both a major component of Barth's theology and a primary source of criticism–the nature of the connection between creation and reconciliation. Barth directly rejects the notion that creation and redemption are connected in a chronological, step-wise order. This historisation of the works of God are reminiscent of late 19th century Liberal Protestantism (and especially the realized eschatology which it produced) which Barth had so strongly rejected. For Barth, creation and redemption are the working out in space and time of the primordial decision of God to be for humanity in the form of the Elect *Logos ensarkos*. Thus our history is the acting out on the stage of creation the eternal will of God in choosing to create and electing His creation against nothingness.[10]

By holding together creation and reconciliation as the working out of the divine election, Barth has produced his answer to the cosmological question of classical theodicy. Barth is able to 'justify' creation not by looking back to an original good intent which went wrong, but by seeing all creation as linked to reconciliation and thus to the eschatological glorification of the triumph of the Son. The justification of creation lies in its future (even if that future is only the revelation of an already-completed past reality) and not in an explanation of its past. We can say that justification is inherently ontic to creation and therefore awaits its noetic *parousia*. This will be taken up later, but here the justification of creation, and therefore of God Himself, must be seen to be a product of the unity of creation and covenant as the outworkings of the eternal decision of God in election.

---

part of man. This is a return to the 'free-will' and 'determinism' debate as well as the root of the Reformed/Arminian controversies. These all fail to see, according to Barth, that fallen man was already assumed when God chose to create, and the justification for His decision is found in His eternal election and nowhere else. Thus we must reject the critiques such as we hear from Berkouwer that this view of Barth's "robs paradise of its historical reality." (Berkouwer, *The Providence of God, op. cit.,* p. 58) Paradise must be seen in its role as witness to the eternal will of God, and not as an historical reality which must be defended. Barth's use of saga here is helpful in indicating the purpose of the creation stories as this witness to God's intention in creation and of the state of humanity. Thus the Fall story is everyone's story, and Barth's point is not to deny that the pre-fallen state ever occurred, but that its historical reality is inconsequential.

[9] CD IV/1, p. 508. Here is the point Barth wishes to emphasise, for all we know of humanity is sinful humanity, and speculation on the 'golden age' is unhelpful.

[10] This has opened Barth up to the charge of 'creation docetism' as he seems to devalue our history and its significance to God's plan. From all that has been said thus far it should be clear why such a criticism is off the mark.

The 'Inevitability-Impossibility' Tension in the Sin and Fall of Humanity

In understanding creation history as 'saga', Barth interprets the Fall as the pre-historical event which preceded our time and which ushered in our time. There was no single historical act which divided pre-fallen and post-fallen time. This view is essential to Barth's entire doctrine of election in the critical distinction between the Supralapsarian view of Christ's election as *homo labilis* and the Infralapsarian view of *homo lapsus*. The pre-historic Fall is assumed in the election of Christ as *homo labilis* which is according to the combination of the two realities of God's eternal self-differentiation and creation as His self-recapitulation. The Fall was assumed by God; His non-divine creation would face and inevitably fall to the rejected nothingness. This does not presuppose that God created humanity in a sinful state nor with a propensity to sin. In dealing with the former idea, Barth rejects a natural evil nature to humanity, for God created it 'good'. The Fall of all humanity is the result of the rejection of our true freedom in place of an alien pride which seeks to bring us up to God's level and make the decisions only He can make. The inevitability of sin in Barth's theology does not necessitate the creation of humanity as either already sinful nor even as potentially sinful. Neither does it play down the utter seriousness of sin or the total depravity which sin brings to the creature.[11] This view is in direct conflict with Hick's thesis which states that man was necessarily created at an 'epistemic distance' and the sinful state of man was God's original intention.[12]

---

[11] The idea of this total depravity as originating in the fallen state of humanity and reenacted in the life of every person is the basis of Barth's view of original sin. He can affirm original sin as the sinful and fallen state into which each person is born and in which they will, of their own volition, inevitably repeat the Fall in their own lives. What Barth rejects is the notion of hereditary sin, for that sets sin one step removed from the tie between action and guilt. Our guilt for sin is not an alien guilt but our own, and thus it is something we bear as a result of our own actions, and not something that can be inherited or passed on separate from our own actions.

[12] Hick's agenda is not unlike Moltmann's but there are some key distinctions. Hick's 'Irenaean theodicy' could be stated as follows: God created the world as a process whereby his creation would grow and mature into the likeness of God; therefore humanity, created according to the scientific understanding of the evolutionary processes, at some point was ready to become the covenant partner of God and was given the soul; God gave to man the free will to choose for God without any natural compulsion or direct evidence of God creating man at an 'epistemic distance' to Himself; the world is then the 'vale of soul-making' where God uses evil and suffering to make us conform more to his likeness and therefore all suffering will be wholly justified in the glory of the new kingdom; yet God's purpose in creation will not be frustrated and therefore all humanity and creation will be saved regardless of the choices made in this life. For Hick it is imperative to understand that man's 'fallenness' is the price God paid for freedom. God created man in a fallen state because only in such a state could man truly have the opportunity to 'come to God'.

Barth's Critique of Schleiermacher's View of Sin

This view is carried on in Barth's analysis of Schleiermacher. Barth rejects Schleiermacher's claim that God was the Author of sin and therefore,"an incapacity for good is the universal state of man... this incapacity for good was present in human nature before the first sin."[13] Barth criticised Schleiermacher for seeing sin as a derangement of human nature, the repression of the God-consciousness, but nothing further. Schleiermacher refutes the whole concept of a fall and sees hereditary sin (as opposed to actual sin) as the natural consequence of the sexual relationship between man and woman and therefore as part and parcel of the original perfection in which humanity was created. Thus Schleiermacher locates the origin of sin in God while giving to it a definite distinct flavour over the origin in God of redemption. So sin is the necessary correlate to grace, for without the former we cannot perceive and receive the latter, leading Schleiermacher to conclude that sin and evil are ordained by God but caused solely by us.

Given this general framework, Barth considers those areas where Schleiermacher has been unfairly criticised. This section is most enlightening! Schleiermacher holds that God is the Author of sin in His negation of sin which gives it its only possibility for existence.[14] This ordination of sin in its

---

Hick unabashedly states the obvious conclusion that sinfulness has a vital role to play in God's providence. This is clearly the influence of Schleiermacher to whom Hick is indebted for the bulk of his eschatological agenda. For Hick, like Moltmann, it is in the *parousia* that the final theodicy answer will be given. However for Hick, that answer will come in a true justification of all suffering as a proper means to the pre-planned end of creation. Moltmann, as we have seen, will have no part in a justification of suffering of any kind. Therefore Hick rests his case on the '*O felix culpa quae talum ac tantum meruit habere redemptorem*'. This is the ultimate statement of God's purpose and desire to bring good out of bad, therefore justifying the evil and, implicitly, the creator of evil. We have many criticisms of Hick. The necessity of his 'epistemic distance' can be refuted by a simple reference to the bond between parent and child. Hick also plays fast and loose with his understanding of 'free will' for as soon as he has painted the most comprehensive picture of free will in relationship to God, he then bases his universalism upon the fact that God, given enough time, will win the hearts of every last human being. We find this highly questionable reasoning, for it must be equally possible that, given enough time, all humans would choose against God, if men are as free as Hick leads us to believe. Yet for Hick all absolutely *must* be saved, and there goes his so-called free-will of man. Just as you cannot have God responsible for evil and hell together, so you cannot have man's free will and *apocatastasis* together. All talk of an 'epistemic distance' in Hick is negated when he arrives at this kind of universalism.

[13] Schleiermacher, *The Christian Faith, op. cit.,* p. 301.

[14] For Schleiermacher, evil exists 'only as attached to good, and sin only as attached to grace'. In this way, God can be called the Author of sin as sin is seen in its relationship to redemption. Schleiermacher saw the dilemma posed by the two extremes of the relationship between God and sin; namely, if sin is independent of God then the result is Manichaeism, if sin is dependent upon God, the result is

negation must not be held in isolation to God's will for man's redemption. In a reiteration of the idea of *O felix culpa*, Schleiermacher states that God makes this negation to hold humanity firmly to his redemption, thus making it an additional decree of salvation. Barth concludes of this discussion, 'so far so good'.[15] Barth believes that the relationship of grace and sin in Schleiermacher would be wholly acceptable if given a proper Christological foundation. Schleiermacher teaches that the consciousness of sin follows that of grace, serving it by producing within us a sense of our need of redemption. So sin is advantageous to us, for as the limitation of our God-consciousness it prepares us and opens us up to our appointed salvation by the grace of God. Thus evil, which is produced from sin, preserves us for our redemption.

Barth counters that although this is right in a sense, it needs the Christological foundation and its corresponding epistemology to talk truly of sin as the antithesis of grace. Yet with these tools *such talk is quite accurate in describing the relationship between sin and grace.* Sin is wholly subordinate to the superior power of the grace of God and it serves it only as its antithesis. Barth returns to his insistence upon the lordship of God over nothingness stating, "God's grace is mightier than sin, evil and death. They are together the enemy of whom it can be said, 'One word shall quickly fell him.'... We do not honour the truth but compound a falsehood and make common cause with the enemy if even momentarily we fail to see nothingness otherwise than in its relativity."[16]

Here Barth provides a critical clarification of this point, accusing Schleiermacher of reversing this relative relationship so that good is also correlative to evil. By doing so Schleiermacher held that sin is essential in human development and advantageous, doing no 'injury' to the creature but operating as a natural step in the unfolding of the power of the God consciousness.[17] Here Barth says no! He accuses Schleiermacher of returning

---

Pelagianism. Thus Schleiermacher concluded that both must be held together, and if God is to be called the Author of sin, this conception must be tied closely to the redemption which provides the justification of God. (Ibid. pp. 327-329)

[15] It is interesting to note here that Barth accepts Schleiermacher's understanding of God as the Author of evil as long as it is conditioned by the fact that He is its Author as He negates it. Because our consciousness of God brings about the guilt for sin, God can be said to be the Author of sin, for only in Him do we see our sin. Thus Barth is again making the epistemological point that the Law is only seen and understood in light of the Gospel, and sin in light of the cross and resurrection. Yet in saying that sin is dependent upon God for its revelation and therefore its 'existence', is there not necessarily implied, in the creaturely sphere, the antithesis of this? Is this not the root of the idea of the *O felix culpa*? It is one thing to say that the self-revelation of God shows us to be the sinners we are. It is quite another to say, as both Schleiermacher and Barth seem to be doing, that without that sin our salvation would not be possible.

[16] CD III/3, p. 332.

[17] Schleiermacher is following the lines of Hegel's idea of the 'upward fall'. For Hegel, sin was a necessary phase in human development and so man must not stay in

to a Leibnizian form in making sin positive.[18] We must carefully define Barth's attack here. His argument is that if sin is made in any way necessary as a positive aspect of human development, in the goal of creation or in the will (the 'Yes' or right hand) of God, then it ceases to be 'real sin', and the grace which is bound to it is not 'real grace'. Schleiermacher, like Leibniz, allowed nothingness to lose its character as a radical opponent by bringing it into an equilibrium with grace. He has failed to keep in mind that the relationship is not between two equals, but between two hostile enemies where all of the proper attributes of existence belong solely to the first and not the second. By not consistently holding to the reality of nothingness only in its rejection, he has given it a positive reality in relation to grace.

What are we to make of Barth's criticism in light of our motif of a 'necessary antithesis'? We maintain that if his criticism of Schleiermacher is properly understood, our claim of the 'necessary antithesis' is strengthened. Barth used this motif in a direct rejection of Schleiermacher's equilibrium and he consistently held to the 'dualism of rejectedness' between sin and grace. Therefore, given all of its Barth-qualified characteristics in relation to grace, nothingness remains the negative half of a 'necessary antithesis' in Barth's theology, not only in the created sphere, but in God Himself. We agree with Barth that the mistake of Schleiermacher was to see sin and grace in a balance, in the same way the orthodox view of Supralapsarianism formulated the *decretum absolutum* as a balance between election and reprobation. Yet he does not reject the whole idea of a necessity of sin as the antithesis of grace, evidence again of the importance of the motif of the 'necessary antithesis' in his theology as a whole, and in his doctrine of sin and evil in particular.

Adam and the Human Capacity to Sin

For Barth, humanity's fall was its own doing despite its inevitability. He holds here to an Augustinian line whereby the origin of sin is in the will and not in the nature of humanity as created by God.[19] Barth rejects Kant's idea that humanity is sinful by nature such that "evil can be predicated of man as a

---

his state of innocence and ignorance (vestiges of Kant here), but must move ahead in knowledge, even if it brings about evil and suffering.

[18] Bernard Ramm cites Schleiermacher for a doctrine of sin which, "is too academic or abstract an approach," and which "is primarily a psychological definition of sin." Ramm rightly criticises Schleiermacher for not having any room in his theology for real, violent evil. (B. Ramm, *Offense to Reason: The Theology of Sin,* (San Francisco: Harper & Row, 1985), pp. 130-131)

[19] St. Augustine writes, for instance "God made man upright, and consequently well-willed: otherwise he could not have been upright. And so this good will was God's work, man being therewith created. But the evil will, which was in man before his evil word, was rather a falling from the work of God to its own works than any positive work." (*City of God, op. cit.,* p. 40)

species."[20] Yet he does agree with Kant that humanity cannot have been created with a propensity to sin, or the guilt of sin would lie not on the creature but the Creator, "evil does not start from a propensity thereto as its underlying basis, for otherwise the beginning of evil would not have its source in freedom; rather does it start from sin."[21] There is a dialectic type of tension here in Barth's view of the necessary goodness of the nature of created humanity and the assumed fallenness of humanity in God's election in Christ. If the former is overemphasized, the unity of creation and covenant is undermined; if the latter is stressed, the responsibility for sin shifts from humanity to God.

This tension is displayed in Barth's teaching that the tree of the knowledge of good and evil represents the creature's opportunity to exercise its God-given freedom to obey and trust, and yet is also the 'possibility' for the creature to forsake the fatherly care of God by taking to itself the discernment of what is good and what is harmful. It is critical to distinguish Barth's idea of 'freedom' from the modern concept of 'free choice'. Barth is not implying that humanity had the freedom to choose good or evil, for that is the folly into which it plunged itself only after eating of the second tree. Instead the true freedom given by God is that whereby His creature obeys and trusts Him as the provider of all its needs, praising and rejoicing in His goodness, without questioning the goodness of His provisions. Humanity is not 'free' in this way to choose to sin, to choose to disobey.[22] It is only in a misuse of its freedom that humanity can do other than choose for God.[23] That this 'impossible possibility' could

---

[20] Kant, *Religion Within the Limits of Reason Alone, op. cit.,* p. 27. Kant understands the evil nature of man as having the two components of sensuousness and moral law. What makes a man evil by nature is not that he has both of these components in his nature, but that he naturally subordinates the latter to the former. To say that a man is evil by nature is to say that "he makes the incentive of self-love and its inclinations the condition of obedience to the moral law; whereas, on the contrary, the latter [moral law], as the *supreme condition* of the satisfaction of the former, ought to have been adopted into the universal maxim of the will as the sole incentive." (Ibid. p. 32)

[21] Ibid. p. 37. Obviously Barth would greatly qualify Kant's use of the term 'freedom' in this statement.

[22] "Man's freedom to decide, as it is given to man by God, is not a freedom to decide between good and evil. Man is not made to be Hercules at the cross-roads. Evil does not lie in the possibilities of the God-created creature. Freedom to decide means freedom to decide towards the only One for whom God's creatures can decide, for the affirmation of Him who has created it, for the accomplishment of His will; that is, for obedience." (Barth, *Dogmatics in Outline, op. cit.,* p. 56)

[23] This point was made most succinctly by Samuel Taylor Coleridge, "A will cannot be *free* to choose evil-for in the very act it forfeits its freedom, and so becomes a corrupt Nature, self-enslaved. It is sufficient to say, that a Will *can* choose evil, but in the moment of such choice ceases to be a *free* will." (cited by J.R. Barth, *Coleridge and Christian Doctrine,* (Cambridge, Mass., Harvard University Press, 1969), p. 110, cited by C.E. Gunton in 'The triune God and the freedom of the creature', in S.W.

and must exist is the necessary correlate to God's creation of the non-divine outside of Himself. He could not create without this 'impossible possibility' actually having possibility,

> The purpose of God in granting man freedom to obey is to verify as such the obedience proposed in and with his creation, i.e., to confirm it, to actualize it in his own decision. It is obvious that if this is His will God cannot compel man to obey; He cannot as it were bring about his obedience mechanically. He would do this if He made obedience physically necessary and disobedience physically impossible, if He made man in such a way as to be incapable of a decision to obey.[24]

Adam was thus put in front of this tree with the opportunity to deny his true existence and rebel against his God-given freedom to obey, and therefore to choose to do the impossible. The irony of the situation is that it is in this relationship, in the free obedience of His creature, that God causes humanity to participate in the fellowship of the Godhead. In this way, humanity actually does share in the judicial office of God, but in the proper way of participation through obedience. Therefore Barth rejects the theodicy question that would have God make Eden trouble-free. By doing so, He would have denied His creation its greatest blessing–namely, the opportunity to participate through obedience in fellowship with the divine.

> He had to be brought to the cross-roads; he had to be shown the possibility denied him for his salvation; that door had to be opened... The tree of knowledge could become a danger to man only if he faced it in a freedom appropriated in misuse of the freedom given him. In face of the realization of this possibility, God the Creator needed no justification.[25]

This decision before the tree in the Garden is seen as saga, as the pre-historical and representative act of disobedience in which we all participate daily. It testifies to the depth of the tension between the impossibility of the concept of sin as humanity stands before this tree, and the inevitability of that sin as seen and known from eternity.[26] The 'impossibility-inevitability' tension is

---

Sykes (ed.) *Karl Barth: Centenary Essays,* (Cambridge: Cambridge University Press, 1989), p. 55)

[24] CD III/1, p. 264.

[25] Ibid. p. 266.

[26] Although flawed in some crucial areas, Berkouwer's analysis of Barth's doctrine of sin is helpful at this point where he states, "The central thrust of Barth's conception is not an irrational paradox (impossibility *and* reality of sin). The emphasis he wishes to make is rather this: man cannot fall from grace because of the prior electing love and faithfulness of God, while at the same time, sin is a reality... We see that the triumph of grace is emphatically placed *before* sin and that for this

seen here in all of its sharpness; a tension which Barth not only allows to stand, but defends as the only proper way to describe the situation of humanity with respect to its created state and the Fall.[27]

For Barth, humanity was not created 'able' to sin, and yet its fall was assumed from all eternity.   Indeed creation itself was enacted that sinful humanity may be reconciled to God in Christ and nothingness may be finally defeated.[28] This is a difficult tension to maintain, for it requires humanity to be both wholly responsible to refrain from sin and yet wholly incapable of doing so.   Even further, humanity was created with the knowledge that that incapability would manifest itself in the Fall; indeed it was created on the very basis that that Fall would occur! Yet only by acknowledging this tension can we see how Barth can affirm humanity as 'immediately fallen' while at the same time being created 'unable to sin', and sin as the 'impossible possibility'. Any lessening in this tension will yield a wholly different interpretation of creation.

The role of evil within this tension is multifarious: it begins as the 'unavoidable' (necessarily the confronter of creation according to the will of God); it then becomes the 'necessary and immediate victor' (humanity is unable to resist because it is inherently non-divine); and then the requisite 'role player' in the history of the creature (as the 'necessary antithesis' to the salvific work of Christ that God's plan for creation may be realized); and finally it is the 'defeated

---

reason sin is anticipated and intercepted and so made ontologically impossible." (*Triumph of Grace, op. cit.,* p. 234)

[27] Far from being a departure for Barth, this understanding of sin as 'impossible' can be traced back to his earliest writings, where it emerged as a dominant theme.   Jüngel has seen this and concludes, "This phrase [impossible possibility], which in the *Church Dogmatics* appears simply as a fitting characterization of the ontological peculiarity of negative phenomena, is in Barth's earlier writings an indispensable expression of the essence of Christianity." (*Karl Barth: A Theological Legacy, op. cit.,* p. 61)

[28]   This idea of humanity as necessarily fallen from creation coupled with the teaching in Barth that true humanity is only found in our union with Jesus Christ causes us to ask again if created humanity was ever 'true' humanity and therefore 'good', or whether, as Kant has said, the goodness in created humanity was not its current state but its ability to 'become good'. Kant noted, "When it is said, Man is created good, this can mean nothing more than: He is created *for good* and the original *predisposition* in man is good; not that, thereby, he is already good, but rather that he brings it about that he becomes good or evil." (*Religion Within the Limits of Reason Alone, op. cit.,* p. 40) If this is the case, then even prior to sinning created man was in need of his union with Christ to become the true humanity for which he was created. As we have already been able to refute an idea that Barth posited the possibility of the incarnation without the Fall, there is here again reason to believe that for man as created 'good' by God to become the true humanity for which he was created, the Fall was a necessary player that the work of Christ as elected from eternity may take place and man, in and through it, may be elevated to the position for which he was created. This is what Jüngel had in mind when he commented, "humanity will be human by being raised to God in this man [Jesus]." (*Karl Barth: A Theological Legacy, op. cit.,* p. 133)

foe'. When applied to the 'right and left hand of God' motif, evil becomes first a strangely unvanquishable foe prior to creation (a difficult subject we have referred to before), then an instrument which God permits to operate within His good creation which results in its fall (evil can only operate with divine permission, even in the temptation of the creature), then the instrument which God uses to move His creation to its appointed end and goal (we see this dominant instrumentalism emerge in Barth's treatment of providence), and finally the hated and eternal enemy whose defeat marks the end of the work of the 'left hand of God'. The tension which is present in Barth's understanding of the created nature of humanity is transferred directly to this difficult tension between the role of evil under the 'left hand of God' and the positive work of His 'right hand'.

The Role of the Fall and the Goal of Creation

In attempting to avoid just this sort of tension, theologies have often sought a positive role for the Fall. Hegel posited an 'upward Fall' by virtue of which men were put on the path to their fuller development. Schleiermacher stated that the manifestation of sin "is ordained by God as that which makes redemption necessary."[29] In Kierkegaard the Fall was seen as the necessary motivator of the salvation of humanity.[30] Berdyaev viewed the paradisal realm

---

[29] Schleiermacher, *The Christian Faith, op. cit.,* p. 335.

[30] Barth's interpretation of Genesis 3 falls generally within this Kierkegaardian understanding of the non-historicity of the Fall saga, and the representative, and archetypal role of Adam. For Kierkegaard, Genesis 3 represents a cross section of the existential act of sin. Adam's fall is the story of the fall of all humanity, of each individual. Instead of a single act in space and time, Adam is a model or archetype for all humanity with regards to sin. Kierkegaard regarded sin as potentiated despair before God. Man stands eternally before God and in this state, as he is made conscious of God, a demand is made upon him which he cannot fulfil, and in which he can only despair. Therefore, sin is not ignorance, for, "If sin is really ignorance, then sin in fact does not exist, for sin precisely is consciousness. If sin is being ignorant of what is right, so that therefore one does wrong, then sin does not exist." (*Sickness Unto Death*, (London: Oxford University Press, 1941) XI, p. 266), and also, "Sin is not a momentary thing, but an eternal fall from the eternal." (*Christian Discourses* 108, (London: Oxford University Press, 1939), X, pp. 126-126) For this reason, the opposite of sin, for Kierkegaard, was not virtue, but faith. In this way there is, for Barth, some (although limited) agreement with Paul Tillich who worked out Kierkegaard's ideas of sin most comprehensively. Tillich views the Fall as a slippage of humanity from its essence (the 'God-intended') into its existence (actuality). The possibility of sinning lies in the tension between these two states, and accordingly Tillich defines sin as unbelief, defiance, concupiscence, and as being both demonic and collective. Yet in all of this it seldom becomes more than what Ramm has called 'existential error'. Barth critiques Tillich as well for having reduced the seriousness of sin in his over-existentialised reworking of Kierkegaard's idea of sin. The linkage between Kierkegaard, Tillich (as well as Reinhold Neibuhr, Emil Brunner and a host of other theologians) and Barth here is in their desire to retain the

as a state in ignorance, 'vegetative and unconscious'. In his use of his created but hidden meonic freedom, God's creature sought the growth available through the suffering of distinction and death to the innocence and ignorance of paradise. "Knowledge was born of freedom" and the Fall enabled humanity to improve and develop beyond the created state of ignorance.[31]

Although Barth finds agreement at points with each of these ideas, he consistently rejects any notion that would see the Fall in a positive light, for evil was manifest in creation and humanity was condemned and lost as a result of the Fall.[32] Does our motif of the 'necessary antithesis' require that the Fall becomes a positive step in God's plan for His creation? Does the fact that the Fall was inevitable and that God planned to overcome its devastation from eternity before creation mean that it changes from something negative and heinous to something positive? Clearly it does not. Barth can assert that the *felix culpa* is in error only in that it attributes *meruit habere* to the Fall instead of seeing the Fall and the consequent sinful state of humanity as that which was assumed in God's election to be 'for' humanity in Christ. That salvation came from the brink of the abyss does not change the Fall into this abyss into a *felix culpa*. Our study of Barth has not denied this, but it has shown that the Fall was a necessary result of the combination of the self-distinction of God and the choice of God to create that which would be a recapitulation of this eternal self-differentiation. The Fall was inevitable, but for that reason alone it was not fortunate.

Barth does not develop this idea only with regards to the Fall. We must be reminded that Barth has said several other things which combine to give us a true picture of his idea of the Fall. Barth has said that the goal of creation was not the paradisal state, but the lifting up of the creature into fellowship with the *crucified and risen* Christ; that the blessings of this union were *higher and greater blessings* than those given in creation; that evil would only be finally destroyed *as a result of* this salvific work of Christ; and that God's own glorification would come not through the maintenance of some pre-fallen state, but through this process of exaltation of his creature in and through the exaltation of His own Son (His *crucified* and risen Son!) for them. We are faced here with a picture in which God's free choice create and to realize His goal in that creation gave rise to a necessary place and role for the Fall. This does not imply any Manichaeistic dualism, but simply a proper interpretation of the instrumentalism of Barth's doctrine of evil which has clearly been emerging. The result is that

---

seriousness of sin without taking Genesis 3 literally, and thus falling back into all of the problems that come with the sharp distinction between an historic pre-fall and post-fall state of creation.

[31] Berdyaev, *The Destiny of Man, op. cit.,* p. 40-41.

[32] Barth will have no part in assigning good to what is evil, even if good is the result. Thus here he is in line with the thought of Berdyaev that, "the very origin of good and evil was in itself a terrible tragedy." (Berdyaev, *The Destiny of Man,* p. 172)

the Fall must be held to be inevitable and indeed a factual necessity in God's eternal purposes when He chose to create humanity for Himself.

Absolute Dualism and 'Necessary Antithesis'

We must take a look again at the fine line that divides our motif of the 'necessary antithesis' and an outright dualism especially with regard to Barth's interpretation of the separating activity of God in creation. In defining creation as separation[33], Barth is careful to point out that this separation does not imply an absolute dualism where darkness is given an independent status to the light. The relationship instead is one of acquiescence, confrontation and subordination. Darkness exists only as light exists, as marked off and distinguished from it and it therefore "necessarily serves that which it tries to oppose."[34] Barth will no more let evil be blamed on God than he will let it be independent of Him. For even Satan and the demons, Barth says, are God's good creation in their original uncorrupt state, and their corruption and the nothingness they manifest are not a part of that good creation.[35] God is then the Author and Creator of only the good, and evil is the responsibility of that which He has created,

> Thus a true and strict analogy to the relationship between light and darkness is to be found only in the relationship between the divine election and rejection, in the eternal Yes and No spoken by God Himself when, instead of remaining in and by Himself, He marches on to the *opus ad extra* of His free love.[36]

There is no dualism here between light and darkness, for both are in one sense from God and He is Lord over both. God is Lord over darkness controlling it for His own purposes. "It is not darkness itself, nor Satan, nor man, but God who gives it its name, assigning it a place and *giving it a role to play and a duty to perform*."[37] All is internal to God, for even in the non-willing of darkness

---

[33] "Here and in the second act of creation, and clearly enough even in the first part of the third, *to create is to separate*." (CD III/1, p. 122, emphasis mine)

[34] CD III/1, p. 123.

[35] This is a most curious statement by Barth (CD III/1, p. 123) as he later rejects all notions of a pre-mundane fall of the angels (CD III/3, pp. 530-531) which we believe is equally odd given his adherence to an exegetical basis for his theology. (See G. W. Bromiley's criticism of the same problems in Barth in *Introduction to the Theology of Karl Barth, op. cit.*, pp. 154-155)

[36] CD III/1, pp. 123-124.

[37] Ibid. pp. 126-127. (emphasis mine)

there is a covenant of sorts with the night as well as the day, which implies that it is wholly under His sovereign lordship and control.[38]

If Barth is successful in supporting his rejection of an absolute dualism, he has also re-affirmed the motif of a 'necessary antithesis' and, we will say further, even that of a temporary dualism. Barth has shown that darkness requires the light for its very existence. In doing so he has implied quite unequivocally the correlate, that light has a sort of dependence upon darkness. Thus Berkouwer calls chaos (nothingness) in Barth's theology the *'material for confrontation'*. "The emphasis on the chaos and on the chaotic does not relativise the joyful message, but *makes possible* its being sounded forth in all its clarity and triumph."[39]

Barth has based his manifestation of nothingness in space and time upon God's eternal self-distinction. This is who God is, He is the God who is eternally self-differentiating. This self-distinction is so central to the ontological nature of God that it is carried necessarily into the created realm in God's self-recapitulation, and as a result becomes a threat to God's creation. This threat is taken so seriously that God could only create based upon the presupposition of His self-determination to suffer and die to save His creation from its inevitable fall. To do less would be for God to act other than according to His own nature. God's 'Yes' requires a 'No' for it to be a 'Yes'. If God is eternally the self-differentiating God, then that from which He makes Himself distinct must have a necessary, even if a negative and non-willed, role to play in the very existence of God.

We recall Fiddes' fitting comment, "God uses death to define his being... the most dreadful assault of non-being has become the most articulate word about God."[40] Could God be God if He were other than the self-differentiating God? Barth has told us no, and thus there is a necessary role to this 'other' which is carried right through to creation, salvation history and eschatology. Barth has lead us to understand God in an eternal relationship of rejection and distinction from nothingness in a way in which the not-God, nothingness, not-good, is the 'necessary antithesis' of God, existence and good. It has been from eternity and it must be and will be through eternity!

This is where Barth is open to criticism in his teaching on the annihilation of nothingness. He has posited the destruction of that by which, even if negatively, God is defined. Good without any existence of not-good is not good but neutral, even evil itself. In this way good requires not-good just as God requires that from which He can be defined as the eternally self-differentiating God. Yet Barth's realism, and the objectivism and actualism of his theology provide the requisite balance in putting evil in subordination to God and allowing a full denial of an absolute dualism. Barth has brought us to the brink

---

[38] "It is certainly consoling that-from whatever angle we see Him-God is above this antithesis [day/night] and gives to both sides their names. But what is really consoling is that it is He who causes it to be day and night." (CD III/1, p. 128)

[39] Berkouwer, *Triumph of Grace, op. cit.,* p. 249. (emphasis mine)

[40] Fiddes, *The Creative Suffering of God, op. cit.,* pp. 265-266.

of this idea in CD II/1, and we must be consistent and carry it through at this point and others.

This is also seen in Barth's positing of an eschatological answer to the Sabbath rest of God on the seventh day of creation. Barth affirms the answer given by Kohlbrügge,

> Could God have rested if He had not done all of these things with a view to Christ? Or did He not know that the devil would soon spoil all creation, including man? But as God created heaven and earth through Christ or in Christ, so He created all things with a view to Christ. On the seventh day God was pleased with His Son. He saw creation perfect through Christ; he saw it restored again through Christ; and He therefore declared it to be finished, and rested.[41]

The seventh day rest is the crown of creation and in it God is pleased and satisfied with this work of creation, only as that through which He will do His ultimate work in it and for it in Christ. It is important for Barth's theodicy to understand that by creation in and through Christ Barth is not affirming simply that the second person of the Trinity was involved in the creation of the world. He is saying that creation was in and for and through *Jesus* Christ, the incarnate Son, the *Logos ensarkos* who will suffer and die and rise again. "The world came into being, it was created and sustained by the little child that was born in Bethlehem, by the Man who died on the Cross of Golgatha, and the third day rose again. *That* is the Word of creation, by which all things were brought into being."[42]

This is evidence again of the role of the Fall in the doctrine of creation and predestination. God was on the cross before Genesis 1:1, the 'Lamb was slain from the foundation of the world', and therefore the cross was presupposed in the rejection of nothingness, the creation of humanity, and the placing of the trees in the Garden of Eden.[43] How else could God be God than if He knew and anticipated the Fall from all eternity? This is what His divine self-determination means and we must not shy away from its implications that God, by the act of creation which put humanity in confrontation with nothingness, predestined humanity to fall and to be saved through Christ. That is an essential part of Barth's understanding of creation as the 'external basis of the covenant'.

---

[41] H.F. Kohlbrügge, *Schriftauslegungen*, Volume I, 1904, p. 23; quoted in CD III/1, p. 222.

[42] Barth, *Dogmatics in Outline, op. cit.,* p. 58.

[43] "Predestination means that from all eternity God has determined upon man's acquittal at His own cost." (CD II/2, p. 167)

The Two-Fold Determination of the Covenant

Taking these motifs a further step, Barth finds the necessity of evil in the very nature of the covenant. In answer to the question of the necessity of the 'No' in the covenant Barth replies,

> The answer is to be found in the fact that the revelation of God the Creator so closely binds the life which He has created with the covenant in which He willed to make Himself the Lord and Helper and Saviour of man; with the reconciliation of the world with Himself to be accomplished in Jesus Christ.[44]

There is therefore a twofold determination in this covenant which binds creation to Creator. On the one hand there is the requisite exaltation of the creature in the sight of the Creator, and on the other there is the 'need and peril' of the creature as it stands in the presence of the Almighty God, who would move to save His creation from this peril and meet this need in His Son. This is humanity's lot in the covenant which is manifest in the world as the 'Yes' and 'No' of God. Here again, and perhaps in its greatest form, Barth returns to his motif of the 'necessary antithesis'. On the one hand he writes that "God created man to lift him in His own Son into fellowship with Himself."[45] This is the goal of creation, the goal of the covenant. This is the 'better' which follows the 'good' of creation. This is what it means that the world was created with a view to Christ, for Him, by Him and in Him. This lifting up of humanity in the Son was the will of God in the eternal divine self-determination to be 'for' humanity. Barth's entire eschatology will be built upon this idea of the ultimate goal of creation finding its completion in the work of Christ in which we participate now only in part, but will wholly and completely in the second coming. This is the positive meaning of our existence as we live in covenant relationship with our Creator.

The negative meaning of this existence, the 'necessary antithesis' to the fulfillment of the goal of creation and the completion of the eternal will of God is demonstrated in that God created us in the shadow of nothingness to which we would inevitably fall. The exaltation of the positive meaning *necessarily* requires and presupposes the wretchedness of the post-fallen state. This is the negative side of the meaning of our existence and it is no less but *equally necessary and important* to the accomplishment of the goal of creation, even though it must be remembered that it is ultimately subordinate to and overcome by grace.

Barth supports this idea with these most important words, "Since everything is created for Jesus Christ *and His death and resurrection,* from the very outset

---

44 CD III/1, p. 375.
45 Ibid. p. 376.

everything must stand under this twofold and contradictory determination."[46] Life on the edge of the abyss and in the contradiction of joy and misery, pain and pleasure, this is how we stand in the presence of God in the covenant relationship He has established with us. Yet this is not a description of humanity only in its post-fallen state, as though this is somehow an aberration of God's original intent, but "This is how He wills it to be. This is how He has *created* it... *Hence the joy and misery of life have their foundation in the will of God.*"[47] We need no stronger evidence of Barth's view that evil has a necessary role to play in the entire event of creation, covenant and salvation history.

The world God created necessarily must involve evil and involve it in such a way that its temporary victory is allowed in order to provide the proper context for the salvific work of Christ for whom and by whom and in whom the world was created. The origin of evil can be found nowhere else but in the eternal self-distinction of God in such a fundamental way that God could only create a world which reflected this eternal internal struggle and which would be played out for good on the stage of creation. Thus the creature was willed and determined to a life that would involve the pleasure of the relationship with the Creator and the sharp attacks of the nothingness which it would inevitably face and to which it would certainly succumb.

The Transcendence of God in the Contradiction of the Positive and Negative Existence of Humanity

The greatness of the incarnation lies in the fact that God is transcendent beyond and above this contradiction of His creation. They neither define nor limit Him but He they. It is critical here to note that this does not, for Barth, mean that the 'Yes' and the 'No' do not exist in God outside of creation, but quite the opposite, that they exist in their most absolute form in His transcendence eternally. This is demonstrated in the recurrent theme in Barth that the humiliation and exaltation of the Son of God are the true self-revelation of the Creator, "For here the majesty and lowliness *(Hoheit und Niedrigkeit)* of God Himself are manifested."[48] In creating the world under the 'Yes' and 'No' of His eternal will, God then assumes its determination in human form. This assumption of the twofold and contradictory distinction of human existence by

---

[46] Ibid. p. 376. (emphasis mine) This speaks further to the link between the pre-determined incarnation and the cross, for it was not only the incarnation which was presupposed and fore-ordained, but everything was created for the incarnation which also means the cross and resurrection. Barth does not see just the incarnation in the predetermination of God to be 'for' man, as though the incarnation in an unfallen world was God's true purpose in creation, but the incarnation in its unbreakable link to Good Friday and Easter.

[47] Ibid. p. 376. (emphasis mine) *"So hat der Jubel und hat der Jammer des Daseins seiner Grund in Gottes Willen."* (KD III/3, p. 431)

[48] CD III/1, p. 377.

its Author and Lord is, for Barth, the meaning and end of creation.[49] What is fulfilled in Jesus Christ is the whole being of humanity in this twofold determination, and since it has been fulfilled as such, we are summoned to take life seriously in this twofold determination. We can add here the assertion that God in the incarnation is taking upon Himself in human form not something grossly new, but a form of what He is eternally in Himself.[50] In the twofold contradiction of good and evil in eternity, God is always the Victor in His self-distinction of God from 'not-God'. Since His creation, being non-divine, was unable to do in space and time what God has done in eternity in Himself, God now embraces this twofold determination in its manifestation in His creation.

The Eternal Relationship Between the Two-Fold Determination of the Existence of Humanity

If there is a necessary twofold determination of the creation which is confirmed and transcended by God, what is the relationship between the two? For Barth, any and every attempt to speak of this conflict must be done from the one, wholly Christian and unequivocal belief that God has embraced this conflict, endured it, overcome it, and that He continues to endure it today. It is due to His objective self-revelation that we can see through the imperfection of being to its perfection. In this conflict, since God in His love has taken it wholly to Himself, we can have faith and freedom before Him even as we live in the continuing conflict of this twofold determination. For before we existed, God took the contradiction to Himself, not in His natural superiority over it (as He has eternally in His divine self-distinction) but in the incarnation where he embraced this antithesis, causing it to be internal to Himself. In God Himself

---

[49] "The secret, the meaning and the goal of creation is that it reveals, is that there is revealed in it, the covenant and communion between God and man, and therefore the fulfillment of being as a whole, which is so serious and far-reaching that the Word by which God created all things, even God Himself, becomes as one of His creatures, being there Himself like everything else, like all the created reality distinct from Himself, and thus making His own its twofold determination, its greatness and wretchedness *(ihre Größe und ihr Elend)* its infinite dignity and infinite frailty, its hope and its despair, its rejoicing and its sorrow. This is what has taken place in Jesus Christ as the meaning and end of creation." (Ibid. p. 377)

[50] John Thompson sees the humanity of God as foundational for Barth's theology, "In the Christian faith we are not dealing with God or man in general, in abstraction or isolation, but in their relationship and unity in Jesus Christ-a relationship and unity eternally willed and decreed, determined by God alone in the mystery of his electing love in which he became and always is the God of man, God with man and for man. This is the significance of the *Logos ensarkos*. There is no depth of deity in which he was other than the God of man, in which man was not with and before God. The two belong indissolubly together, not by man's choice but by God's, not because it is in the nature of God or man to be so determined but because of God's action and will." *(Christ in Perspective in the Theology of Karl Barth, op. cit.,* p. 99)

from all eternity there was the Elect man, the *Logos ensarkos* who was also the *homo labilis*. In so doing, the contradictory elements of the twofold determination of human existence find their origin in God Himself. For Barth, "This is how we must put it if on the basis of His self-revelation we affirm that His covenant with man is the meaning and the goal and therefore the primary basis of creation."[51]

Thus, by taking it wholly to Himself, the problem is primarily God's own problem which is answered and solved in the death and resurrection of Jesus Christ. For Barth, there can be no accusation brought against God concerning this contradiction in which we live, for God has already embraced the fullness of this contradiction and has overcome it in His own sacrificial death in the Son. It has ceased to be our problem; no, it never was our problem, but it was the divine problem handled in full by God before creation.[52] The problem of human existence is embraced and solved by God, not in some secret, mysterious way, but in the way revealed by Him, in His Son.

Here again Barth takes us back to the idea of the eternal will of God including the Fall of humanity and its restoration as the ultimate goal of creation, "from the realized intervention of God for His creation we have to learn that no less than this was in fact sufficient to bring creation to this goal; or conversely, that *this goal is so high that its attainment demanded nothing less than this intervention of God Himself.*"[53] The goal of creation from eternity would necessitate the intervention of God in the incarnation of His Son, and His subsequent death and resurrection. This theme is so recurrent in Barth that we have by now proven its place in his theology. Here, however, he goes one important step further. If this intervention is predetermined in the goal of creation, then is there not a necessary and even a positive, yes, good and perfect role for creaturely imperfection? Barth can only say 'yes' given what all he has said previously.

> When we realize this clearly, we cannot deny that there is a transparency, meaning and even perfection of creaturely imperfection... Is there any more perfect world[54] than that which, in its imperfection, is the arena, instrument and object of this divine action?[55]

---

[51] CD III/1, p. 380.

[52] Barth gives evidence of this in *The Christian Life* when he talks of the cry of the Old Testament over the victory and good fortune of the ungodly. He writes, "the psalmists, or those for whom they speak, have no intention, as they also have no possibility, of avenging themselves on their oppressors, or even of defending themselves against them. This is obviously because they realize that in the struggle with them the serious and final issue is the problem of theodicy, which it will be God's affair to answer and solve and not theirs." (*The Christian Life, op. cit.*, p. 209)

[53] CD III/1, p. 382. (emphasis mine)

[54] A few pages later Barth will make the same point by stating, "If the created world is understood in light of the divine mercy revealed in Jesus Christ, of the divine participation in it eternally resolved in Jesus Christ and fulfilled by Him in time; if it

Here we have a return to the idea of *felix culpa,* for the imperfection of the world is the 'arena, instrument and object' *(der Schauplatz, das Werkzeug, der Gegenstand)* of the salvific work of God which is the goal of creation, the fulfillment of the covenant and the achievement of the goal of the divine self-determination of God. This imperfection is a required element for this perfect world. And by being so, this negative determination of human existence is justified by God. We remember that Barth has rejected the idea of *felix culpa* because ascribed to the *culpa* is the *meruit habere.* What Barth certainly does not reject is the idea that the *culpa* was the 'necessary antithesis' to the *salvatorem.*

Evil in Creation Under the 'Right and Left Hand of God'

The pattern of the ontic-noetic movement in Barth's theology regarding evil has been firmly established and it emerges again here in the consideration of the act of creation itself. The movement from the ontic basis of evil in the 'necessary antithesis' to its noetic manifestation in the 'right and left hand of God' is echoed in two further movements; 1) in the move from the Fall (the ontic necessity) to the sinful state of humanity as the *homo lapsus* (the noetic manifestation of the Fall), and 2) in the move from creation out of nothingness but in confrontation with nothingness (the ontic basis of the 'impossible possibility' of evil) to God's providence as the necessary correlate to the rebellion of humanity which allowed chaos into the creation (the noetic manifestation of the 'inevitable' choice of the 'impossible'). Since God's providential care of the fallen creation is seen as making possible the time and place of the fulfillment of the covenant, creation and covenant are inextricably tied, and Barth's discussions of the creation-covenant link must be understood in terms of this ontic-noetic theme and the underlying doctrine of evil which has so strongly influenced it.

In Barth's theology, creation was manifested to serve the divine eternal purposes of the covenant which, as we have seen, were to enact in space and time the divine self-determination to be for all humanity in Jesus Christ. The whole of this picture must be kept in view. God chooses in His eternal divine freedom and love to create out of the overflowing of his glory. This creation of another which will be necessarily non-divine involves a risk for the Creator, for the eternally rejected nothingness will now confront the non-divine creature, and this creature will inevitably yield. For God to create, there had to be a prior, in fact the ultimate *a priori* self-determination to be for this inevitably fallen humanity in Jesus Christ, the incarnate Son who would suffer and die to save

---

is thus understood as the arena, instrument and object of His living action, of the once for all divine contesting and overcoming of its imperfection, its justification and perfection will infallibly be perceived and it will be seen to be the best of all possible worlds." (Ibid. p. 385)

[55] Ibid. p. 382.

humanity from its destined fall.[56] This God chose to do, and therein lies the justification for creation. Therefore creation becomes the preparation of the stage upon which this great cosmic drama will be played out in time and space.

> This is the creation chosen, willed and posited by God; the creation which, for this reason, is 'good', indeed 'very good', in His sight. It is so because, in virtue of this typical superiority and subordination, it is adapted to be the theatre of the covenant which is the purpose of the divine volition and accomplishment; and because, in virtue of its nature, it is radically incapable of serving any other purpose, but placed from the very first at the disposal of His grace.[57]

The covenant was the purpose of creation, the covenant in which humanity would be the unequal partner, the covenant in which humanity would fail and God would triumph in that failure. Creation looked beyond the garden of Eden and immediately to the cross and resurrection where God would fulfill the covenant and realize the goal of His eternal self-determination to be for humanity in Jesus Christ, bringing all humanity in the Son into participation of the Sabbath rest of the Trinity.

Tohu wa-bohu and the Critical Interpretation of Genesis 1

If this interpretation is correct, we would expect to find evil as a necessary component of creation, and in this assumption we are not disappointed. The key to Barth's understanding of the relationship between evil and creation lies in his heavily disputed interpretation of Genesis 1:2. We will attempt to construct his line of reasoning and then will venture a criticism.

In God's act of creation, for the purposes stated above, everything which was either neutral or hostile to God was rejected, becoming utterly past and making its the presence in God's good creation 'impossible'. The only *Wirklichkeit* that this utterly past can have is tied wholly to its nature as that

---

[56] The link between creation and incarnation is again emphasized by Barth when he writes, "if this is true... that God was in Christ, then we have a place where creation stands before us in reality and becomes recognisable. For when the Creator has become Himself the creature, God become man, if that is true (and that is the beginning of Christian knowledge), then the mystery of the Creator and His work and the mystery of His creation are open to us in Jesus Christ, and the content of the first article is plain to view. Because God had become man, the existence of creation can no longer be doubted." (*Dogmatics in Outline, op. cit.,* p. 53) He continues later, "Here the second article reaches back to the realm of the first; here creation and redemption are united. From this standpoint we must say that creation itself, God's existence itself, prior to the whole world from eternity, is unthinkable apart from His will as it has been fulfilled and revealed in time. The eternal will of God has this form." (p. 69)

[57] CD III/1, p. 99.

which has been rejected by God in creation. It survives only as and because it is rejected.[58] God faced the imposing problem of the confrontation of His good creation with the nothingness and He acted in and for His creation (which does not have the power to do so for itself) at the beginning to both reject and push aside that which threatens it. This pushing aside is demonstrated in the description of creation as a process of separation of light from darkness, land from the waters, and the earth from the sky in which the former terms are the good and positive will of God and the latter are the forces of chaos. Barth enjoins the argument of the interpretation of the *tohu wa-bohu* ,

> The first and basic question is obviously this: Does verse 2 (with or without reference to verse 1) speak of the *tohu wa-bohu*, of darkness and flood, as a primeval condition which preceded creation, and therefore a primeval reality independent of creation and distinct from God? Or does it affirm that creation commenced with the fundamental positing of *tohu wa-bohu*, of darkness and flood, as the primeval state–a positing not included in the work of the six days, but promisingly accompanied by the Spirit of God brooding over this dark and disorderly totality. The first explanation must surely be rejected.[59]

Barth rejects the first point in line with his understanding of the sovereignty of God and the impossibility of anything having existence that is outside or independent of God. What is referred to in verse 2 can be given no independent status in relation to God, nor a condition or pre-existing 'reality' with which

---

[58] George Hendry's article, 'Nothing' (*Theology Today*, Volume 31, Number 3, 1978) is helpful here, as well as a bit misleading. Hendry points to the difficulty of locating the origin of nothingness in the effectual non-willing of God. He says of Barth's idea of elective divine action, "it demonstrates its electivity by negating its contrary; but in so doing, it confers a strange kind of negative reality on it. He [Barth] seeks to dampen the dualistic, or Manichaean sound of his construction by naming the contrary that is negated 'the nothing', or 'nothingness'; it is that to which God has said no; nevertheless, he ascribes to it a very positive and active character as a theat to God's good creation; it is not merely un-creation, it is anti-creation." (pp. 283-284) Hendry shows here both an inherent dualism in Barth and how the negated reality of nothingness becomes a positive player in God's eternal plans. However, Hendry is unable to see how this negated nothingness pre-exists the act of creation in God's eternal self-differentiation, and therefore he criticises Barth for a two-stage creation, which he claims is due to his [Barth's] failure to distinguish between absolute *(ouk on)* and relative *(me on)* nothingness. He concludes against Barth that he "fails to make it clear how the negated possibility of a chaotic or formless world could turn into a reality which threatens God's creation and even the being of God Himself." Hendry has missed the critical link in Barth's theology between God's eternal self-differentiation and His eternal self-determination; a link which we have consistently shown to be all-determinative for Barth.

[59] CD III/1, p. 102.

God must now deal. There is no independent 'reality of chaos' which confronts the Creator from without at the point of creation.

In assessing Barth's rejection of the first position, the distinction between reality and non-reality must be kept in mind. For Barth, nothingness has no 'reality' or 'existence' apart from its nature as that which has been rejected and therefore it can be said to 'exist' only according to His will (the negative non-willing) and therefore as a servant of God. Again we see how God has done temporally in creation what He does in Himself eternally. The eternal divine self-distinction of God from 'not-God' is manifested in the first act of creation which was to continue that distinction, now in space and time, between that which is God's positive will, and therefore good, and that which is rejected by God, and therefore evil. Again we see the move from evil's ontic basis in the 'necessary antithesis' motif to its noetic manifestation in the motif of the 'right and left hand of God'.

In this way Barth can say that God passed over and rejected the chaos of the past, pre-creation state, while maintaining that it was not independent of Him but that its 'reality' was only by virtue of its rejection, and therefore only in its relationship to and dependence upon God.[60] As he did in his doctrine of election, Barth seeks here to keep the absolute sovereignty of God intact while at the same time exonerating God for any responsibility for evil. In addition he is attempting to give to evil both a form in which it can be taken seriously and a reality which is seen in its absolute subordination to God. Finally, Barth is setting the stage for the Fall and salvation history where humanity can be seen to bear the responsibility for sin, and where God in Christ can be shown to have the power and authority to overcome sin, death and evil on the cross. All of this is built and dependent upon Barth's ability to hold together these ideas of evil and creation.

It is not surprising here that Barth also rejects the second statement concerning the *tohu wa-bohu*.[61] Barth argues that Scripture does not support the idea of a creation of chaos prior to the creation of God's good creation, but

---

[60] "Had He not been the Creator of light, there would have been no darkness. As He is the Creator of light, darkness, too, is not without but through Him." Ibid. p. 106.

[61] Here Barth parts company with Augustine as well as a major portion of Reformed and orthodox teaching regarding the *creatio ex nihilo*. Augustine taught plainly that God created the formless and void world of Genesis 1:2 which was defined as the *privatio* of the light, and from it he separated the light. "For Thou, Lord, madest the world of a matter *without form*, which is out of nothing, Thou madest next to nothing, thereof to make those great things, which we sons of men wonder at." And later, "With regard to the understanding of the words following, out of all those truths, he chooses one to himself, who saith, *But the earth was invisible, and without form, and darkness was upon the deep*; that is, 'that corporeal thing that God made, was as yet a formless matter of corporeal things, without order, without light." (*Confessions, op. cit.,* pp. 253, 265)

exactly the opposite, for God is not the God of chaos but of order.[62] The spirit which broods over the waters then is not the Spirit of God, but the spirit of that which is wholly rejected by Him.[63]

Barth's controversial point is that the *tohu wa-bohu* is that which God rejected and passed over at the beginning of creation, and therefore Barth equates the *tohu wa-bohu* with *das Nichtige* or nothingness.[64] By equating the

---

[62] See CD III/1, pp. 103-104 for Barth's main argument against Luther is his connection of verse one and two. Luther saw the creation spoken of in verse one as indicating the origin of the *tohu wa-bohu* of verse two. Barth denies any such connection and, instead, will posit that these two verses are two different views of creation, with no such connection as Luther proposed.

[63] In the New International Version of the Bible, the spirit in Genesis 1:2 is given the capital 'S'. Likewise in the New American Standard Version it is the 'Spirit of God', where the Today's English Version translates this as the 'power of God'. None of them deny that this Spirit or power was of God and not in any sense the antithesis or rejected of God. With regard to these modern English translations, Barth's exegesis stands alone at this point.

[64] We must stop here and look at some other exegetical comments concerning verse 2. Walter Brueggemann suggests that there is a tension between the *creatio ex nihilo* suggested (but not stated outright) in verse one with the creation from the *tohu wa-bohu* of verse two. This tension can and should be allowed. "We need not choose between them, even as the text does not. Both permit important theological affirmation. The former asserts the majestic and exclusive power of God. The latter lets us affirm that even the way life is can be claimed by God... Perhaps for good reason, this text refuses to decide between them." (W. Brueggemann, 'Genesis', in *Interpretation: A Bible Commentary for Teaching and Preaching,* (Atlanta: John Knox Press, 1982) pp. 29-30) Claus Westermann identifies the three clauses of verse two as the 'before' or opposite of creation. "The Hebrew expression *tohu wa-bohu* indicates a desert waste, analogous to the Greek *chaos*; its darkness is uncanny, something like what animals experience during a solar eclipse; and a 'violent wind', encountered in many cosmologies of the ancient world, intensifies the sense of chaos." (Claus Westermann, *Genesis,* (Edinburgh: T & T Clark, 1987), p. 8) Gerhard von Rad provides Barth with support for his unique interpretation. Von Rad sees the 'spirit' which moves over the waters as belonging "completely to the description of chaos and [it] does not yet lead into the creative activity." The chaos which it does help describe is that "of a reality that once existed in a preprimeval period but also of a possibility that always exists." This threatening abyss must be seen through the eyes of creation faith in which the marvel of the creation is seen with regards to this abyss, "thus it speaks first of the formless and abysmal out of which God's will lifted creation and above which it holds it unceasingly." (G. von Rad, *Genesis: A Commentary,* (London: SCM Press, 1957), pp. 47-48) Finally, a much more conservative approach is taken by Edward Young. Seeking to interpret Scripture as 'truth in propositional form' Young approaches Genesis as actual literal history. He concludes directly against Barth that the chaos of verse two was the first step of God's *creatio ex nihilo* and that even as it was formless and void, it belonged to God's good creation. Accordingly, the *tohu wa-bohu* "is the first picture of the created world that the Bible gives and the purpose of the remainder of the chapter is to show how God brought this world from its primitive condition of desolation and

condition of the earth as the *tohu wa-bohu* with the Scriptural description of the horrors of the final judgement, Barth portrays God as having acted on behalf of humanity in creation to save it from this nothingness, and acting again in salvation history to save it from the final return to nothingness. Between the two stands the cross where this nothingness was faced in its fullness and overcome.[65] The darkness of Calvary is the Son's embracing and submission to the full force of the nothingness which He rejected in the creation of the world.[66] On both sides, in front and behind, humanity is on the frontier of nothingness. Yet it is always that nothingness which has been rejected in creation, defeated on the cross, and whose annihilation will be revealed in the final *parousia*.

Creatio ex Nihilo and the Space for Creation

By choosing this third option, Barth is building upon a combination of points which he has previously developed, including primarily the strict distinction between the immanent and economic Trinity, the relationship

---

waste to become an earth, fully equipped to receive man and be his home." (E.J. Young, 'Interpretation of Genesis 1:2', in *Westminster Theological Journal*, (Volume 23, May 1961), p. 174) Clearly von Rad's interpretation is the only one which gives to Barth any help whatsoever, and in a further examination of commentaries on the verse it becomes clear that Barth's exegesis is a major anomaly among Old Testament scholars.

[65] Of this R. Ruether says, "God's left hand of wrath and judgement over evil is sounded from the beginning in his triumph over chaos in creation, and all subsequent expressions of God's wrath and judgement in history and eschatology grow directly out of this original wrath and judgement of chaos in creation." (R. Ruether, 'The Left Hand of God in the Theology of Karl Barth', *op. cit.,* p. 4)

[66] Barth ties these together without losing the importance of their distinction. He states that it is on the cross that judgement fell upon the world in the person of the Son, the high priest and servant who died in our place. He adds, "Here-in exact correspondence with what He did as Creator when He separated light from darkness and elected the creature to being and rejected the possibility of chaos as nothingness-He pronounced His relentless and irrevocable No to disordered man." (CD IV/1, p. 349) This is why the Lord became a servant, was obedient unto God, and went into the far country and died as the Judge who was judged in our place, who bore our judgement and thus atoned for our guilt. Here Barth ties together the main parts of his section on the priestly work of Christ as well as showing the connection and yet distinction between creation, covenant, reconciliation and atonement. When these relationships are kept in mind, the cross can be seen as a separation in the *same exact manner* as creation. Nothingness is again, but this time finally and conclusively, separated from the good creation of God, which has never lost its goodness even in the midst of its fallenness and under its lordship to the power of nothingness. This point is vital for Barth for his understanding of the preservation of God, the covenant and the work of the cross as separation 'in exact correspondence' with his separation of light from darkness in creation.

between God's omnipresence and His freedom, the primordial electing grace of God and the idea of God's eternal self-differentiation. What arises from this foundation is a structure which is able to integrate this controversial exegetical position into the rest of Barth's theology, whether or not it is hermeneutically correct. This foundation and integration is as follows:

1. God's eternal internal reality includes His eternal rejection of that which is 'not-God'.

2. "The immanent Trinity can neither be identified with, separated from nor synthesized with each other or with the sphere of history."[67]

3. God's omnipresence means that God's space for Himself includes all space, and therefore the space of creation is "space which is given out of the fulness of God."[68]

4. This making of space for creation is a function of the freedom of God (God is able to do it) and the love of God (He is willing to do it).

5. Since creation is both that which occurs in God's space and thus is a self-recapitulation of God in space and time, and also that which is according to His economic work, and thus not itself necessarily divine, it is inevitably confronted by that which God has rejected in His own self-differentiation.

6. This nothingness was both rejected by God in His act of creation (Barth's third option) and, at the same time, its inevitable victory over God's creature was the basis of the covenant made with humanity in God's eternal election in grace of Jesus Christ as *homo labilis*, an eternal decree which now is to be played out on the stage of creation.

7. The state of creation is then one of fallenness in which God holds it above the abyss of nothingness from which it was separated and, despite humanity's disobedience, from which He also has saved it in the final defeat of that nothingness on Calvary.[69]

---

[67]   This statement is from an article by Paul Molnar which is very helpful in illuminating the integral role which this distinction plays in Barth's theology, and how it forms a critical distinction between Barth and other theologies, especially that of Moltmann and Pannenberg. (P. Molnar, 'The Function of the Immanent Trinity in the Theology of Karl Barth: Implications for Today', in *Scottish Journal of Theology,* Volume 42, Number 3, 1989, pp. 371-372)

[68]   CD II/1, p. 474.

[69]   This line of thought is supported by a sub-section in the *Church Dogmatics* which deserves to be quoted. In CD III/1, pp. 108-110, Barth moves along the following line of thought. "The only primal and rudimentary state which calls for consideration is that of evil, of sin and of the fall and all its consequences... Our only option is to consider v. 2 as a portrait, deliberately taken from myth, of the world which according to His revelation was negated, rejected, ignored and left behind in His actual creation... it is the epitome of that which *was* ... It is only behind God's back that the sphere of chaos can assume this distinctive and self-contradictory character of reality. This can, of course, happen. The creature can be so foolish... and thus drawing upon itself the wrath instead of the love of God the Creator... All this can happen because in its distinction from God the creature as such, while it is not ungodly, is non-divine, so that to posit it at all is undoubtedly a risk, since it is

Barth's soteriology is heavily dependent upon the two ideas here of *creatio ex nihilo* and His rejection of *das Nichtige* prior to creation. Again we see how the relationship between creation and chaos and, as we have shown, before creation to the eternal election of Jesus Christ, is a cohesive theme which runs the length and breadth of the entirety of Barth's theology. The central concept in that theme is Barth's use of nothingness as a 'necessary antithesis' to God, creation and salvation (the goal of creation through its final glorification of God in the establishment of perfect fellowship with His creature). The further one goes in the *Church Dogmatics*, the more dominant and important this motif becomes.

For Barth, the *creatio ex nihilo* destroys all concepts of dualism by showing that God used no primordial or pre-existent matter.[70] The chaos of verse 2 is not to be misinterpreted to mean a pre-existent matter, but possibilities and potentialities which God chose not to realize, rejecting them and consigning them to utter 'pastness'. They do not cease to exist in their 'peculiar ontology' of rejectedness, but they cease to be possibilities. Thus when God's creature chooses for them over the grace of God, Barth can say that they are choosing what is 'impossible', what is past and what has been rejected already for them, for their own good.

There are three points in Barth's understanding of God's making space for creation which must be noted here. First, nothing is ever outside of God, and

---

to posit a freedom which is distinct from the freedom of God... He [God] will not permit Himself to be obstructed by man's misuse of his freedom from actually making use of His own holy freedom in such a way that... He will not cease to be the Creator of Genesis 1 and to abide by His Word as spoken in Genesis 1... As this Word is spoken and repeated in the history of the covenant which begins immediately after the fall of man, it is thereby constantly decided that, in spite of all appearances to the contrary, the *hayethah* of chaos is final - this world *was*... If in Genesis 1:2 judgement upon a world alienated from Him is indicated as at least a possibility, it can actually be executed only at one point in the cosmos created by Him and in one creature. And at this one point and in this one creature God is Himself the One who is judged and suffers in the place and for the salvation and preservation of the rest of creation. This - the moment of darkness in which His own creative Word, His only begotten Son, will cry on the cross of calvary: 'My God, my God, why hast thou forsaken me?' - will be 'the moment' of His wrath... In this way, and in no other, God will allow men and their world to reap the fruits of wrath which they have brought upon themselves... he will exalt this one creature, the man Jesus Christ, as a sign of the promise given to the cosmos, so that His end in this vulnerable form will be the beginning of a new form in which He is no longer assaulted by this sinister possibility." Here you have the linkage fully displayed between Barth's doctrines of God, Election, Creation and Reconciliation a well as the indicator of why this interpretation of Genesis 1:2 is so important to the continuity of Barth's whole theology.

[70] Aquinas made a similar point. He rejected the *nihil* as a substance 'out of' (from the preposition *ex*) which the world was created. There was, instead, no pre-existing substance, but only true nothingness, true *nihil*. *Creatio ex nihilo* then is taken by Aquinas to mean *creatio post nihil*. (*Summa Theologica, op. cit.,* I, a, p. 45)

this includes nothingness in its 'peculiar ontology'. This does not mean that things in God's space are identical with God Himself, for creation is within this space. What it does mean is that all sense of dualism is to be rejected, but even more importantly, that God's will controls all things, even nothingness. This understanding of space in relation to creation is a key to Barth's doctrine of the providence of God. Nothing, not even hell or Satan are outside of this space, and therefore independent of God Himself.

Secondly, because of Barth's distinction between the immanent and economic Trinity, as well as his understanding of the freedom of God, Barth is not forced to say that God and creation unite in a pantheistic or panentheistic way.[71] We have seen in the perfections of God how Barth is able to hold to a strong idea of the proximity of God in creation while also demonstrating God's distinction and remoteness. Here is the heart of the tension between God's ability to be self-bound to His creature without consequently tying His own fate to that of His creation. God can do this because creation is 'in Him' and yet He is not 'in creation'.

Thirdly, we may ask just what does it mean when Barth sees the *creatio ex nihilo* as the separation of creation from these rejected potentialities? It means that we are ever faced with the abyss as the threat to our existence, but it does not mean for Barth that nothingness defines our nature. We were created in the *imago Dei* which for Barth means that we were created as those elect in the relationship and fellowship of the covenant. This relationship is eternal and the

---

[71] Moltmann asks the question, 'if God is omnipresent, then *where* is the universe?' To answer, Moltmann picks up, as we have shown, on the work of Isaac Luria and his use of *zimsum*. (*God in Creation, op. cit.,* pp. 86-87) Creation takes place in the space made by an 'inversion of God into himself'. The key to this idea is that, even for God to have the space in which to create, God had to limit himself. There was already prior to creation the commitment and willingness in God to suffer and undergo self-limitation and to allow his creation to dwell in a place that is *in* himself. "God already renounces his honour in the beginning at creation." (*The Crucified God, op. cit.,* p. 273) Yet we must go a step further. What is this space that is made for creation? If it is devoid of God, then the very space that God makes for creation is Nothingness. "The *nihil* in which God creates his creation is God-forsakenness, hell, absolute death; and it is against the threat of this that he maintains his creation in life." (*God in Creation,* p. 187) By creating a space for creation through his own self-limitation, God also makes a space for that which is 'not created'. In an incredible statement Moltmann says, "Only if all disaster, forsakenness by God, absolute death, the infinite curse of damnation and sinking into nothingness is in God himself, is community with this God eternal salvation, infinite joy, indestructible election and divine life... If one describes the life of God within the Trinity as the 'history of God' (Hegel), this history of God contains within itself the whole abyss of god-forsakenness, absolute death and the non-God." (*The Crucified God,* p. 246) Although parting with Barth in his use of panentheistic language, Moltmann stays on a strict Barthian line in his use of the term Nothingness and in setting it in direct confrontation with God through his creation. Moltmann describes the creation of the possibility of evil and concludes that it was a necessary aspect of God's *creatio ex nihilo*.

covenant is irrevocable (from God's side–and therefore from our side as well) and therefore the *imago Dei* cannot be lost. We err if we conclude from our *creatio ex nihilo* and God's rejection of *das Nichtige* that our created nature which, although constantly faced with the rejected nothingness, is less than the fullest expression of the *imago Dei*.[72]

In referring to providence as the Divine Preserving, from his interpretation of the *creatio ex nihilo*, Barth re-affirms that the 'nothing' from which we were created was not the non-existence of matter, but the non-willed nothingness of the *tohu wa-bohu* of Genesis 1:2. God preserves the distinction He created in the 'making space for' and separation of creation, and in so doing He preserves the creature. We see here the wrath of God as it continues against chaos, and therefore Barth, in a continuation of his understanding of the righteousness of God, rejects any notion of a 'genial providence'.[73] We are then preserved from nothingness[74], the threat of evil at the frontier of our created sphere by which, if it were not for God's preservation, we would be overwhelmed and fall into non-being.[75] God does not abandon us on the edge of the abyss but, from all eternity "His merciful will was to take up the cause of the creature against non-existence."[76] This eternal will of God was decided in favour of humanity and it is worked out in the ministry of Jesus Christ. This is the dominant picture of

---

[72] In the words of Augustine, this fallen man who was made out of nothing, now as a result of the Fall "grew not to be nothing, but towards nothing." (*City of God, op. cit.,* p. 43)

[73] Heppe states, "since all things are made of nothing they cannot of themselves have the power of continuance and operation... It is the condition of created things, that as they are partakers of nothingness, they have no power of subsistence or activity of themselves, and if the Hand by which they are sustained in being and activity be withdrawn, they cannot subsist to do anything even for a moment." (H. Heppe, *Reformed Dogmatics*, (London: George Allen & Unwind Ltd, 1950), pp. 255-256)

[74] Here Barth defines nothingness as "the devil... the world of demons and sin and evil and death." (CD III/3, p. 74) In an important statement he goes on to say, "from all eternity judgement has been pronounced and executed upon it by God." (Ibid) This gives additional evidence that Barth is thinking of an eternal self-distinction in God whereby the knowledge of evil and the act of the self-distinction brought also the judgement of God upon it. Yet it also opens up serious questions. If God had judged evil from all eternity, and if He had supreme power over it, why wasn't the sentence executed in full prior to creation? If evil has no perpetuity, as Barth will develop later, then why must its annihilation only occur at the end of the space/time sphere of created history? Is Barth implying that God could only carry out the final defeat of his eternal enemy in a created setting which included a fallen creature, the cross and resurrection? This will be developed in full in Barth's section on the temporality of nothingness, but we will raise it hear in anticipation of the strong criticism that must be made against this idea.

[75] "Everything outside God is held constant by God over nothingness." (Barth, *Dogmatics in Outline, op. cit.,* p. 55)

[76] CD III/3, p. 79.

grace and election which Barth has painted for us throughout this book. Again here the reason for this merciful work was that the creature may fulfill its destiny to participate in the work of salvation, that we may respond and participate in the covenant of grace.[77]

This preservation on the edge of the abyss of nothingness will end in the final *parousia* of Christ where we will experience the eternal preserving of God which will allow us eternal fellowship with Him. Again here we see Barth tending strongly in the direction of *apocatastasis* when he says of God in this eternal preserving, "He will not allow anything to perish, but will hold it in the hollow of His hand as He has always done, and does, and will do."[78] This statement comes just after he has stated that when 'the totality of everything that was and is and will be will only have been', God will preserve it all. This is a clear indication that truly God 'will not allow anything to perish' *(wird von Allem nichts fallengelassen haben)* but that all will be included in the eternal preservation of God.[79]

We ask finally, how can nothingness, as that which was set aside and wholly rejected in creation and that from which we are preserved under God's providential care, enter and dominate creation? Barth's answer is essentially the *homo lapsus* where humanity's violation of its God-given freedom allowed evil to cross that frontier at which God's grace holds it at bay, and through the creature it entered and dominated God's good creation. As a result, "it may be presupposed that man's fall and alienation from God is the root of all evil."[80]

> All this can happen because in its distinction from God the creature as such, while it is not ungodly, is non-divine, so that to posit it at all is undoubtedly a risk, since it is to posit a freedom which is distinct from the freedom of God... This is the undeniable risk which God took upon Himself in the venture of creation—but a risk for which He was more than a match and thus did not need to fear.[81]

It is us who allow nothingness (which is wholly past) to have a present and a future, but only and always as that which is controlled and rejected by God. The nature of nothingness as only that which is past is assured in the covenant of God with humanity and the salvation history which follows. Thus the risk in creation was in one way no risk at all, for God had already pre-determined Himself to be for humanity to the point of the cross. We remember that the *homo lapsus* was the assumption taken by God in His eternal election in Jesus

---

[77]   Ibid. pp. 81-82. Here Barth talks of this participation and the covenant of grace, and this section contains one of the most beautiful expressions of Barth's soteriology we have found in the whole of his writings!

[78]   Ibid. p. 90.

[79]   KD III/3, p. 102.

[80]   Barth, *The Christian Life*, *op. cit.*, p. 213.

[81]   CD III/1, p. 109.

Christ as *homo labilis*. The sin which inevitably was manifested in His creation was pre-destined in Christ to be overcome. In this way it is still the good God who created despite the inevitability of the Fall and all of the suffering it would wreak upon His creation.

The Fall as the Commencement of *Heilsgeschichte*

If in Genesis 1 the stage was constructed for the great cosmic drama, in Genesis 2 the play actually begins. Here God operates outwardly as He is in Himself,

> It is in the same free love that He Himself is God, i.e., the Father in the Son and the Son in the Father by the Holy Spirit. Again, it is in the same free love that He has resolved in Himself from all eternity in His fellowship with man in the person of His own Son. As this free love is revealed, i.e., made visible outside His own being, His hidden glory is revealed.[82]

The internal love of God and the decree to be for His creature now reaches out and embraces its external object, and so Barth views the covenant as the 'internal basis of creation'.[83] It is towards God's goal and for the fulfillment of

---

[82] Ibid. p. 230.

[83] Moltmann concludes that the covenant cannot be the 'inner ground of creation' for it is solely for the coming glory of God in the kingdom that God created. Therefore, and fundamental to his whole theology, it is the kingdom of God that is the 'inner ground of creation' and nothing else! (*God in Creation, op. cit.,* pp. 7-8) Moltmann states elsewhere, "The concept of the unity of God in the unity of meaning of his created activity can, in my view, only be preserved through the concept of the coherent, eschatologically oriented process of creation... Creation is then not a *factum* but a *fieri.*" (*The Future of Creation,* (London: SCM Press, 1979), p. 119) Here is the heart of the strong divergence in Barth's and Moltmann's eschatology. Moltmann describes eschatology as the future that has come in the midst of history, "In the midst of the history of death, the future of the new creation and the glory of God has already dawned in this one person." (*The Church in the Power of the Spirit, op. cit.,* p. 99) He develops a comprehensive understanding of history as God's history with the world which is, in the end, the eschatological history of the Trinity. God's history is the world's history and vice versa. He can say the world's history is God's history by virtue of the participation of creation in the inner-trinitarian relationships in the power of the Spirit. Therefore, "the history of the world is the history of God's sufferings." (*The Trinity and the Kingdom of God, op. cit.,* p. 4; see also *The Crucified God, op. cit.,* p. 270) The new future, the qualitatively new era has begun in the very midst of the old. It is the 'daybreak of the new creation'. In this new messianic time, Moltmann sees a transition not to a linear concept of time, but to a distinctively messianic concept of time. He also defines eschatological time as the time determined by the universal fulfillment of what was promised historically and of which has dawned in messianic time. In this eschatological time, the present

God's purpose that the world is created and the history of the covenant moves, and as such it is the best of all possible worlds. The history which commences after creation is the history of the covenant which will include the history of Israel, the incarnation and work of Christ, and the Church *post Christum* until the final *parousia*. Thus, "whatever objections may be raised against the reality of the world, its goodness incontestably consists in the fact that it may be the theatre of His glory, and man the witness to this glory."[84]

God's covenant with humanity pre-dates creation as we saw in Barth's adopting and amending of the Supralapsarian position in election.[85] However, the enactment of the covenantal relationship between God and humanity in human history starts not with the creation of humanity; instead the commencement of the covenant, the first steps of fellowship between creation and its Creator, (and we should not be surprised by this time to discover this) is located in Barth's account of the Fall.[86] Even the creation of Adam from the dust is a prefigurement of the Fall as seen in Barth's restatement of F. Delitzsch's view where, "the creation of man is understood and portrayed in the light of his later fall and its consequences."[87] What is equally prefigured is the eternal readiness of God to "perfect that which is utterly unattainable and to give life to that which is intrinsically dead."[88] These two must always be held together, for the justification of God for having created humanity in this way is

---

time is defined by the future. That is the essence of eschatology. The future breaks back upon the present in its anticipations of the coming future of God. For Barth, the present is defined by the past-the completed work of Christ on the cross and the resurrection, and the future if the noetic revelation of that completed work. For Moltmann, creation has an eschatological end in mind and eschatology has the purposes of creation in mind, both having their centre in messianic time. These divergent eschatologies both evolve from the divergent views of either creation or the kingdom of God as the 'inner ground of creation'.

[84] Barth, *Dogmatics in Outline, op. cit.,* p. 58.

[85] In Barth's commentary on John 1 he writes, "So great is the Revealer that in him we see not merely a later, ad hoc fellowship between God and the world, set up merely for the purpose of redemption, but a fellowship that is *original*." (*Witness to the Word, op. cit.,* p. 31)

[86] CD III/1, pp. 232-233. As we have shown from the outset, Barth has little time with discussions of the pre-fallen state. We remember the very important statement that 'created man was immediately fallen man'. Therefore, that the covenant history began after the fall is the same as saying that covenant history begins after the Sabbath rest. Not that he discounts the account of the Fall, but that the duration of the pre-fallen state is speculation and what is revealed to us is only the reality of post-fallen man in his relationship to God.

[87] CD III/1, p. 244.

[88] Ibid. p. 244.

seen only and wholly in salvation history.[89] The cross is the great vindicator of God in the accusation brought against Him by theodicy in relation to creation.

This view also distinguished God's providence from predestination, where predestination is the specific act of God in His covenant relation with humanity, and providence deals with God's creation generally. Yet here there is a definite order which Barth establishes in his rejection of the Thomist teaching that predestination must be understood according to providence. Barth insists the very opposite, that providence can only be rightly understood in light of predestination and never *vice versa*. This is indicated again in Barth's order of the *Church Dogmatics*, where the doctrine of election precedes that of creation and providence. In the latter, the distinction and distance between God and creation is important only and properly because it is in creation that God carries out His decrees made in the transcendence of the Godhead.

For this reason Barth chooses to use *videre* or *curare* instead of *destinare* in speaking of providence as the general divine government of the world.[90] In a similar distinction Barth sees providence not as *continuata creatio* but as *continuatio creationis*.[91] Thus God continues His creation but He does not continue to create.[92] That God continues His creation and supports and governs

---

[89] "For by the covenant we mean Jesus Christ. But it is not the case that the covenant between God and man is so to speak a second fact, something additional, but the covenant is as old as creation itself. When the existence of creation begins, God's dealing with man also begins... The covenant is not only quite as old as creation; it is older than it. Before the world was, before heaven and earth were, the resolve or decree of God exists in view of this event in which God willed to hold communion with man as it became inconceivably true and real in Jesus Christ. And when we ask about the meaning of existence and creation, about their ground and goal, we have to think of this covenant between God and man." (*Dogmatics in Outline, op. cit.*, pp. 63-64)

[90] CD III/3, p. 4.

[91] Barth's strict distinction between the process of creation and providence is a break with much Reformed doctrine. For example, Heinrich Heppe states, "There is a single divine act by which God creates the world and determines its government. That is why Providence may be conceived as a continuous world-creation... hence *conservatio* is to be conceived as a *continuata creatio*, resting upon the same command of God as creation." (*Reformed Dogmatics, op. cit.*, p. 251, 257) In support of his point he uses a quote from Johannes Cocceius, "By reason of the things which have begun to be, creation is a kind of creation continued." (Cocceius, *Summa Theologiae ex Scriptura repetita* XXVII, p. 9, in Heppe, p. 257) We hear this also in Salomon van Til, "Providence is the perpetual creation of God, differing only relatively from creation." (S. van Til, *Compendium Theologiae*, (Bern, 1975) in Heppe, p. 256)

[92] This distinction is held by Reformed scholars as well. For instance, Berkouwer attempts to clarify the Reformed position that there can be no thought of a continuous *creatio ex nihilo*. "We must reject the thought of a continuous creation out of nothing, though this should not keep us from asking whether a continuous creation may be spoken of in a better and more correct sense." (*The Providence of*

it, indeed the fact that creation is wholly dependent upon God for its continued existence is revealed in its creation. The first act necessarily required the second, and so providence is inextricably tied to creation.[93] This leads Barth to affirm the depth and breadth of the sovereignty of God, for the creature and all of creation can never escape His lordship.

> Whatever occurs, whatever it does and whatever happens to it, will take place only in the sphere and on the ground of the lordship of God, not only under a kind of oversight and final disposal of God, and not only generally in His direct presence, *but concretely in virtue of His directly effective will to preserve, under His direct and superior co-operation and according to His immediate direction.* [94]

Barth is constructing a view of providence which is airtight with regards to the activity of creation and the control of God. This holds true even for the

---

God, op. cit., p. 61) Berkouwer provides a helpful clarification of the Reformed position stating that when its dogmaticians use the term *creatio continua* they meant to stress that Providence is as great an act as creation. This leads H. Bavinck to conclude that the link between creation and providence is a mystery, and A. Kuyper to find that the two are 'at once similar and dissimilar'. The similarity for Kuyper's position is that God's sustaining power which constantly holds the created world above the abyss is a continual act of empowering, "from the hour of original creation until now, God, the Lord, has done the same thing as in the moment of creation: He has given all things power of existence through His power." Kuyper states that the dissimilarity is as follows, "Creation refers to what comes into existence: Providence to what, already existing, is continuously upheld by God's power." (Kuyper, '*Locus de Providentia*' in *Dictaten Dogmatiek*, quoted in Berkouwer, *Providence of God*, p. 62-63) This understanding is in line with Barth's desire to keep providence and creation linked without dissolving them into a single act of God.

[93] This tie, however, does not constitute one act, but two. Barth's point is that both creation and providence are outward acts of God which are manifestations of His inward acts of self-differentiation and self-determination. What was said in Barth's doctrines of God and election is determinative for what is now being created and preserved in space and time. Thus where predestination is "a matter primarily and properly of the eternal election of the Son of God to the the Head of His community and all creatures," providence has no such corresponding root in the eternal decree of God, but it instead, "belongs to the execution of this decree." (CD III/3, p. 4-5) The break between the work of creation (as seen in the Sabbath rest of the seventh day) and the beginnings of God's providence (in the sustenance of the fallen creation) is reflected in the relationship between Creator and creature. Thus the real difference between them is, "In creation we have to do with the establishment and, in providence with the guaranteeing and determination, of the history of creaturely existence by the will and act of God." (CD III/3, p. 8). In the end, the beginning of providence is the beginning of the covenant; or in using Barth's metaphor, if creation was the stage for the drama of *Heilsgeschichte*, then providence is the assurance that the drama will be played out until the end.

[94] CD III/3, p. 13. (emphasis mine)

voluntas permittens, for even where God permits He still holds the initiative, He still chooses the 'when', 'where' and 'how' to permit. Nothing, absolutely nothing is ever for one single moment outside of the providence of God.[95] Here the discussion of the *voluntas permittens* from Chapter III re-emerges under the doctrine of providence. We saw earlier how God's willing and God's permitting were essential to His being the God who operates from both His right hand and His left. Both the willing and non-willing, or permitting, are displays of the divine will of God as everything comes wholly under His control. We concluded that for Barth, God's non-willing is a necessary aspect of His divine will–God could not be God unless He permitted as well as positively willed. The justification for this permitting of evil and its consequences is the overarching goal of creation to which all things move and which will be accomplished not in spite of evil, but through and by the employ of evil under this divine *permittens*. Only by seeing God's permission of evil as falling within this determination of creation towards its ultimate goal can Barth conclude that we must see the *voluntas permittens* as wholly and fully *voluntas divina*.[96]

The break Barth has made with the orthodox Reformed doctrine of Supralapsarianism is troublesome to Barth's position here. The Reformed doctrine could teach a divine permission according to the eternal duality it saw in God's eternal decrees. However, when election is seen as the election of all humanity in Christ as Barth has developed it, and when all sense of a duality in God's decrees in election are stripped away, as Barth has successfully done, then the ability to posit a positive sense to the necessary divine permission to evil is greatly impaired. That Barth continues to attempt this is a major problem which we have seen emerging in his 'right and left hand of God' motif.[97] We have shown how the problem of dualism which Barth rejects as being outside of God re-emerges as a problem within God Himself because of this motif. If God must of necessity permit evil, then the work of the left hand of God creates problems for the ideas of constancy and holiness which Barth expressed earlier. What has emerged is the idea that evil was so necessary and such a contingent part of creation, and even of God Himself, that the justification of creation, and along with it *of God Himself*, was the necessary work of Christ. This is the fullest expression of the 'necessary antithesis' motif which must stand behind the motif of the 'right and left hand of God'.

---

[95] This is Calvin's point, "providence means not that by which God idly observes from heaven what takes place on earth, but that by which, as keeper of the keys, He governs all events." (Calvin, *Institutes of the Christian Religion, op. cit.,* pp. 201-202)

[96] See CD II/1, p. 595.

[97] Berkouwer sees this as well and he takes exception to the idea in Barth that permission is somehow a necessary aspect in the divine will. "His [Barth's] identification of the idea of God's permission with the notion of concessions, and his accent on the Divine *necessity* of permission are fruits of speculation. They give a solution which only raises further problems at another point." (*Providence of God, op. cit.,* p. 140, emphasis mine)

The Justification of Creation in Barth's 'Noetic Eschatology'

God has created and has said 'Yes' to His creation, and within that 'Yes' lies the rejection of the 'No', and the justification of creation.[98] In contrasting the 'Yes' with the 'No' of God, Barth must hold that that which God has rejected He "cannot even tolerate as a reality distinct from Himself."[99] Here again we see the two roles of evil in relationship to God. We have been told that evil is a necessary result of creation, it is the tool of God, the instrument in service to Him. We have had evil described as a servant, as a role player in the will of God, and at all times as that which derives from the left-hand of God. Now we see the other side of evil as that which God cannot tolerate and which Barth describes as being wholly in battle against God, His dire enemy and powerful foe. Barth paints a picture of the power of evil which can only be defeated by the sacrifice of God's own Son, destroying it on Golgatha. Yet after this, evil is suddenly returned to the role of servant, given a role in the life of the Church and

---

[98] It is noted here how Barth's understanding of the 'good' of creation is similar to and yet differs with the optimism of the 18th century as best articulated by G. W. Leibniz's *Essays de Theodicée* of 1710 (London: Routledge and Kegan Paul, 1952). This is the philosophical counterpart for what Barth sees as the goodness in creation and Barth is far from unsympathetic to Leibnizian optimism stating, "He [Leibniz] must be taken seriously in dogmatics because he too, although in a very different way, tried to sing, and in his own way did in fact sing, the unqualified praise of God the Creator in His relationship to the creature." (CD III/1, p. 405) Despite this, Barth criticises Leibniz for attempting to assimilate evil, sin and death into human existence and for taking the positive aspects of creation too lightly. This is a key epistemological point as Barth finds this form of 18th century optimism as having only the anthropocentric reference in creation and man as the basis for its understanding of good and evil. The sphere in which it sought to understand both sides was fundamentally restricted to human judgement. Thus the goodness of creation had to be intrinsic to it and evil was merely the privation of this good. The two were seen in balance in this system and neither could be taken wholly seriously or regarded in their unconditional reality. What is missing is the transcendence of God above the judgement of man. Barth saw the replacement of the sovereignty of God with the sovereignty of man and the insulation of the optimists' thesis as its ultimate downfall. It was the Church's lack of a Christocentric epistemology and theology, which pre-dated Leibniz, which paved the way for the Enlightenment and its rejection of this dual system. If we are to keep from making the same mistake again, we must ensure that covenant and creation, nature and grace, revelation of creation and revelation of salvation all remain inextricably linked together and revealed solely in Jesus Christ. If this knowledge is able to be found elsewhere, it will relegate the Christian message to a footnote.

[99] CD III/1, p. 331.

viewed as impotent and heading for annihilation. All of this produces a confused picture of evil as Barth is presenting it.[100]

Creation and Covenant and the Justification of Evil

In this confusion we must see that Barth is seeking to maintain the critical link between creation and covenant such that to deny it is to bring into question any benefit of creation at all. This is the error of Marcion[101] and Schopenhauer,[102] for if you ignore the covenant, there is no benefit in creation, and without the cross the benevolence of the Creator can be seriously questioned. The covenant must be seen as the eternal will of God demonstrated before creation in the election of Jesus Christ.[103] For only if the Creator came and stood in total solidarity as a fellow creature with His fallen creation to save it

---

[100] We need only compare pages 287-288 to p. 331 in CD III/1 to see a striking example of how Barth can define evil as both intolerable and inimical to God, and as that which God uses freely in the administration of His own righteousness.

[101] See CD III/1, pp. 334-335. Barth argues that Marcion, in seeing creation as the origin of sheer darkness and horror, of falsehood, shame and evil, focuses on a counterfeit covenant. Marcion's docetic Christ makes null and void his attempt to interpret creation from a covenantal stance. His overemphasis of the divinity of Christ at the full expense of His humanity caused Marcion to elevate the New Testament over the Old and restricted him from finding the true Christ in the history of Israel. So creation was carried out by the inferior God of the Old Testament who was confronted and overcome by the true God in Jesus Christ in the New. Marcion did not, then, err by separating creation from covenant, but his radical misinterpretation of the covenant along highly docetic lines made the outcome of his theology equally flawed. (See also pp. 337-338)

[102] See CD III/1, pp. 335-340. Schopenhauer saw the world and creation as an idea which is objectifiable as will and action. Because this will is the will for life itself, in its aimless striving after the better life, it will manifest itself as suffering. Far from the 'best of all possible worlds', for Schopenhauer this is as bad as it can possibly be, and any talk of optimism is absurd in the face of the depth and inevitability of human suffering. It can only be addressed through the renunciation, quietude and resignation taught my Christian mysticism. Barth criticises Schopenhauer for being "as godless as Marcion's view is world-less." (p. 338) Schopenhauer sees the world from a God-less point of view. What he sees is the actuality of the world without the covenant in all of its abstractness and evil. He sees what man has wrought upon himself outside of the grace and love of God. He sees plainly the suffering of man and the seeming depravity of creation, but he sees all of this in its abstractness, i.e., outside of the reality of the revelation of God in Christ. Seen concretely from the standpoint of the covenant in Christ (not the docetic Christ) creation is seen differently and in its proper form in its relation to the Creator and His commitment to His creation in Christ. Thus to view creation abstractly and not concretely will lead to one or the other of these two heretical views.

[103] "For this reason it cannot be denied that the triumph of *creation* is of one piece with the triumph of *election*." (Berkouwer, *Triumph of Grace, op. cit.,* p. 60)

and bring it back to Himself, only in this Christian scenario can creation be seen as the great benefit of God's loving-kindness.

> The fact that this covenant and union came into being shows the benefit enjoyed by the creature as such because bestowed in the act of creation... We have to realize that any loosening or obscuring of the bond between creation and covenant necessarily entails a threat to this statement, and that it collapses altogether if this bond is dissolved.[104]

Simply put, "where the covenant is no longer seen in the creation, or the creation in the covenant, the affirmation that creation is benefit cannot be sustained."[105] This critical position bears heavily on a modern day theodicy, for the goodness of creation is the starting point for many critics of Christianity's God. Barth must be credited with providing a helpful insight into the centrality of the cross not only in response to the human suffering in contemporary society, but in answer to the questions of the goodness of creation itself. It fits again with his soteriological picture which puts the decision to save humanity in Jesus Christ back into the eternal self-determination of God and it ties together his section on election with that of creation, justifying the placing of the former in respect to the latter.[106]

In a way, Barth can be said to describe providence as the preservation and maintenance of the theatre of creation until all of drama of salvation history is complete.[107] Providence has a two-fold relationship to the special salvific

---

[104] CD III/1, p. 332.

[105] Ibid. p. 334.

[106] This tie between election and creation is rejected by some who see it as an attempt to justify the bad as a necessary by-product to bring about good. Or worse, to see the decision to do good made at any price. If God is seen here in Barth's theology to have decided to create and save His creation regardless of the suffering which that would entail, then for the likes of Berdyaev and Dostoyevski, God is not the God of love. This idea lead Berdyaev to state, "There is nothing more evil than the determination to create good, no matter what the cost." (Berdyaev, *The Realm of the Spirit and the Realm of Caesar,* (London: Centenary Press, 1949), p. 94) It also lead Dostoyevski, through the voice of Ivan Karamazov in his confrontation of the God of his brother Alyosha, to conclude, "If the sufferings of children go to make up the the sum of sufferings which is necessary for the purchase of truth, then I say beforehand that the entire truth is not worth such a price." (Dostoyevski, *The Brothers Karamazov, op. cit.,* p. 285) This idea will be taken up in more detail later. Here we must see that the tie between election and creation, and on to reconciliation as the justification for creation and its consequent sufferings and evils does not solve the whole problem of theodicy for Barth.

[107] "The created cosmos including man, or man within the created cosmos, is this theatre of the great acts of God in grace and salvation. With a view to this he is God's servant, instrument and material. But the theatre obviously cannot be the subject of the work enacted upon it. It can only make it externally possible." (CD III/3, p. 48) Barth also calls creation a mirror as in the same way the mirror only reflects an image

history of the covenant. On the one side, it maintains the world until the grace of God made manifest in the special history of the covenant becomes universally revealed. The preservation of creation from nothingness is the link between providence and salvation.[108] On the other side, providence does not reduce the history of the covenant to a single common denominator with general world history. There is an 'astonishingly thin line' which separates world history under God's providence from covenant history under His predestination in election. The former must be seen in its relationship to the latter and not *vice versa*, for in the end the line of world history will run in the same direction as the line of the history of the covenant. For Barth, "This is the theme of the doctrine of providence."[109]

Although creation history and covenant history are two distinct lines, they are connected and coordinated and stand in a positive relationship to one another. For they both came from God in His faithfulness and thus they are, while distinct, also indivisible.

---

and is never the subject of the image. (Ibid., p. 49) Moltmann takes great exception with Barth's view of creation as the *theatrum gloriae Dei*, and especially in the form it takes here. If creation is the theatre, Moltmann asks why the entire theatre itself is not also the subject of the drama, for are we not to expect a new heaven and a new *earth*? It is in Moltmann's later writings, where he is becoming increasingly concerned for the cultivation of an understanding of the transformation of all creation in the second coming, and our subsequent responsibility for God's creation and stewardship of it, that Moltmann finds reasons for attack of Barth here. This is seen in one of Moltmann's strongest challenges where he writes, "Barth certainly tries to 'see together' things that are in fact incomparable: the *gloria Dei* and the *theatre mundi*; the eternal light and the little created lights. But this is only possible if (to keep to the stage metaphor) the theatre itself is part of the play that is being performed. It is impossible if the theatre is declared to be merely the 'setting and background' for the drama. But in the theological context, the theatre and the play are one and the same, because the drama of salvation is only played out once-once and for all." (Moltmann, *God in Creation, op. cit.*, p. 62) Yet this must be seen as an over-use of this metaphor against Barth's position. For Barth, too, sees a new heaven and a new earth, but he is using this metaphor for creation to illustrate the activity of man in relationship to God. In doing so he does not, by implication, deny the role of all creation in the coming new day of the Son. It may be good for Moltmann to issue such a criticism merely for the sake of ensuring that the proper balance is maintained in this idea of the theatre of the glory of God, but his criticism of Barth is far too rigorous at this point based on the whole of what Barth has to say of creation.

[108] Berkouwer is helpful here. "The doctrine concerning divine preservation [Barth's] does not teach a metaphysical, neutral *conservatio* or *sustenatio*, but a *servatio*, a *rescue from* and *out of* the danger by which the creature would be overwhelmed and turned into a chaos-element if only its *own* power *existed* to protect it. Preservation as *salvation*-that is the theme around which Barth's doctrine of providence is concentrated." (*Triumph of Grace, op. cit.*, pp. 70-71)

[109] CD III/3, p. 36.

The faithfulness of God is that He co-ordinates creaturely occurrence under His lordship with the occurrence of the covenant, grace and salvation, that He subordinates the former to the latter and makes it serve it, that He integrates it with the coming of His kingdom in which the whole of the reality distinct from Himself has its meaning and historical substance, that He causes it to co-operate in this happening.[110]

Because all of creation is made serviceable to the grace and will of God in this inner connection between world history and the history of the covenant, all creation can be called 'good'. We recall that Barth has said that even the imperfections in creation are 'good' because they are able to be used by God to bring about His will and good purposes for creation.[111] This is a return to that point, now under the providence of God. Yet here it is given an even more positive role. In God's providence He uses and co-ordinates creation in all of its imperfection into His work and His kingdom. "He causes it to co-operate in the history of this kingdom, this is the rule of His providence."[112] Thus His

---

[110] Ibid. p. 41.

[111] It is important to distinguish Barth's idea here of God's turning evil into good from that of 'Process Theology' which features this as a central idea in their cosmology. Process theology return to a quasi-equilibrium which Barth has rejected in his challenges to Schleiermacher and Leibniz. In process thought, evil is both good and bad, "Evil is positive and destructive." (W. Whitla, 'Sin and Redemption in Whitehead and Teilhard de Chardin', in *Anglican Theological Review*, Volume 47, January 1965, p. 84) Whitla comments that Whitehead sees evil as 'good in itself'. This good comes about as evil plays its role in creation through the process of creative transmutation. This transmutation is the work of God, turning what is for Whitehead an equal component of the universe, evil, into the good. The struggle in which God is at work turning evil into good makes evil "an element to be woven immortally into the rhythm of mortal things." (A.N. Whitehead, *Religion in the Making*, Northrop and Gross, p. 526) In this way, both good and evil are realities of the created world. Whitla can conclude, "Evil, then, in the process-way world-view, is as necessary to the development of the cosmos as evolution." (Whitla, p. 90) We have shown Barth's rejection of evil as 'positive' and 'necessary' in the process way of thinking. God's turning of evil into good is an act of total grace which is both unmerited and which should be always unexpected. Evil is not necessary for the good development of humanity, but it nonetheless is the inevitable result of creation. For this reason, because of the inevitability of the Fall, God has chosen to save His creation through the Cross, and in it evil is changed to good. The key distinguishing feature is that while evil can, in this sense, be said to be the 'necessary antithesis' to God, it is never anything but the inimical foe to be routed and extirpated. It never takes on the form of good or positive because it is never considered in a state of equality or equilibrium with creation. By keeping this critical distinction in mind, we can see how Barth can use the motif of a 'necessary antithesis' and how he can talk at length of God's turning evil into good, while avoiding any identification with process theology.

[112] CD III/3, pp. 42-43.

providence is not only sustaining and furthering creation, but bringing the imperfection of creation into line with His will and work.[113]

In keeping the covenant and creation together under God's providential care, Barth can posit creation as justification in the sense that what God has created is good and as such God has justified it. Creation is the best it can possibly be as it was created as the theater of the glory of God. It is God and His judgement which justify creation in this way despite the seeming contradiction in our world of the goodness or perfection in which we were created.[114] Yet despite the goodness of creation and God's justification of it, the one thing which is better than creation as it was made is *creation as it will become*. The fellowship and participation of creation with the Creator made available in the covenant is the greater goal towards which the good creation now moves. "The only thing which can be better than what is by God (apart from God Himself) is what is to develop out of what is in its communion and encounter with God. The only thing which can be better than creaturely existence is the goal of the covenant for which the creature is determined in and with its creation."[115]

God created and justified His creation with a view to its future glorification in the achievement of the goal of the covenant, namely Jesus Christ.[116] Again Barth is seeking to justify creation through its inextricable link with the salvific work of Jesus Christ as the goal of the covenant. When creation is seen in the work of the Son, it is genuinely and in the widest sense of the term beneficent. Barth's realism allows him to see that God's view and our view are wholly different in this respect. That which we see as marred, sinful and corrupt God

---

113 Whitehouse has correctly seen this vital connection and provides the well-phrased comment, "*Creatio*, in other words, is preceded by a *servatio*, and guaranteed by a *conservatio*." (*The Authority of Grace, op. cit.,* p. 38)

114 This view is in direct opposition to the modern day 'protest theodicies' which advocate a provocative response by humanity to the seeming senselessness and waste of an apparently less than wholly sovereign God. We find this in Moltmann, Dostoyevski, and most recently in John Roth who writes, "Everything hinges on the proposition that God possesses-but fails to use well enough-the power to intervene decisively at any moment to make history's course less wasteful. Thus, in spite and because of his sovereignty, this God is everlastingly guilty and the degrees run from gross negligence to murder." He continues later, "the fact remains: the net result of God's choices is that the world is more wild and wasteful than any good reason that we can imagine would require it to be. Thus, to be for such a God requires some sense of being against him as well." (John Roth, 'A Theodicy of Protest', in *Encountering Evil: Live Options in Theodicy*, ed. Stephen Davis, Atlanta: John Knox Press, 1981, pp. 16, 19) Only by taking the 'right' to judge ourselves, can we find such room for protest, and this line of reasoning must be kept in sharp distinction from Barth's understanding of the justification of creation and the Creator.

115 CD III/1, p. 366.

116 "If we enquire into the goal of creation, the object of the whole, the object of heaven and earth and all creation, I can say only that it is to be the theatre of His glory... this purpose of God 'justifies' Him as the Creator." (Barth, *Dogmatics in Outline, op. cit.,* p. 58)

views from the vista of the covenant of grace. Therefore our response is to rejoice and praise God for His creation regardless of how god-less it may seem to us, and "to accept its silent or negative testimony, and thus to recognise its perfection not only in individual details but in its totality."[117] Without the 'Yes' of God in the goal of the covenant, the 'No' would compromise any understanding of the goodness of God and, consequently, of His creation. The 'No', therefore, echoes, underlines and gives force to the 'Yes'.

The Problem of the Divine Accompanying

Any proper understanding of the concept of the 'freedom of humanity' in Barth's theology must accommodate his view of God's divine accompanying of humanity's decisions; a view which in turn is deeply influenced by the motif of the 'right and left hand of God'. That God accompanies humanity means that every moment of life is a momentary preservation, that God affirms humanity in his God-given autonomy, and that God accompanies humanity as its Lord. This lordship precedes humanity (*praecurrit*), accompanies humanity (*concurrit*) and follows humanity (*succurrit*). In interpreting this difficult subject it is important to see that these three 'moments' of the lordship of God form a dialectic in the sense that each in itself can represent the whole of God's lordship without taking anything away from the other two. Thus Barth can say that everything necessary to humanity's salvation happened in the *praecurrit* without diminishing the role of the *concurrit* or *succurrit*. This is his attempt to show how God's lordship is complete in each, without inferring any subordination in the process.[118]

This lordship is defined by Barth in seemingly highly deterministic terms. According to the *praecurrit,* God rules over humanity "with the absoluteness which is possible only for the Creator ruling over the creature. This is how it is provided that His will is done on earth as it is in heaven, that nothing may or can take place as the action of the creature which is not in a very definite sense His own action."[119] God created the pre-conditions and even the pre-pre-conditions for all of the works and ways of the creature. Yet the foreordinations of God are sovereign and, because they are *His*, they are gracious and work for humanity's exaltation. The one freedom allowed to the creature is the freedom to be wholly and fully the creature as God created him in the fulness of His divine will.

This freedom is given its context of operation in the divine *praecurrit*, and in this way it is the freedom of the creature and not its limitation. Of more difficulty is the consideration of the *concurrit* about which Barth remarks, "the 'concurrence' of God with the creature, being His own and absolutely supreme means that the activity of God conditions absolutely the activity of the

---

[117] CD III/1, p. 372.

[118] These categories correspond to the Reformed three-fold doctrine of sustenance, concurrence and government, or preservation, co-operation and government.

[119] CD III/3, p. 93.

creature... and nothing can be done except the will of God."[120] Yet Barth is not embracing a wholly deterministic understanding of God's lordship, for the freedom of the creature is maintained, but in its defined limits.

The key for Barth is in the proper understanding of the God who is the Accompanier. Since this God is defined in Christian terms, since He is the gracious Father of the eternal Son, His will is only that of fatherly good-will. Here Barth maintains the subject-predicate order where God's work is according to His grace towards us.[121] Barth can conclude that the action of God and the action of humanity not as two separate operations but a single action under the *concurses simultaneus.*

The idea of cause and effect must also be altered when used in this context.[122] The creaturely activity which corresponds to the divine lordship of the Father cannot be thought of merely as effect, and in the same way the almightiness of this God cannot even in the fulness of His rule and lordship destroy the free activity of the creature. That is, the free activity to be the creature of the Creator, to live in obedience and respond to the gift of grace with a life of witness and service. The true freedom of the creature in its relationship with its Creator is given to it in its fulness when it is under the supreme lordship of its Creator.[123]

---

[120] Ibid. p. 113.

[121] C.E. Gunton makes a critical distinction in this sense in linking the freedom to the creature under this determination of the *concurses* to Barth's understanding of the revelation of God in the Trinity as over against a modalistic God, "there is all the difference between determination by a triune God, who, because he has space in himself, can therefore give to his creatures space to live in, and by an abstract, impersonal control, whether that control be a unitary God or a mechanical universe (and, as Samuel Taylor Coleridge saw, they are essentially the same). According to Barth, creation is a giving of space for autonomous human reality; reconciliation the work of omnipotence of the cross within that authentically worldly space. The creaturely person is not violated by the action of God as Son and Spirit. In reconciliation, therefore, we are *determined* to be the children of God, but not... *compelled.*" (Gunton, 'The triune God and the freedom of the creature', *op. cit.,* pp. 58-59)

[122] Barth's view is similar to the Reformed understanding of 'second causes', where for instance Heppe points out that God does not use second causes in an instrumentalist way, for God is not limited to second causes as a vehicle for working His will. "So second causes are related to the governing activity of God not merely passively, but also actively, since God is active in them not 'subjectively' but 'effectually'." (*Reformed Dogmatics, op. cit.,* p. 261)

[123] Whitehouse sees this clearly in Barth, "This particular Christian doctrine of the divine *concurses*, which matters so much, yet is so hard to state, makes sense only with the belief that in every creaturely event there is an *encounter* of two radically different realities, an encounter such as we know about in our own meeting with God by means of His Word and Spirit. Can we understand the general workings of God, with and over His creatures, from that focus? It is the obligation to do so which faith recognizes... which has produced the elements of this doctrine-that all creaturely

Since God's lordship over His creation is a fatherly operation, it requires the corresponding work of the people of God which is unconditional and irresistible, meaningful and not empty, freeing and not binding.

> We can therefore conclude our exposition of the *concurses simultaneus*, the sovereign and overruling accompanying of the creature by the divine operation, with the proposition that even under this divine lordship the rights and honour and dignity and freedom of the creature are not suppressed and extinguished but vindicated and revealed.[124]

Finally the *succurrit* follows from the first two in that God not only controls the pre-conditions of human action and works in and through all human actions, but he also controls the effect of human actions.[125] "God accompanies the activity of the creature as its Creator and Lord. And this means that even the effects of this activity, even the changes brought about by it, are still subject to His disposing and control."[126]

If this is Barth's position on the sovereignty of the lordship of God and the freedom of the creature, then we ask about the impact this view has on God Himself? Barth holds that God, in His lordship over His creature, is simply acting out the work of His 'right hand' and the work of His 'left hand' in His creation. Can we therefore take seriously any idea of a battle with evil in a world so all-determined by God? Can we envisage a situation in this picture where evil could ever win, and if not, is there really a battle at all, or is Barth parading a 'straw man' under the guise of evil?[127] This criticism emerges here in Barth's use of the 'right and left hand of God'.

A second problem arises where Barth has maintained that the *homo lapsus* was not willed by God. However, given what he has said here, can we envisage the Fall in any respect outside of the will and work of God? Surely humanity cannot be said to have acted in a way outside His will, beyond His control, or not in accordance with the *concurrit*. If Barth has made God a co-author of every decision made by humanity is there left any room for responsibility for sin outside of God Himself? Fiddes finds only these options available concerning sin, "Either it was something strange to God, or it was an instrument for the

---

being is good, and to the glory of God, and directly produced by His action out of the richness of His grace, and yet is produced as the proper act of the creature, achieved in genuine freedom and spontaneity." (*Authority of Grace, op. cit.,* p. 40)

[124] CD III/3, p. 145.

[125] Heppe makes this point, "By government all things are so guided by God that they serve the purpose of the world and thereby achieve their own purpose." (*Reformed Dogmatics, op. cit.,* p. 262)

[126] CD III/3, p. 152.

[127] Barth states for example, "there has to be confessed as in no other teaching the absolute superiority with which God controls and conquers nothingness even in the form of human sin, not in any sense being arrested by it, but setting it to serve His own glory, and the work of His free love." (CD IV/2, p. 398)

good, necessary for man's moral growth and development, part... of God's providential 'plan'."[128] Barth's emphasis on the justification of the Creator, of the permission of evil and of all human suffering which results from sin must be seen as his attempts to justify God Himself in the face of just this sort of dilemma.

Along similar lines the motif of Barth's 'noetic eschatology' is employed in the dilemma found in Barth's view of the Divine Ruling. In this Divine Ruling, God rules the world by ordering it, He Himself is the goal of His ruling, and therefore "He rules in transcendence over the cosmic antitheses of freedom and necessity."[129] In ordering the world God controls creaturely activity meaning that God makes creaturely activity correspond to His own activity. Thus our activity is free in that it is the activity of God, for we as creatures are given permission by God to exercise the freedom given to us in our co-action in God's work. Our freedom, which is given to us as a series of permissive acts, is truly freedom because these acts are controlled by God. In this way Barth finds no contradiction between the sovereignty of God and the freedom of the creature.

> Both in general and in particular God Himself fixes for the creature its goals, that is, the goals that it will actually attain. In one way or another it will ultimately realize the divine decree. This, then, is the divine order of world-occurrence; the controlling of creaturely activity in its execution and also its results. Since this control is universal, and embraces and concerns all creaturely activity and its effects, *it is actually an ordering of everything that happens.*[130]

This all leads in one direction. God controls and rules all things, including all of the activities of His creation, solely and totally that all creation will move in the direction of its goal,[131] which is "His own glory as Creator, and in it the justification, deliverance, salvation, and, ultimately, the glorification of the creature."[132] Barth anticipates the charge that the world in the time *post-Christum* cannot be seen as moving in a positive direction under the control of God. He counters that this movement of world-occurrence can only be seen through the eyes of faith. Yet God's rule is operative, if hidden, in world-

---

[128] Fiddes, *The Creative Suffering of God, op. cit.,* p. 220.

[129] CD III/3, p. 164.

[130] Ibid. p. 167. (emphasis mine)

[131] The goal of creation in Barth's theology differs quite distinctly from that of orthodox Reformed theology, which is seen most sharply in the earlier discussion of Supralapsarianism. Here we see the results of Barth's re-definition of election. For where Barth can talk of the goal of creation in the union of all humanity in Christ-and that being the essence of the glory of God, Heppe states that "This supreme purpose [of providence] is to glorify God by the blessing of the elect. 'The end of providence is the glory of God and the salvation of the elect, which all subserve'." (*Reformed Dogmatics, op. cit.,* p. 263)

[132] CD III/3, p. 168.

occurrence, just as world-occurrence is subjected to salvation history, although again only in the eyes of faith.[133] The Christian is then distinguished from the non-Christian by what he or she sees and knows including the understanding of evil as an already defeated foe whose annihilation will be revealed in the final *parousia*.

God's Use of Evil and Human Suffering

A final word must be said here regarding the role of evil in Barth's doctrine of providence with regards to the suffering it brings. We have set out five categories of suffering in Chapter I and we must revisit them here in order to help us define more closely what Barth is proposing. These categories which we have developed are intended to serve as a framework in which Barth's doctrine of evil can be analysed with regard to its particular view of suffering. Thus far it has been apparent that Barth's overall intent is to justify the presence of evil in creation through the salvific work of God in Christ as the foundation and eternal

---

[133] Barth spoke of a divine ordering in his earlier polemical writings in *Against the Stream*. Speaking of the problem of poverty he wrote, "Throughout the Bible, however, the fact that there are both rich men and poor, in either sense of the word, appears to be a kind of divine ordering of events, which ordinance must serve as a basis for all further thought - just as in this world we have to accept the facts of illness, war, and other such human deeds of violence, without question and without concerning ourselves with ideas of an essentially 'better future'." (*Against the Stream,* (London: SCM Press, 1954), p. 243) Barth goes on to say that poverty is a result of sin, and yet God associates Himself with the poor, requiring the rich to be like the poor in dependence. Here there can be seen the early and deep respect Barth had for the sovereignty of God and the idea of the divine ordering under God's providence. This idea of divine ordering is also seen in two other writings worth mentioning here. In *Fragments Grave and Gay* Barth is discussing with a group of the *Bruderholz* the appeal to the German Churches made in response to the rise of Hitler. He is bemoaning the church's deaf ear which was turned towards these warnings, and he concludes that the Church of Germany should have heeded these warnings, "But God willed otherwise." Similarly, in response to a question put to him by one of those attending (Herr Weitbrecht) concerning the use of the State by God, Barth concluded, "The State somehow functioned on the left hand of God." (*Fragments Grace and Gay,* (London: Collins Fontana, 1971), pp. 76-77) We also see this in his address to the first Assembly of the World Council of Churches where, in speaking of the refusal of Rome and Moscow to join the Assembly, he commented, "Why should we not simply recognize in these refusals the mighty hand of God outstretched over us?... I propose that we should now praise and thank God, that it pleases Him to stand so clearly in the way of our plans." (Barth, 'The World's Disorder and God's Design', in *Congregational Quarterly*, Volume 27, 1949, p. 14) Finally, we see this idea of God's ordering in a comment Barth made in his tract *Theological Existence Today* where, in discussing the correction of the errors of the Church, he uses the phrase, "*hominum confusione et Dei providentia* (by the blundering of men and the providence of God)." (*Theological Existence Today, op. cit.*, p. 29)

decree of God. However, as we have asked before, if this answers (perhaps) the 'why?' of evil, then to where do we turn for the answer to the 'why so much?' Again the issue is confused in part because of the lack of identification of suffering in Barth's theology along the lines of the categories we have posited. Therefore, we will look at what Barth has said about suffering and relate it to the appropriate category. Only in this way do we believe that we can construct a clear enough picture of suffering in Barth's doctrine of evil to enable us in the end to formulate a 'Barthian theodicy'.

1. *Suffering as the result of (wages of) sin* Barth has posited a clear tension between the 'impossibility' of sin and its 'inevitability'. By doing so, he can see the election of Jesus Christ as *homo labilis* and yet hold humanity wholly responsible for sin. In this way Barth can still affirm the suffering for humanity as a result of its sin. If God were made the Author of sin, there would scarcely be any justification for suffering as a result of sin, and the protest cries of the likes of Berdyaev, Camus and Dostoyevski would be unanswerable. If humanity is responsible for sin (because of its impossibility), then when it is manifested (as it must be according to its inevitability) suffering results.

When nothingness crosses the frontier and enters creation, it brings the chaos and threat which God rejected at creation. However, as much as this chaos is allowed (under divine permission) to operate in this way, it is always limited and under the full sway of the providence of God. This is the best illustration of the divine permission, simply an allowing of evil to operate according to the open door given to it by humanity's rebellion. And as a result we suffer.[134] It is the divine love in operation which creates good out of human suffering for sin. Therefore, evil is allowed to operate under the limiting control of the left hand of God, but it can never escape its ultimate use of it to bring about the good work of His right hand. It is and can be put to such a use because it is the defeated enemy, and as such is God's instrument even when it is permitted to be so apparently harmful to His creation.

2. *Suffering as chastisement and correction from the hand of God* and

3. *Suffering for the sake of testing and strengthening faith.* These ideas are closely tied to each other in this section. Whether God uses the evil which occurs as a result of sin to chastise and correct, or whether He sends suffering specifically to test and strengthen our faith is uncertain. By his omission of the idea of the 'sending of evils' from his commentary on the Heidelberg Catechism it can be assumed that Barth does not see God's direct sending of evils in this

---

[134] Hauerwas takes issue with this point in recalling his story of the death of a young girl named Carol Wanderhope, concluding, "Even if one assumes rather physicalist accounts of the inheritance of 'original sin', it still does not follow that Carol Wanderhope 'deserved' leukemia; nor does it comfort us to believe that leukemia is the result of humankind's sinfulness and thus denotes the general disruption of God's 'good order'." (Hauerwas, *Naming the Silences, op. cit.,* p. 73) We would disagree to the extent that disease and death are the result of sin which in fact creates a disruption of God's 'good order'. Whether or not this brings comfort depends on your view of God's future, and we hear Barth saying that God will justify all things in that future, including disease and death.

way, but instead of His bending of the suffering we bring on ourselves to be a correction and chastening rod for our good.[135] Again there is not an inherent conflict with the 'right and left hand of God' motif here, for what God allows under His left hand He then brings into the service of His right hand.

4. *Suffering as a result of our faith and faithful obedience.* Little has been said here on this topic, but at first it seems to fit well within Barth's general understanding of suffering under the divine providence. Because evil is allowed in the world, the suffering of the Christian is an inevitable state which should not be shunned but accepted. Our suffering as allowed by God again works for our good and thus is a comfort. We do not think ill of God because the evil we suffer is from (permitted by) His left hand, for the same permitted evil crucified Christ, and we suffer with Him. Here, however, lies the problem. In what sense can we see evil, nothingness, as the true enemy of God? Is there room left, in light of the overwhelming sense of control Barth has articulated here in the divine providence, for a truly inimical sense of evil? If we posit that evil is not inimical to God but only His creation, we must return to Barth's point that God became vulnerable in His creation.

If it costs God the life of His Son to defeat evil in creation, if this was the price that had to be paid, if this is the risk that God took, then can we continue to find the source of this nothingness in the providential control of God's left hand without either, 1) robbing evil of any and all real evilness or 2) creating a dualism in God? Barth has strongly criticized both Schleiermacher and Leibniz for watering down the seriousness of evil and its consequences, yet can he escape a similar, if restated criticism? If he is to give to evil the depth of wretchedness it requires to be Scripturally correct, and as we will see, if he requires us to understand the depth of evil from the horrors of the cross, then the duality in God which results is a problem for Barth.

5. *Suffering as a result of the sinful state of the world in which we live.* By now it is clear that all suffering falls under the providence of God either by the right or left hand. The allowance of evil effects the guilty and the 'innocent', and it results in natural and moral evil. Barth will not have us focus on the evil itself, but on the justification for it, for all creation, in God's eternal self-determination for be 'for' His creation in Jesus Christ. Barth's entire theodicy is dependent upon this justification! He can only hold to an absolute sovereignty and this resultant doctrine of providence if the God who is sovereign and providentially reigns is the God of the cross.[136] This he has done and his answer to the theodicy question hangs upon it.

---

[135] In his commentary on the *Heidelberg Catechism* Barth rewords the phrase from Question 26, "Moreover, the evils he sends upon me in this troubled life he will turn for good," into "He governs also over evil which, though it does not come from Him, has the dangerous being of non-being." In this way Barth seems to sidestep the direct implications of the original wording of the catechism. (*The Heidelberg Catechism for Today, op. cit.,* pp. 59-61)

[136] This answer to theodicy is one which is rejected by theologians like Moltmann who will allow no justification of suffering. Yet this is a philosophical protest along

the lines of Berdyaev, Camus and Dostoyevski. It is also found in Dorothee Soelle, *Suffering*, (Philadelphia: Fortress Press, 1975). The question at the heart of this rejection, and one which will feature strongly in our conclusion, is the seriousness of this earthly life. Where the *parousia* is dismissed as being unable to justify earthly suffering, Barth's position in untenable. We will seek to show that this, however, is an invalid criticism.

CHAPTER VI

Das Nichtige

The Limited Scope of CD III/3 § 50

Barth has formulated his doctrine of creation in direct relationship to chaos, and has shown God's providence as that which preserves us on the frontier of nothingness and which wards off the peril of its evil and death. Now Barth directly addresses the nature and role of nothingness itself as that which, although repelled by God, still constantly threatens to corrupt us. In view of this, the brevity of our chapter on this all-important subject must be addressed.

The development of his doctrine of evil has been given fundamental and structural definition and clarity in his doctrines of God, election, creation and providence which point to the folly of attempting to understand Barth's doctrine of evil by looking only, or even primarily to his section on *das Nichtige*. Barth's intention here was not to take up the subject of evil for the first or even the definitive time. Instead he sought to provide clarity on the role of evil within the creation especially as it relates to his insistence on a shadowy side of the created world. This section, with its very narrow and defined purpose, has mistakenly been treated as the best and final word from Barth on evil. It is instead simply a further exposition on a topic which has been an integral part of his theology from the beginning, and which here receives yet another treatment with regards to the 'good' of creation. Therefore we find only a few new pieces of new information here which we have set out in this brief but important chapter.

Language and Nothingness

Barth begins this section with a most extraordinary statement in speaking of nothingness in relation to providence, "We did not take into account that it is not only inimical to the creature and its nature and existence, but *above all to God Himself* and His will and purpose."[1] At the start of this important discussion Barth raises what is for him a real dilemma when he seeks to articulate the true reality of the extremes of the 'right and left hand of God' in his doctrine of evil. For as we have seen, the tension between the servanthood and defeat of evil on the one hand, and the imposing threat of evil on the other, is difficult for Barth to maintain. To this he adds a second conundrum. If on the one hand God's lordship is acknowledged in its supreme sovereignty as lordship over nothingness, then how do you keep nothingness from deriving from the positive will and work of God? The other option is equally troublesome, that it should instead derive solely from the activity of the creature. This is the

---

[1] CD III/3, p. 290. (emphasis mine)

theodicy question in other terms, for Barth asks here "How can justice be done both to the holiness and omnipotence of God when we are faced with the problem of nothingness?"[2]

By putting the question in this format Barth is able to say that nothingness neither proceeds from the positive will of God nor from the creature, but from the non-willing of God. It is only because it comes from the left hand of God, from His 'No', from that which He has not-willed, that nothingness can take on that unique character of being both wholly under the lordship and control of God, originating, existing, operating, armed, empowered and permitted solely and fully by Him, while at the same time exonerating God of all responsibility for its origin, existence, operation, power and actions. In addition, evil is also hostile, a true threat, wholly inimical, a dreaded enemy and a 'serious antagonist' *(schlechthinnige Ungehörigkeit)*, not only to creation but to God Himself. All of this is maintained within this 'right and left hand of God' motif. Yet we have seen how difficult this position is for Barth to maintain, for what comes from God from His right hand, the place of Jesus Christ, and His left hand, the place of Satan and his kingdom, are both from God, according to His will, even if positive and negative, and, as we have shown beyond all doubt, according to His eternal will and in line with His goal for creation. In the face of these critical dilemmas, Barth re-introduces the fourth motif of his 'revelatory positivism' under the banner of the brokenness of theological language.

Theology faces a unique problem in articulating its belief concerning God's lordship and nothingness, for while we are transformed by the former, we remain bound up in the latter. The fact that we are influenced by the very subject we are trying to study, indeed that we are under its power and corrupted by its sway over us, means that we cannot expect to produce a tight and complete dogmatic statement with regards to it. All of our talk takes on a uniquely and necessarily broken and incomplete character when we attempt to deal with that which so influences us. "It may be said at least that it can be so only as we soberly acknowledge that we have here an extraordinarily clear demonstration of the necessary brokenness of all theological thought and utterance *(notwendigen Gebrochenheit alles theologischen Denkens und Redens)*."[3]

Even finding the correct term is problematic. By using *das Nichtige* Barth sought to define this nothingness not as a negative entity, as in Augustine, nor as a mental illusion. Instead he sought to give to it its true identity as that which exists only by virtue of its negation. Barth knows from the outset that even naming and defining this nothingness in its 'peculiar ontology' is fraught with difficulties.[4] For this reason this talk must be 'logically inconsequent',

---

[2] Ibid. p. 292.

[3] Ibid. p. 293, and KD III/3, p. 332.

[4] G. V. Jones, writing on God and Negation in Barth's theology, stated, "because we have to reckon with it [*das Nichtige*] we cannot speak simply of God's direct relationship to His creation in terms of straight vertical lines *(geraden Strichen von oben nach unten)*, for this negational element originates neither in the Creator nor in the creature... And in so far as it is a creative activity theology itself must admit that

and the contradictions posed by it must be consigned to the *"mysterium iniquitatis."*[5] This is so because the subject, nothingness and its operation, are objectively the break in the relationship of humanity and God in the covenant. It is both the frontier at which creation is poised and the break itself between the creature and its Creator. For this reason we are swayed by it especially when we seek to objectify and articulate it.

Using this motif, Barth can say that, in the end, all theology is a record of the history of this break which he defines as the fundamental basis for the history of the covenant and of theology's role as the witness to that history. So in talking of nothingness, we must reject all attempts at a systemization and stay true to the role of theology as a 'report'; a report on covenant history, the history of this break, and here more specifically on the break itself.[6] This idea of the impact of nothingness upon all theological discussion brings us back to the principle role of faith, God's lordship *must* be believed despite all existential evidence to the contrary. Because of this brokenness of theological language, we must set aside all expectations that a reconciliation between God's sovereignty and the problem of nothingness can be finally and fully articulated; theological language "must not strain after completedness and compactness."[7]

Barth is saying that in place of a definitive statement of this sort, the absolute lordship of God is the axiomatic *a priori* which is to be accepted in faith in the face of all seeming contradictions and dilemmas. "This is the general and formative answer to the question how the *simple recognition of God's universal lordship* is rightly to be applied in view of the presence of nothingness as opposition and resistance to that lordship."[8]

The question to be asked here regards the role of the Holy Spirit in enabling theological language to actually and accurately expound the Truth. Must we see an impenetrability in evil and thus conclude it to be an inaccessible *ratione* ? The dialectic of revealedness and hiddenness does not give us license to fall back on hiddenness and mystery as a final position, even with regards to evil and nothingness. If there is revelation, if there is revealedness, we must seek answers here in the midst of so much mystery and hiddenness.[9] We must

---

it, too, is in the grip of the negational of the anti-creation, from which it neither can nor may escape." ('God and Negation', in *Scottish Journal of Theology*, Volume 7, September 1954, pp. 233-234)

[5] Barth, *Credo, op. cit.,* pp. 36-37.

[6] *"Eben diese Geschichte, in deren Verlauf sich auch jener Bruch ereignet, is der Gegenstand der Theologie. "* (KD III/3, p. 334)

[7] CD III/3, p. 295.

[8] Ibid. p. 295. (emphasis mine)

[9] Here we can take a lead from Hans Frei who sees in Barth's understanding of revelation a two-tiered system of sorts where there is a language and logic of Christian faith (first-order Christian statements) which takes priority over the pragmatic application of that language to the Christian life (second-order Christian statements). "In other words, the situation of the Church, to Christian life in our culture in our day, is such that Christian subjectivity, or how to become a Christian,

always probe a little further where Barth's theology leads to contradiction and dilemma, regardless of his use of his 'Jobian ace in the hole'.

The 'Necessary Antithesis' as the Ontic[10] Basis of Nothingness

The ontic basis of nothingness is derived from its peculiar nature which, on one side, cannot be identified in any way with God or creation and yet, on the other side, cannot be defined as simply that which is not God nor His creation. Nothingness carries a third nature.[11] It exists in a definitive form with special characteristics. In a classic statement Barth concludes, "Nothingness is not nothing."[12] Barth rejects the idea that nothingness can be dismissed or minimized once it is denied an identification with either God or the creature. It is true nothingness in its own ontology and cannot be dismissed as illusory on the grounds that it is neither created nor divine.[13] Similarly, that God is 'not'

---

must be-not existentially, but theologically-subordinate to the *what* of Christianity." This duality does not, however, form a necessary paradox or contradiction, "No, the internal coherence of the two modes of discourse is fragmentary; its fulness as the logos or rationale of faith, hidden but not absent." (Frei, *Types of Christian Theology, op, cit.,* p.43) This understanding of the hiddenness of the coherence between the reality of our faith and its existential experience in our Christian lives is helpful in seeing how Barth wishes to speak of both not in terms of a contradiction, but in the revelation-terms of revealedness and hiddenness.

10 Berkouwer criticizes Barth's use of the term 'ontology of chaos' on the grounds that it is simply not Scriptural. "Such a conception can never find a legitimate place on the basis of the revelation concerning creation. It bears, rather, the earmarks of speculative thinking wherein the human choice of one possibility, involving the rejection of other possibilities, is transferred to God and is turned into an independent conception from which all kinds of conclusions are drawn." (*Triumph of Grace, op. cit.,* p. 246) This is the heart of the critique of Barth's exegesis of Genesis 1:2 and, especially, of our own critique of his association of the separated darkness with the shadow side of creation. Both ideas are certainly built on speculative exegetical grounds. However, where Barth has had some success in associating the idea of the *tohu wa-bohu* with *das Nichtige*, he certainly has not been successful in identifying the *Nichtige* with *Schattenseite*.

11 This third nature has some similarity with Augustine who saw that evil "is not any substance: for were it a substance, it should be good." And also when he states, "I enquired what iniquity was, and found it to be no substance, but the perversion of the will." (*Confessions, op. cit.,* pp. 122, 124)

12 CD III/3, p. 349.

13 In his book comparing Barth and Schelling, Kurt Lüthi writes, *"Der Sieg des Lichts ist von der heilsgeschichtlichen Mitte her so umfassend, dass sich die von uns empfundenen Probleme als Scheinprobleme enthüllen. Zugespitz gesagt: Barth ist so überwältigt vom Sieg Christi und Hereinbruch der Lichtwelt, dass hier alles Reden und Denken zum Loben und Preisen werden muss; und wo hätte, wenn gelobt wird, Reflexion über abstrakt Böses und über abstrakt Finsternis ihren Raum?"* (*Gott und*

the creature but distinct from it in its necessary non-divinity does not prescribe to the latter the nature of nothingness. This was the error of Leibniz as he confused this non-divinity, the imperfection of creation or, for Barth, the shadowy side of creation, with nothingness.[14]

Barth makes the important point that, "all conceptions and doctrines which view nothingness as an essential and necessary determination of being and existence and therefore of the creature, or as an essential determination of the original and creative being of God Himself, are untenable from the Christian standpoint."[15] This is true. As we have asserted, the 'necessary antithesis' which we have claimed as a recurrent theme in Barth does not make evil and sin a necessary determination of either creation or God. Neither God nor the creature are determined in their being by nothingness. This does not however counter the idea that God is, in a negative sense, defined as God in His self-differentiation from the 'not-God'. God is always the Determiner and never the determined. Yet there is a necessity in this relationship. In the same way, the destiny of the creature and the fulfillment of God's will towards it require that nothingness have its place and role, even if that is a non-willed place and a role as that which is

---

das Böse, (Zurich: Zwingli Verlag, 1961), p. 261) In light of Barth's understanding of the reality of *das Nichtige*, we must reject Lüthi's idea here that Barth's triumphalism creates an illusory sense of evil.

[14] Barth criticises Leibniz for identifying metaphysical evil with the necessary imperfection of the creature in creation, and all suffering and pain as well as pleasure and joy as a product of this necessarily dualistic nature. Thus we can have the best of all possible worlds and evil without reflecting negatively on God. Leibniz sees a very positive role in the imperfect side of the creature, for it is necessary to show the true magnitude of the good side. Good is dependent upon the possibility of sin. In this way, sin is made an important part of creation with a positive role to play. Barth criticises Leibniz for confusing the shadowy side of creation with metaphysical evil, and allowing real Nothingness to masquerade as imperfection. At blame is Leibniz's use of the Augustinian idea of *malum est privatio boni* which loses the radicalness of the *privatio*. Where Augustine saw privation as an attack upon the *boni,* Leibniz has pacified it to a mere privation of good. Nothingness in its radical, detestable and deplorable form ceases to exist in Leibniz's system and in the end, "it is not just nothingness but nothing." (CD III/3, p. 319) What Barth does not point out here is that Leibniz has no theology of the Fall. Therefore to account for evil, man must be created in a state which includes imperfection. This is the key to understanding Leibniz's dualistic nature of the creature and his consequent understanding of sin as privation of the good. For God to be vindicated in Leibniz's picture, for it to be the best of all possible worlds and yet account for evil, man had to be created with this imperfect side and yet that imperfect side must be shown to serve the good purposes of God. It is this reason why it loses its radical form and Barth is quite right to level this critique. Yet he misses the crucial point that Leibniz does not allow for a perfect creation before the Fall. The result is for Leibniz, that the created imperfection must account for sin and evil without implicating God, thus leading him to domesticate nothingness. It is this, rather than a confusion of a shadowy side of creation with nothingness, which accounts for Leibniz's position.

[15] CD III/3, p. 350.

rejected. In this way the Fall is a pre-determined part of the drama of salvation history for which creation was prepared as its theatre and stage. Thus Barth's warning here is sound and does not impair the motif of the 'necessary antithesis'.

Barth reiterates his Christological epistemology as the sole basis for knowledge of nothingness where humanity is incapable of any true knowledge of nothingness independent of God's rejection of it. This is how we know it, we know it defeated, the enemy of God and thus the enemy of His creation. Only because it is against Him is it against us. And only because He is victorious over it can we stand firm in the face of it. Nothingness 'is' only in this way and according to this knowledge. Thus nothingness has an ontic *Wirklichkeit* which is expressed in the way it is revealed to us. As God acts according to His eternal election, He acts in grace and mercy, and also in wrath and judgement. In the latter, God separates Himself from nothingness in the exercise of His positive will. In this separation His wrath is manifested towards nothingness and on this basis, as the rejection and separation by God in His holy activity, nothingness has an ontic 'reality'. Nothingness 'is' only in its negative relationship to the holiness of God, and it has no substance or stability outside of this relationship.[16]

Here again Barth gives us evidence of a 'necessary antithesis' even in God Himself as in the following quote, "Nothingness is that from which *God separates Himself* and in the face of which He asserts His positive will... God wills, and therefore opposes what He does not will. He says Yes, and therefore says No to that to which He has not said Yes."[17] This is not God's activity in the creaturely sphere alone, but in His eternal self-distinction. That He separates not just His creation in Genesis 1:2, but *Himself* from nothingness is a confirmation that Barth is thinking of an eternal subordination of nothingness in the very existence of God. God exists as that which is not 'not-God'. Regardless of how strong Barth conceives of the distinction between God and nothingness, no matter how utterly impotent the latter is in the face of the former, God is still defined by that from which He is in eternal distinction by virtue of His rejection of it. So His creation can only attempt to do the same, in time and space, and so in its non-divinity its fall is inevitable.

---

[16] Jüngel adds an important qualifier to this lack of permanence, "*Als das von Gott a priori Verworfene ist das Nichtige zwar ohne Bestand und ohne Substanz, aber in seiner Unbeständigkeit und Substanzlosigkeit - man könnte auch im Anschluß an Augustins Bestimmung des malum als corruptio boni sagen: in seiner ganzen Korruptheit - ist das Nichtige das den Bestand der Welt Gefährdende und also theologisch auf keinen Fall zu unterschätzen.*" Jüngel, '*Die Offenbarung der Verborgenheit Gottes*', *op. cit.*, pp. 177-178. "*Das Nichtige* is what was negated *a priori* by God, although without permanent substance, but in its impermanence and lack of substance one could say, following on St Augustine's definition of evil as *corruptio boni*: in all its corruption, *das Nichtige* threatens the permanence of the world and is not to be underestimated theologically."

[17] CD III/3, p. 351. (emphasis mine)

This picture continues to emerge as does Barth's desire to reconcile the sovereignty of God and his total exoneration from sin and evil. By using the terms *verwerfen, unwille, widerwille,* and *nein,* and by basing nothingness' ontic reality in the holy wrath of God, Barth is trying to deny any such potentially dualistic role to nothingness. Yet he cannot completely do so, for in the end, nothingness is a manifestation of the left hand of God, acting as His servant to bring about His good will. Barth is forced to conclude that even when evil is pushed to the extremes of the 'left hand of God', in the end, "Even on his left hand the activity of God is not in vain."[18] We have here an internal war of sorts between the two hands of God; the right hand in wrath and judgement separating itself from and finally annihilating the work of the left hand.[19] In this way Barth's understanding of lordship continues to exist in tension with his desire to paint nothingness as true enemy of God. It still remains that nothingness has its origin in the eternal self-distinction of God from 'not-God', and therefore, "not only what God wills, but what he does not will, is potent, and must have a real correspondence. What really corresponds to that which God does not will is nothingness."[20]

The 'Shadowy Side' of Creation

A main feature of Barth's excursus on *das Nichtige* is his insistence that there is a created shadowy side to God's good creation which, as it is part of this creation, must not be confused with true nothingness. The main reason for this is clear; since Barth sees this shadowy side as an essential and necessary aspect of God's good creation, to identify it with nothingness is to give to evil the status of 'created' and therefore a positive existence by making it the necessary partner in the positive will and work of God.

Barth has stated earlier that the imperfections of creation can be called 'good' because they are serviceable by God in His work and will to bring about the goal of creation. Because they are useable as His instruments, they are 'good' despite their seeming, and sometimes glaring imperfections. Barth is keen to draw a clear distinction between this side of creation and nothingness, and to do so he builds a three-tiered system of sorts. First, there is God's creation from His positive side, that which was perfect and therefore 'good'. Second, there is the creation from His negative side, but still from His positive will, which is imperfect but useable and is therefore 'good'. Finally, there is nothingness which is the product of His non-willing, his negative will, and this is not good but evil. Barth calls the result of the positive will but negative side of God the 'shadowy side' of creation *(Schattenseite)*. This imperfection in creation is near

---

[18] Ibid. p. 351.

[19] Berkouwer comments, "The purpose of God's *proper* work is to make an end to His *alien* work." Thus nothingness can only play the role of the "*defeated* enemy" and as a result, it is "*not a dangerous* force." (*Triumph of Grace, op. cit.,* pp. 74-75)

[20] CD III/3, p. 352.

to, yet wholly distinct from the nothingness from which it was separated and from which it is preserved.

The Roots of the Evidence for die Schattenseite

Barth draws from two prior sections in holding to this highly suspect view. He has stated earlier (CD III.1, §41, 2) that in the creation of the world as the external basis of the covenant, God's separations of light from darkness and land from water, etc., were separations of what God positively willed in the 'Yes' of His creative act, from that which He did not will but rejected in His divine 'No'. Here darkness, water, air and the like take on a shadowy character in relation to light, earth and land, which reflect His positive will. As such, Barth believes he has laid the foundation for this shadowy side of creation as that which, while representing the rejected nothingness, is yet incorporated into the positively-willed creation and which, even in its imperfections, is used by God and thus praises Him.[21] It is on account of this shadowy side that creation is bordered by and threatened by nothingness. Yet this darker side cannot be equated with nothingness but must be distinguished from it in the same way as that which is positively willed is distinguished from that which is non-willed and thus rejected.[22]

The other section is the critical discussion of Creation as Justification (CD III.1, §42, 3), where Barth has shown that God has justified His creation even in its imperfections by using it to bring about the goal of creation. As they reflect the 'No' of God, as they are signs of His judgement and result in misery and sorrow, they are what were wholly taken up into the Son and reconciled in Him, and as such they serve a positive purpose in giving relief and contrast to the 'Yes' of God.[23] Instead of being results of the Fall, Barth is saying that they

---

[21] R. Ruether comments that the relationship of radical evil to the shadow side of creation is "the most difficult problem in Barth's treatment of evil." She goes on to speak of the difficulty of the left hand-right hand metaphor. "There is a left hand to creation, but one which is balanced by a right hand within the totality of God's affirmation. This left hand can make us sigh, but it does not make us draw our breath in horror." She concludes quite rightly that the frontier between this shadow side and real nothingness in Barth's theology becomes confused and blurred. "It is hard to draw this border and to distinguish between natural tragedies which can be borne and tragedies which are the expression of a disorder to be combated." ('The Left Hand of God in the Theology of Karl Barth', *op. cit.*, pp. 14-15)

[22] Berkouwer makes this point in a succinct statement, "In this way the joy but also the misery of existence have their ground in the will of God." (*Triumph of Grace, op. cit.*, p. 64)

[23] This idea certainly pre-dates the *Church Dogmatics*. It is given a full expression in Barth's Gifford Lectures of 1937-1938, where he writes concerning the two realms of heaven and earth, "neither of these realms is absolved from the duty of gratitude, however much the idealists may despise nature and the materialistic spirit. But this is true also *mutatis mutandis* of the antithesis between *coming into being* and *passing*

are a part of God's *original creation*, which produces a second, created 'necessary antithesis'. In addition to the antithesis of God and evil which, as we have seen, is the manifestation in space and time of the eternal self-distinction within God Himself, there is also now the created antithesis between creation and its shadowy side.

The Problems of the 'Shadowy Side of Creation'

Given this background, the shadowy side of creation is troublesome. Barth states that included in this created but shadowy side is "an abyss...obscurity...impediment...limitation...decay...indigence...ashes...end...wo rthlessness...darkness...failure...tears...age...loss...death."[24] None of this, it must be pointed out with the greatest of clarity, is a result of the Fall of humanity, but it is a picture of the created world which God called 'good' and over which He was content to rest. Barth defends this interpretation with his Christology, for all of this was created with a view to Christ and the justification of it which His salvific work would bring. The creature is involved in the struggle brought about by the antithesis of the light with the shadows in creation. Yet this struggle does not imply that the creature has the character of nothingness, but that it is involved with the creation as it was made for and in Jesus Christ. Therefore,

> it is irrefutable that creation and creature are good even in the fact that all that is exists in this contrast and antithesis. In all this, far from being null, it praises its Creator and Lord even on its shadowy side, even in the negative aspect in which it is so near to nothingness. If He Himself has comprehended creation in its totality and made it His own in His Son, it is for us to acquiesce without thinking that we know better, without complaints, reproach or dismay.[25]

In fact, our existence in this shadowy side and all of the misery it brings should be cause for rejoicing, for it is out of such that God will bring light and life. In and of itself, this shadowy side is God's instrument and in its own way it sings the praises of God.

Therefore we must not confuse *die Schattenseite* with *das Nichtige*, for it is the guise of nothingness to pretend that this shadowy side of creation is real

---

away. Both of these extol the glory of God-not only the majesty of what we call growth, progress and fulfillment of life, but also the darkness of what we call decay, destruction and death. On the other hand, it would be the sign of a narrow outlook to look for God's glory only on the dark side of creation and not on the bright side also. Both coming into being and passing away stand in equal need of the overflowing grace of the Creator, in order to possess their own particular glory." (*The Knowledge of God and the Service of God, op. cit.,* p. 64)

[24] CD III/3, p. 297.

[25] Ibid. p. 297.

nothingness, diverting our attention away from the true evil, the real threat. "We do not really come to grips with true nothingness, with the real adversary which menaces and corrupts us as long as we look in this direction."[26] What is at risk is the giving to Satan and the kingdom of true nothingness a participatory form, and therefore a positive role, which is only rightly assigned to the shadowy side of creation. Thus Satan and his kingdom become part of the created world and therefore a part of that which falls under the salvific work of God in Jesus Christ. Because Jesus died for and brought up into Himself the shadowy side of creation, Barth can conclude, "in the knowledge of Jesus Christ it is inadmissible to seek nothingness here."[27]

There exists a created antithesis between the positive and the negative side of creation which Jesus Christ took up into Himself in His salvific work on behalf of creation, and this shadowy side as well as the positive side is part of God's intended creation and instruments to the accomplishments of His divine will and goal for creation. This 'created antithesis' is distinguished by Barth from the 'necessary antithesis' motif which is between God and nothingness, saying of the latter, "This antithesis has no substantive existence within creation... It is the antithesis which can be present and active within creation only as an absolute alien opposing and contradicting all its elements, whether positive or negative."[28] This antithesis transcends the creaturely world and is strictly between God and evil. Yet because we are God's creation, it is hostile to us as a means to attack God. In a re-statement of our motif of the 'necessary antithesis' Barth states unequivocally that God is Master of it, and has been from all eternity.

> God alone, the God who from all eternity has decreed its defeat, transcends the antithesis, comprehending, envisaging and controlling it. For us it remains the antithesis which we can neither conquer nor comprehend, neither envisage nor master and control either in theory or in practice. It is the antithesis which is impatient of any legitimate synthesis. God, but He alone, can deal with it and has already done so, in accordance with the fact that He transcends it from all eternity in His essence as God. But it must be clearly understood that He has treated it as His adversary, as the No which is primarily and supremely addressed to Him, as the nothingness which is true nothingness in opposition to Himself and His will and work. But if this is the relationship between God and nothingness, we cannot and must not include it in the creaturely world.[29]

---

26 Ibid. p. 299.
27 Ibid. p. 301.
28 Ibid. p. 302.
29 Ibid. pp. 302-303.

The great impact which Barth's understanding of the *tohu wa-bohu* has on his entire interpretation of evil can be seen here. It provides him not only with the basis for his doctrine of providence, but with his understanding of the shadowy side of creation. He uses the two together to define sin as the crossing the the frontier at which humanity is preserved in the providence of God and the direction to which it is poised in the shadowy side of creation, as well as the basis of the reconciling work of the Son. Here Barth is building for us a picture in which the justification of all creation is based upon the work of Jesus Christ. Because God makes good out of bad, the bad can be seen as His instrument and thus a part of His good creation. This is curious from two standpoints.

First, the Fall of humanity, which plays such a critical role elsewhere in Barth's theology, is mysteriously absent here. It is not as a result of the inevitable fallen state of humanity that God eternally chooses in His self-determination to make good come from the bad (an idea embraced in other places where Barth seems to raise the idea of *O felix culpa*) but it is that God *created* the bad, the shadowy side, in order for the good to come. We are given a picture which, at one level, makes the Fall inconsequential. It was the antithesis within the good creation which God took up into Himself in Jesus Christ.[30] Yet Barth insists that it was nothingness "which brought Jesus Christ to the cross."[31] And we have seen that Barth would not conceive of the incarnation without the cross, and therefore without the Fall. By destroying the link between sin and the shadowy side of creation, Barth has created a breach between creation and the covenant, the latter of which was inaugurated *as a result of the Fall*.

This is problematic for the consistency in Barth's doctrine of evil, and it is magnified in Barth's subsequent view of humanity's relationship to and responsibility for plants and animals. In CD III/4, Barth draws the necessary distinction between the human, as the 'animal' God chose for fellowship, and the world of animals and plants. They are not the same and yet they are closely related, so much so that the creature has great responsibility to each, for the animals and plants make up, "the indispensable living background to the living-space divinely allotted to man and placed under his control."[32] Yet with regards

---

[30] "It thus follows that though its existence is under doubt and shadow it is not of itself involved in opposition and resistance to God's creative will. On the contrary, this will is fulfilled and confirmed in it. The creature is not unnatural but natural. It is good, even very good, in so far as it does not oppose but corresponds to the intention of God as revealed by Him in the humiliation and exaltation of Jesus Christ and the reconciliation of the world with Himself effected in Him. For in Him God has made Himself the Subject of both aspects of creaturely existence. And having made it His own in Jesus Christ, He has affirmed it in its totality, *reconciling this inner antithesis in His own person.* The creature does not have the character of nothingness as and because it is a creature and partakes in this antithesis. On the contrary, this is its perfection and the proof of its creation in and for Jesus Christ." (Ibid. p. 296, emphasis mine)

[31] Ibid. p. 305.

[32] CD III/4, p. 350.

to the animals especially, control does not mean ownership, but "requisitioning, disciplining, training, harnessing, exploiting, and making profitable use of the surplus forces of nature in the animal world."[33] Here Barth offers us a basis for a 'green theology' in his portrayal of the responsibility of humanity towards the animals and plants which God has created and provided. The distinction between lordship and ownership is essential in seeing how Barth would have us use, but not abuse, the creation of God.

The problem for his idea of creation's *Schattenseite* comes when Barth turns to the idea of the killing of animals. Seeing this as 'annihilation' in distinction from the harvesting of plant life, Barth turns to a strict, almost historical understanding of the pre-Fall paradisal garden in which, "man and beast find their table furnished by the world of plants and cannot come into collision."[34] Barth acknowledges that Scripture shows that "animal slaughter and the *general struggle for existence* emerge *only after the account of the fall of man.*"[35] This leads him to conclude,

> it is evident that we have to do with a new and different order as regards the peace of creation of Genesis 1 and 2, if from now on the killing of animals seems to be permitted and even commanded. This new order is *not yet possible and real in the pre-historic realm of the creature's fashioning by the Word of God* , but only in the *historical sphere of sinful man* to whom God is still gracious.[36]

Barth proceeds to speak of three 'periods' in the life of the animal world; the 'period of peace' which is broken by the Fall, the 'interim period' where the peace is replaced by a struggle for existence, and the 'last times' when this struggle will cease. Again Barth gives us an excellent basis for a theology of animal rights and welfare, especially with regards to his compassionate treatment of the killing of animals. The problem here lies with a great confusion between what Barth wants to refer to as creation's *Schattenseite*, where misery and the struggle for existence is part of the good creation of God, and this 'new order' which has come about as a result of the Fall. We have here again the tension of the 'inevitability-impossibility' of the Fall, and the ambiguity between the creature created as 'immediately the first sinner' and the need in Barth for 'at least a golden Sunday morning'. With regard to the animal world, Barth seems to return to the idea of a primordial time when the peace which will be ushered in by the final *parousia* was, even if momentarily, an actual reality in creation. If this is so, then isn't Barth confusing the fallen state of creation with a positively-created *Schattenseite* ?

---

[33] Ibid. p. 351.
[34] Ibid. p. 353.
[35] Ibid. p. 353. (emphasis mine)
[36] Ibid. p. 353. (emphasis mine)

Barth may respond that what nothingness has added to the shadowy side of creation is a threatening aspect. Thus the natural suffering of the shadowy side of creation becomes the suffering of evil which leads to death. And this death is not the natural, God-given limitation to life, but the "intolerable, life-destroying thing to which all suffering hastens as its goal."[37] The place of revelation of nothingness is in the salvific work of Christ. Here it is suffered and routed, endured and defeated. It is seen in its absolute negating sense and here it is made impotent. What humanity is saved from is the threat of nothingness which was manifest in its sin.

In addition to the inconsistency of this approach, the further question must then be raised, what is the state of humanity in the time of the Church, the time *post Christum* ? It is clear that in Christ evil has been defeated, and with it the suffering it brings upon us. Yet what of the shadowy side of creation? Presumably it still remains as a part of God's good creation. Thus, with evil utterly defeated and the shadowy side of creation still intact, we can trace all suffering, pain and misery to the heart and will of God, as a result of His willed creation and its instrumental use in His hands. This would appear to make God responsible for all natural evils.[38]

Barth will not allow this, however, for although evil is routed, he will go on to say that it is still allowed to operate by the permission of God. What then are we to make of suffering? Is it from God by permission (from His left hand), from God by direct decree (from His right hand), from God by means of the continuation of the shadowy side of creation, or from all three? In either case, we have a muddled picture from which we must draw conclusions about the suffering of humanity in the time between the resurrection and the second coming.

The root of these problems lies in two places; first with this idea of a shadowy side of creation itself, and, secondly, a deficiency in the eschatological understanding of the defeat of evil in the work of Christ. The latter debate will be taken up in Chapter VII. Here we must reject the first idea that God created a world in which there existed, side-by-side and according to His good and perfect will, a light side and a dark side. No sense of a dark side of creation can be found

---

[37] CD III/3, p. 310.

[38] We agree with Fiddes here who sees Barth's *Schattenseite* as "a good example of the tendency to smooth away the offensive shock of natural evil" with the result that Barth "seems to trivialize the impact of natural evils." Fiddes cannot see how Barth can be so sure of God's attitude with regard to natural evil, "how does he [Barth] know that God's participation in the shadow-side of creation was an approving one, in which he found that is 'sang the praise of God just as it was?'... How does Barth know that God was not also there protesting against and challenging the natural evils of disease and death?" Fiddes concludes, "if God experiences hostile non-being when he shares the life of the world, then he must speak of the fall of nature, like that of man, as being a strange factor to God." (Fiddes, *The Creative Suffering of God, op. cit.,* pp. 223-225) We agree with Fiddes that there must be affirmed the fall of the creation as well as the creature, and that what Barth sees as a positively created dark side is actually the fallenness of that creation.

in the creation saga except in Barth's interpretation of the *tohu wa-bohu* as 'nothingness' which was rejected and passed over by God. To be clear, we are not rejecting Barth's equating of the *tohu wa-bohu* with *das Nichtige*. What we are rejecting is the idea that the consequent creation by separation required that the two-fold nature of the separation (light and darkness, land and water, etc.) correspond to good and chaos. The darkness, water and air described in the creation saga are erroneously understood by Barth to coincide with, although they are distinct from, the *tohu wa-bohu* of verse 2. It must be seen instead that all of God's creation, as it was made distinct from nothingness as light and darkness, land and water, etc., is God's good and perfect creation.

Given this interpretation, we have no evidence whatsoever to assert a negative aspect to creation prior to the Fall. In fact the whole of the creation saga suggests exactly the opposite. Barth is trying to interpret the creation saga Christologically by finding good in the shadowy side of that which is separated by God because of its future use by God and its justification in the salvific work of Christ. Yet this attempt, under the compelling influence of Gerhard von Rad, has created not good exegesis but eisegesis and must be rejected.[39]

We assert that what Barth calls the shadowy side of creation is only creation under the influence of nothingness. This does not mean that Genesis 3 cannot be interpreted as saga, for there is certainly room for the primordial, pre-historic Fall in a scenario which sees a transition of creation from a perfect state to one under the influence of that nothingness which was allowed to enter it on account of the Fall. We must remember that there is a tension here between the integrity of the election of Jesus Christ as *homo labilis* and the created humanity as not 'able to sin'. It is the 'impossibility-inevitability' tension which means we must say both that the fallen state of creation was assumed from eternity and that humanity was indeed created in a state in which sin was seen to be impossible. We posit that it is this state in which creation itself was created without a shadowy side, but that this shadow accompanied humanity's choice of the impossible, even if this is understood to be 'immediately' after it came on the scene. Therefore, if we must assert and proclaim a distinction in the loudest of terms, it must be between God's original intention and the characteristics which Barth has labeled as the shadowy side of creation. These are not the necessary correlates in God's creation but the product of the fallen state of humanity, and

---

[39] We think here of Hick's critique, with which we only partially agree, where he states, "Barth's exegesis of Genesis 1:2-3 is a classic example of theological *eisegesis*, or reading into the text, for he equates the *tohu wa-bohu* (without form and void) of verse 2 with *das Nichtige*, and thus discovers his own theory of evil in the biblical account of creation... Again he interprets the 'darkness' of verse 3 as referring to the primitive chaos which God put behind Him and which now exists only as the rejected, hostile *Nichtige*, in contrast to God's good creation." (*Evil and the God of Love*, op. cit., p. 140) Hick is right in the latter criticism of the interpretation of the 'darkness', yet he gives insufficient evidence as to why we should also reject the former idea of Barth's interpretation of the *tohu wa-bohu*. In addition, he seems to tie the two together necessarily, which is not required, as we have shown.

to keep us from seeking nothingness in them is to force us to find nothingness in God![40]

We are not rejecting the idea that God can and does send upon His creation trials and experiences which may have the look and feel of evil. We have treated such an understanding of suffering of this sorts under our own categories of suffering (see categories 2 and 3 in our discussion). What we do reject is the idea that suffering was a part of God's good creation, for there is clearly no place for the suffering of God's creation outside of the Fall. Sin, evil and suffering are inextricably bound! We agree with Barth that creation is justified in Jesus Christ, but we must be sure that it is *das Nichtige* which required the incarnation and not simply the justification of the duality of creation itself.[41] We must reject such an idea and see God's salvific work wholly on behalf of His good creation which has fallen of its own disobedience, and thus ushered nothingness onto the scene of creation. Only thus can we affirm that God did not abandon His creation to the nothingness it had chosen for itself, but justified creation in Christ and for Himself. In this way the muddle is resolved as there can be no confusion between what is the result of sin, leading to death and eternal perdition, and what is experienced as the necessary shadowy side of creation; for there is simply is no evidence for a shadowy side of creation, and its inclusion is a most troublesome and unfortunate feature of Barth's doctrine of evil.

The Problem of the Annihilation of Evil

As Barth has developed his understanding of evil throughout the *Church Dogmatics*, we are told that there is an eternal transcending of nothingness by God and a determination for its annihilation. Yet this antithesis between God and evil outside creation leads us to several questions as to the destruction of evil. If God has authority over evil, if He is eternally disposed to its destruction and if He has power not only over its very existence but power to annihilate it for all eternity, why must it be present to the creaturely sphere at all? Why didn't God carry out His eternal will of its destruction in the proper sphere of this antithesis, namely, outside the creaturely world?[42] Do we have reason to

---

[40] We remember how the idea of a fallen creation is given an ambivalent treatment in Barth, as seen in his statement, "I am not ready to say that there is a fallen creation. I would not deny it, but I cannot affirm it." ('Table Talk', *op. cit.,* p. 46)

[41] G.V. Jones makes the point that Barth, too, sees this distinction, "For what becomes evident is this: that the Incarnation of the Word of God in Jesus Christ merely as a revelation of the goodness of the divine creation in its double aspect would not have been necessary... The *Nichtige* is that 'reality' because of which God Himself became a creature of His own creation." ('God and Negation', *op. cit.,* p. 235)

[42] We hear the same question from Augustine when he questions the origin of evil, "If it [evil] were from eternity, why suffered He it so to be for infinite spaces of times past, and was pleased so long after to make something out of it? Or if he were suddenly pleased now to effect somewhat, this rather should the Almighty have

assume that it was necessary that evil be destroyed only in relation to a created world where it could reign only to be destroyed by the sacrifice of the Son of God for creation? If this really was required for the annihilation of evil, then evil necessarily must be seen in its relation to creation and intimately included in the creaturely world. Isn't Barth saying that creation, as the theatre for the glory of God, is also necessarily the only possible but divinely appointed theatre for the annihilation of evil? Could one not draw from this that God must create in order to destroy His eternal antagoniser once and for all?[43]

This same dilemma arises in Barth's understanding of what he calls the 'opponents of the ambassadors of heaven'. Barth does not deny the existence of demons or the devil, but he defines them wholly and completely as *das Nichtige*. Barth is determined to give demons only a brief glance, for they deserve nothing more. In this glance, we see in Barth an identification of demons with nothingness in every respect, for they are not creatures, they have no independence vis-á-vis God, and they are only related to God and the angels in the same rejected relationship as nothingness. Barth rejects any notion that would put angels and demons in the same *genre*, for they are as dissimilar as 'sense' and 'nonsense', as *die Wirklichkeit* and *das Nichtige*. In this way Christian faith must 'demythologise' its demonology in such a way as to posit towards it a 'radical unbelief'. In Christ, the reality of demons is a past and finished subject, and now their activity is so impotent that their very being is rejected in the light of the true reality of Jesus Christ.

The demons then are identical with nothingness and as such they are both the inimical foes of creation and the defeated enemy turned servants of the left hand of God.[44] What is peculiar in this idea of Barth's is his outright rejection of any sense of a pre-mundane fall of the angels. Barth sees this older demonology as a 'bad dream' and emphatically states that Satan was never an angel. "He was a murderer *ap archs*. He never stood in the truth. No truth was ever in him."[45] Barth denies not only that the angels did indeed fall, but he

---

effected, that this evil matter should not be, and He alone be, the whole, true, sovereign, and infinite Good." (*Confessions, op. cit.,* p. 113)

[43] For evidence of this, "In plain and precise terms, the answer is that nothingness is the 'reality' in whose account (i.e., against which) God Himself willed to become a creature in the creaturely world, yielding and subjecting Himself to it in Jesus Christ in order to overcome it." (CD III/3, p. 305)

[44] Barth's words are so strong here they must be quoted as evidence of the radical 'pastness' with which he views evil. "What is revealed [in Scripture] is the kingdom of Satan and his angels as this is already assaulted and mortally threatened, and indeed *radically destroyed*; demonic being, not in its concealment and therefore powerful, but unmasked and therefore disarmed; not its march and attack and even victory, but its defeat and withdrawal and flight; not an earth and humanity controlled, visited and plagued by demons, but liberated from them; not a world bewitched but exorcised; not a community and Christendom believing in demons but opposing to them in faith that resolute disbelief; in short, the triumph of truth over falsehood." (Ibid. p. 530, emphasis mine)

[45] Ibid. p. 531.

denies the very idea that the angels *could* have fallen. The freedom of humanity does not include the freedom to sin, however sin, even as the impossible, is yet a possibility in all of its absurdity. Yet even this sense of true freedom which is given to created humanity is denied the angels, for they can do no other than obey and worship God.

Barth is open to criticism here at two levels. The first is a straightforward critique of his exegesis concerning the demons. The crux of this critique is Barth's rejection of the passages which certainly speak of a fall of the angels, especially Jude 6 and 2 Peter 2:4. Barth rejects these verses outright as too 'uncertain and obscure' to lead us in any positive direction. This decision is dubious to say the least.[46] What lies at the heart of Barth's decision is less the interest of true exegesis than the realization that if such a doctrine were able to be sustained, it would undermine his entire section on angels and demons.[47] Secondly, however, is the point that Barth is nowhere able to give an answer to the origin of evil. Barth insists that the devil himself is some indistinguishable component of all that he calls nothingness, with no proper understanding as to his origin, but only the certainty of both his necessity and sure demise. If, as Barth has repeatedly said, it is the 'not-God' which God rejects eternally, and if there were no pre-mundane fall of the angels to explain the origin of this nothingness, then we must conclude that the origin of this 'not-God' is found in its negative existence as the eternal correlate (in antithetical if not dualistic terms) to God.

Barth concludes that this nothingness 'is' and will continue to 'be' only as and so long it is against God. To see it in another determination other than in its character of enmity with God is not to see it as it is. Again we will ask here, anticipating Barth's later point, if this doesn't necessarily require that nothingness is eternal? Can God ever cease to be against it, against Satan, against nothingness? If He can, does He not cease to be known as God, especially his inability to posit any origin of evil save for its antithetical role as the (eternal?) rejected 'not-God' of God's eternal self-differentiation? Given this, it is highly questionable from what Barth has said here that nothingness can ever

---

[46] Bromiley is highly critical of Barth at this point. In his guide to Barth's work, Bromiley states here, "Barth does not expunge the verses that hint at a fall of the angels. He simply objects to the way they are expounded. Unfortunately he does not back up the objection with any direct biblical material. His interpretation stands, then, under the shadow cast by these verses... in doing so he lays himself open to criticism at a vital point... it is a pity that the whole discussion should end with so questionable a thesis and procedure." (*Introduction to the Theology of Karl Barth, op. cit.*, p. 155) Berkouwer sounds a similar critique, "The sharp issue which Barth took with the bad dream of dogmatics (that the demons are fallen angels) robs the revelation about the demons of its *concrete character.*" Berkouwer also notes that Barth is never able to say why man *can* fall and the angels *cannot.* (*Triumph of Grace, op. cit.,* p. 239, 239n)

[47] "Literally all the insights which we have gained concerning the being and ministry of angels, and developed at least concerning the character and activity of demons, are necessarily false if this doctrine is correct." (CD III/3, p. 531)

be annihilated, leaving God nothing to reject in His self-distinction which is for Him also a self-definition. Will there be a time when God will cease to non-will and reject and separate? And to return to a previous question we have raised, if such a time can be envisaged, why didn't God bring it about prior to creation?

This is the real theodicy question which must be raised against Barth. If God could have but didn't, is He benevolent? If He couldn't, if it required the creation of a theatre and stage, of fall and sin and the threat of creaturely perdition in order for God to finally conquer and annihilate His eternal enemy, then is God the absolute sovereign as Barth has depicted Him? Barth is in difficulty here for behind these two antitheses as Barth has proposed them is nothing but a return to the same problem of theodicy. Far from moving to a solution, Barth has only succeeded in pushing the questions back one step.

It must be said here that all of this is dependent upon two highly questionable theses of Barth's which, if altered or rejected altogether, change this scenario completely. These are 1) the interpretation of Genesis 1 which gives Barth his whole basis for the shadowy side of creation, and 2) his idea later in this section that evil has no perpetuity, which makes its total annihilation possible and brings much of the above criticism to the fore. We have given good reason to reject the first of these here and we will offer the same with regard to the second one when we reach Barth's discussion of the end of evil in his eschatology.

The Battle Against Evil Under the 'Right and Left Hand of God'

Having re-stated and clarified the ontic basis of nothingness and the humility and faith which is required in its examination, Barth returns to the motif of the 'right and left hand of God' to show how evil operates according to its 'peculiar ontology' as privation.

Barth can speak of evil as privation and does so in a more forceful way than Leibniz because he sees this privation as the adversary of grace. He is staying to a true Augustinian line in citing the radicalness of the privation in its enmity to the grace of God. The reason evil is evil is because it is in opposition to grace, and in this way it is intrinsically evil. It attacks God by offending Him, and humanity by threatening our very existence which is dependent upon the grace of God. It is not a part of either God or creation and as such it is inexplicable, outside of any norm or standard and unable to be systematized. Again Barth gives us a key statement in this section as he writes, "It cannot even be viewed dialectically, let alone resolved. Its defeat can be envisaged only as *the purpose and end of the history of God's dealings with His creature, and in no other way.*"[48] The purpose of God's creation and His history with and in it, and indeed its very end and goal includes the defeat of nothingness. This may be posited as a likely answer to the question asked above. God chose the sphere of

---

[48] Ibid. p. 354. (emphasis mine)

creaturely existence of time and space in which to do battle and defeat His eternal enemy.[49]

We must never lose site of the fact that in all of this talk of battle, the foe is always that whose very existence, power and place in creation are sustained under the administration of the 'left hand of God'.[50] Therefore, since creation was to be the stage for this final battle between God and nothingness, Barth sees its inevitable outcome as solely God's affair. We are only involved because the battle takes place in our own created sphere of space and time. As the enemy of God is allowed access to creation, he seeks to destroy it on the way to the destruction of God Himself, and as he finds us as non-divine creatures, our defeat seems both effortless and inevitable.

What Satan did not count on was God's eternal self-determination to be 'for' this creature. Thus even when we are thrust into the depths of nothingness by our sin and rejection of the grace of God, we are still the creature of God under His care and existing solely by His providence, and as His creatures we are summoned to His side in this battle. In His contending for us He is in confrontation with nothingness, His grace engaged in the battle with its adversary. The end goal is the absolute and final separation which is the end and destruction of nothingness. This defeat in the final separation as grace's victory over evil is the "meaning of the history of the relationship between God and His creature."[51] God alone masters nothingness and moves the history of His creation to the final victory over it.

---

[49] Yet prior to creation Barth has told us God had the power to destroy this nothingness. His sovereignty demanded that He always has possessed such power. Why then involve creation as the stage of its defeat? And corresponding to that, can we ever again think we see in Barth any other idea concerning the role of the Fall than the fact that it was the pre-determined and necessary lot of the creature? Otherwise nothingness would remain on the frontier and the cross of Christ would be meaningless or unnecessary. God's 'purpose and end' for His creation would be thwarted. In this picture which Barth has painted the Fall has supreme importance, for it allows the entrance onto the stage of the all important co-star, without whom the entire construction of the theatre would have been in vain.

[50] Of this situation Ricoeur asks, "Can this coordination without conciliation between God's left and right hands make sense? If it is not a covert concession to the failed theodicies of the past and accordingly a weak compromise substituted for a broken dialectic, does it not reopen the way to speculations such as those of Giordano Bruno and Schelling on the demonic aspect of the deity?" (Ricoeur, 'Evil, A Challenge to Philosophy and Theology', *op. cit.,* p. 644) Ricoeur is right to question the sensibility of this 'coordination without conciliation', yet his critique that Barth may be sliding back into the demonic God of Schelling is clearly wide of the mark. Ricoeur fails to consider the other motifs of Barth's doctrine of evil which provide the framework in which Barth talks of the 'right and left hand of God'. Our final acceptance of this second motif can only be made in the context of the four motifs taken together.

[51] CD III/3, p. 355.

Because He is for the creature, the creature can choose the one true 'good' and as a result can stand with God in His opposition to nothingness. Therefore our struggle with evil, as it operates from the 'left hand of God', can find its only meaning in the fellow-battle with God over the nothingness which has pervaded the world through sin. This is the only way in which we have a meaningful role in this battle which is entirely God's affair. It is He who is primarily effected by it and it is He alone who can and does confront it and overcomes it. Any belief which fails to hold to this critical point is, for Barth, a 'non-Christian conception of nothingness'.

> The whole theological concept of nothingness depends upon the fact that the primal antithesis or encounter in which it has its being is its confrontation with God Himself, which God freely allows because His freedom is that of His grace and love and faithfulness, and His glory is that of His condescension, to His creature. Everything ultimately depends on this one point, and we remember that it is not a theory or notion but the concrete event at the core of all Christian reality and truth–the self-giving of the Son of God, His humiliation, incarnation and obedience unto death, even death on the cross. It is here that the true conflict with nothingness takes place. And it is here that it is unmistakably clear that it is God's own affair.[52]

The whole of the picture which we have seen emerging in Barth is articulated here. Barth affirms of nothingness that "*daß der Urgegensatz und die Urhegegnung, in der es sein Wesen hat, seine Gegenüberstellung zer Gott selber ist.*"[53] This primal antithesis has its origin in the eternal self-distinction of God from nothingness as the 'necessary antithesis'. Here, in the creaturely sphere, God allows it to have form solely because God has pre-determined Himself to be God for humanity in the salvific work of the Son. Thus the eternal conflict, in which God was never in fact threatened, now is played out upon the stage of creation. Again we see how the noetic form of nothingness under the 'right and left hand of God' motif flows from the ontic basis of nothingness in the motif of the 'necessary antithesis'. The eternal enemy of God is given ground to operate within His creation, but only because God has fixed the outcome which will be its defeat at Golgotha. Creation is saved and the eternal enemy of God is slayed on the cross of Christ, and it is this end for which God created the world.

The Defeat of Nothingness and the Problem of Theodicy

Barth's exposition on *das Nichtige* leads him to this final point that the goal of creation is the salvation and reconciliation of humanity via the

---

[52] Ibid. p. 360.

[53] (KD III/3, p. 416) "the primal antithesis or encounter in which it has its being is its confrontation with God Himself."

annihilation of evil which was accomplished on Calvary. This occurs in that nothingness, as the negative work of God, as the *opus alienum Dei*, no longer has a purpose or role in the face of the fulfillment of the positive work of God.

This negative activity of God has as such, in accordance with its meaning and nature, a definite frontier, and this is to be found at the point where *it attains its goal and accomplishes its purpose*. With the attainment of the goal the *opus alienum* of God also reaches its end. God is indeed eternally holy, pure, distinct and separated from evil which is nothingness. But this does not mean that He must always strive with this adversary, enduring its opposition and resistance, and Himself exercising His jealousy, wrath and judgement upon it. Surely He will also be holy, and all the more so, when judgement is executed, when the triumph of His love is unchallenged and boundless, and therefore when He is the God who no longer has to do with an enemy but only with His creature.[54]

Nothingness has achieved its purpose in making necessary the salvation of creation through the death and resurrection of Jesus Christ and by bringing about the security of the future of creation in Him. The positive work of God, once it is fulfilled, makes His negative work dispensable. Thus evil is destroyed in the salvific work of Christ and what is left is God's new and restored relationship with the creature.

Two points attract our criticism. One is the assignment of nothingness to a role player as Barth has done. The talk of the defeat of God's great enemy has subsided into the elimination of an actor when his lines have been read. Nothingness has played its part and God has completed the goal for which He created the world and allowed evil its temporary reign. The inevitable outcome of the covenant drama has been achieved and the foe can now be dismissed. The main question we must ask here is one we have raised often before. Is nothingness tied only to creation, or to God Himself? Both answers are highly troublesome for all that Barth has said thus far. If it is tied only to creation, then we must ask quite pointedly of the origin of the *tohu wa-bohu*. If nothingness was not a necessary manifestation in space and time of that from which God exists eternally in His self-distinction, then where do we find the basis for a 'No' in God? The non-divinity of the creature can only be in jeopardy if it stands before something which necessarily confronts it in its existence as the non-divine. The 'No' of God, His left hand and the *opus alienum Dei* lose all credibility if there is no sense of nothingness prior to and outside of the sphere of creation. Then we must return to the question of the 'best of all possible worlds' and we find ourselves again entangled in the web of theodicy.

If on the other hand Barth is holding to what he has said previously about nothingness and its necessary position with regards to creation, then we must ask why God can cease to be the God of self-distinction and still be God? If

---

[54] CD III/3, p. 362. (emphasis mine)

Barth wants to take the defeat of nothingness in the creaturely sphere and bring it up into God Himself, then He is destroying the negative backdrop which supplies the necessary contrast for the holiness and goodness of God. As we have shown, without the 'not-God', God is not the God revealed to us in Jesus Christ! Fiddes states, "God uses death to define his being," and therefore "The most dreadful assault of non-being has become the most articulate word about God."[55] A final idea might be that nothingness is only defeated in the creaturely sphere and remains in its role as the 'not-God' which gives God his definition. This is a position which we find much more in keeping with Scripture while also being viable within Barth's theology as a whole, but Barth rejects it outright. The only conclusion that can be drawn is that Barth's teaching of the non-perpetuity of evil is a most problematic element within the rest of his theology.

The second critique has to do with the simple question, if nothingness is wholly defeated and routed on the cross, what are we to make of 1900+ years of human history which seems to exude evil in all imaginable depths and forms? If this is not evil, if this is not the continuing work of nothingness, what is it? Barth's position is clear and it carries with it major eschatological problems which will arise in greater depths in Chapter VII from his wholly 'noetic eschatology'. Here Barth argues that nothingness is the past, the defeated old foe who in Jesus Christ was destroyed as the end of His non-willing. "Because Jesus is Victor, nothingness is routed and extirpated."[56] Barth hopes to ensure that nothingness in the time *post Christum* is not taken with any seriousness, but that the attention of the Christian remain solely on the resurrection and the second coming in faith and hope.

Barth is surely right when he says that it is wholly un-Christian to hold in awe the present day manifestations of evil as though nothingness was the lord of the world. Here we return to Barth's realism and we must see true reality not in our experiences but in the revealed Word. Only when our experiences are united with the true Reality do we sense the reality of God in His hiddenness. He is also surely right when he chides those who feel they are serving the Christian cause by admitting that evil is the only true possibility. Yet he has given us only the two options at the extreme. We either see nothingness as the lord who is to be held in awe, or we see it as that which no longer exists, which is destroyed and past and insignificant.

We believe that in not interpreting the defeat of nothingness eschatologically, Barth has failed to consider a temporal separation between the cross, where the sentence of death was passed upon evil, and the execution of that sentence in the final *parousia*. Such a view would allow that in the final *parousia* Christ will annihilate nothingness from the realm of the created world, sending it back to its detached void, to true nothingness from which it was allowed to emerge in the creation of time and space. By holding to his view of

---

[55] Fiddes, *The Creative Suffering of God, op. cit.,* pp. 265-266. Barth would change the 'has become' to an 'always was' in the sense of the 'necessary antithesis'.
[56] CD III/3, p. 363.

an utter and final defeat in space and time as having been finally accomplished on the cross, Barth is left open to the criticism levelled against him that he does not take sin seriously. He is forced to talk in such instrumental ways about sin and evil in the time *post Christum* that they lose their character as real evil. Yet we have to remember Barth's 'revelatory positivism' in that he is not seeking a metaphysical construct or logical system but he is only concerned with being a faithful witness to what has been revealed. Barth will only allow for the one-way movement in revelation with the result that evil can only be described in these terms, regardless of the paradox which results.[57]

Finally, we will look at Barth's discussion of theodicy in this section. He insists, and rightly, that all talk of God, evil and humanity in their respective relationships must not be based on philosophical notions or general world-occurrence, but only on covenant history in the revelation of Jesus Christ. Only such a truly theo-logical (as opposed to a detached academic) discussion will be concrete and not abstract. This concrete discussion yields the all-determining point for Barth that to talk of nothingness is to talk of something that is past, judged and defeated. This is the only talk of nothingness which is legitimate given the cross. The only way in which nothingness can truly be 'seen' is in this backward glance, and to it as the defeated and routed past enemy of God. According to Barth's 'noetic eschatology', what we await in the second coming is the general revelation of this past and ultimate defeat.[58]

This is not to say that nothingness plays no role in our present day. It still acts as the adversary, it still acts as that which can visit us with mortal danger and can threaten us as of old. But in all of this it can only act, for its real and destructive power has been defeated. It is then only a shadow, an echo which exists in fragmentary form. Barth makes it clear that the ultimate routing of evil in the past is a fact which extends throughout the universe and its activity. "This is not yet recognizable, but it cannot be doubted and does not need to be

---

[57] This led S. Gottschalk to conclude of Barth, "He does not move from the problem of theodicy back to the understanding of God; rather, he moves out from the conviction that in the light of the revealed and experiencable reality of a sovereign and good God, evil *must* be described-both with respect to its ontological status and its operative character-in terms of its sheer negation, as what he calls 'das Nichtige'." ('Theodicy After Auschwitz and the Reality of God', *op. cit.,* p. 81) Here Gottschalk has identified three of our motifs as Barth's 'revelatory positivism' demands only that evil be described as it is revealed; in its ontology as the 'necessary antithesis' and in its operative character or noetic manifestation under the 'right and left hand of God'.

[58] In his article, G.V. Jones asks, in dealing with nothingness according to this understanding of it as wholly defeated and past, "is Barth writing about something actual, or is he toying with what he himself describes as *Gedankengespinst*?: a question suggested by his paradoxical method of writing and by the difficulty of providing an exact rendering of his terminology." ('God and Negation', *op. cit.,* p. 239) This is the danger in Barth's over-emphasis on the completedness of the work of Christ at the resurrection and the consequent down-grading of the salvific role of the final *parousia*.

repeated, fostered, augmented or extended."[59]　According to Barth's intense realism, we are required by faith to hold together the two facts that evil is manifested around us in all of its most hideous forms, seemingly increasing daily in its hold over us, and yet it is impotent and only an echo and shadow, having been destroyed and resigned to the past. If we see evil in the world it is because of the "blindness of our eyes and the cover which is still over us."[60] This cover will be removed in the second coming when the defeat of nothingness, as it was accomplished and completed on the cross, will be unveiled to all. Thus Barth stays true to his wholly noetic understanding of the nature of the second coming.[61]

The inevitable point to which we are led is that nothingness now operates solely and completely under the decree of God as its instrument, according to His will and for His own good purpose. This is the cumulative net result of Barth's development of his understanding of evil according to his doctrines of creation, providence and nothingness. "What it now is and does, it can be and do only in the hand of God."[62]　And we must understand this as the 'right hand' of God. We may then ask in a re-statement of the theodicy question, if evil is in the hands of God as its defeated foe, why must it be manifest in such an intolerable way in the world? Barth's answer for this is indicative of what will follow in CD IV. Returning to the idea of 'permission' Barth states that God "still permits His kingdom not to be seen by us, and to that extent He still permits us to be a prey to nothingness."[63]　God thinks it good that we should live our lives as if evil is not defeated, but understanding that it actually has been.

The question that must be asked here is 'why?' What possible reason could God have for defeating nothingness on the cross, with all that it cost Him, only then to pretend it never happened while His creation is forced to continue to suffer the pain of its continued activity? If ever the benevolence of God were called into question it is in this dubious idea, yet Barth is unable to escape it as a logical end to his understanding of evil. If it has been utterly defeated in our past, and now is under God's control as His submissive servant, and yet if it still is able to wreak such havoc on His creation, God must have a reason for withholding the second coming and allowing such evil to grow and fester in His creation.

---

[59]　CD III/3, p. 367.

[60]　Ibid. p. 367.

[61]　Again we see how G.V. Jones rejects this idea of the liquidation of evil as being a wholly past event. "The fact remains that the kingdom of the *Nichtige*, the rule of Evil, has not been liquidated. If the term 'defeat' has any meaning it is that the enemy is no longer there or has been disintegrated or has capitulated, that is, it has no more power. This is manifestly not the case. The sinister is as potent as ever." ('God and Negation', *op. cit.,* p. 243) This is typical of the criticisms leveled at Barth at this point and one which we shall employ as we look in Chapter VII to the role of the community in Barth's doctrine of evil.

[62]　CD III/3, p. 367.

[63]　Ibid. p. 367.

The ultimate justification for this 'permission' lies in the final *parousia* at which time God's glory will greatly overshadow all suffering which was manifest from his 'left hand', thus justifying His creation and, in the process, justifying Himself. Our faith and hope in this noetic unveiling of the new creation and its consequent justification of all evil and suffering is, in the end, Barth's theodicy.

CHAPTER VII

Evil, the Work of Christ and Barth's Eschatology

What is made clear in the incarnation of the Word of God and the offering up to death of the Son of God is that evil is not an element in the orderly course of the world, but an element, indeed *the* element which absolutely threatens and obscures it - the sowing of the enemy in the good field, the invasion of chaos, the nihilist revolution which can result only in the annihilation of the creatures.[1]

The Two Separations of Evil in Barth's Doctrine of Reconciliation

Barth's doctrine of reconciliation is a vast subject spanning some 2,600+ pages of the *Church Dogmatics* and care must be taken to understand its structure so as to do justice to its overarching themes in as succinct a way as possible. Barth gives three parallel treatments of the doctrine of reconciliation which correspond to the three Offices of Christ:

	Priestly Office	**Kingly Office**	**Prophetic Office**
Office =			
Truth of Christ =	Christ as God	Christ as Man	Christ as God-Man
Work of Christ =	Lord as Servant	Servant as Lord	The True Witness
Fulfillment =	Verdict of the Father	Direction of the Son	Promise of the Spirit
Sin =	Pride & Fall	Sloth & Misery	Falseh'd/Condemnat'n
Work against sin =	Justification	Sanctification	Vocation
H.S. in Community =	Gathering	Upbuilding	Sending
H.S. in Individual =	Faith	Love	Hope

Barth's ordering of these sections is again significant to his message. While Calvin and the Reformers held to the order of prophet, king and priest, and the Lutheran tradition to prophet, priest, and king, Barth explains his order of priest, king, and prophet,

For me the priestly and kingly offices in the narrower sense are the doings of Christ. The humiliation of God in becoming man and the exaltation of man up to God are respectively Christ's priestly and Christ's kingly work. Christ the prophet is Christ revealing Himself as King and Priest. To make clear what happens when He reveals Himself, I have to know what He is and does... Christ's priestly and

---

[1] CD IV/1, p. 411.

kingly offices are the subject-matter, the content of His prophetic office, because He reveals Himself.[2]

It is in the prophetic office where Barth's eschatology is most fully developed especially with regard to the role of evil in the time of the community and with a view to the second coming. Yet this eschatology is built upon the understanding of what happened to evil in the priestly and kingly work of Christ. These two works have much to say of evil which is the focus of this discussion of Barth's eschatology.

In Barth's doctrine of reconciliation we have the completion of the interconnected theme of his entire theology, both as a whole and with respect to his doctrine of evil. The striking picture which finally emerges concerning evil is its treatment within all three of the doctrines we have studied (God, Creation and Reconciliation) under the idea of *separation*. The overarching theme of evil is its 'peculiar ontology' in its state of rejection and separation from God and his creation. This picture emerged under the doctrine of God as God's eternal self-differentiation in His distinguishing Himself from 'not-God'. In eternity God *separated Himself* from all that was 'not-God'. As God's eternal state, this separation is a component of God's self-definition according to the motif of the 'necessary antithesis'.

We saw a similar separation in the doctrine of election where God rejected all possibilities of the perdition of the creature He had chosen to create in the positive election of all humanity in Jesus Christ. Future humanity was to be separated from evil in this election. Moving to the doctrine of creation, this separation was necessitated when creation, as the self-recapitulation of God, necessarily was met with the 'not-God' of His eternal self-differentiation. This required God to set His good creation off in opposition to what now in the space and time of creation became chaos. God's providence is the process of holding creation above the abyss of nothingness, ensuring this created separation remains as the outworking of the motif of the 'right and left hand of God'.

Now we turn to reconciliation and here we find two additional separations. Both are predicated upon the destruction which humanity has brought upon itself in choosing the impossible, the abyss over grace, and therefore nothingness over life. Humanity in its fallen state has opened the door for nothingness to enter the created realm and corrupt it. It is in this fallen, damned and lost state that reconciliation occurs.

As such, the first separation is a recapitulation in space and time of the primordial separation that took place on behalf of the creature as the first and fundamental act of creation. Genesis 1:2 is re-enacted on Calvary, but this time once and for all, objectively and eternally in Christ. What humanity overturned in the fall can no longer ultimately be overturned with regard to this separation. Thus in his doctrine of reconciliation Barth returns to the 'necessary antithesis'

---

[2] Barth, 'Table Talk', *op. cit.,* p. 17. It is interesting to note that this order has changed from Barth's earlier Göttingen Dogmatics where the sequence was prophet, priest and king.

motif and uses it to show how the completed work of Christ is the final separation between God and evil, and thus between humanity and evil. Corresponding to this divine act of separation, there is a second separation of the old nature of sin and the new person of grace in Jesus Christ and for us. The old nature of sin, which we all are, is set aside and destroyed in the salvific work of Christ. The work of His left hand is completed and the new person now emerges under the work of His right hand, and as God's creatures we are now involved in the process of moving from the one to the other. This strict division and separation is closely related to the cosmic separation of evil affected on Calvary, yet it is important in its own right and form as that separation in the life of the creature.

These four separations are the backbone of Barth's doctrine of evil. They flow throughout his work and operate within his positive theme of God's eternal covenant with humanity. Evil shadows the covenant in its inception in God's eternal election, for the elect Son was the elect Saviour of the cross and resurrection, the elect Suffering servant, the elect *homo labilis*. Evil shadowed the covenant in creation as the necessary backdrop for the working out of the covenant as a result of the fallen state of sinful humanity. And evil will shadow the covenant in reconciliation as the covenant is restored through and by the final separation of evil, and as humanity realizes its goal as God's creation through the salvation which such a separation requires. The 'necessary antithesis' motif can nowhere be more clearly seen than here, as evil is the 'necessary antithesis' to the covenant, a theme which we seen consistently throughout the *Church Dogmatics,* and which will come to its completion in this final chapter.

The Separation of Evil from Creation

We made the point earlier that the Fall of humanity into sin was both 'inevitable' and 'impossible'. We have shown how this tension allows Barth to hold together the cohesive theme of the covenant from election through reconciliation (according to the inevitability of sin) while at the same time exonerating God from the charge of being the Author of sin and instead placing full responsibility for sin on the humanity who made the absurd choice of sin (according to the impossibility of sin). Thus the fallen state of humanity is met by God neither with surprise nor with complacence, for God can be said to both know that this sin would occur and thus is prepared to overcome it, and that He holds humanity responsible for it and therefore reacts against it. This tension and its contributions to Barth's understanding of reconciliation is crucial lest we shift the emphasis too far in one or the other direction and run into the difficulties which emerge when the tension is lost. Barth employs this understanding when he posits that reconciliation is presupposed in the covenant. What takes place in Jesus Christ, in the historical event of the atonement accomplished by Him in time, "maintains and fulfills His Word as it was spoken at the very first. He affirms to us and sets among us His original promise and

His original command in the concrete reality and actuality of His own being as man."[3]

The atonement is assumed in the establishment of the covenant according to the election of humanity in *Jesus* Christ. It is the great act of God's covenant faithfulness, and therefore Barth can call the atonement, "His faithful execution of the plan and purpose which he had from the very first as the Creator of all things and the Lord of all events, and which He wills to accomplish in all circumstances."[4] The cohesiveness of election, creation and reconciliation cannot be lost, and neither, we may add, can the interconnectedness of the covenant and the shadow cast upon it by evil. The covenant is the presupposition of the act of reconciliation also because the inevitability of sin in creation was disabled by the election of God in Christ. And as election and the covenant are related, in a similar way so are the Fall and reconciliation. Barth affirms this connection,

> Even in a Christian doctrine of sin, although there can be no question of an innate potentiality for evil in accordance with creation, we have to reckon with the fact that, unlike God, man is indeed exposed to the assault of chaos by reason of his creatureliness, that he confronts the nothingness which is intrinsically alien to him, not with the superiority of God, but... with a certain reversionary tendency. Nor can it be contested, but only asserted, that within the created order it is the place of man to be not only the field and prize of battle, but himself the contestant in the divine conflict with nothingness which began with creation.[5]

The conflict with nothingness which involved humanity at the beginning of creation is now to be decided once for all in the final separation of it from creation. God chooses to do this according to His covenant faithfulness, God was free to act in this way to save humanity, and, "not to go back on His choice between chaos and the world which He created good, even in view of its corruption and in His righteous anger; not to resign as Creator and Lord of the creature, but to act and confirm Himself as such."[6] Humanity is a loser in this battle even as created and under the providential and parental care of God. Left to itself humanity has fallen, and as a result it is "rushing headlong into nothingness, into eternal death."[7] It will require nothing less than the direct involvement of God Himself to correct this wrong and to affect this ultimate separation. Therefore, "God Himself engages the nothingness which aims to destroy man. God Himself opposes and contradicts its onslaught on His creation

---

[3] CD IV/1, p. 47.

[4] Ibid. p. 47.

[5] CD IV/2, p. 398.

[6] CD IV/1, p. 307.

[7] Ibid. p. 213.

and triumph over His creature."[8]   In doing so God opposes sin for it is sin which "opens the door for the invasion of His creation by nothingness, because in sin the creature delivers itself up to it, itself becoming futile and chaotic."[9]

The Annihilation of Nothingness in the Death of Christ

In order to effect this separation, nothingness must be taken up by God Himself and finally destroyed in Him. This is the only way in which evil can meet its end, in Him, in God, in Christ. The two-fold work which affected this separation was that of death and resurrection.[10] Death was required, for the old nature, the sinful nature, the 'man of sloth and falsehood' had to die in the face of the wrath of God. This death was borne by God in Christ, and with His death came the death of sin, the death of chaos, the final defeat and separation of evil from creation. This death is the final *opus alienum*, the final activity of the left hand of God.[11]   Christ fulfils the overcoming of sin in the atonement, "in its

---

[8]   CD IV/2, p. 225.

[9]   Ibid. p. 225.

[10]   Jüngel says of evil under Barth's understanding of death and resurrection, "*Das Ziel und Ende des opus alienum Gottes ist aber im opus proprium Gottes, in Werk seiner Gnade gegeben. Und dieses Werk der Gnade Gottes gescheiht da, wo Gott sich in Jesus Christus selber dem ganzen Unwesen des Nichtigen ausgesetzt hat.*" (Jüngel, '*Die Offenbarung der Verborgenheit Gottes*', *op. cit.,* pp. 178-179) "The goal and end of God's *opus alienum* is given in God's *opus proprium* in the work of his grace. And this work of God's grace happens when God in the person of Jesus Christ himself dispels the whole horror of *das Nichtige*."

[11]   Barth's intense instrumentalism emerges here with regards to the duality of this old man - new man and the pre-figuring of such in creation. Despite the great emphasis given to the threatening quality of evil, the groundwork laid in providence and even before in the perfections of God is never forgotten. Barth states that the epistemology of evil in all of its breadth and depth comes only through Jesus Christ and the price He paid for its defeat. This definition of evil is also its limitation, and in the end, its conformity to the will of God. "Hence in the light of the One to whom all this was done, who had to suffer all this, we see plainly the man of sin. Here we have the actuality and totality of evil... of course it is shown to be limited here - not limited itself, as the being and activity of man, but limited by God whose gracious will is supremely served by this evil instrument." (CD IV/1, pp. 399)   In this way Barth can state that "according to the disposition and in the service of God death and nothingness are brought in and used for the reconciliation of the world with God, as instruments in His conflict with the corruption of the world and the sin of man." (CD IV/1, pp. 306)   Again we see the tension of the 'right and left hand of God' motif which requires both the confrontation of evil and the instrumentality of its cooperation with the positive work of the right hand. This goes back to Barth's rejection of all forms of dualism and, in the end, when coupled with God's sovereignty and the desire to take evil seriously, such a tension must be maintained. Therefore in this final section Barth continues to paint a confusing picture with regards to evil. For example, in the Sloth and Misery of Man, Barth contends, "God

limitless anguish of separation from God, by delivering up sinful man and sin in His own person to the non-being which is properly theirs, the non-being, the nothingness to which man has fallen victim as a sinner and towards which he relentlessly hastens."[12] This work is definitive and final.[13] In Christ this 'man of sin' and the present *Wirklichkeit* of evil in the world, "was taken and killed and buried in and with Him on the cross."[14] This is the 'No' of God which was sounded at the creation in the rejection of the *tohu wa-bohu* and which is sounded here again once and for all. "Here - *in exact correspondence with what He did as Creator when He separated light from darkness as nothingness* - He pronounced His relentless and irrevocable No to disordered man. Here, in and with this No, he made an end of that man once for all."[15] The separation which happened there happens here again, but definitively. "The omnipotence of God in the world, without and against the world, and therefore creating order for the world, is concretely identical with this righteous man, this second Adam who took the place of the first and put right what he had perverted."[16] As Christ took on our judgement, he fully and wholly died our death, the death to sin, which means the return to nothingness, to chaos.[17] He became in His death the non-being which was the destiny of all of us, and God's wrath was upon Him, as it should have been on us.

The Second 'Yes' of God the Creator

This saving of Christ is our salvation, and it is demonstrated in the resurrection, in which both God and humanity are justified. That the resurrection is the justification of God in creation includes what is described by Barth as a 'second Yes', "He has spoken a second Yes which creates and gives them new

---

Himself is affected and disturbed and harmed by it [evil]... His own glory is called into question. He Himself finds Himself assaulted by it in His being as God, and He hazards no less than His being as God to counter it." (CD IV/2, p. 401) Yet with regards to the Pride and Fall of Man he states, "God has broken evil in Jesus Christ. And since He has done this, it is settled once and for all that it can exist only within limits which were fixed beforehand and beyond which it cannot go." (CD IV/1, p. 409)

[12] CD IV/1, p. 253.

[13] "That is the great exchange which gives life to the world. The old is gone. Satan has fallen from heaven like lightening. The kingdom of God has come near. 'It is finished': what had to happen for the reconciliation, salvation, and peace of men, has really, radically, and fully been fulfilled." (Barth, *Christliche Gemeinde im Wechsel der Staatsordnungen*, 1948, p. 31, in Berkouwer, *Triumph of Grace, op. cit.,* p. 75)

[14] CD IV/1, p. 254.

[15] Ibid. p. 349. (emphasis mine)

[16] Ibid. p. 257. This separation is given its fullest development under the heading, 'The Judge Judged in our Place' (CD IV/1 §59.2).

[17] "God abandoned Him to chaos, as had to happen because of our transgressions, only in order to save Him from it." (CD IV/1, p. 307)

life; a Yes which He did not owe them, but which He willed to speak, and which was the gracious confirmation of His own original will to create and His act of creation"[18] This new 'Yes' is life because it calls forth the One who died in complete and utter solidarity with sinful and lost humanity.[19] The effect of this work was the annihilation of the nothingness which died with Christ but was not raised with Him. This radical exchange of God for humanity has brought the end of that which could destroy humanity but not God. In thinking it could destroy God with His creation, nothingness accomplished neither, but was itself destroyed.[20] All that is left is the exaltation of the new creation in the One in whom is has this newness.

> He became and was and is in this very act of His suffering and dying, the Conqueror, the Victor: exalted as man; entering into that above; passing from dereliction by God to perfect fellowship with Him; being set as a man at the right hand of the Father; and therefore putting into effect in our place and for us that alteration of the human situation... No one can alter the fact that he, too, is a brother of this One, and that this One lives for him.[21]

This then is the first separation found in Barth's doctrine of reconciliation.

The 'Necessary Antithesis' Re-defined and Defended

In this first separation there is the re-emergence of the motif of 'necessary antithesis', except here Barth offers a challenge and a qualification which we must address. The sinful nature is so because humanity has chosen the absurd and impossible in a direct denial of its created freedom. In rejecting any form of dualism either between God and evil or as an equilibrium between sin and grace, Barth states that evil can in no way be regarded as 'necessary'. Evil cannot be seen as a correlate to God or as an "original and indeed creative counter-deity which posits autonomous and independent facts... we cannot legitimately deduce this from a mere contrasting of the idea of evil with the idea of good."[22] He goes on to reject a necessary role to sin in the working of God which he

---

[18] Ibid. p. 308.

[19] "As the act of God's grace in the resurrection of Jesus Christ from the dead confronted His being in death, that is, His non-being as the One who was crucified, dead, buried and destroyed, as the One who had been and had ceased to be... The One who was exalted was the One who as abased." (CD IV/1, p. 305)

[20] "The conversion of the world to God has therefore taken place in Christ with the making of this exchange. There, then, in Christ, the weakness and godlessness and sin and enmity of the world are shown to be a lie and objectively removed once and for all." (CD IV/1, p. 76)

[21] CD IV/2, p. 383.

[22] CD IV/1, p. 408.

identifies with the optimism of Leibniz. "We say too much even if we say that this event [sin] may take place according to the divine will and appointment... There is no inner or outer necessity and therefore there is no inner or outer possibility."[23]

In doing so Barth is intent on supporting two critical points in his theology. One is that while evil is the eternally differentiated 'not-God' and thus is inevitably allowed access to creation, it nonetheless must never be seen as an independent reality alongside God. Evil is not related to God as in the philosophical constructs of good and evil, nor is evil the necessary and equal counter-balance to God. As we said earlier, evil is a factual necessity and never a logical necessity. We have seen that according to the 'necessary antithesis' motif the necessity does not derive from any idea of balance or equilibrium, but that even in its peculiar ontology of 'being in rejectedness' it must necessarily have this 'existence' in relation to God. This distinction must be maintained, and according to this distinction it continues to be supported by Barth's exposition here on reconciliation.

Secondly, Barth's denial of the necessity of sin is wholly in line with his view of sin as the 'impossible possibility'. This is a rewording of the 'inevitability' - 'impossibility' tension which we have demonstrated. Sin must always be seen as the absurd choice of humanity and never as a necessary part of God's work. Yet this absurd choice was inevitable and as such God's work assumed it in the eternal election of humanity which preceded the creation and determined the reconciliation of the creature. So Barth is able to say both that sin is never to be seen as 'necessary' and, in the same paragraph, "We must not go beyond the negative statement, that since man is not God he can be tempted along these lines and therefore it was not, and is not, excluded that this event [sin] will take place."[24] And surely, as Barth has repeatedly said elsewhere, this event was inevitable! Thus this motif is further substantiated in these qualifications by Barth.

This motif is further evidenced in Barth's section on the fulfillment of the broken covenant. We have made the point that an integral part of the development of this motif has been Barth's claim that the redeemed and reconciled humanity, the humanity saved from the edge of the abyss and from the fallen state of sin, is put in a greater position than what could have been hoped for for unfallen humanity. Barth claimed earlier that there was a greater blessing for the humanity saved in Jesus Christ than for the humanity which was simply the creature of the Creator, even if the non-fallen creature. The essence of this idea is that the goal of creation, the ultimate purpose for which God created the world was fulfilled not in the original creation, nor could it have been, but it was fulfilled only as a result of the salvific work of Christ in the sphere of the fallen race. In this way, without needing to embrace necessarily the optimists outlook or the full meaning of the *felix culpa*, evil and its manifestation as sin is indeed

---

23 Ibid. p. 410.
24 Ibid. p. 410.

necessary to the goal of creation. It is the required foe in the drama of *Heilsgeschichte*.

Here in Barth's doctrine of reconciliation he returns to this idea. The sending of the Son into the world was certainly to save it from sure perdition, "but that was not all. Eternal life as the continuance of man in fellowship with God Himself, in the *consortium divinitatis*, is not in any way assured to man simply because he is the creature of God. It is rather the particular promise of that light which lighteth every man from the beginning, the light of the covenant which God made with man."[25] This covenant, as we have surely demonstrated, is instituted in the history of *fallen* creation, for outwith this fallen state, there would be no covenant. Barth is tying together again the idea that fallen and redeemed humanity is able to achieve the goal in creation, the *consortium divinitatis* , which was not possible for unfallen humanity.[26] Here we see again this motif as the necessity, as understood according to its peculiar ontology as a 'being in rejectedness', of evil to the eternal goal of God for creation.

The Separation of the Old Sinful Nature From the New Person of Grace

What took place for all humanity for all time in Christ takes place for each of us individually as we are ontologically united with Christ. His victory is our victory, His exaltation is our exaltation. Yet what for Christ was a 'once for all' great event, is for us both a 'once for all' and a process of 'becoming' who we are objectively. To illustrate this Barth uses the orthodox idea of the death of the 'old man' of sin and the life of the 'new man' of grace and hope, reintroducing the motif of the 'right and left hand of God'.

Sin is developed in Barth's doctrine of reconciliation according to the threefold treatment of the work of Christ. In the first section, sin is the pride of humanity in response to the humiliation of the Servanthood of the Son which results in the fall of humanity; in the second, it is the sloth of humanity in response to the Kingship of the Son which results in the misery of humanity; and in the third it is the falsehood of humanity in response to the True Witness of the Son which results in the condemnation of humanity.

Sin can only be defined and discussed according to its Christocentric epistemology, for only in Christ do we see the extent and the depth of sin, and

---

[25] Ibid. p. 72.

[26] We must not be lead astray here by thinking that the idea of 'unfallen man' has no place in Barth's theology. Although he sees no pre-fallen time, he must affirm its possibility and even its absolute probability if he is to stay true to the understanding of sin as the 'impossible' and the absurd. That man was not in any way created as 'able to sin' and that his sin was his choice of the 'impossible' requires an unfallen creation in the primordial saga. We quote Goetz again, "There was no golden age for Barth, but there had to be at least a golden Sunday morning." (Goetz, 'In Search of the Illusively Enigmatic', *op. cit.,* p. 15)

consequently, who we are as sinners.[27] What such a look will tell us first and foremost is that sin is pride, disobedience and, ultimately, unbelief in the true 'goodness' of this fatherly care. This is seen in that the 'Word became flesh' to overcome humanity's sin in its self-orientation and self-alienation in which it looks to itself and not to God for help. In doing so, humankind creates its own god in this pseudo-divinity and as such it falls. In seeking its own glory it finds shame, in desiring to be its own judge, humanity is itself judged and condemned, in seeking to be free from a fictional bondage, the creature loses its real freedom. In the end, humanity wills what is objectively evil, in seeking its own right, it chooses the ultimate wrong. The result is the wrath of God which must now be directed at fallen humanity, although Barth consistently keeps to his line that sinful humanity is ever and always the *imago Dei*. For all of the depths of its fallenness, humankind is never at any time other than the creature who exists for God, and as a result of the salvific work of Christ, we must say it is never other than the one who is saved in Christ. "There is no heaven or hell in which he is out of the reach of God's Spirit or away from His countenance", and therefore the state of fallen man is such that "He can neither live with God nor can he die before Him."[28] This is the basis of the duality in man according to Luther's idea of *simul iustus et peccator*.

It is upon such an idea (although qualified from Luther's original intent) that Barth develops the second separation of evil in his doctrine of reconciliation. It has at its heart the distinction between the goodness of the creature and the utter sinfulness of his fallen state. We remember that the *imago Dei* is defined by Barth as the relationship within the covenant of grace which God has established with humanity. Therefore, since this relationship depends upon God and not humanity, even in the depth of the depravity of its fallenness, humanity can neither nullify nor escape the consequences of being within this covenantal relationship. This does not mean God does not reject humanity in His wrath, but it does mean that there is a distinction in this rejection. "We can indeed say that God hates sin but does not cease to love the sinner. But it is only as we see God in Jesus Christ that we can really say this."[29]

This duality in humanity is shown on the one hand in that through sin evil is given its nature and form, for humanity's sin is the door through which evil crosses the frontier and enters the created sphere. "Man is the dark corner where wrong can settle and spread and flourish in all its nothingness as though by right."[30] Humanity's sin therefore attracts the wrath of God against this manifestation of evil, and yet humanity remains the covenant partner of God.

---

[27] "Only when we know Jesus Christ do we really know that man is the man of sin, and what sin is, and what it means for man." (CD IV/1, p. 389)

[28] CD IV/1, pp. 482-483.

[29] Ibid. p. 406.

[30] Ibid. p. 539.

This puts humanity in the serious position of being taken seriously by God[31] and, "If it is the case, then, that as a wrongdoer man has fallen victim to the strict and radical and definitive judgement of God but still continues to belong to Him as the good creature and elect of God, this means that the righteousness of God comes upon him as a crisis."[32] This crisis is the dividing of the existence of humankind at its very roots between the right and left hand, between its determination as the wrongdoer before God and its even greater determination as one on the way to the goal for which it was created.

> On the left hand, therefore, he is the man who can only perish, who is overtaken by the wrath of God, who can only die, who has already been put to death and done away, and on the right hand he is the same man who even in this dying and perishing, even as the one who has been put away, is still the one who stands over against God, object of His purposes, surrounded and maintained by His life.[33]

The dialectic between this right and left hand existence of humanity could not be drawn more sharply. On the left hand humanity is truly and utterly destroyed by the wrath of God, and on the right it is saved as the elect and good creature of God's good creation. God makes this division in humanity and draws this deeply dividing line in its existence, and yet the situation is not static or else it would constitute a true dualism within humanity. Instead it is a fluid and dynamic movement from the one to the other, a life-long process of identification with the former man of sin, but also and already solidarity now and in the future with the new creation in Christ. These two sides in this movement coincide with the righteousness and grace of God, the 'Yes' and 'No' of God which occurred in the separations at creation. "The dividing of the righteousness and grace of God as we have described it is an event: a dividing which is forcefully prefigured by the Creator's dividing of light and darkness, of the waters above the firmament and the waters below the firmament, of the sea and the land; a dividing to the left and right which is comprehensive, total and definitive."[34]

The righteousness of God in the justification of humanity assumes this left side on behalf of the right, dealing with the 'No' on behalf of the 'Yes', and therein lies humanity's salvation. This left and right hand, this 'No' and 'Yes' correspond to the death and resurrection in the work of Christ, forming the basis for the salvific work of Christ as He bears the wrath we should have borne and wins the victory over evil which humanity inevitably lost at the commencement of creation. Humanity, then, has a past and a present state which correspond to the work of the right and left hand of God and to the two sides of the antithesis

---

[31] Man is still God's possession, "even when that catastrophe breaks upon him, even in the consuming fire of the wrath of God, even in his mortal sickness, even when he has to perish, even in his dying and destruction." (CD IV/1, p. 540)

[32] Ibid. pp. 540-541.

[33] Ibid. p. 541.

[34] Ibid. p. 547.

of light and darkness as they were separated at creation. In this way there occurs the second separation in Barth's doctrine of reconciliation. We must look closer at the two sides of humanity in this separation.

The Death of the 'Old Man' Under the Left Hand of God

The wrath of God against humanity is meted out according to the work of the left hand of God, and there the 'old man' dies and is destroyed, and with him the evil which was the root of his fall. We must be clear here to see that for Barth, the 'old man' is dead and destroyed in all of the reality with which Christ died and was buried. Therefore,

> the God against whom the man of sin contends has judged this man, and therefore myself as this man, in the self-offering and death of Jesus Christ His own Son, putting him to death and destroying him; and He has revealed and continually reveals him as the one who is judged and put to death and destroyed in the resurrection of Jesus Christ from the dead and His being and living and witness for all ages.[35]

On Calvary, the sinful nature of humanity is, in the same way as the rejected nothingness of creation, resigned to a state of utter pastness. The sinner under the wrath of God had to suffer and die and be destroyed and, in the fullest and most profound way, he did and was. All of this happened not to us but 'for' us in Jesus Christ.

> The Son of God died in our place the death of the old man, the man of sin... the containment of sin as it has taken place on the cross of the Son of Man, the complete replacement there of the man of sin, took place in the conflict of an unreconcilable and unbridgeable opposition in which only the one or the other could remain and one or the other had necessarily to give place... the divisive No of the wrath of God, which is the consuming fire of His love, lay on the old man, destroying and distinguishing him... an unequivocal and intolerable and definitive enemy of God was treated as he deserved and *utterly destroyed*.[36]

All of the ways of our old humanity are now the impossible and absurd choices of that which is annihilated. This allows Barth to say that history as we know it, human history actually ended with the death of Christ. What is opened up to us is the new creation, new life in Christ and the hope of our full redemption in the second coming. This 'right and left hand of God' motif coincides with the death and resurrection and, as we can now see, to the separation of the old life, the sinful and fallen state of humanity, the corruption

---

[35] Ibid. p. 390.
[36] CD IV/2, pp. 399-400. (emphasis mine)

of nature and the destruction of the man of sin in the wrath of God, from the new life in Christ, the life of the new creation and the hope of the new world to come.

This radical separation is the result of the coalescence of all four of the separations in Barth's theology.[37] It brings together the eternal separation of God in His self-differentiation, for in this final separation the eternal will of God is realized and the eternal enemy is defeated. It includes the separation in creation where the enemy of creation and the rejected *tohu wa-bohu* are finally truly destroyed and no longer able to be a threat to humanity or, through humanity, to God. And it combines the two separations of evil and creation and the old and new state of the individual. All four are portrayed here in this radical understanding of the final and great 'once for all' separation in the death and resurrection of Jesus Christ. This is the cohesiveness of Barth's doctrine of evil in the *Church Dogmatics*.

The Ontological Reality of the 'New Man' in Christ

As the death of Christ is the basis for the death of the 'old man' and we with him, so the resurrection is the basis for the new life in Christ, and our subsequent exaltation and life.[38] Yet this new creature is not a completed reality for us but only in Christ and here we can see Barth's realism emerge. We are on our way to being who we are ontologically already in Jesus Christ. This must be kept in mind if Barth's discussion of this issue is not to become nearly incomprehensible. We *are* ontologically and objectively this new creation. Yet we are also *becoming* this new creation and this state (fluid state) of becoming will continue until the final *parousia*. We must anticipate Barth's eschatology and add that this does not mean that something of ontological or salvific significance will happen in the second coming. Barth's eschatology is wholly noetic and revelatory. What it means is that the objective reality of who we are,

---

37 "Nothingness has its reality and character, and plays its past, present and possibly future role, as the adversary whom God has regarded, attacked and routed as His own enemy. All that makes it threatening and dangerous, all that it can signify as disturbance and destruction in the relationship between God and creature, all its terrible features, all the hostility to God and nature which characterizes and proceeds from it, can be summed up in the fact that it is that which God did not will and therefore did not tolerate but which He Himself removed. Indeed, we may say that if nothingness is not viewed in retrospect of God's finished act of conquest and destruction, it is not seen at all." (CD III/3, p. 366)

38 "The resurrection of Jesus Christ from the dead is at once the fulfillment and the proclamation of this positive sentence of God. Man is a suitable human partner for the divine partner. He is the one in whom God delights. He is a faithful servant and a friend and a dear child of God. This man was brought in with the resurrection of Jesus Christ from the grave, and with just the same energy with which the old man of contradiction and opposition was done away with in the death of Jesus Christ." (CD IV/1, p. 95)

our true ontology in Christ will be revealed and we will then be able to become in full who we already are but cannot fully become in our time.

This means that we are still living in the contradiction of this radical division, and this must finally be explained in further detail. Barth gives an indication of this dilemma by calling it "necessarily puzzling."[39] In fact, he sees this puzzle as the proper result of our justification, "It [our justification] is genuine and complete, but contradictory, concealed under this contradiction. It is only in the being together of that which is antithetical, in the form of a riddle, in the mystery of the *simul peccator et iustus*."[40] We stand between our 'whence' and 'whither', between our past which is still present and our future which is already here. He describes this as, "his coming out of the wrong which is removed and destroyed, his coming, therefore, out of his own death, and in that coming - this is his present - his going forward to his new right and therefore to his new life."[41] This process is our sanctification which is brought about through the Holy Spirit who works death in us to the old man and life of the new, in the understanding that for all of the fluidity of this process, it will be for us a movement unto death. Using the 'right and left hand of God' motif, Barth explains this movement in the Spirit,

> From the right hand there is that which proceeds from the Spirit... and on the left hand here is that which stems from the contradiction of the being of man in Jesus Christ; that which is done is a relapse and apostasy into unfreedom, into the nothingness which is already abolished and done away with, that which involves a return to the closed kingdom of the dead... The Holy Spirit knows and distinguishes and separates in the man to and in who he works the new man which he is created and elected and determined and called to be... from the old man who is already superseded in the existence of the man Jesus, who continually stirs and moves in us as if he still had a right and place there... and the Holy Spirit affirms the one man and negates the other.[42]

What the Holy Spirit works to destroy in us is any sense of balance between the two states of human existence, and here we see Barth return to his understanding of the relationship of sin and grace. It emerges here as the same distinction between the old sinful nature and the new creation in Christ where the two are not equals or in a state of equilibrium which would give credibility and a sense of necessity to the old nature by virtue of such a stability in its relationship to the new. There is not only no such balance, but there is no

---

[39] CD IV/1, p. 548. "*Sie muß uns schon rätselhaft sein.*" (KD IV/4, p. 611)
[40] Ibid. p. 602.
[41] Ibid. p. 545.
[42] CD IV/2, p. 368.

connection at all between these two states.[43] Instead our new life is held under a two-fold determination which produces a radical division and a very convoluted state of existence.[44] In this state as *simul iustus et peccator* humanity can only hope to survive by understanding that it is "prevented from understanding this *simul* as something lasting and definitive."[45] Thus the hope of humanity is that this is not its final state, but that it is and must be and will become wholly the one and none of the other. The left hand is becoming truly past, and the right hand, now separated from the inimical left, is its true and objective reality towards which humanity moves, it is the new creation in Christ. Just as God separated the light from darkness, just as He rejected the 'not-God' by and through the work of His Son as the eternally elected *homo labilis,* so here God separates the old sinful humanity from the new. In the process of this separation, evil is destroyed and no longer able to be a threat to this new creation again. This is the justification of creation, and with it, the justification of the Creator Himself.

The Status of Evil in Light of These Two Separations

We must now determine what this means for Barth's doctrine of evil, and we must carefully define the consequences of the fact that the old sinful nature is dead, destroyed and utterly past and gone, and, consequently, what we are to make of the presence of evil and sin in our world. There are three conclusions which we can draw from the impact which is brought to bear on evil in the priestly and kingly work of Christ.

First, evil must now and forever be seen as no longer a threat to humanity. The ontological union of all humanity in the salvific work of Christ assures us that the threat of nothingness is gone, it cannot pose to us the abyss, for the 'atonement filled the abyss of nothingness', and that atonement was universal, effectual and final. Barth will have us see a return to sin in this way as the 'absurd' (*absurd*) and 'impossible' (*unmöglichen*) choice which faced humanity at creation. Yet it is still a choice and will be until the final *parousia.* The question we ask is, can the results of such an absurd choice be, in the end, truly detrimental? Is there room left anywhere for evil to rise up again, now for a second time, and prove to be a threat? If so, then the effectualness of the priestly and kingly works of Christ, and the efficaciousness of these two critical separations are in peril. This is the first point we must always keep before us, for it is incontrovertible and unequivocal.

---

[43] "There is no continuity or harmony or peace between the death of that old man and the life of this new." (CD IV/2, p. 399)

[44] "The situation can be understood, therefore, only in the following terms. In the twofold determination of the man engaged in conversion we have to do with two total men who cannot be united but are necessarily in extreme contradiction. We are confronted with two mutually exclusive determinations." (CD IV/2, p. 571)

[45] Ibid. p. 573.

Second, if evil still remains, which we must affirm on both exegetical and existential grounds, then according to the providence of God, the omnipotence of God and the sovereignty of God, evil must 'exist' wholly and solely in absolute subservience and subordination to God. The very fact that evil does still 'exist' is in itself problematic given the forcefulness of Barth's exposition on its banishment and removal. Barth gives evidence to the tension and paradox he faces in statements such as, "It [sin] is present only as something which has been eternally removed and destroyed."[46] The logical inconsistency of this statement is a preview of the difficulties which lie ahead as Barth attempts to square the completedness of the work of Christ with the justification for the time of the community. Whatever nothingness may be allowed to do in its present existence, it can never again be inimical to God's creation. Any talk of evil as still a threat to God and His creation must be regarded as fraudulent, or Barth's talk of these two great separations is a charade. If we take the terms 'utterly destroyed', 'abolished and done away with', 'extinguished', 'defeated', 'conquered' and 'banished' at all seriously, then the enemy of God can no longer in any possible way be considered to be anything but the impotent puppet of a victorious Lord.[47]

Finally, if evil does exist, as we affirm it does, then it must do so for a reason. It must have a role to play, for its existence hangs by a thread based upon our two conclusions above. If God empowers it and arms it as we were told in the providence of God, and if it remains armed and empowered after the two final separations of the cross and resurrection, then it must have a reason, a purpose and a goal for doing so. God is not a God of arbitrariness or concupiscence. We can only look to evil in our world as a necessary means to some end which God has so decreed, without losing sight of the fact that this 'means' is having a catastrophic effect on God's new creation. Put in terms of the theodicy question, there must be some ultimate and all conclusive justification for every single moment of evil in the time *post Christum* given Barth's exposition of evil in his theology.

These three conclusions bring us to the question of the time of the community and Barth's eschatology. The point we have reached brings into sharp critique the very existence of this time between the resurrection and the

---

[46] CD IV/1, p. 553.

[47] G.V. Jones echoes this critique, "Nevertheless, the fact remains that the Kingdom of the *Nichtige*, the rule of Evil, has not been liquidated. If the term 'defeat' has any meaning it is that the enemy is no longer there or has been disintegrated or has capitulated, that is, it has no more power. This is manifestly not the case." This is the essence of the problem in Barth's use of these terms. Jones ends his article by offering a dialectical answer to this problem in the form of paradox, "the truth of God is the only instrument in routing the *Nichtige*; but it is nevertheless not yet routed. The sinister twist in creation exists by the permission of God, yet in reality only in a permitted opposition to it. The Incarnation has not yet routed the demonic manifestation of the *Nichtige*, but it alone can do so." ('God and Negation', *op. cit.,* pp. 243-244) This is a good statement on the paradox presented by Barth, and Jones should be commended for allowing it to stand as such.

final coming of Christ. The question is put most simply; if evil is no longer inimical to God, nor to humanity nor to creation, and if the salvific work of Christ is both complete and conclusive, what is the justification for this time of such intense evil and such overwhelming suffering? In this time, neither the defeat of evil nor the completion of God's salvific work for us lies ahead of us, but wholly and completely and ontologically behind us. If this is true for all humanity, as Barth has surely stated with great emphasis, then Barth's eschatology poses problems in his theology with regards to his treatment of evil.

Evil in the Time of the Community

There are three issues which will determine how we interpret and critique Barth's discussion of eschatology under the Prophetic Work of Christ. The first has been determined by our look at the two separations in his doctrine of reconciliation and the resultant status of evil as it now faces the Church and the world in the time of the community. The second is how much latitude can be given to Barth in his dialectical approach when he develops key issues which seem to conflict with the preponderance of his thought. This is also the question of our fourth motif in Barth's 'revelatory positivism' and the 'happy inconsistency' which he is willing to allow. The third is the clear tendency towards *apocatastasis* in Barth's theology, and here it becomes vitally important that we look at this issue in more detail. A main critique of Barth's 'noetic eschatology' depends to great degree on this interpretation.

Apocatastasis and the Condemnation of Humanity

There is in Barth's theology a strong tendency and an inner logical movement towards the stance of universalism. We have seen it emerge with strength in Barth's doctrine of God (especially with regard to election) and in his doctrine of creation, and here, under the prophetic work of Christ, it receives its definitive treatment.

In distinction to Jesus Christ as the True Witness, humanity has engaged in the falsehood of sin which has brought about its own condemnation. This condemnation is the life which humanity has chosen for itself in its pride and sloth. The creature refuses the truth, the prophetic Word, and as a result it refuses its own pardon. By turning this truth into untruth, it turns its pardon into its judgement and condemnation. By 'condemnation' *(Verdammnis)* Barth means that humanity, "stands under the threat and danger of being damned. His condemnation hangs over him like a sword. Less cannot be said in relation to his falsehood."[48] Yet this condemnation still 'hangs' and the sword has not yet fallen. The condemnation is not yet pronounced, the threat not yet fulfilled, the

---

[48] CD IV/3.1, p. 465.

creature is not yet damned, not yet lost.[49] Humanity still has time before the threat becomes reality. What there is now over it is only the threat.

The tension Barth creates here is between the position that the threat of damnation has not yet been carried out, and that, try as it might, humanity in its falsehood can never succeed in turning truth into untruth, thus canceling its objective reality by denying it in its subjective activity.[50] This objective reality is on the offensive causing confusion in the untruth of humanity and confronting it with the real truth, the truth of its objective reconciliation before God in

---

[49]   There is evidence for Barth's strong tendency towards *apocatastasis* in his discussion of those who are 'totally unredeemed'. Despite his statement that the term 'unredeemed', "describes their ontic situation as well as their noetic, their external as well as their internal, their objective as well as their subjective" (CD IV/3.1, p. 338), even in this ontic and objective unredeemed state Barth goes on to say, "Nevertheless, it is true for them, too that the work of Jesus Christ precedes and follows all being and occurrence in our sphere and therefore their own ignorant and enslaved existence, that He Himself is not conditioned by the valid and effective conditions which are their judgement, but is their Lord. They can find no hope in their freedom actualised in bondage. But He is their hope too. For He is on the way from His commencement to His goal. No competition is offered to His work by any situation which arises and persists in our sphere, however objectively or subjectively corrupt. This work cannot be destroyed or arrested." (pp. 338-339) We strain for words which would clarify this statement but no such definitive statement is to follow. We conclude from this that even in an ontic and objective unredeemed state of the non-Christian as it stands under the judgement of God, the non-Christian in all of his rebellion cannot offer any true competition to the Son's completed and completing work of reconciliation and redemption. In spite of sin and rebellion, rejection and self-inflicted isolation, 'this work cannot be destroyed or arrested' *(zunichte gemacht oder auch nur aufgehalten werden kann).* (KD IV/3.1, p. 391) As in the majority of places where Barth handles issues relating to universal salvation and eternal perdition, there is only enough here to allow us to speculate as to his final position. Yet it seems clear that when these statements are combined with the numerous other accounts, we have a strong case for concluding that Barth anticipates the redemption of all humanity in the final *parousia.*

[50]   Throughout his soteriology Barth is keen never to let the noetic determine the ontic. He is consistent here for in his commentary on the Heidelberg Catechism and in his article on Romans 5 he stays to this all important line. In the former, after basing the Christian's assurance of heaven on his knowledge of who he is in Christ, Barth asks who are the enemies of God who are condemned before the Judge? He answers, "If we want to understand condemnation correctly, we must hold fast to the fact that all men (we too!) are his enemies - but that we all go to meet the Judge whom we Christians may *know*... We certainly should not weaken the seriousness of condemnation, but we should hold fast to the fact that Christ *suffered also for them.* Then the contrast between the elect (us) and the damned (them) can continue to concern us only humorously." (*Heidelberg Catechism, op. cit., p.* 82) In the latter reference, Barth seeks to show that the rule of grace is not for those only who have the mark of the Christian, but it is for all of those who are in Adam. "What is *Christian* is secretly but fundamentally identical with what is *universally human.*" ('Christ and Adam in Romans 5', *op. cit.,* p. 43)

Christ. This is the pain of humanity in its falsehood, this constant truth and reality which strives against this humanity and confronts this humanity. Because this and not the untruth of humanity is reality, there is set a limit on its falsehood and the resultant condemnation.

We are prompted to ask if there is in this scenario a true threat to this humanity in its falsehood? This is again, but most pointedly, the question of *apocatastasis* which Barth takes head on,

> Can we count upon it or not that this threat will not finally be executed, that the sword will not fall, that man's condemnation will not be propounded, that the sick man, and even the sick Christian will not die and be lost rather than be raised and delivered from the dead and live?[51]

Barth's answer is wholly conditioned by the key words 'count upon' *(rechnen)*, for God's universal grace in the face of the our falsehood cannot be assumed or counted upon, but if it does happen it is "a matter of the unexpected work of grace."[52] Barth will not allow for a withdrawal of the threat which hangs over human falsehood in a doctrine of certain *apocatastasis*. Barth's words are crucial here,

> No such postulate can be made even though we appeal to the cross and resurrection of Jesus Christ. Even though theological consistency might seem to lead our thoughts and utterances most clearly in this direction, we must not arrogate to ourselves that which can be given and received only as a free gift.[53]

Barth is concerned that grace should remain grace, that the freedom of the gift should never be compromised by the assumption of humanity that in some way this universal salvation is owed to it or must logically be bestowed upon it. He is not denying that God can save all, nor that God desires to save all. He is denying only that all *must* be saved, and it is the 'must' which is the key in his words of warning.

Thus his warning is balanced with the idea that we should be open to the very good possibility that God's grace will extend to all and that, as we are all reconciled in Him, this final threat may be withdrawn. "If for a moment we accept the unfalsified truth of the reality which even now so forcefully limits the perverted human situation, does it not point plainly in the direction of the work of a truly eternal divine patience and deliverance and therefore of an *apocatastasis* of universal reconciliation?"[54] Here is the critical balance - we are forbidden to

---

51 CD IV/3.1, p. 477.
52 Ibid. p. 477.
53 Ibid. p. 477.
54 Ibid. p. 478.

count upon universal reconciliation and we are also commanded to pray for it and hope for it.[55]

We must discern between Barth's guarding of the grace of God in his seeking this balance, and in the underlying assumption by him in his theology that this is indeed what will come about.[56] To his credit, Barth can and does do both. He is able to stay one step back from an outright avowal of *apocatastasis* while within his theology he develops the unstated but clearly understood assumption that this universal grace will actually be realized by all creation.[57]

---

[55] Yet further evidence is available to support Barth's tendency towards universalism. Barth asks what the Christian should expect in the final coming of Christ when his (the Christian's) eyes will be fully opened, "Not his eyes alone, but those of the whole community which has hoped in Him in every age and place, and indeed of all men who have lived, or live, or will live, will see this great light, will be terrified by it, but will also be made to rejoice by it... to all men and all creation, there will then come the great change of the overthrow of all contradiction in which they now exist and the necessary bending of every knee to Jesus Christ and the confessing of Him as Lord by every tongue. This then is what the Christian expects." (CD IV/3.2, p. 931-932)

[56] This balance, when it is sought by Barth, always in the end gives way to what we will call his 'logically required' and 'implicitly affirmed' universalism. This was seen in his discussion of the fate of Judas from his doctrine of election in CD II/2. Barth's desire to keep a real tension, a true 'contrast' which the Church is called to keep, is overcome in his overwhelming emphasis on the victorious grace of God over all sin and human folly. If human wickedness is truly powerless in the face of the grace of God, and if we know from Scripture that God desires it that all men be saved, the conclusion of universal salvation is inevitable. Yet for Barth, as much as we believe he truly believes this, there is benefit in the tension, and that is his point. As we will continue to show, the tension is vital if grace is to be preserved. Our point here is that his attempts to preserve this tension must not divert us from the unequivocal conclusion that universalism in Barth's theology is both 'logically required' and 'implicitly affirmed'.

[57] We will again give evidence for our case that Barth tends strongly in this direction. This time the evidence seems overwhelming. In the Promise of the Spirit Barth talks about the determination of the non-Christian as he faces the power of the Holy Spirit. In a statement reminiscent of the Calvinistic doctrine of irresistible grace Barth writes, "And when there comes the hour of the God who acts in Jesus Christ by the Holy Ghost, *no aversion, rebellion, or resistance on the part of non-Christians will be strong enough to resist the fulfillment of the promise of the Spirit which is pronounced over them too,* which applies to them, which envisages and comes to them, or to hinder the overthrow of their ignorance in the knowledge of Jesus Christ and therefore of themselves as creatures reconciled in Him, or to prevent the discovery of their freedom as such, and therefore the beginning of its exercise, and therefore the Christian alteration and renewal of their existence. Their blindness and deafness still stand like a dam against the surging and mounting stream. *But the stream is too strong and the dam too weak for us to be able reasonably to expect anything but the collapse of the dam and the onrush of the waters.* In this sense Jesus Christ is the hope even of these non-Christians." (CD IV/3.1, pp. 355-356, emphasis mine)

Thus the strong tendency towards *apocatastasis* does not conflict with his desire to keep to this balance where he is forced to address this topic directly. Therefore, in Barth's theology, the universal salvation of all humanity in Jesus Christ is both 'logically required' and 'implicitly affirmed'. It is logically required by Barth's rationalism which makes requisite a consistency in doctrine. It is implicitly affirmed as the *eschaton* of all of God's creatures as they are held in the covenantal faithfulness from which they can never escape. There are two further pieces of evidence to support this conclusion.

Barth's Doctrine of Hell and the Day of Judgment

Barth's understanding of the Biblical idea of hell is not in conflict with his underlying universalism. In his doctrine of election Barth posited the absurd possibility of unbelief in which we must take the thought of hell seriously. "We must certainly take their punishment and suffering in all seriousness. The judgements which fall on them and us are not merely merited, but are, in fact, hard and severe... It is a serious matter to be threatened by hell, sentenced to hell, worthy of hell, and already on the road to hell." Yet Barth quickly follows with his now-familiar qualification, "On the other hand, we must not minimize the fact that we actually know of only one certain triumph of hell - the handing-over of Jesus - and that this triumph of hell took place in order that *it would never again be able to triumph over anyone.*"[58] There remains no possibility for any triumph of hell over anyone given the effectual work of Christ. This is Barth's first point.

In Barth's doctrine of creation he again shows that there is a hell where the wrath of God burns directly upon humanity and where humanity perishes in the very separateness of that alienating wrath. This is the place of hopelessness and despair; it is our place, the place of sinners, and because and as it is poised against God and God against humanity,

> Here it becomes 'hell'. Here the alienation from God becomes an annihilatingly painful existence in opposition to Him. Here being in death becomes punishment, torment, outer darkness, the worm, the flame - all eternal as God Himself, as God Himself in this antithesis, and all positively painful because the antithesis in which God here acts cannot be a natural confrontation, but must inevitably consist in the fact that infinite suffering is imposed upon the creature which God created and destined for Himself when God reacted against this creature as it deserves.[59]

Barth could show in no more perspicacious fashion the reality and horror of hell. He takes it with the utmost seriousness that sinful man, condemned man,

---

[58] CD II/2, pp. 495-496. (emphasis mine)
[59] Ibid. pp. 603.

rejected and judged man is clearly and rightfully here in this place. However, in a most critical focus of our attention, Barth proceeds directly to tell us *who this man in hell is,*

> It is, of course, true that this man is the Son of God. In Him God Himself suffers what guilty man had to suffer by way of eternal punishment. This alone gives the suffering of this man its representative power. This is what makes it the power by which the world is reconciled to God.[60]

The man in hell is this man and *only this man.* That Jesus suffered true hell for us, and that that suffering reconciled us means that we will never have to stand where Jesus stood, and we must affirm this if the *pro nobis* is to have its real efficacious meaning.[61]

In Barth's doctrine of reconciliation he returns to this subject under the priestly and kingly work of Christ. By affirming the irrevocable covenant God has made with humanity means that for rejected and condemned sinful humanity, there is no escape from God, not even in hell itself. If humanity were destroyed or annihilated, it would serve as a relief from this relationship with God which has, for the sinner, turned into a hellish relationship in his rejection of the grace and fatherly care of God. Barth's point is clear, hell is no place of refuge in a final separation from God, "there is no heaven or hell in which he is out of the reach of God's Spirit or away from his countenance."[62]

Hell is an eternal state of a relationship of rejection and rebellion against the grace of God in which God's love must have *den Charakter verzehrenden Feuerst (the character of a consuming fire)*.[63] Humanity is delivered up to its own disobedience and as such the state of fallen humanity is serious indeed. Then comes the expected balance and emphasis on the grace of God in the face of this

---

[60] Ibid. pp. 603-604.

[61] This all-important point is made again by Barth when he states that the judgement of God upon sinful humanity was absolutely essential and requisite. "God would not be God, the Creator would not be the Creator, the creature would not be the creature, and man would not be man, if this verdict and its execution could be stayed." (*Dogmatics in Outline, op. cit.,* p. 118) Indeed this verdict was executed, and hell had its sinful man as it rightfully must. God's judgement is fully and completely executed, "but in such a way that what man had to suffer is suffered by this One, who as God's Son stands for all others... In Him God makes Himself liable at the point at which we are accursed and guilty and lost." (p. 119)

[62] CD IV/1, p. 482.

[63] KD IV/1, p. 540. "The grace of God is still turned to man, but this now means that it is non-grace, wrath and judgement to the one who despises and hates it and will not live by it." (CD IV/1, p. 483)

dire situation of humanity.[64] God has acted on behalf of humanity with the result that, "His forgiveness makes good our repudiation and failure and thus overcomes the hurt we do to God... His forgiveness repels chaos, and closes the gulf, and *ensures that the will of God will be done on earth as it is in heaven.* What, then, is the guilt of man in light of the fact that God encounters him in this way, as the One who pardons his sin?"[65]

In this way, "the wrong of man cannot in any way alter the right of God."[66] God has a right over humanity as the Creator and faithful covenant Partner of humanity, and humanity can never escape the ramifications of this right of God.[67] God's right over humanity is grounded in the internal right of His very Godhead, it is truly His eternal right. What is the result of this being in the *Rechte Gottes*? There is only one possible meaning, "what other right can it be than that of grace, and what else can the exercise and application of it be in His righteousness but in its very essence and at its very heart the realization of His grace?"[68] We remember in Barth's doctrine of creation that space for creation is made in God Himself, and therefore any ideas of hell must never be posited as being somewhere 'outside' of God. In his doctrine of election He elected all humanity in Jesus Christ, and with this election God claimed all humanity; all humanity then is under his right. The combination of these two doctrines with the ontic work of Christ bring Barth to these conclusions which again show that hell cannot be conceived as a possible eternal place of condemnation for the creature. To be so would be for God Himself to forfeit His own right and purpose in creation; it would be for God to forsake Himself in his own eternal Godhead, from which this right flows.

Finally, Barth portrays hell as an alibi for the person who would reject his or her ontological salvation and union with Christ. It is the choice a person makes to his or her own shame, but it is a false and, in the end, it is as impossible a choice as unbelief itself.[69] Our choice to reject our own

---

[64] "God is too intimately bound with man for Him not to be affected by man's repudiation and failure, for Him not to be genuinely disturbed and hurt and wounded by it." (CD IV/1, p. 485)

[65] Ibid. p. 486. (emphasis mine)

[66] Ibid. p. 534.

[67] "Man may fall. Indeed he necessarily falls, and into the abyss, when he sets himself in the wrong and against God. But in this fall into the abyss he cannot fall out of the sphere of God and therefore out of the right which God has over him and to him... even in the lowest depths of hell, *whatever that might mean for him*, he is still the man whom God has elected and created, and as such he is in the hand of God." (CD IV/1, p. 534, emphasis mine)

[68] Ibid. pp. 536-537.

[69] Berkouwer provides a helpful comment here. "As sin is ontologically impossible because it cannot achieve what it aims to achieve - man's separation from the grace of God - so unbelief is an *impossible* reality because it cannot touch what in God's decision has become *irrevocable* truth, namely, that God's grace is for *all men*. This line of thought is plain. Even though the expression 'ontological impossibility' is

sinfulness, and therefore to reject our own salvation as one rescued from the abyss, is to choose hell. "The only alibi that he can find is hell. If we are not ready to be in the far country, we are not ready to allow that the Son of God has come among us. We want to be in hell."[70] But this desire simply cannot be fulfilled, for Barth makes it clear immediately thereafter that although only Christians can see why we must affirm our sinfulness to know our salvation, that salvation in Christ, "is valid and momentous for all men. For it is for all men that the Son of God has become lowly, and takes their place in lowliness as the new man, and is their hope and confidence."[71]

This is Barth's understanding of hell. Whatever it is, or was, there is left no room for a conception of hell being the eternal destiny of fallen humanity; neither as a place of judgement, of torment, of perdition or of annihilation. We must add to this view two final points concerning the role of hell in Barth's soteriology. The first point is that God is so intimately bound to His creation that He cannot allow anyone to perish. The great tension in Barth's entire theology between the freedom and love of God must not cause us to cast a jaundice eye on those sections where Barth talks about God's being bound to and compromised by His creature. Barth has allowed for such an intimate relationship between God and humanity, even though the theological/philosophical pressures of his day required that he constantly over-emphasize the transcendence and sovereignty of God. Because Barth develops such a very keen sense of God's proximity with the creation, we can and must give credence to these important points he makes concerning the risk of God and the impact which the sin of humanity had upon Him. We cite the following as representative examples of his point; "To satisfy His righteousness they [sinful humanity] would have to perish genuinely and finally, to fall from His hand. But then God would not be the God who has sworn to be faithful to them, for He for His part would not have kept His oath and covenant with them."[72] "We are not dealing with merely any suffering, but with the suffering of God and this man in face of the destruction which threatens all creation and every individual, thus compromising God as the Creator."[73] "It is a matter of saving his [the sinner's] life and being, and of doing this for the sake of God's glory. For the glory of God is threatened by man's destruction. Hence God cannot tolerate that man should perish."[74] "He will not allow anything to perish, but will hold it

---

an obscure one, it is clear that the actuality of God's decision and the irrevocability of the election of all leads Barth to his view of the *factuality* of salvation." (*Triumph of Grace, op. cit.,* p. 266)

[70] CD IV/2, p. 396.

[71] Ibid. p. 397.

[72] CD IV/1, p. 553.

[73] Ibid. p. 247.

[74] CD IV/2, p. 226.

in the hollow of His hand as He has always done, and does, and will do. He will not be alone in eternity, but with the creature."[75]

The second point is that the work done in Christ cannot be undone even in the face of the rejection and rebellion of humanity. It is ontic, objective and absolute, and much as in the previous defense, if humanity could perish, the efficacy of the work of Christ, and therefore the omnipotence and glory of God would be compromised. "By permitting the life of a rejected man to be the life of His own Son, God has made such a life objectively impossible for all others. The life of the uncalled, the godless, is a grasping back at this objective impossibility, an attempt to expose oneself again to the threat which has already been executed and consequently removed."[76] And even more directly,

> The world and every man exists in this alteration [death of old man and life of new]. Note that it is not dependent upon whether it is proclaimed well or badly or even at all. It is not dependent upon the way in which it is regarded, upon whether it is realized and fulfilled in faith or unbelief. The coming of the kingdom of God has its truth in itself, not in that which does or does not correspond to it on earth.[77]

The conclusion to be drawn is that the orthodox view of hell has no place in Barth's soteriology nor his eschatology. The actual existence of hell is only seen and known in its defeat through the work of Jesus Christ on behalf of us sinners. There is no ontic basis for its presence now or in the future, there is no subjective ground for us to separate ourselves from the grace of God which would be required for entry. There is no power of hell over humanity that was not broken by Christ. Finally, when these are coupled with Barth's teaching of the non-perpetuity of nothingness - which can only be hell itself - then clearly the perdition of humanity to a state of eternal death or torment is an anathema to Barth's theology. On this point we will give Barth the final word, "all pictures of judgement day are wrong. They are profoundly *un-christian* pictures."[78]

We will turn briefly to Barth's position on the last day and what it holds for the Christian and the world, for this, too, demonstrates Barth's 'implicitly affirmed' *apocatastasis*. Without doubt the future holds the judgement of God, the division of the sheep and goats, but as we have seen, the orthodox understanding of the division to salvation and perdition can only be a wholly 'unchristian' one in the face of Barth's theology.[79] The judgement faced by all

---

[75] CD III/3, p. 90.

[76] CD II/2, p. 346.

[77] CD IV/1, p. 312.

[78] Barth, *Heidelberg Catechism for Today, op. cit.*, p. 82.

[79] John Thompson seems to get caught up in Barth's own dilemma here. He sides with Barth's latent universalism in the coming judgement day, "For Christians the judgement of Christ is thus a comfort and a hope. The place to Christ's left hand may possibly remain unoccupied since on the cross God has barricaded the door of Hell." (*Christ in Perspective, op. cit.*, p. 132) Yet he also affirms that indeed

humanity is the judgement of the One who was judged in our place. It will be the great unveiling of our redemption accomplished for us and now given to us in that Judge. "Already, in celebrating Easter, the Christian may celebrate the dawn of the Last day on which the veil will be taken away and everything that ever was and is and will be will be set in the light of God, divested of its dubiety and frailty and therefore redeemed."[80] Our future is bound up with Jesus Christ, for it is Him whom we await in the final *parousia*.[81]

Barth's picture of the final day includes no place for yet a fifth separation involving his creature and evil. There is no departure of the heathen into everlasting fire and torment, there is no hell, there simply cannot be, for we stand before the Judge who was judged for us.

> *Venturur judicare* : God knows everything that exists and happens. Then we may well be terrified, and to that extent those visions of the Last Judgement are not simply meaningless. That which is not of God's grace and right cannot exist... That there is no such a divine No is indeed included in this *judicare*. But the moment we grant this we must revert to the truth that the Judge who puts some on the left and others on the right, is in fact He who has yielded Himself to the judgement of God *for me* and has taken away all malediction from me. It is He who died on the Cross and rose at Easter... That does not lead to *Apokatastasis*. There is a decision and a division, but by Him who has interceded for us.[82]

---

condemnation and damnation would have been the results of an immediate final coming at the resurrection, "The answer lies not in any necessity there is for God to redeem nor in a temporal delay in the *parousia*, but in the nature of the *parousia* itself as God's revelation of his will to reconcile and redeem man. Were it the ultimate end it would mean destruction and condemnation and not salvation. But the goodness and patience of God give time for the salvation of men and therefore for the Church and its work." (p. 130) We have shown that it certainly would <u>not</u> have meant the destruction of the creature, but only an immediate universal revelation of the 'barricading of the door to Hell' and the completion of the redemption of humankind. Therefore, there is no justification here for 'the Church and its work', nor for.the God who permits that which is seemingly unnecessary and even harmful.

[80] CD IV/3.2, p. 916.

[81] "Any future life other than that of the Word and so of Jesus Christ Himself could only consist in our condemnation and eternal death... but this can only be mentioned as a warning, an indication of what might be if left to himself and thus lost, but what in Jesus Christ cannot be, a reminder of the fact that outside the Word of God there is no life but eternal torment. If we adhere to the Word of God, we can and shall think of this torment, of which the Confession speaks, only as something that has fallen into oblivion for time and eternity." (*The Knowledge of God and the Service of God, op. cit.*, pp. 242-243)

[82] Barth, *Dogmatics in Outline, op. cit.*, pp. 135-136.

This then is the picture of the final day in which Barth's universalism is so 'logically required' and 'implicitly affirmed'. It is a picture which Barth leaves with us in the closing pages of the *Church Dogmatics* and one which is so critical to his entire theology. At the end of CD IV/3.2 he returns to the alteration actualized in Jesus Christ and concludes that it was for '*der ganzen Menschen - und Weltwirklichkeit* ' (the whole of human and cosmic reality effected by Him).[83] It is in the event of the revelation of the final coming that this universal alteration will be made manifest, and not just a revelation to the Christian. "Not his eyes alone, but those of the whole community... and indeed of all the men who have lived, or live or will live will see this great light, will be terrified by it, but will also be made to rejoice by it." What this means is that "to all men and all creation, there will then come the great change of the overthrow of all contradiction in which they now exist and the necessary bending of every knee to Jesus Christ and the confessing of Him as Lord by every tongue."[84]

The universal salvation of all humanity needs to be treated as a foundational theme in Barth's theology, a theme that is not claimed outright, but which is 'logically required' and 'implicitly affirmed'.[85]

The Prophetic Work of Christ

We have now come to the final and conclusive section in the development of an understanding of evil in Barth's theology. We must be reminded of three points Barth has made concerning evil in the time *post Christum*; 1) it can no longer be inimical to humanity nor God, 2) it must be wholly subjected to the

---

[83] KD IV/3.2, p. 1069.

[84] CD IV/3.2, pp. 931-932.

[85] To support this conclusion we cite Barth's statements in the *Humanity of God*, which was written in 1956 near the end of his career, and at the same time he was working on CD IV/3.2. "I wish here to make only three short observations, in which one is to detect no position for or against that which passes among us under this term [universalism]. 1) One should not surrender himself in any case to the panic which this word seems to spread abroad, before informing himself exactly concerning its possible sense or non-sense. 2) One should at least be stimulated by the passage, Colossians 1:19 which admittedly states that God has determined through His Son as His image and as the first-born of the whole Creation to 'reconcile all things (ta; pauta;) to himself' to consider whether the concept could not perhaps have a good meaning... 3) One question should for a moment be asked in view of the 'danger' with which one may see this concept gradually surrounded. What of the 'danger' of the eternally sceptical-critical theologian who is ever and again suspiciously questioning, because fundamentally always legalistic and therefore in the main morosely gloomy?... This much is certain, that we have no theological right to set any sort of limits to the loving-kindness of God which has appeared in Jesus Christ. Our theological duty is to see and understand it as being still greater than we had seen before." (*Humanity of God, op. cit.,* pp. 59-60)

will and purpose of God, and, therefore 3) it must have a positive purpose given its existence and the continuation of the history of creation. This leads us to the theodicy question which is posed in this time and to this God concerning this evil. We will state it here as follows: if evil was destroyed on the cross, why is it still amongst us?; if the salvific work of Christ was completed on the cross, why is there still this interval of time when evil is allowed to cause such suffering?; and in this time, if evil is this impotent servant, then must we not trace all suffering back to God, either as a means to some eternal end, or, as the great question mark placed against his benevolence and omnipotence? With these conclusions and these burning questions for theodicy, we will now turn to Barth's eschatology as he presents it under the third office, the prophetic work of Christ.

Barth claims that the prophetic work of Christ is the work of one who is the 'Victor', and it is critical that we understand in what sense Barth uses this term since we will find here a whole new idea of the victorious Lord than might be expected. This may be due in part to changes in Barth's position towards the end of his life and his increasing interest in eschatology. Whatever his reason, we clearly see a shift in Barth's view of the completeness of the work of the Son and the role of evil in the time of the community. Some of the old themes we have cited will still emerge, but the overall context has definitely changed.

The Prophet in the World of Darkness

In this third office, Jesus Christ is the prophet who comes to us today not unlike the prophets of old came to Israel and called for repentance and obedience. Jesus is that prophet in the world of darkness and the relationship between the two is fluid.[86] This does not imply an absolute dualism, but it does allow for the antithesis which in reality is present. In the world there is light and darkness, good and evil and the powers behind each. They are not dualistic in the sense that they are equal powers, but they do both exist in battle with one another.[87]

In this battle the power of the light is greater than the power of the darkness, but in a surprising statement Barth adds, "The power of light is not so overwhelming in relation to that of darkness that darkness has lost its power altogether, as though its antithesis were already removed, its opposition brushed aside, its challenging and restricting of light of no account."[88] Instead of the utter destruction of nothingness and the total defeat of evil and chaos which

---

[86] In Barth's interpretation of John 1:4 he sees the 'light' as God's self-revealing in a new and distinct action that goes beyond creation. *"phōs is a new and different light which is only rising. It is the light of dawn, not the full light of eternity already present."* (*Witness to the Word, op. cit.,* p. 40, emphasis mine)

[87] Barth will use the idea of battle frequently in this section. Given what we have said of evil as a 'straw man' in Barth, we will have to look carefully at the credibility of this military language.

[88] CD IV/3.1, p. 168.

seemed to be the result of the final two separations in the work of Christ, there still remains a 'dynamic teleology' *(dynamisch-teleologisch)*, which is to be thought of,

> in relation to the power of light, Word and revelation as this is active in great superiority yet has not so far attained its goal but is still wrestling toward it, being opposed by the power of darkness, which even though it yields in its clear inferiority, is still present and even active in its own negative and restrictive way. A history is taking place here; a drama is being enacted; a war waged to a successful conclusion.[89]

Thus the sign 'Jesus is Victor' hangs over the prophetic, historical work of Christ *despite* the content of the current battle. This battle, as it is historical, requires narration and this narration must be shot through and through with the understanding that the One who is the Prophet is the One who is the Victor. For Barth, this means that the outcome of this *dynamisch-teleologisch* is certain and in this sense we cannot deal with light and darkness with equal seriousness, for it is Jesus with whom we are dealing, and Jesus is Victor.

The Revelation of the Atonement

This victory has come through the atonement which is the fulfilling and healing of the covenant of grace; the great obstruction is overcome, sin and evil have been dealt with and defeated. In the process, humanity has been saved from a return to chaos from which it was separated at creation. Thus "the atonement is the filling of this abyss of nothing, of human perdition."[90] In the prophetic work of Christ this atonement is revealed to humanity as knowledge where God Himself is the mediator and the subject and content of the knowledge which is mediated. As this knowledge is mediated to humanity, humanity is confronted with it and therefore with Jesus Christ Himself. Along with this confrontation, the opposition of the world to the prophetic work of Christ also emerges and thus in the time *post Christum* there is not only the opportunity for humanity's grateful response to the gracious love of God in Christ, but there is also the opportunity for it to offer 'futile resistance'.

Here Barth offers a clearer picture of the state of the 'not yet' in relation to the salvific work of Christ. The opposition to God characterises the state of a world which, while it is reconciled to God in Christ, is "not yet redeemed and consummated by His coming glory, i.e., in His final, definitive and universal revelation."[91] Ranged against God's reconciliation in Christ are the forces of nothingness which "still have their own shape and freedom of action in the world

---

[89] Ibid. p. 168.
[90] CD IV/1, p. 89.
[91] CD IV/3.1, p. 186.

and among men."[92] Barth builds a picture of nothingness which is a real threat
in a near dualistic clash with the prophetic work of Christ. Here evil "opposes
the prophecy of Jesus Christ, *meeting it on its own level,* calling in question
the declaration and recognition of what God has done and achieved for His
creature in Jesus Christ at the very point where it comes to the world and man as
the proclamation of His saving grace."[93] As the light of life shines out in the
darkness, the darkness will and must resist it, for only in its rejection of the
light does it continue to be darkness. The important point is that it is the *"noch
nicht ausgetilgte Finsternis* (not yet dissipated darkness)".[94]

We ask here, given all that Barth has said previously, 'why not?' How can
there still be darkness after its utter defeat and destruction on the cross of
Golgatha?[95] We remember Barth's response that it is now present only in its
provisional form, as a fleeting shadow, an echo and, ultimately, as a tool and
instrument at God's bidding actually working to bring about His own good
will.[96] This is Barth's picture of evil in the time *post Christum,* and we must

---

[92] Ibid. p. 186.

[93] Ibid. p. 186. (emphasis mine) Barth builds this idea of a true threat to the creature
by nothingness in the time *post Christum,* and we must ask again here as to the
justification of this time as given to the creature. If there is a true threat to humanity,
then there is no reason why God should have allowed this time. If this time is just for
the carrying out of the pre-determined will of God in which evil will be destroyed and
all humanity saved in Christ, then the attempt to build evil up as a real threat is but
the construction of another straw man. Either way, Barth must be questioned as he
speaks in such threatening tones of evil in its relationship to the prophetic work of
Christ.

[94] KD IV/3.1, pp. 212-213. There are strong vestiges of Kant's idea that the work of
Christ did not defeat the evil principle, but only broke its power. Kant's words here
are remarkably close to the very idea Barth is developing in 'Jesus is Victor'. "The
moral outcome of the combat, as regards the hero [Jesus] of this story (up to the time
of his death), is really not the *conquering* of the evil principle - for its kingdom still
endures, and certainly a new epoch must arrive before it is overthrown - but merely the
breaking of its power to hold, against their will, those who have so long been its
subjects." (*Religion Within the Limits of Reason Alone, op. cit.,* p. 77)

[95] "In exercising judgement and thus reacting in his grace to the rebellion of man,
God *covers over* sin from His sight (q. 36). He does not want to see it. He puts it out
of his sight. He banishes it to where it came from - into real 'nothingness'."
(*Heidelberg Catechism for Today, op. cit.,* p. 70) How can sin stand under the
twofold determination of being 'banished into nothingness' and 'not yet dissipated'?

[96] Berkouwer finds this talk of the impotence of evil difficult to square with
Scripture. "We do not in the Bible gain the impression that the battle is all 'an
emptied matter' in the sense in which Barth speaks of it. On the very contrary, we are
warned against a danger that is still very real. When Barth continually speaks of
'not-dangerous' and 'apparent power' it is difficult to harmonize this 'objective
situation' with the New Testament." (*Triumph of Grace, op. cit.,* p. 237)

not let that picture escape us for one moment.[97] The question we have raised is to the purpose and reason why this time must exist at all, since there is nothing left to be completed that will not be completed in the final *parousia*. Even the necessity of humanity's response is moot when considered alongside Barth's strong tendency towards *apocatastasis*. Here too we ask this fundamental question of Barth's understanding of the future and role of evil in the time of the community. Barth's answer is crucial and we will quote it at length.

> With man and his history, therefore, there is drawn into the history of Jesus Christ the nothingness or evil still present and active in the world which is not yet redeemed. As Jesus Christ confronts man, He confronts with His prophetic Word this element which is quite unworthy in its sinister sordidness and shame, integrating it into its own history, letting it play the role of its opponent, allowing it to show its nature, desires and ability in contrast with Him, exposing Himself to its opposition yet also constituting Himself the Opponent of this opposition, causing this adversary to put to Him the question and the problem for which He has an answer... As He reveals Himself and gives Himself to be known as the One in whom God's gracious decision has been made concerning the world and man, the devil is let loose on the side of the world and man.[98]

The movement of thought goes like this; the world was allowed to continue after the resurrection as the unredeemed (although already reconciled) world in which nothingness is still present; as Jesus confronts humanity with the grace of God, the residual nothingness in the world attacks that Word of grace as it must according to its nature as true nothingness; God allows this in order to show how impotent it really is, in order to show that He is its match, that He is the real Opponent and in the face of Him nothingness will fail and no longer be a threat. How are we to understand this permission of evil after the cross?

---

[97] Barth will allow for evil to be present in this aftermath of the resurrection, but in many places it is given the role of a hapless and rather pathetic opponent. "Easter... is the proclamation of a victory already won. *The war is at an end* - even though here and there troops are still shooting, because they have not heard anything yet about the capitulation. The game is won, even though the player can still play a few further moves. Actually he is already mated. The clock has run down, even though the pendulum still swings a few times this way and that. It is in this interim space that we are living: the old has past, behold it has all become new." (*Dogmatics in Outline, op. cit.,* pp. 122-123, emphasis mine) It is comments like this that pose such problems for Barth's answer to any theodicy question. For the great and heinous evils of this life and these times, the barbaric and monstrous evils that are manifested every day in every land almost relentlessly, all must be accounted for as the result of the last few swings of a pendulum or the futile moves of a beaten chess player. The contrast here is striking, and it points in some ways to the criticisms of Barth as not taking sin, and we may say the evil of our present day, with due seriousness.

[98] CD IV/3.1, p. 187.

What are we to make of the idea that the devil is let loose by the prophetic work of Christ?

Barth depicts the world as a battleground and we are in the midst of a great conflict, opposed by nothingness on the one side and confronted with the Word on the other. It is critical to keep in mind at this point that this whole idea only has credibility if there is something truly at stake. The idea of a conflict and battle presuppose that there is something to be 'won' or at least something not to be 'lost'.[99] This is where Barth's eschatology is open to criticism.[100] For

---

[99] Barth follows this section with an exegetical discussion of the parable of the sower from Matthew 13:3-8. The work of the Sower is threatened as He casts His word out to the nations. Here Barth seems to critique himself as we have only to answer this by returning to the very basis of the critique. He asks, "It might seem that the result of this work is inevitable. Is not the world in which it takes place the world which is known by God? Has it any option but to know the One by whom it is known?" (CD IV/3.1, p. 190) We agree, this is indeed the situation which Barth has created, and which makes evil the straw man. But how does Barth answer? First by stating that although the fact that the Sower will not go out in vain is "eternally settled", it is "by no means self-evident." Then he states that the defeat of evil in the prophetic work of Christ "has to take place... It has to happen that he is driven from the field." (p. 191). The drama has to take place, the event has to be enacted. But hasn't it already? Hasn't 'The Event' taken place where evil was utterly defeated and wholly destroyed? If the battle is eternally settled and historically settled, why must it continue to be fought?

[100] This is also Berkouwer's criticism as he could not live with the tensions of the relationships posed by Barth. The use of the term 'triumph' speaks to Berkouwer's critique that Barth's triumphal theme of the sovereign lordship of God over evil and nothingness reduces the latter to such a degree that it ceases to be evil, threatening or dangerous at all. Barth responds that, viewed christologically, the relationship between evil and God cannot be anything else but that between the superior and victorious power of Jesus and the inferior and defeated power of evil. It is triumphant because it is christological. Thus comes evil as non-willed or nothingness whose reality is expressed only in its negative and opposing relationship to God. For Barth, far from taking the sting out of evil, this opposition to God and God's denial and rejection of it gives to nothingness its true and real 'evil' nature. Barth defines 'ontological impossibility', the most troublesome term for Berkouwer, as meaning that "the nature of evil as the negation negated by God disqualifies its being, and therefore its undeniable existence as impossible, meaningless, illegitimate, valueless and without foundation." (CD IV/3, p. 378) Barth presses the point that none of these terms nor the foundation upon which they are built undermine the historical character of the encounter between God and evil. The reason for this is again christological. In the interpretation of the work of Christ we are right to see that the defeat of evil was accomplished in the eternal will of God. Thus he can rightly say that 'from the very outset' evil was determined for defeat as that which was rejected by God at the beginning of time. How do we know this? "We know it because we take seriously the manner in which the conflict is waged in Him as the source of our sure and certain knowledge of this matter. In other words, we know it because we try to be consistently christological in our whole thinking on the subject." (CD IV/3, p. 179) Barth is satisfied with the various 'dialectical tensions' which he has constructed to support this idea of evil. These tensions were too much

if there is a pre-determined outcome, if evil must lose, if in the end we must affirm a universal salvation, then we are left to question the real credibility of this whole discussion. Indeed the talk of battle in Barth's theology is a difficulty simply because of the power of the overarching cohesiveness of election - creation - reconciliation. From all eternity the battle was decided, in the creation the defeat was pre-figured, on the cross it was actualized in space and time. The four separations have taken place, evil is banished into the nothingness from which it came. In all of this, in the whole tenor of Barth's theology, we must simply ask, where then is the battle? This led Fiddes to remark that in Barth, "non-being is not really alien to God at all. It is only his own, though hapless, work."[101]

If we are to side with Barth we must adopt his degree of comfort with the tension of these relationships which seem ready to blow apart under the pressure.[102] We must be willing to let this critical contradiction sit comfortably in the mystery inherent in the dialectic of revealedness and hiddenness, in Barth's 'revelatory positivism', and the resulting brokenness of theological language.[103]

---

for Berkouwer, as they are in a different sense for us. Yet believing his own interpretation to be purely christological in its approach, Barth maintains these tensions against all attempts to synthesize them or change them into a form which, while perhaps more palatable, would be less christological.

[101] Fiddes, *The Creative Suffering of God*, *op. cit.*, p. 219. Fiddes continues with the important point which again supports our 'necessary antithesis' motif, "Moreover, God is not really free over his own being, which obliges him to give non-being actuality." (Ibid.) This is also a bit misleading because Fiddes never saw the important dialectic of Being and non-being as going back to the eternal distinction of God from 'not-God' where God's freedom is defined as the freedom to eternally self-differentiate Himself from non-being. Therefore he also did not see that non-being is not consigned to a role only in and with the creation, but also prior to it. Had Fiddes interpreted Barth better here, his criticisms could have been even sharper at this point.

[102] Barth himself finally reverts to mystery as the only way to accept this teaching in the end. In a telling statement he compares this time between the times with the three days of Christ in the tomb, concluding both as a "puzzling interval between the two great acts of God by and in Jesus Christ." (CD IV/1, p. 324)

[103] This is what Jüngel meant when he said, "*Die entscheidende Frage, die sich sofort erhebt, lautet: Wie kann sich 'unter Gottes Verfügung etwas ereignen, was sich doch gegen seine Verfügung richtet? Barth versucht den hier sichtbar werdenden Widerspruch nun seinerseits mit Hilfe der von Luther her bekannten Unterscheidungen von Gottes linker und Gottes rechter Hand, von seinem opus alienum und opus proprium wenn nicht aufzulösen, so doch dem Denken als Widerspruch verständlich zu machen.*" Jüngel, '*Die Offenbarung der Verborgenheit Gottes*', *op. cit.*, p. 178. "The crucial question is, how can something take place under the power of God which is nevertheless directed against this power? Barth tries, if not to solve, then to make understandable as a contradiction, the contradiction becoming apparent here with the help of the distinction between God's left and God's right hand, known from the times of Luther

Finally, the prophetic work of Christ also includes the idea that the historicity of the atonement is not alongside or outwith world history, but it includes world history within itself. The history of the covenant and its culmination in the atonement as revealed in the prophetic work of Christ places all humanity in the antithesis of knowing and not-knowing, of either siding with Him or against Him. This antithesis is bordered on both sides by a fluid frontier which is a threat to Christians and a hope to non-Christians. Barth makes it clear that this is a very *necessary antithesis*,

> If the Word of God spoken in Jesus Christ had completely destroyed the opposition and contradiction which withstands it; if it were thus no longer spoken in this antithesis, this would necessarily mean that we should all be those who know, and nothing more. Conversely, if the opposition and contradiction were a match for, or even superior to, the Word spoken in Jesus Christ, this would mean that we should all be those who do not know, and nothing more. But neither of these assumptions is valid. There is no opposition of contradiction which is superior to the Word of God, or even a match for it. Yet the Word of God has not so far removed the hindrance and questioning, but is still spoken in this antithesis.[104]

This is what it means that the prophecy of Jesus Christ takes place in our history, and thus in the darkness which is still present. Into this darkness the light of the Word is proclaimed, placing all humanity into the antithesis of light and darkness, of knowing and not-knowing.

There seems nothing objectionable about the picture Barth paints of light and darkness nor of the antithesis in which every person finds themselves with regards to Jesus Christ. Where the objection is raised is with the need for, or the ultimate value of this antithesis given the two horns of the dilemma; the completed work of Christ and universal salvation as Barth has articulated them. If it could be assumed that humanity's response to the grace of God in Christ was a necessary and indispensable component in the covenant relationship, then Barth's statements here would be acceptable. However, the whole thrust of Barth's soteriology, his objective salvific work and ontological union of all humanity in Christ, combined with an implied *apocatastasis*, leads us to ask what value there is in this antithesis? Those who do not know, will, must at some point become 'knowers'.[105] So why this interval of light and darkness

---

as the *opus alienum* and *opus proprium*." Jüngel's idea of 'making understandable a contradiction' is a good definition of Barth's use of the 'revelatory positivism' motif at this point.

[104] CD IV/3.1, p. 192.

[105] This is not in contradiction to but wholly in keeping with Barth's personalism as God's confrontation from without will come to all humanity in such a way that all will come to the knowledge of their objective union with Christ. God could not tolerate that anyone should perish, His glory would be diminished and evil would have both a victory and perpetuity.

when the light will prevail? Why the need for the response of the creature when that response will necessarily be heard in its perfection for eternity? If the objective and ontological side of humanity's salvation is sure and final and complete, why must there be this annexation of a time in which nothing really happens which will have any eternal consequences? The burning theodicy question with which we began this final section re-emerges here.

The Eschatological Completion of the Prophetic Work of Christ

Barth makes the point that this antithesis is moving towards its own overcoming. The *simul* of the *homo iustus* and the *homo peccator* is not static but fluid and moving in the determined and undeniable direction. This antithetical relationship must be understood "dynamically and teleologically."[106] We must be careful if we interpret Barth as saying here that the completion of our salvation must be seen eschatologically. For all of the talk of the dynamic and teleological character of this antithesis, it is still the antithesis of absolute sovereign and the straw man. It still moves in the direction not of an eschatological completion of the prophetic work of Christ, but towards the noetic unveiling of the fact that we were all bound to be 'knowers' all along. The old man <u>has</u> died, <u>has</u> been utterly destroyed. Evil is now the tool and instrument of God, impotent and defeated and no longer a threat.

In making this statement we must take into consideration what Barth does say about the completion of the prophetic work of Christ, for he does affirm that a final Word is still to be spoken which does not belong to the work of reconciliation but to the final work of redemption. This final word is an eschatological word as Jesus the Victor is still enmeshed in the battle of today, never losing ground or suffering loss, but also not yet at the end of the battle, "He cannot yet be manifested to the world or to them as the One who has completed His prophetic no less than His high-priestly and kingly work, and is thus at the goal. He is not yet at this goal... The victory of Jesus the Victor is not yet consummated."[107] This consummation may even look as though it is in jeopardy. "In relation to the 'still' and 'not yet' which are our sphere and circle of vision there seems little prospect of the continuing advance and final triumph of Jesus."[108] Thus we must rely on our faith that the One who battles is the already victorious One of Calvary and Easter Sunday. He was victorious at the beginning and He will be so at the end.[109]

---

106   Ibid. p. 197.

107   Ibid. p. 262.

108   Ibid. pp. 262-263.

109   The certainty of this final victory comes by virtue of the fact that He is the Word of God. As such He is superior to the "devastating interposition" (*wüste Zwischenfall*) of nothingness which stands between Himself and His creature (CD IV/3.1, p. 267) We must be reminded that that which is here a 'devastating

Barth does, then, posit a future completion to the prophetic work of Christ which seems to include the completion of His priestly and kingly work as well. Yet we must ask here what Barth means by 'not yet consummated'? Is there an ontological or objective work which is yet incomplete with regards to the fulfillment of the covenant, the salvation of the creature, the eternal will of God for humanity? Clearly not! Barth is not thinking here of a completion of this sort, but by *vollendet* he is pointing to the noetic event of the final *parousia* where reconciliation is revealed as redemption.

What will be complete will be the *knowledge* of the reality which is now hidden, and that reality is that everything is already complete. It will unveil for us that the battle between God and evil was already won on the cross and that our opposition to God's grace was already overcome in the one great Opposition settled in the rejection of the Son of God on Calvary. It will unveil that the status of all humanity before God rests under the verdict 'not lost'. We must understand that when we see Barth use the word 'completed' (*vollendet*) with regards to the prophetic work of Christ, it is this idea of final unveiling which he has in mind.

In this 'noetic eschatology' there is nothing for which we wait and work and hope that will give to this current time a reason for its existence, nor a justification of the suffering and misery which has been meted out since the resurrection. Since the 'completion' is noetic, the question still stands as to why such a 'completion' could not have happened along with the resurrection. We must be clear here on the nature of this problem. The question is not whether Barth develops an eschatology that includes a continuance of evil. This he certainly does. The question is just how it can fit within the rest of his theology. It is the cohesion of his eschatology with is overarching themes of election - creation - reconciliation all under the umbrella of the covenant, and the resultant impact each has through the four separations they affect on evil, which leads to question of how Barth can discuss evil as he does in his eschatology. This is the dilemma which is seen here in all its sharpness.

Evil and the Justification for the 'Time of the Community'

Barth addresses this question from a different angle by stating that this time between Easter and the final *parousia* is distinctly the 'time of the community'; and its the activity of the community which gives definition to this unique time. There was a *real end* of creation and the fulfillment of its purpose in the resurrection of Jesus Christ. "Human history was actually terminated at this point. The resurrection of all the dead had already been indicated. Enclosed in the life of this One, their eternal life had already become an event."[110]

---

interposition' is also and at the same time that which is 'armed and empowered by the left hand of God', which is 'under His control and used by Him to bring about His own good will and purpose'. To what extent then can we really believe that this interposition is 'devastating'?

[110] Ibid. p. 734.

Here we see the unity of the idea of *parousia* in Barth which cannot be interpreted chronologically.[111] All was fulfilled, now in provisional form but also in its fullest at the moment chosen by God to reveal it; and therefore all *could* have ended at the resurrection, for nothing else was required, and nothing else ever will be required. Indeed it is only the 'invisible hand' of God which holds off the second coming and allows this time of the community to continue.

The question which arises, first perhaps in its abstract form but certainly for us as a direct statement of the theodicy debate, is why this time is allowed and given to us? Wouldn't the good purposes of God and the world have been better served if the resurrection and second coming had been a single historical event, as indeed Barth has fully indicated they could certainly have been? In a classic statement of Barth's 'revelatory positivism', he responds, "Strangely enough, for what more can God will and work when everything has already been accomplished? But that is how it is. And if that is how it is, it is obvious that He still has a goal and goals, that He still expects something in the world and humanity created and preserved by Him."[112]

This 'something' according to Barth is the response of humanity, for had the resurrection been the true end of history, in some strange way we would have had to regard God as a dictator who overpowered creation with His will rather than graciously calling it to respond and participate in His work. It would not have been the exercise of the grace of God but of an abstract and godless grace, a "unilateral decision and exercise of force... a declaration of will, and the whole [act] a sovereign overpowering of humanity to His own glory."[113] It would have been a world in which there would have been no room for thanks on the part of the creature, nor for a show of gratitude and the response of faith and trust.[114] In addition, it would have meant that God would never have heard the 'Yes' of His creation to His own acts of grace on their behalf.[115]

---

[111] Gotthard Oblau points out, "*In Analogie zur Perichorese der Trinitätslehre gilt, daß die Auferstehung Jesu Christi antizipierend seine Parusie in endgültiger Gestalt mitenthält, und gilt auch der reziproke Satz, daß Jesu Christi Wiederkunft im Eschaton rekapitulierend die Ostererscheinungen mitenthält.*" Gotthard Oblau, *Gotteszeit und Menschenzeit: Eschatologie in der Kirchlichen Dogmatik von Karl Barth*, (Düsseldorf: Neukirchener Verlag, 1988), p. 264. "In analogy to the perichoresis in the teachings on the Trinity, what is true is that the resurrection of Jesus Christ contains within it and anticipates His *parousia* in its final form and the reciprocal proposition is also true that the second coming of Jesus Christ contains within it the Easter appearances recapitulated in the last days."

[112] Ibid. p. 736.

[113] Ibid. pp. 735-736

[114] Oblau states, "*Schon die Entfaltung der Prophetie Jesu Christi, die Barth als Übergang der Versöhnung zur Erlösung apostrophiert (IV 3, p. 303), macht deutlich, was das Generalthema seiner Erlösungslehre gewesen wäre: Gott läßt sich nicht daran genügen, daß seine Schöpfung und die Menschheit, der er sich verbündet hat, ihre komprimierte und repräsentative Erfüllung in der Geschichte des Einen finden, sondern daß auch alle Bereiche seiner Schöpfung und der Menschheitsgeschichte, die sich außerhalb des besonderen zeitlich-geschichtlichen Raumes seines Sohnes*

In analyzing this justification three points emerge which form the backdrop to this discussion. First, this time is not needed by God.[116] It is seen exclusively as a gracious act of God and not in any way as requisite for His eternal goal for creation. God's desire to hear the 'Yes' of creation is only that, a desire, but not in any way of salvific significance. This time contains nothing which for God is a part of *Heilsgeschichte*. Indeed Barth has called this time a 'postscript' *(Nachgeschichte)* to history, in the understanding that 'real' history ended at the resurrection.

Second, it is also not necessary for humanity. The 'Yes' which we can and might speak to God in this time is a 'Yes' of gratitude and thanks and has no bearing on our eternal destiny.[117] Barth posits the same type of justification in CD IV/2 in the spreading of the Gospel and the work and witness of the Church. We must go back to our section on Barth's *apocatastasis* and affirm the same criticism. This time is not necessary for humanity, for whether He hears it in this life or not, we know that the last day holds for God (and us) the promise that 'every knee shall bow and tongue confess that Jesus Christ is Lord, *to the glory of God the Father'*. (Philippians 2:10-11) The point here is that this 'Yes' and 'Amen' and praise to God for His salvific work and fatherly care of the creature is the eternal destiny of all creation in the new heaven and the new earth. However, given the picture which seems to be emerging here, we can say that

---

erstrecken, noch einmal für sich und als solche zu ihrer Erfüllung gelangen. " (Oblau, *Gotteszeit und Menschenzeit: Eschatologie in der Kirklichen Dogmatik von Karl Barth, op. cit.,* p. 266) Here Oblau sees that 'God does not allow Himself to be satisfied that His creation and mankind, to which He has bound Himself, find their condensed and representative fulfillment in the history of the One'... but they must find it 'in themselves as such'. Oblau seems happy with this point and here we must protest that while it is certainly acceptable doctrine, it carries with it unsurmountable problems with theodicy. For had God 'allowed Himself' to be satisfied, our present day suffering would not have had the stage upon which it could become the devastating reality as we find in our world. Again we have a rather heinous picture of God emerging; a God who, purely for His own self-satisfaction, holds back the universal revelation of His glory in order to allow a time of indescribable human suffering, all so that He may hear the affirmations from the few of His grace and mercy. Oblau has correctly interpreted Barth here, he is only remiss in accepting it.

[115] Thus our time is given to us because, "God will not allow His last Word to be fully spoken or the consummation determined and accomplished and proclaimed by Him to take place in its final form until he has first heard a human response to it, a human Yes; until grace has found its correspondence in a voice of human thanks from the depths of the world reconciled with Himself." (CD IV/1, pp. 737)

[116] "He [God] did not need it. He might have done without it. But it is a further dimension of His friendliness to man." (CD IV/1, p. 738)

[117] This strong statement takes us into the whole discussion of conversion and the subjective/objective controversy which revolves around Barth's theology. We believe we have provided more than sufficient evidence to support the claim that the objective work of Christ and the consequent impact on a universal position in Barth means that although God graciously allows, invites and calls men to respond to His grace, there is no absolute need for him to do so.

perhaps it was best for humanity to be given the chance to make this affirmation, to give its praise to the Creator in some provisional, annexed time.

Without considering the third point, there seems some justification for God to ask this thanks from us, and for us to be given the time to render it, to participate in his work, to enjoy the peace and blessings of life lived in the Spirit under the providential care and grace of God. Yet behind all of this, we must be firm in the understanding that for all of its apparent benefits, this time for humankind was not absolutely necessary to its salvation.

Thirdly, if this time, although not necessary, was yet allowed by God *solely* because of its benefits to humanity and God, should we not expect a world in which all of this is the dominant, if not exclusive theme of its existence?   This question is absolutely critical!   For if God had chosen otherwise, as He could have done without detriment to the creature or Himself, this time would be, instead, the fulfilled time of eternal joy, the full participation of the creature in the presence and glory of God.   This is what was and is held back by God's *unsichtbarer Hand* in order for this time of ours to 'be'.   Therefore, if the true justification for this time is to serve as an opportunity for the joyful and thankful response of the creation to the Creator, bringing fulfillment to the former and glory to the latter, then we could only expect a world in which this activity was the centre and focus.[118]

This then is our opportunity as citizens of God's kingdom, that we may have the time to rejoice and praise God in the living out of our citizenship in this new kingdom.

Now we must turn to the reality of the world in which we live and make this third and conclusive point.   For this is certainly not a description of the world in which we live!   This is the day of the theodicy question uttered from the depths of a world gripped and seized by evil and suffering of every shape and form.   The history of the manifestations of evil in this world from the time of Christ to the present renders this justification a misguided and detached piece of speculation at a most profound level.   It is extremely difficult to view our modern day as the time which glorifies the Creator, for it is this time of ours in

---

[118]   Thus Oblau concluded, *Das ist der besondere Sinn des Daseins der Welt und der Menschheit in der Zeit neben und nach der Zeit des Einen: nicht nur gemäß der Versöhnung in der Passivität eines durch Jesus Christus repräsentierten Daseins auf dem Plan zu sein, sondern kraft der eschatologischen Neuschöpfung aktiviert zu werden zur Erkenntnis Jesu Christi;   zur lobenden und dankbaren Antwort auf das Werk der Versöhnung, das Bürgerrecht im Reich Gottes nicht nur zu haben, sondern selbst wahrzunehmen und auszuleben* . Oblau, *Gotteszeit und Menschenzeit: Eschatologie in der Kirklichen Dogmatik von Karl Barth, op. cit.,* p. 266. "That is the special sense of the world's and mankind's existence in the time near and after the time of the One: not only to be in the design in accordance with the reconciliation in the passivity of an existence represented by Christ, but by virtue of the eschatological new creation to become activated to the knowledge of Jesus Christ, to the praising and grateful response to His work of creation, to have not only the right of a citizen in God's kingdom, but to be aware of it and live it out."

which the justification of creation and the Creator was never a more burning question.

The problem in Barth's eschatology here is the inevitable dilemma which is faced when the thrust of all of his theology comes together in this time of ours. The historically completed work of Christ, the objective salvation of all humanity, the defeat of evil on the cross, the future salvation of all creation and the wholly revelatory *parousia* combine to leave Barth struggling to justify the time of the community *post Christum*. And most significantly, it leaves him in a very difficult position to answer the question of theodicy which is sounded from the midst of the struggle with evil in this very time. As long as the election - creation - reconciliation cohesion is seen to be all completed in the historical work of Christ, and not in an eschatological fulfillment which still lies ahead, then this problem will remain and Barth's answer to the evil of our present time will suffer as a result.

The Eschatological 'Now' and 'Not Yet'

Finally, Barth seeks a justification of the time of the community within a proper understanding of the work of the community as it continues in the tension between the true *Wirklichkeit* of its new creaturely status (only seen by faith according to Barth's realism) and the 'not yet' of its present existence. One aspect of Barth's objectivism led Hunsinger rightly to posit "the counterintuitive, eschatological nature of the objective soteriological claim" where Barth posits the 'real, hidden and yet to come'.[119] Barth is able to affirm that our reality lays hidden with Christ in God and what we see is not the reality which we are in Christ. We are objectively the reconciled and true humanity in Jesus Christ, yet we do not see what we are but must walk by faith and not by sight.

Barth has endeavored to show that the prophetic work of Jesus Christ is the work of revealing, in the sphere of our own history, in our own darkness, the work of reconciliation which has been affected for all humanity. He does this by coming into the very midst of the darkness to proclaim this Word.[120] Here, in the darkness, "sin necessarily retains its place and power."[121] In this proclamation, humanity is given the knowledge of its reconciliation which is already accomplished for it, and the consequent true status of evil which is only

---

[119] Hunsinger, *How to Read Karl Barth, op. cit., p.* 38.

[120]   Barth sees that by coming in humiliation, God came to us in Christ in concealment. It is by faith that we see him in this concealment. This is an aspect of the hiddenness of God in the dialectic of hiddenness and revealedness. Humiliation was such a component of Christ's state for us that "He would not be the One He is for us, nor we those that we are for Him, if not in this concealment." (CD IV/2, p. 296)

[121]   CD IV/3.1, p. 280.

'past'. This knowledge brings freedom in which we participate in its provisional form in this 'not yet' time of the community.[122]

This theme is carried on as Barth discusses the future of humanity and evil in this time between the times. Here is Barth's realism coming again to the surface in line with a wholly noetic understanding of the final *parousia* and again a strong tendency towards an outright *apocatastasis*. The positive side of the time of the community is the reality of the resurrection revealed in the prophetic work of Christ.[123]

---

[122] We must be careful not to misunderstand Barth at this most crucial point. It would be a gross error if we were to posit any significance to this knowledge in the actual attainment of the freedom it brings. It is not a work of man in the attainment of this knowledge which results in his freedom from sin and liberation from darkness. We are not talking here about an additional and necessary step which man must take himself if he is to be free from sin and able to participate in the glory of God. Even here, and perhaps especially here, man has no ability to affect such a change. This knowledge is given to man by the Spirit and the knowledge itself is only the revealing of man's total dependence upon the grace of God. It leads not to man's exaltation as the one who achieved this knowledgeable status, but exactly the opposite. It leads to man's humiliation and despair at which he can only throw himself upon the mercy of God and respond with the gratitude that in that mercy God has saved him in Christ. This is important for our purposes because we must see that there is no decision or act of man in the post-resurrection era which has any bearing whatsoever on the efficiency of effectiveness of what was done and accomplished and completed for us in the work of Christ. Barth is not adding a second necessary step in the salvific process where the knowledge which comes to man completes the objective work done by God in Christ. (See CD IV/3.1, p. 328; and Hunsinger, *How to Read Karl Barth*, *op. cit.*, pp. 40 - 41)

[123] In the resurrection of Jesus Christ the salvific work of Christ was revealed as a completed and finished work. The covenant is fulfilled and God has acted to save His creature. Barth sees Easter as the definitive event, and all that follows is the noetic work of repeating, developing and confirming this one great ontic event. In this sense, Barth can say that the divine noetic event has the force of the divine ontic. Barth sees in the resurrection the confirmation of the completion of the salvific work of God in Christ to such a complete and final degree that he concludes that "the new creation has taken place in the resurrection of Jesus Christ." (CD IV/3.1, p. 300) The key term Barth uses here is that the reconciliation of man to God and God to man as taken place in Jesus Christ and confirmed in the resurrection has 'irrevocably happened once for all' "*(Geschehen: ein für allemal, unwiderruflich geschehen! haben wir nun mehr als einmal betont).*" (KD IV/3.1, p. 346) Although Easter had unique qualities, it is one and the same event as His coming in the Spirit and the final coming to which we look in hope. There was a determination given to the world and man that they are not now nor can they ever be again as they were before the cross. They are the new creation in Christ. The universal determination of creation in the revelation of the Resurrected Lord at Easter is this absolute, definitive and 'irrevocable once for all'. We must be clear that there is nothing future which will or could happen in all of the prophetic work of Christ which could add to this complete and definitive act. Even the second coming will not bring about the fulfillment of Isaiah 25:8 or the answer to Romans 8:19, but will unveil the fact that the fulfillment

Having made these foundational points Barth takes up a defence against a criticism wholly in line with our own concerning the justification of the time of the community. He does not directly confront here the question as to the 'why' of the continuation of creation after the resurrection, but he takes up a closely related point of the 'why' of the limited scope of the self-revelation of Jesus Christ in the resurrection. Barth maintains the revelatory nature of the tension between the present day reality of evil and sin (the 'not yet') and the ontological absolute of the resurrection (the 'now'). We simply do not see that all of what God has objectively done is actually done, and thus we do not see the true reality behind our experiences in the world. The transformation from the old to the new creation is accomplished but hidden from our view. "The alteration of our situation effected in Him is concealed as it were by a veil which our eyes cannot penetrate."[124] This veiling does not alter the fact that it is truly and really accomplished and finished for us, and therefore we walk by faith and not by sight.[125]

This view of Barth's has been referred to as an 'eschatological realism' by Ingolf Dalferth. This realism is eschatological because it calls us not into a

---

is already accomplished and the answer already given in the resurrection of Jesus Christ. Finally, this coming of Jesus at Easter is a radically new coming than that of His incarnation and the priestly and kingly work of His earthly ministry. There is the greatest distinction between the cross and the resurrection, for the former is the end of the history of creation and the latter is the beginning of the last times. His resurrection was no extension of his earthly work, but a new revelatory work which ushered in a whole new age. This is the basis for our hope, for He broke out of His transcendence in the incarnation and now he breaks out of it in the glorified form of the resurrection. This opens up to us our participation in that glory, for He was with us in His own glory. That same form which vicariously represented all humanity on the cross now represents us all in glorified form towards which we now move in faith. This glorification in space and time of the God-man pronounces the world as 'not lost'.

[124] CD IV/3.1, p. 318.

[125] Barth sees two sides to the revealing and concealment of this truth. "He is the Crucified who as such closes Himself off from us, and He is the Resurrected who as such discloses Himself to us." (CD IV/2, p. 299) Thus God is constantly hiding and revealing, closing and disclosing Himself. His disclosing is the joy of the Gospel, for he discloses Himself as the Royal Man, in His majesty as the Resurrected and exalted Son of Man. This is the disclosure which demands our response. It is in the power of the resurrection that we can move in the positive direction demanded by this disclosure. Therefore there is a transition taking place from closure to disclosure in which God reveals Himself as the Crucified and Risen Lord. Both sides continue to exist, the hidden and the revealed, the self-closure and the disclosure. In this we become Christians, and our corresponding action is a movement from darkness to light, from the beginning to the goal of our redemption. "In the last resort it consists in the fact that in all of the limitation of his assaulted and oppressed existence he [the Christian] is confronted by the fact that the beginning of his re-constitution has been made, and that he can live on from this beginning. The night has not yet passed, but he moves towards the morning." (CD IV/2, p. 319)

faith in a past figure in our history but into a relationship with the present and living Lord, the risen and victorious Jesus Christ. It is in this relationship that we can know this reality, and from this knowledge that we can make theological statements concerning it. Here also lies the problem, for as Dalferth rightly sees, the evidence for this presence, and certainly of the lordship of the risen Christ in our present day and age is "positively not given."[126] This is the root of the problem of theodicy, for the power and glory, the lordship and goodness of God are excruciatingly absent in the experiences of this present day world of suffering and misery. This must not and cannot, however, alter the ontological truth and reality itself, "the eschatological reality of the resurrection which Christians confess in the *Credo* has ontological and criteriological priority over the experiential reality which we all share. The truth claims of the Christian faith are the standards by which we are to judge what is real, not vice versa."[127] Thus experience is not devoid of reality, but the reality of our experience transcends that experience and breaks into it externally.

Concrete reality is not then a component of what we experience from within, but it is an objective and transcendent reality which must come to us from without (here we see the continuing influence of Kierkegaard and Zündel). What we experience apart from its connection with that ultimate reality is not real at all but abstract. Thus Barth can set that which appears to be reality, namely our experience, against that which is true reality, the Word of God. This does not infer a sense of obscurantism, but it posits a dialectic between what we experience as real and what is ultimately real.[128]

---

[126] Dalferth, 'Karl Barth's Eschatological Realism', *op. cit.,* p. 22.

[127] Ibid. p. 22.

[128] Dalferth is attempting to refute the criticism that Barth's theology produces a dichotomy of sorts between our human, fallen 'reality' and the work of God in Christ. This critique has been made by, among others, Wolfhart Pannenberg (see *Jesus - God and Man,* (London: SCM Press, 1986), especially pp. 383-387); Rosemary Ruether (see 'The Left Hand of God', *op. cit.,* pp. 25-26); and Jürgen Moltmann (see, for example, *Theology of Hope, op. cit.,* especially pp. 50-58), and it has found its most recent ally in Richard Roberts who sees in Barth's doctrine of time that there is a "key to a structure which contains serious flaws, that in their turn reflect the illusory security of a theology which unfolds itself *apart from the natural order* and which, in an attempt to recreate everything, appears to find itself in possession of nothing." (Roberts, 'The Ideal and the Real in the Theology of Karl Barth', in *A Theology On Its Way?,* (Edinburgh: T & T Clark, 1991), p. 64.) This statement is indicative of Roberts' misinterpretation of Barth at numerous key points. In one example among many, Roberts' seeks to build his critique on an 'understanding' of Barth's thought in the *Church Dogmatics* which he sees as having been built on several factors. Among them is the claim that "the transition from the dialectical theology of crisis to the *Church Dogmatics* proper can be legitimately seen as a continuation in temporal terms of a series of contrasting idealist resolutions of the antinomy for finite and infinite existence. Thus Barth's synthesis in the *Church Dogmatics* may be understood as the culmination of Hegelian and Kierkegaardian dialectical progression." (Roberts, p. 65) This statement is simply incorrect for Roberts has failed to see that in Barth's use of both Hegel and Kierkegaard their theology

This is a critical understanding of the relationship of the reality of God in Christ to the statements of faith made about that reality and its implications for all Christian epistemology. With regards to theodicy, Barth is not seeking to synthesize the contradictory elements in the God-evil debate, nor allowing for either a dualistic construct or a mutually-interpreting methodology. Instead, the true reality of God for us in Jesus Christ will be the determiner even, and we may say here especially in its relationship with the non-reality of nothingness in its forms of sin, suffering and death. In addition, because it is not just realism, but an *eschatological* realism espoused by Barth, the seemingly contradictory nature of the existential experience of our day with the true ontological reality of the defeat of evil and death is overcome through faith.

The question to be put to Barth is the purpose and reason for this time of dichotomy between what is experienced as evil and what is true reality - the kingdom of God. Why is our experience necessarily the "preliminary, penultimate, abstract reality which as such is in permanent danger of relapsing into nonexistence?"[129] We also ask about the efficacy of the completed work of the concrete reality. Barth is forced to find all evil as impotent under the left hand of God after Calvary, for there it met its 'real' end. It is only that this victory has not yet been made manifest to creation. So Barth is working with a difficult picture when he attempts to justify this time *post-Christum* through his exposition of the prophetic work of Christ (his 'noetic eschatology') and the brokenness of human language (his 'revelatory positivism').

The 'Not Yet Accomplished' Work of Christ

Barth also poses what appears to us as a tautology in seeing the revelatory work of Jesus Christ as complete in its own sphere but still in its commencement to its final consummation in our world. In its own it is present in all of its fullness, definitive and complete. "But this does not mean that it has ceased to be the future in another sphere outside this event, i.e., in the sphere of our own existence and that of the rest of the world."[130] This is true only because we have been given this space and time, but it does not make this space and time necessary. As we are in this time of the community we can and must look back to the resurrection in faith and forward to the second coming in hope. Yet the fact that we can and must do so does not tell us why we have this time in the first place. We cannot say that the purpose for this time is that we may look forward to the second coming, for we would counter that there would not be the need for this hopeful looking in the face of the world's despair if the second coming had been synonymous with the resurrection. Barth has accurately described our current state, but he has not given a justification for its existence.

---

underwent radical reinterpretation and his final use of their theology in the *Church Dogmatics* can in no plausible way be regarded as a 'culmination of Hegelian and Kierkegaardian dialectical progression'.

[129] Dalferth, 'Karl Barth's Eschatological Realism', *op. cit.,* p. 29.
[130] CD IV/3.1, pp. 318-319.

In seeking to answer the question of the self-revelation of the risen Christ, "how could it commence there without at once reaching its goal everywhere and perfectly?"[131], Barth confesses that there is here a definite contradiction which we cannot evade or escape, nor should we attempt to do so. For this contradiction is 'light and not darkness', and we are to embrace both sides of it with a "radical acceptance" *(grundsätzliche Bescheidung)* if we are to "proceed with confidence."[132] From this point Barth builds his eschatological understanding of the tension between the completed work of Christ in the resurrection and the continued groaning and sorrow of the created world.

As the Revealer of His work He has not yet reached His goal. He is still moving towards it. He is marching from its beginning in the revelation of His life to the end of His not yet accomplished revelation of the life of all men and all creation as enclosed in His life, of their life as the new creation, on a new earth and under a new heaven. In His prophetic work He moves from the one Easter Day to the day of all days, to the last day, to the day of His final and conclusive return... By way of anticipation, it is already reached in His resurrection, in Him as the Subject of the Easter event. The eternal light has already gone out into the world. *The new and future redeemed and perfected world is already present.* In this commencement, however, the goal is not yet reached except in Him. It is not yet reached in the situation of the world and man. It does not yet have the form of a world enlightened and irradiated by His revelation, of a redeemed and perfected man. It is to this goal which is still to be reached outside Him, to the revelation of His own glory as the glory of the world reconciled to Him, of the man justified and sanctified in Him, that He moves in and from this beginning... But He has not yet accomplished it. He is on the way, moving and marching from the commencement to the completion.[133]

This is the core of the contradiction, that the world is both redeemed and perfected absolutely and once for all in Christ, and yet that it must also move towards its redemption and perfection in His second coming. We see here that the prophetic work of Christ never loses its exclusively noetic character. What has yet to be accomplished is the revelation of this transformation to all the world. Yet Barth is not looking for an earthly movement of humanity in the Spirit where, prior to the second coming, this universal revelation will be

---

[131] Ibid. p. 324. Hear again also as Barth states of the time of the resurrection appearances of Christ, "His completed being and work, and its completed revelation, were sufficient then, and they are sufficient to-day (sic), and they will be sufficient for all times, and even when time shall be no more." (CD IV/2, p. 142)

[132] CD IV/3.1, p. 326.

[133] Ibid. p. 327. (emphasis mine)

accomplished.[134] He can only affirm of this world of ours, "*noch nicht in Gestalt einer durch seine Offenbarung erleuchteten, von ihr durchleuchteten Welt, noch nicht in Gestalt eines erlösten und vollendeten Menschen.* " nor will it this side of the second coming![135] Barth only sees this universal knowledge of the salvific work of Christ for humanity as coming with the universal unveiling of the final *parousia*. "It is the Word of God which forbids us to dream of any golden age in the past or any real progress within Adamic mankind and history or any future state of historical perfection."[136] There is then still no meaningful work given to humanity, and therefore no justification for this annexation of time between the first and second coming. The Son is moving from Easter to the second coming without the need for, nor with the anticipation that anything will happen, in the time between. Humanity will not realize the 'not yet accomplished' revelatory work of Christ this side of the final *parousia*.

Two Final Justifications

Barth cites two final reasons why this time is allowed and given by God to humanity in his 'not yet' existence. He uses the terms of combat to say that the world as we know it has not yet ended because the warfare between the Son and darkness has not yet ended. Jesus is described as "being still engaged in conflict with the darkness which contests the peace established in Him."[137] Emerging from the tomb Jesus is "surprised and startled that it is not removed."[138] Therefore Jesus' suffering is not at an end but He continues to bear the burden of the wickedness of the world and the "resultant evil and the death which darkens everything."[139] Far from having been routed, evil and nothingness have grown in their intensity in the world and so He continues the battle which began before

---

[134] We are reminded of this by the early Barth, "by 'God's Design' is therefore *not* meant the existence of the Church in the world, its task in relation to the world's disorder, its outward and inward activity as an instrument for the amelioration of human life, or finally the result of this activity in the Christianization of all humanity and, connected with this, the setting up of an order of justice and peace, embracing our whole planet... While we observe our office as political watchmen and do our service as social Samaritans, we wait for the immovable City which God will build - *not* for a future political State to be set up with Christian assistance, whether it be of liberal or authoritarian character." ('The World's Disorder and God's Design', *op. cit.,* pp. 11, 16)

[135] KD IV/3.1, p. 377. "It does not yet have the form of a world enlightened and irradiated by His revelation, of a redeemed and perfected man." (CD IV/3.1, p. 327)

[136] CD IV/1, p. 511.

[137] CD IV/3.1, p. 328.

[138] Ibid. p. 328. The German is "*Gefremdet und entsetzt*" which is better translated 'surprised and horrified'. This points even more strongly to the devastating tension in Barth's theology between the competed work of Christ in the utter defeat of Satan on the cross, and the continued role and operation of evil under the divine *permittens*.

[139] Ibid. p. 328.

the resurrection, for He remains the only One who can win.[140] This is God's battle, He is the One who is still on the way to the final victory - His final victory.[141] We, as His people, are simply on the way with Him.

The conflict is still incomplete, and so the Son is "giving Himself time and place for combat."[142] The 'good' in this scenario is that humanity is given a chance to speak and respond as God's partner in the world,[143] for our participation is the mark of the graciousness of God and the independence of the Creature. Thus had God not given us this time He would have proven His lack of interest in us as partners and seen us only as 'objects and spectators' *(Objekte und Zuschauer)*.[144]

Secondly, Barth states that this time between the times has its own particular glory. Today is the day of the living and present Jesus Christ, thus regardless of the sin and misery which surround and overtake us, this time stands under the sign *par excellence*. As all humanity is included in and bound by the relationship they have with God in Christ, so He comes again in this time as the One moving on the way to unveil this reconciliation. As such this is His time and therefore it is necessary and has its own glory. This fact is in and of itself sufficient, for Barth can conclude,

> It may well be a day on which the earth is covered, as once before the flood, by so much merited and unmerited suffering. It may well be a day when no moment passes in which death does not make what seems

---

[140] Barth takes a similar line in his later work, *The Christian Life* where he makes the seemingly contradictory statement, "It would be better for us if we were to learn again with the same fearlessness and freedom to see and to reckon with the fact that even today we still live in a world that has been basically dedemonised already in Jesus Christ, and will be so fully one day. But in the meantime it still needs a good deal of dedemonising, because even up to our own time it is largely demon-possessed." *(The Christian Life, op. cit.,* p. 218)

[141] "In short, it is not in the first instance the world, or the Church, or an individual man suffering under and either rebelling against or in some way enduring the conflict, but He Himself, the Resurrected, who is still on the way, still in conflict, still moving towards the goal which He has not yet reached." (CD IV/3.1, p. 329)

[142] CD IV/3.1, p. 330.

[143] "We live in this brief, dark, and yet not totally dark world. It is brief and semi-dark because from its beginning and its end there streams the light of banished night from two brilliant Days of God, which in truth are not two Days, but one Day of Jesus Christ, the Day that was and the Day which is coming. It is! In the midst of the night which is our day, that Day is! The only foundation of the Church consists in the fact that this night is encompassed by this Day of Jesus Christ and that this Day of Jesus Christ is our Day of life. *This makes us to be ministers of the Word!* " (Barth, *God in Action, op. cit.,* pp. 72-73)

[144] Instead, "the way between commencement and completion of His presence, the distance between Easter Day and the day of the consummation of His return, the ground which He has still to traverse and creation with Him, is the great opportunity which He has given to creation freely to enter His service." (CD IV/3.1, p. 333)

to be an irrevocable end of some human life. It may well be a day of the devil and demons, of yielding but still resisting darkness. This is true. But this is not decisive. The decisive thing is that it is also a day of Jesus Christ, a day of His presence, life, activity and speech.[145]

Both of these justifications are troublesome given what Barth has said in the priestly and kingly work of Christ. We must always remember that evil is the utterly defeated and routed enemy of God ("the decisive No of the wrath of God... lay on the old man, destroying and extinguishing him... [therefore] an unequivocal and intolerable and definitive enemy of God was treated as he deserved and utterly destroyed"[146]) which now exists as the servant of God ("there has to be confessed as in no other teaching the absolute superiority with which God controls and conquers nothingness even in the form of human sin, not in any sense being arrested by it, but setting it to serve his own glory and the work of His free love"[147]) under His controlling providence in the service of His good will ("In this world Satan can have only the power which is given and allowed him as he is powerfully upheld by the left hand of God."[148])

In this dramatic and unequivocal understanding of evil, we must also and with equal force affirm evil in its role as the continuing inimical enemy of God, the ongoing threat to the creature, and the final reason and purpose for the continuation of creation. Can this defeated enemy still incite such a call to battle? Surely God is battling His own servant; His right hand in combat with His left! Barth is in danger once again of putting the contradiction of this mystery into the very being of God and making Him a God of confusion. We agree with Fiddes that, "when Barth considers the origin of *das Nichtige* he defuses it of all real alienation," which in the end means, "this notion of a hostile non-being as the *opus alienum* of God comes down heavily on the side of the *opus* of God. It is too much 'his own' and not enough 'most alien'."[149]

The second problem is this, what is God on His way towards which is so necessary not just for humanity, but for Himself? It cannot be for the accomplishment of His own divine will which requires this time, for "Jesus Christ *is* the eschatological realization of the will of God."[150] If it is for the defeat of evil, we pose the previous dilemma even more strongly. For now God is suffering today with His creation that which He thought He defeated on the cross. He is truly a God who is 'startled and surprised' (*entsetzt* - horrified!) to

---

[145] CD IV/3.1, p. 362.

[146] CD IV/2, p. 400.

[147] Ibid. p. 398.

[148] CD IV/1, p. 267.

[149] Fiddes, *The Creative Suffering of God, op. cit.,* pp. 217-218.

[150] CD IV/1, p. 34. John Thompson echoes this view of Christ's completion of the totality of the work required for the salvation and glorification of humanity, "Thus he is in his Person the covenant in its fullness, the Kingdom of heaven which is at hand." (Thompson, *Christ in Perspective, op. cit.,* p. 100)

find evil still in the world. Yet this is certainly not the God Barth has portrayed in the Perfections of God, the Providence of God nor in the entire thematic presupposition which runs throughout the *Church Dogmatics* that God has revealed Himself *as Lord*.

If on the other hand, it is to give to humanity the space and time to respond, to share in the harvest and to exercise its freedom, we turn to Barth's strong tendency towards *apocatastasis* and ask if this is not a moot defense? Barth's doctrine of evil at this late stage forces us to the point of stating that if we can perceive of a scene at the second coming where all will respond to the grace of God, where all will glorify Him and acknowledge Him as Lord, and where all will confess Him and live eternally in the service and praise of His people, we can find no reason for the supposed necessity for humanity's fragmented, partial and sinful response in the world which is still unredeemed and in bondage to nothingness. It is difficult to imagine that there is something inherently necessary about this temporal response that would justify the suffering and misery of the world, given a sure future in which all will render this response and confession in perfection for eternity.[151]

This also calls into question the simple conclusion that because Jesus Christ is present in this day, it is a day which is justified. This is arguing in a circle. There is no doubt that He is present and active and at work, and there is no doubt that this is the Day of Jesus Christ. This does not, however, justify any interpretation we may give to what else this day might mean. In fact, that Christ is present and active, that this is truly His day leads us in the opposite direction, that there truly is a purpose and reason and justification for this time.

Thus neither the 'field of battle and the exercise of freedom' nor the 'day of Jesus Christ' arguments are acceptable in answer to this dilemma. Barth is left with a number of very difficult and seemingly impossible tensions in his eschatology. He must hold together the ideas of the destruction of evil and the present existence and reality of evil; evil as under the preserving and controlling providence of God and evil as the inimical enemy of God which he must still engage in battle (which is the heart of our critique of the motif of the 'right and left hand of God'); the new creation won for us through the work of Christ and

---

[151] We understand that Barth certainly sought to build a genuine doctrine of the response of humanity. Our contention is not that such a doctrine is wrong, only that in terms of the theodicy question, and in light of Barth's soteriology and the elements of his 'noetic eschatology', it poses great problems for him. We cannot disagree with Oblau who provides us striking images of Barth's desire to give full force to our response (see Oblau, *Gotteszeit und Menschenzeit: Eschatologie in der Kirklichen Dogmatik von Karl Barth, op. cit.,* p. 267-268), but we can and must continue to question how such a response fits in a picture in which we must add the suffering and evil which we experience. If either Barth's universalism were abandoned or his view of the defeat of evil made more eschatological, then the place Barth gives to our response would be wholly acceptable. However as we have seen, these two positions are integral to Barth's entire theology, and as they are, the justification for the time of the community will remain a major problem to any 'Barthian theodicy'.

the hiddenness of that new creation; and the completed work of Christ with its 'logically required' and 'implicitly affirmed' universalism and the justification of this time of suffering and evil. Indeed it is in this time and as a result of this dominance by evil that the theodicy question is raised.

CHAPTER VIII

Theodicy, Suffering and the Church:
A Conclusion to Barth's Doctrine of Evil

The Four Motifs and a 'Barthian Theodicy'

The 'Necessary Antithesis'

Through his use of the motif of the 'necessary antithesis' Barth has labored to keep the relationship between God and evil from either a Manichaeistic dualism or the total dissolution of all distinction resulting in the equating of God and evil. Barth has also avoided the idea that evil was 'necessary' in the same positive way in order to combat all ideas of contingency and to preserve the sovereign freedom of God. Nonetheless, it has been shown repeatedly the unique way in which the term 'necessity' can and must be used to describe the relationship which develops in Barth's doctrine of evil. It has been defined according to Barth's usage in such a way so as to avoid the problem of contingency and also to allow it to function as Barth intended as an invaluable component of his 'dualism of rejection'. Thus the 'necessity' of evil is upheld and fully integrated in Barth's theology without devolving the relationship between God and evil into the type of equilibrium or *Aufhebung* which Barth has criticised in Schleiermacher, Leibniz, and the Reformed understanding of the *decretum absolutum.*

Therefore in Barth's theology, evil is necessary, but it is never positive or good, even where the Fall can only be seen as the 'necessary antithesis' to *Heilsgeschichte.* This 'peculiar ontology' of evil is the essence of its 'existence'. Jüngel retorts that such an ontology is the result of the misguided desire to satisfy the human need to understand the ways of God—in short, to give a logical answer the problem of evil.[1]

---

[1] *"Die Dogmatik darf dieses menschliche Urbedürfnis nicht einmal befriedigen wollen . Denn sie müßte dann, wie auch immer sie es anstellt, Gott und das Böse in einen ontologischen Zusammenhang bringen: und sei es in den Zusammenhang der Entstehung des Bösen durch den Akt göttlicher Verneinung."* Jüngel, '*Die Offenbarung der Verborgenheit Gottes*', op. cit., p. 180. "Dogmatics should not even *want* to satisfy this human need. For then it would have to bring about an ontological connection between God and evil, no matter how it went about it, even if it meant a connection between the origin of evil through the act of divine denial." Although we are sympathetic to Jüngel's intent here, we do not agree with his view that no connection can be made between God and evil, for it then becomes impossible to avoid the type of absolute dualism which Barth sought so hard to reject. Barth's 'peculiar ontology' is far more an asset to the Christian understanding of evil than is offered by cutting evil lose from God altogether. Jüngel responds, *"Es gibt nur einen, allerdings entscheidenden Zusammenhang zwischen Gott und dem Bösen. Und das ist das Kreuz Jesu Christi, das ist die Urtatsache des christlichen Glaubens: daß Gott das*

One possible reason for why Barth didn't develop this idea more overtly is his insistence upon the non-perpetuity of nothingness. Here we see a tension in Barth between his understanding of the role of darkness to the light, or as he has stated, the critical role of the 'No' of God to the work of the 'Yes', and his overwhelming emphasis upon the completedness of the victory of Christ over the 'No'. Had Barth presented a more consistent view of nothingness outside of creation, he could have provided a much clearer doctrine of evil at this critical point. The picture which could have emerged based upon his understanding of the eternal rejection by God of all that is 'not-God', is one which would see nothingness at the final *parousia* being wholly defeated and banished from the created sphere and sent back into the void where it has known only defeat and 'non-existence' from all eternity. In this way its defeat can be described in the most extreme terms without raising the greatly troublesome objection that if nothingness was truly able to be wholly annihilated prior to creation, God was clearly remiss for not doing so.

The central importance of the eternal, pre-creation 'existence' of nothingness as the 'not-God' must be maintained, for to abandon such an idea in Barth would mean the dissolution of the critical link between God's self-differentiation and His self-determination in election. With this loss would go the overarching significance of Barth's doctrine of election to the whole of his theology. The important tension between the 'impossibility' and the 'inevitability' of the Fall and the similar tension between the positive willing of *homo labilis* and the non-willing of *homo lapsus*, upon which so much of Barth's theology is built, would also be sacrificed if nothingness is not seen as the eternal 'not-God' which is readily rejected by God outside creation. For these reasons the non-perpetuity of nothingness remains a central problem for Barth's theology.

Any theodicy which results from Barth's doctrine of evil must be built upon this motif of the 'necessary antithesis'. According to Barth, both creation and Creator are justified in Christ and will finally be vindicated in the final *parousia*. The very fact that Barth talks of the 'justification of the Creator' is a product of this 'necessary antithesis', for God's desire to create included the Fall, suffering and death. That this is the best of all possible worlds is affirmed by Barth because of the tie between God's self-differentiation and his self-determination; between the eternal non-willing of that which would inevitably win a temporary victory within any non-divine creation, and God's eternal election to destroy evil within that creation in His Son. In this way, by maintaining this tie, Barth can make God ultimately responsible for evil because He is also ultimately responsible for its destruction in a way which will justify His creation and with it, Himself.

Thus Barth's theodicy here is both soteriological and eschatological; it looks back to what has been done for us in Christ (and even further back to what was

---

Böse besiegt, indem er es selber erleidet." (p. 180) This however is really no answer at all unless one is willing to hide the myriad of problems and questions which arise from this 'one crucial connection' behind the veil of mystery. That Barth was unwilling to do so is to his credit and it provides an opportunity to be of service to the Church in a far more effective way than that proposed by Jüngel.

decided for us in God), and it looks forward to the justification which we await with confidence solely because of what has happened for us in the past. In this way, the 'necessary antithesis' motif serves as an answer to the 'why?' question of theodicy.

The 'Right and Left Hand of God'

When the 'necessary antithesis' motif as the ontic basis of nothingness is developed within Barth's supreme sense of God's sovereignty, a mechanism must be used to describe the noetic basis of evil and how evil is related to and subordinate to God. Barth's use of the 'right and left hand of God' motif for this purpose provides both a clarification and a central problem for his theodicy. Barth must contend that God ultimately controls all evil and that evil is truly inimical not only to creation but to God Himself. Even this may be granted according to Barth's view of the freedom of God. However, the nagging question is whether there is, ultimately, any actual threat to God or creation given the all embracing and eternal character of election prior to creation. The question concerning the conflict in God appears at four levels.

1. Can evil ever be real evil? Can the depths of the suffering of the Son on the cross be authentic given that evil is controlled under the left hand of God?

2. Can the negative or non-willing of God, His 'No', actually be distinguished in the end from His positive will (it must be remembered here that *both* are effectual!)? Or put another way, doesn't the positive and negative will of God simply describe two aspects of His will, such that in both cases we are talking about the 'will of God' which is His nature and act? In all Barth's development of the justification of God in the work of Christ and the destruction of evil, there is a strong indication that Barth was thinking along these lines, that evil was ultimately God's responsibility and the work of Christ was, along with the salvation of the creation, also the full and necessary justification of the Creator.

3. Can the operation of evil under the left hand of God account for the experience of evil in the times *pre-* and *post-Christum* ? If evil was allowed an instrumentalist role, if the 'No' was allowed for the sake of the 'Yes' as leading up to Christ's ultimate 'Yes', then how do we account for evil after that event? If the cross is the final justification of God, how do we view that justification in light of the subsequent history of evil in all of its depth and breadth experienced by humanity after that justifying event.

4. Finally, there remains the question of the annihilation of nothingness which takes place as the role of the left hand ceases. This points seems both inconsistent with Barth's theology and un-Scriptural. The heart of this criticism is in the notion that if God's non-willing or 'No' is in fact a part of His will and act, then His nature (being eternal, unchanging, immutable, etc.) is also revealed in this 'No'. For God to cease to say 'No', for Him to terminate His non-willing, would be for Him to change His nature, so closely has Barth tied the nature and will of God.

In terms of theodicy, this motif is a critical interpretation of Barth's doctrine of evil. In Barth's motif of the 'right and left hand of God' there are aspects to be accepted and those to be rejected. What is most objectionable are the problems raised when it is combined with the rest of Barth's doctrine of evil. By not developing the defeat of evil more eschatologically, the work of the left hand of God in the time of the community is unjustifiable. In positing the non-perpetuity of nothingness, God becomes the God of confusion and complaint. In these two respects, the motif of the 'right and left hand of God' is problematic.

Yet when divorced from these concerns, as it must be, Barth's motif of the 'right and left hand of God' is a credible and useful description (which is all Barth intended it to be), for it is the product of the defense of the sovereignty of God and the rejection of a unifying of God and evil. If God is ultimately always in control of evil, which His nature demands, then we must defer to Barth's picture and affirm it with all of its difficulties, as a description of God as He is revealed in Jesus Christ. Thus, in theodicy terminology, Barth is affirming God's sovereignty and His benevolence, and locating evil somewhere within and strangely outwith this God. This is Barth's answer, within the motif of the 'right and left hand of God', to the 'how?' question of theodicy.

Noetic Eschatology

A great deal of time has been devoted to this third motif which, along with the criticism of the 'shadow side of creation' and the 'non-perpetuity of nothingness' which emerge remain the principal weaknesses in Barth's doctrine of evil. Simply put, Barth cannot justify this time of ours except to offer the tautology that its existence is its own justification. This criticism is the product of the two motifs above; in the justification of God having taken place in the defeat of evil on the cross and of the subsequent manifestation of evil being confined to the role of servant under the left hand of God. The picture which emerges for the time *post Christum* is very unclear. All explanations which point to the witnessing role of the community and the proliferation of the Gospel ultimately fail due to Barth's 'logically required' and 'implicitly affirmed' universalism. It is only Barth's insistence that *apocatastasis* cannot be claimed but only hoped for that we find a thin thread of hope that such a justification can indeed be found. However, the overwhelming nature of Barth's doctrine of election on the one hand, and the pervasiveness of evil in the past 2,000 years on the other prove far too heavy for this thread to bear.

This problem also comes up in Barth's uniting of creation and covenant. If the covenant was fulfilled in the historic work of Christ, why must the creation continue 'as if' nothing happened? The sharper question arises here with regards to God's justification as we have already shown. The problem for Barth is that the final *parousia* is wholly revelatory and thus there is no future event which has any salvific significance to offer this final justification. We have shown how Barth has struggled for an answer and how it is, for him, ultimately problematic. This one objection remains the weak link in Barth's theodicy and it can only be overcome by taking a more eschatological view of the destruction of evil.

Revelatory Positivism

This motif has emerged from the core of Barth's entire theological methodology which is founded upon his view of revelation. Barth's insistence upon the nature of revelation and the result it has on humanity's attempt to 'talk about God' are foundational for his doctrine of evil, and it must be so for any resultant theodicy which emerges from it. Our concern has been simply to question when and how it is appropriate to resign a contradiction or paradox to this motif. Barth's affirmation of accessible and inaccessible *rationes* demonstrates his belief that God the Holy Spirit can illumine our understanding of aspects of the *Deus absconditus*. Barth's movement within the dialectic of hiddenness and revealedness seems at times to be quite arbitrary. However the question can be raised as to whether it is the hiddenness of revelation or an inherent weakness in Barth's argument which at points produces these inaccessible *rationes* ?

On the other side, there are a few instances where we see Barth as all too ready to provide an explanation when the assent to the hiddenness of God may have been more appropriate.[2] We can think especially of his discussion of Judas where, in dealing with the highly deterministic sin of Judas and his ultimate responsibility for that sin unto damnation, Barth attempts an explanation of how Judas can be the prototype rejected and also, in the end, elect. This seems to us to be an attempt by Barth to offer an explanation where mystery may have been better affirmed.[3]

---

[2] Jüngel criticised Barth at this same point, *"Hat Barth nicht das Dasein des Bösen letztlich vom Tun Gottes her verstehbar zu machen versucht und damit das Tun Gottes, gerade weil er es nicht als verborgenes Werk Gottes gelten ließ, ins Zwielicht gebracht ?"* Jüngel, *'Die Offenbarung der Verborgenheit Gottes'*, op. cit., p. 177. "Did not Barth, in the end, try to make the existence of evil understandable by the action of God, thereby bringing the action of God into the twilight, just because he would not let it be seen as the hidden work of God?" We agree in part with Jüngel here, however as we have seen above, his final intent is to reject Barth's desire to witness to the relationship of God and evil, and creation and evil as revealed in Jesus Christ. It was according to this revelation and with the desire to be a witness and not a metaphysician that Barth constructed his doctrine of evil. We agree that at times he overstepped his own limits and was tempted by solutions and explanations. However it goes too far to say with Jüngel that Barth's doctrine on *das Nichtige* involves *"geniale systematische Konstruktionen."* (p. 177)

[3] We agree here with David Ford, "There seems here to be a misuse of typology which spoils the realism of the literal story for the sake of trying to know more of God's purposes than can properly be elicited. In his desire to support the possibility of an ultimately favorable verdict on Judas Barth presses his method to the point of producing contradictions." (Ford, *Barth and God's Story,* op. cit., p. 91)

Barth's 'revelatory positivism' provides an important context for all theological inquiry, and yet it is in need of further refinement in its use and application to the doctrines of theology. For Barth's theodicy, this motif plays its most positive role in affirming faith as the ultimate answer to the problem of evil. We are to be witnesses to the God who reveals Himself to us in Jesus Christ. Hauerwas is certainly right when he says,

> It is clear that something has gone decisively wrong for Christians when we underwrite the widespread assumption that there is a so-called problem of evil which is intelligible from anyone's perspective–that is, when we turn the Christian faith into a system of beliefs that can be or is universally known without the conversion of being incorporated within a specific community of people.[4]

Where Barth keeps to this wholly descriptive line, and where he allows mystery and paradox in connection with the reality of the hiddenness of God, his doctrine of evil is both lucid and applicable for use by the Church. Where he is led away from this purpose into either too hasty a retreat to mystery, or into metaphysical or logical speculation[5], his doctrine of evil stands in need of the type of corrections which we have offered in this study.[6]

Barth's Theodicy in Light of His Doctrine of Evil

To help construct a 'Barthian theodicy'[7] we will attempt to apply Barth's doctrine of evil as a response to three thinkers who have raised the theodicy

---

[4] Hauerwas, *Naming the Silences, op. cit.,* p. 53.

[5] What else could be said of his ideas of the non-perpetuity of nothingness, the *Schattenseite* of a good creation, and the lack of a truly eschatological understanding of the defeat of evil, than that these are the products of just such a divergence from Barth's original and laudatory intent?

[6] Jüngel provides a clear case for this motif, "*Das menschliche Urbedürfnis gerade nach Erklärung des Bösen und also nach der Rechtfertigung Gottes angesichts des Bösen, das menschliche Urbedürfnis, die Frage nach der Theodizee nicht nur zu stellen, sondern auch zu lösen, macht zwar vor den heiligen Hallen der Dogmatik nicht halt. Die Dogmatik kann dieses Urbedürfnis nicht ignorieren.*" ('*Die Offenbarung der Verborgenheit Gottes*', *op. cit.,* p. 180) We wonder if Jüngel does not himself 'ignore this basic need' by rejecting those areas where Barth speaks of the 'peculiar ontology' of evil in its being in rejectedness? By refusing all such ideas, Jüngel may escape the charge of being tempted to un-Christian solutions to theodicy, but he has certainly not provided anything for the Church in its place, and in this way he seems to have ignored this problem altogether. This is surely evidenced in his comment which follows, "*Aber sie kann es auch nicht befriedigen. Und sie sollte auch nicht so tun, als könnte sie es.*" (Ibid.)

[7] In Chapter I of this thesis we have made our case for such a term and such an undertaking given Barth's rejection of the need for a theodicy. The reader must

question in four different forms: David Hume in its theoretical and its empirical forms; Fyodor Dostoyevski in its eschatological form; and Elie Wiesel in its existential form

A note of justification needs to be made concerning our choice of Hume. In Hume's *Dialogues Concerning Natural Religion* he is speaking in the voices of Philo, Demea, Cleanthes and Pamphilus in an effort to find a position with regards to God and evil that is somewhere between the dogmatism of Demea and the skepticism of Philo.[8] Hume's interests are not rationalistic but epistemological and so he developed Cleanthes' famous teleological argument in an unabashed anthropocentric form.[9] This is not the shout of the protest atheist nor the passionless probing of the logician. It is a measured challenge from a credible thinker who is neither an enemy of religion nor an avowed believer.[10] Hume's formulation is chosen because it offers a tenable challenge on epistemological grounds to all Christian thinkers on the theodicy question.[11]

Barth's Theoretical Theodicy

The question posed by Philo is strikingly lucid when, speaking of Cleanthes' God, he re-asks Epicurus' question,

---

remember that justification and consequently that the term 'Barthian theodicy' is not necessarily an oxymoron.

[8] Although the debate over 'who speaks for Hume?' is outside our remit, we will say that we are holding here to the measured analysis of J.C. Gaskin who concludes that although Hume's voice can be heard in all four voices, "Hume is still Philo except when Cleanthes refutes Demea." (J.C. Gaskin, *Hume's Philosophy of Religion*, (London: MacMillan Press, 1978), p. 218)

[9] Gaskin's point is that Hume did affirm some belief in God, and so his *Dialogues* were centred on the question of the nature and not the existence of God, "the *Dialogues* can be understood as a discussion of the nature of god (sic), what can be known about him, not a discussion of the question whether a god exists." (Gaskin, *Hume's Philosophy of Religion*, p. 222) Gaskin does see that Philo's argument that little can be known of this god is actually Hume's own position which places Hume somewhere between a total agnosticism (a god with no knowable attributes) and the Christian God.

[10] For a discussion on Hume's regard for religion, see B.M. Laing, *David Hume*, (London: Ernest Benn Limited, 1932), pp. 174-187.

[11] Further justification for our choice of Hume is provided by T.W. Tilley, "First, in the *Dialogues*, Hume displays a sophisticated view of the relations between the reality of evil and faith in God... Second, the *Dialogues* also shows a most important aspect of a religious position for which the existence and nature of God cannot be at issue... Third, moral evils are not an issue for Hume." (T.W. Tilley, 'Hume on God and Evil', in *Journal of the American Academy of Religion*, Volume 56, Winter 1988, pp. 722-723) We believe these characteristics of Hume make him a helpful dialogue partner for Barth.

Is he willing to prevent evil, but not able? Then he is impotent. Is he able but not willing? Then he is malevolent. Is he both able and willing? Whence then is evil?[12]

Hume asks first of the sovereign power of God; 'is God willing but not able?' To this question Barth's theodicy posits a question of its own. When speaking of God's 'ability', we must ask further about what kind of world God was both able and willing to create. Barth has stated that God's sovereignty certainly allowed Him to create a world which would be inaccessible for evil, but the cost would be the freedom of humanity to participate in its relationship with its Creator.

A creature freed from the possibility of falling away would not really be living as a creature. It could only be a second God-and as no second God exists, it could only be God Himself.[13]

The question is shifted from the sovereignty of God to the sovereign will of God to create a being which would have a relationship with its Creator, and Barth states clearly that to create such a being meant that the impossible possibility of evil entering the world through sin indeed did have a possibility. What Hume seeks is the combination of free humanity and no evil, and this must be seen to be impossible for Barth because of the motif of the 'necessary antithesis'.[14] To say 'God' is to say the eternal self-differentiator from all which is 'not-God'. Thus to say 'God and creation' is, for Barth, to affirm the unity of self-differentiation and self-determination in election, and thus to make way for the ultimate justification of God. What God is 'able' to do is to create the best of all possible worlds in which humanity is free and in which God chooses to destroy the inevitable evil which comes as the result of humanity's misuse of that freedom. Therefore God is not impotent, but neither is there the possibility of a world of free beings and devoid of evil.

The purpose of God in granting man freedom to obey is to verify as such the obedience proposed in and with his creation, i.e., to confirm it,

---

12 David Hume, *Dialogues Concerning Natural Religion*, (New York: Bobbs-Merrill Co, Inc., 1970) pt. X, pp. 88.

13 CD II/1, p. 503.

14 We must be reminded that Barth affirms that indeed such a world is exactly what God created-free humanity and no evil, and therefore sin and evil are man's responsibility and not God's. Yet we must also remember the tension between the 'impossibility' of sin and its 'inevitability' because of the non-divine state of the creature. For this reason, there is a shift in Barth of the responsibility for evil from man to God. What God could do is create a world in which humanity was free and in which there was no evil. What God could not do was to create a state where the non-divine creature could resist the temptation put to it by nothingness, and it was because of this 'inability' that Barth makes his doctrine of election such a central player in his theology.

to actualize it in his own decision. It is obvious that if this is His will God cannot compel man to obey; He cannot as it were bring about his obedience mechanically. He would do this if He made obedience physically necessary and disobedience physically impossible, if He made man in such a way as to be incapable of a decision to obey.[15]

Hume's second part of the theoretical question concerns God's goodness, 'is he able but not willing?' The benevolence of God is never in question in Barth's theology generally nor in his doctrine of evil specifically. To the contrary the love of God is seen in the primordial election to save His rebellious creation to the extent that Barth re-introduces a sense of *theopaschitism* where God suffers the penalty which was borne on behalf of fallen humanity. God's grace is always taken more seriously than sin and the true heart of Barth's doctrine of God may be found in his 'logically required' and 'inherently affirmed' universalism where there will be no ultimate victory for *das Nichtige* or sin over the grace of God.

This is not to say that Barth does not affirm the wrath of God nor the existence of hell as we have shown. However it is only the One Rejected who must bear the full wrath of God, and the One Judged who must descend into hell on behalf of God's beloved covenant partner. Indeed it was the love of God which binds together His self-differentiation with His self-determination in election according to which God chose to save His creation in Christ before the world was formed in its distinction from the *tohu wa-bohu* . In Barth's theodicy there is no room to question the benevolence of God if the whole question is kept on this theoretical level.

'Whence then is evil?' Hume asks. In Barth's theodicy evil is permitted to play its role and then it is annihilated. Yet it must be said as we have clearly shown that evil's place in the world was inevitable, and in that sense God is responsible for it, having chosen to create. Thus "without evil as 'permitted' in this sense there can be no universe or man, and without the inclusion of this 'permission' God's decree would be something other than it actually is."[16] The 'whence' of evil finds it under the administration of the left hand of God, in His non-willing, in His 'No'. For all of its problems, this is the only possible place for evil given Barth's rejection of dualism and the clear need to distinguish between God and evil.

Thus Barth answers Hume that God is both willing and able to prevent evil, but only according to the route of the cross, and He is willing to do so as testified in the historical work of Jesus Christ according to the eternal will of God in election. The 'whence' of evil is then a past, defeated foe who now only operates under the left hand of God, and its future lies under the revelation of its annihilation in the final *parousia*. It is here that the 'willing and able' will equal the total absence of evil from the sphere of creation. In this way, although thoroughly noetic, Barth's answer to the theodicy question of Hume is based

---

[15] CD III/1, p. 264.
[16] CD II/2, p. 170.

squarely upon faith, and according to faith Barth can affirm, "If God is greater in the very fact that He is the God who forgives and saves from death, we have no right to complain but must praise him that His will also includes a permitting of sin and death."[17]

Barth's Empirical Theodicy

From this classic theoretical question, Hume through Philo also takes on the 'balance' between misery and joy, finding not only that there is more misery than joy in the world, but asking the underlying empirical theodicy question,

> Why is there any misery at all in the world? Not by chance, surely. From some cause, then. It is from the intention of the deity? But he is perfectly benevolent. It is contrary to his intention? But he is almighty. Nothing can shake the solidity of this reasoning, so short, so clear, so decisive...[18]

Hume's second question asks of the cause of misery in relation to the sovereignty and goodness of God. He bypasses the idea that the presence of joy in the world offsets misery and asks as to the cause, and therefore the justification of misery at all. Barth has no place in his theology for the idea of chance, for all occurrence falls under either the *praecurrit, concurrit,* of *succurrit* of God's providential care. The argument that this heavy-handed providence results in an outright determinism has been taken up and the place within God's providence for the free response of the creature has been defended at length by Barth.

In his doctrine of evil, the misery in the world results from two places; from human sin and therefore from evil itself, and as a natural result of creation's 'shadowy side'. We have rejected Barth's insistence on a created, 'good' and positively-willed dark side to creation and we have demonstrated the myriad of problems with such a doctrine, including mainly the constant blurring and inevitable obliteration of the line between what is part of God's good creation on its shadowy side (and therefore 'caused' by God according to His good and perfect will), and that misery and suffering which is a result of sin (and therefore the responsibility of humanity in its rebellion and disobedience to God).

Gottschalk is certainly correct when he states, "Which of these two interpretations of suffering expresses Barth's basic viewpoint is difficult to determine... A clue to Barth's most basic impulse is that in those often impassioned passages where he speaks of the work of Jesus Christ in defeating the power of nothingness, physical suffering and pain are portrayed explicitly as expressions of *das Nichtige*."[19] When this is coupled with Barth's view that the

---

[17] CD II/1, p. 595.

[18] Hume, *Dialogues Concerning Natural Religion, op. cit.,* p. 91.

[19] Gottschalk, 'Theodicy After Auschwitz', *op. cit.,* p. 82.

shadowy side of creation includes, "an abyss... obscurity... impediment... limitation... decay... indigence... ashes... end... worthlessness... darkness... failure... tears... age... loss... death,"[20] it is clear to see the problem which arises, and Barth's theodicy is rendered useless if such a distinction cannot be made. For this and the other reasons stated earlier, we have rejected a *Schattenseite* in creation and we will look at Barth's theodicy outwith this teaching.

If misery is the result of the disobedience of sinful humanity, then the question of responsibility takes a step back from the idea of cause to that of possibility. Does the phenomenon of misery require a justification of the Creator of a world in which this suffering occurs? Here again we enter into the difficulties of the tension between the 'inevitability' and the 'impossibility' of sin. God, says Barth, cannot and is not responsible for sin (for it is 'ontologically impossible' for created humanity) and yet he is willing to see the need for the justification of the Creator as a result of the inevitability of sin (as a result of the combination of the non-divine state of the creature and the unavoidable temptation of evil). We must remember that this tension requires that both sides be affirmed, and thus we must conclude that humanity is responsible, is the cause of its own misery as it rebels against God in disobedience. In this sense, pain and suffering are a part of the fallen state of humanity and are not traceable to the Deity as its 'initiator'.

The potency of God is not demonstrated in Barth in the destruction of evil prior to creation, but in the defeat of evil within the space-time history of the creature as the covenant partner of God. God has justified Himself and His creation in this defeat, and the theodicy question returns to the realm of faith as we await the revelation of this defeat in the final *parousia*. This two-fold view is the proper way to understand Barth's response to the question of 'cause' with regards to the phenomena of suffering and misery.[21]

Yet we have here as well the re-emergence of two of our strongest criticisms of Barth which significantly weaken his theodicy at this point. Barth's insistence on the non-perpetuity of nothingness puts the question of cause back into God by positing that God had the power to annihilate evil but chose to do so only in the midst of human history instead of prior to its creation. The questions of the freedom of the creature and the 'necessary antithesis' which arise here are overwhelming and, we must say again, unnecessary. The non-perpetuity of nothingness in the extreme sense in which Barth proposes it leaves him with no alternative but to admit that God is the cause of evil directly, and of sin and its resultant misery and suffering indirectly; all simply because He could but did not do prior to creation what He has done and will do at its end in annihilating evil.

---

20 CD III/3, p. 297.

21 In terms of 'cause' we remember Barth's distinction between what is willed and that which exists because of His non-willing. Thus Barth concluded, "God in His foreknowledge is the Lord and source of being, and He is also the Lord *but not the source* of non-being." (CD II/1, p. 560, emphasis mine)

A correction of Barth's idea of the non-perpetuity of nothingness avoids these problems by speaking not of the termination of the eternal non-willing of God, but in the banishment of nothingness from the created sphere back into the meaningless void from which it emerged at creation. Barth's powerful construction of the peculiar ontology of nothingness in its form of a 'dualism of rejection' allows for this interpretation, and we affirm it as a better and more scriptural description of evil than what Barth has offered in its non-perpetuity.

Secondly, and closely related, modernity can only be justified if this final defeat of evil and its annihilation (banishment) are understood as having been sealed and secured in the historical work of Christ, but are not yet to be manifested until the *eschaton*. By shifting the enactment of the sentence passed upon evil to the final *parousia*, we avoid the devastating problem in Barth's theodicy concerning the justification of the time *post Christum*.

With these three alterations to Barth's doctrine of evil (the rejection of the shadowy-side of creation, the modification of the idea of non-perpetuity, and the eschatological understanding of the ultimate defeat of evil) misery can only be ascribed to the sinful rebellion of humanity, and its very possibility in creation is justified first in the desire of the Creator to create another for free fellowship and participation with Himself, and secondly in its defeat and future annihilation in the work of Jesus Christ. Hume's empirical question is answered ultimately within the realm of faith. For it is still in faith that this is accepted and believed, and here we must stand firm with Barth in rejecting a theodicy in which God's justification lies in the reason and logic of humanity.

Barth's Eschatological Theodicy

In the voice of Ivan Karamazov, Fyodor Dostoyevski provides a third challenge in the form of the theodicy question posed against the idea of a future justification of suffering. In rejecting what he called the 'higher harmony' of this future justification of evil, Ivan protests to Alyosha that no final harmony or bliss is worth the price of the sum total of human suffering. Ivan turns especially to the suffering of children which he finds ultimately indefensible. He seizes upon the two stories now famous in *The Brothers Karamazov* ; of the boy torn to pieces by dogs in front of his mother as punishment for the slightest offense, and of the little girl brutally and repeatedly abused and finally shut up in a dung-filled room by her nearly insane parents. Ivan rejects the idea as abhorrent that these evils are the price which must be paid for the future harmony and bliss of humanity, "if the sufferings of children go to make up the sum of sufferings which is necessary for the purchase of truth, then I say beforehand that the entire truth is not worth such a price." And even more pointedly,

> Imagine that it is you yourself who are erecting an edifice of human destiny with the aim of making men happy in the end, of giving them peace and contentment at last, but that to do that it is absolutely necessary, and indeed quite inevitable, to torture to death only one tiny

creature, the little girl who beats her breast with her little fist, and to found the edifice on her unavenged tears–would you consent to be the architect on those conditions?[22]

The part of this protest which is applicable for us here is Barth's strong teachings on the justification of creation and, along with it, the justification of the Creator. If we return to the inevitability of the Fall and the eternal self-differentiation of God as the basis for His self-determination in election, we remember that Barth has never sought to exonerate God for the presence of evil in the world, but only for the sinful rebellion of humanity which ushered that evil into the sphere of creation. And even there we find an indirect link, a line of responsibility of sorts which we have seen Barth address in several places where he finds it necessary to emphasise the justification of God in the work of Jesus Christ. The question can be asked here, echoing Ivan Karamazov, if this ultimate justification of God is able to bear the sum total of human misery encountered in the history of creation? Have we not already reached the point where the talk of future justification of evil is incomprehensible and even abhorrent?

Barth's response is surely a return to the cross and a re-look at what happened there. He will remind us that there is only one true suffering which plumbed the depths of agony and pain and that was the death suffered for us in Christ. So great is that one vicarious suffering for all humanity, that the sufferings of this world can only be understood as *Zeichen und Schatten, Ankündigungen und um die Nachwehen,*[23] of this one great suffering, and they are therefore only to be considered *Zeichen des göttlichen Gerichtes*.[24] Barth's exposition here must be understood as an expression of his realism and the resultant dichotomy between our personal experience and the ontological reality of the Truth of our existence.

In answer to Ivan's challenge, Barth would have the laid the foundation to be able to say 'yes' with one great amendment, it was not the torture of one little child, but the sufferings and death of the very Son of God who won for us the hope of the future and in whom we have the final justification for the sufferings of humanity. That this justification is not built on anything less than the suffering of God, that God took the responsibility for the sum total of suffering of all humanity for all time squarely upon Himself and suffered the results, this is the grace and love of God which is far greater than any compilation of human misery. The 'No' of God is only a mystery to those who have not yet heard His 'Yes', for in the 'Yes', the 'No' is defeated and God is justified.

---

[22] Dostoyevski, *The Brothers Karamazov, op. cit.,* pp. 286-287.

[23] *Nachwehen* is translated here as 'echoes' which is not as strong as the word would imply. The better translation would be 'after-pains'. (CD II/1, p. 406)

[24] Suffering for our faith too is a "faint but not obscure reflection of His [suffering]." (CD IV/1, p. 44)

God has justified Himself in our presence and us in His presence. The theodicy has occurred, beside which all our endeavours to justify God are merely taunting ridicule. Speaking with His own voice, and encircled by the glory of His brightness, God has done once for all the existential deed–He has received men as His children.[25]

As we have seen, the justification for this *time* in which suffering and evil continues to be manifest is highly troublesome for Barth. Yet it is certainly affirmed throughout Barth's theology that God in Christ has secured that final justification, and that we can look forward to it in faith and hope. Barring the great weakness in Barth's doctrine of evil concerning the justification of the time of the community, Barth's theodicy is well-equipped to answer the eschatological question of the justification of evil as put forth here through the character of Ivan Karamazov.

Barth's Existential Theodicy

No theology must be allowed which is not credible in the presence of burning children.[26]

With this powerful and disturbing challenge put before us by Irving Greenberg, we turn to the writings of Elie Wiesel who posits our final form of theodicy in his post-Auschwitz writings. Wiesel speaks from vivid personal experience when he relates the story of a hanging in Auschwitz in which a young boy suffered for more than half an hour because he was too light to have mercifully died as suddenly as the heavier adults hung alongside him. As Wiesel was forced to face the struggling boy, he recalls his now famous thoughts, "Behind me, I heard the same man asking: 'Where is God now?' And I heard a voice within me answer him: 'Where is He? Here He is–He is hanging here, on this gallows'."[27] We will avoid the debate as to whether this was for Wiesel the actual 'death of God' in a loss of faith or the final intolerability which is confronted when the absolute existence of God collides with the horrible depth of the actuality of evil.[28]   What is clear is that Wiesel experienced the

---

[25]   Barth, *The Epistle to the Romans, op. cit.,* p. 300.

[26]   Irving Greenberg, 'Cloud of Smoke, Pillar of Fire: Judaism, Christianity, and Modernity after the Holocaust', in *Auschwitz: Beginning of a New Era?*, (ed) Eva Fleischner, (New York: KTAV Publishing House, Inc., 1977), p. 23.

[27]   Elie Wiesel, *Night*, (London: MacGibbon and Kee, 1960), p. 83.

[28]   R. Bauckham takes the former view, "To me at least it is clear that within the book the story marks the final, crucial step in Wiesel's loss of faith in God. God hangs on the gallows because the possibility of faith in him is dying with every moment the dying child suffers and the God of Israel fails to deliver him. God is dead because the holocaust makes theodicy impossible." ('Theodicy From Ivan Karamazov to Moltmann', in *Modern Theology*, Volume 4, October 1987, p. 87) R.A. Brown takes the latter, "Ever since that first night, Wiesel has struggled with

irreconcilable convergence of the reality of God and the reality of Auschwitz. Does theodicy become impossible in this situation?

Barth's theodicy takes a very strong stance on the understanding of evil as a present 'reality', and we must be careful to give his view an exact representation. Although on the theoretical or metaphysical level it appears as if Barth is assigning a sense of non-reality to evil, he is careful to delineate between the eternal reality of evil and the actuality of the experience of evil in our world. Thus Barth wants to keep from evil any sense of a real form of existence which is equated with either God or creation. If evil 'exists', it does so according to a thoroughly different ontology, and it is to that 'ontology of rejectedness' that Barth readily assigns the titles 'non-existent', 'pseudo reality', and 'utterly past'. In its relationship to God, and by virtue of it in its relation to humanity and creation, evil can and must be described in these terms.

Yet Barth has been unfairly criticised for making evil illusory or less real than what we actually experience.[29] This error comes in missing the connection between evil's eternal defeat on the cross and its temporal actuality in the world. We have shown that Barth's own doctrine of evil is partly to blame for this confusion. However, he does construct an adequate picture in which both 'realities' of the existence of evil can be affirmed. It is according to Barth's realism that we can understand both the actuality of our experience of evil and its state of pastness and defeat in which it will exist until the final *parousia*. Yet Barth will not point us to the peculiar ontology of evil, or to Satan or even to the future justification of evil and the annihilation of nothingness in response to to the kind of challenge which we have in Elie Wiesel. Barth will instead point us directly back to God through the figure of Job.

The consistent, and perhaps consistently shocking picture which emerges in supreme form in Barth's interpretation of Job is the fact that all evil, and thus all suffering must be finally traced back to God! Barth's final theodicy regarding suffering must be found here. Barth's interpretation of Job takes us along the following line of thought.

1. Although it is Satan who actually carries out the persecution of Job, "it must be remembered that Satan could have done nothing at all without God's permission... even in the severest trials which he undergoes, Job is thus in the ruling and protecting hand of God."[30]

2. God does, in the end, bless Job with more than he had previously, however, "the point is that He does not have to do so... without being untrue to

---

two irreconcilable realities-the reality of God and the reality of Auschwitz. Either seems to cancel out each other, and yet neither will disappear. Either in isolation could be managed-Auschwitz and no God, or God and no Auschwitz. But Auschwitz *and* God, God *and* Auschwitz? That is the unbearable reality that haunts sleep and destroys wakefulness.'" (R. A. Brown, *Messenger To All Humanity*, (Notre Dame: University of Notre Dame Press, 1983), p. 54).

[29] For a good comparison between Barth's view of evil and that of Mary Baker Eddy and Christian Science, see Gottschalk, 'Theodicy After Auschwitz', *op. cit.*, pp. 83-89.

[30] C.D. IV/3.1, p. 385.

Job, He can reduce His blessing to the bare minimum of preservation... He can do so to such an extent that God Himself can and actually does appear to Job to be an enemy and persecutor. He did not owe him a favour, nor will He do so. He can also allow disaster to fall upon him...God would not be God if He were not free to both give and take away."[31]

3.   Job's true suffering comes about in the convergence of the God he knows with this enemy God whom he struggles to understand, "his [Job's] true sorrow in all his sorrows, and therefore the primary subject of his complaints, consists in the conjunction of his profound knowledge that in what has happened and what has come upon him he has to do with God, and his no less profound ignorance how far he has to do with God... we see this knowledge and ignorance of God in headlong collision and unbearable tension. This is the depth and essence of the sufferings of the suffering Job."[32] It is the fact that Job knows that in this suffering he is dealing with this God whom he knows and loves that "almost drives him mad" since he is encountering his own God "in a form in which He is absolutely alien."[33]

4.   Job's complaint comes in the context of this relationship, and as such it is "in the name of God that he complains against God." By doing so Barth declares that "the clearly declared meaning of the Book of Job is that he put himself both in the right and also in the wrong in doing so."[34] He is in the right by taking his protest to no one else but God, seeing Him as the actual source of his oppression, and here Barth allows the idea of 'permission' to go to its logical end, for "If God is greater in the very fact that He is the God who forgives and saves from death, we have no right to complain but must praise him that His will also includes a permitting of sin and death."[35] Therefore we are called upon always to affirm that the *voluntas permittens* are fully and wholly the *voluntas divina*.[36] Job is in the wrong in that, after affirming God's right to both give and take away, he protests that God should have dealt differently with him than He has in this 'taking away'. If God had, according to Barth, "exercised His freedom towards him by reducing to the cheerless minimum of actual preservation the blessing which He had hitherto undeservedly blessed him", then Job was in the wrong to insist that God, "ought really to have exercised His freedom very differently."[37]

5.   This constitutes what Barth affirms as Job's "flight from God to God" insomuch as God is both his Liberator and his Opponent, and it is remarkable that Job never considers the role of Satan in his persecutions. Instead Job flees to the bosom of the One who torments him and seeks refuge and deliverance

[31]   Ibid. p. 387.

[32]   Ibid. p. 401.

[33]   Ibid. p. 402.

[34]   Ibid. pp. 405-406.

[35]   CD II/1, p. 595.

[36]   Ibid. p. 595.

[37]   C.D. IV/3.1, pp. 405, 407.

from the One who crushes him. In a spectacular understatement Barth concludes, "This is a hard saying." Yet he will not let us seek answers or help anywhere else than in the eternal cry to God, a cry which, "can neither begin nor continue without clinging to the One to whom and against whom it is directed with the certainty, grounded in Him alone, of His decision not only against but also for the man who hopes and trusts in Him. Of His decision!"[38] The decision is God's and His alone, and Job's 'wrong' is in seeking from God the decision of 'for' rather than 'against'.[39]

6. We come to the climax of this interpretation when Barth anticipates the protest which arises as we consider that we should be content to accept crushing rejection from God hand in hand with His care and blessing. How can both come from the same God, the God in Christ, the God of the covenant? Barth's sharp reply is fundamental for his theodicy, "He does not ask for our understanding, agreement or applause. On the contrary, He simply asks that he should be content not to know why and to what end he exists, and does so in this way and not another."[40] This is God's message as He speaks out of the whirlwind, reminding Job of his true relationship before God. We are reminded here of Paul's same forceful message,

> What then shall we say? Is God unjust? Not at all! For he says to Moses, 'I will have mercy on whom I will have mercy, and I will have compassion on whom I have compassion'. It does not, therefore, depend on man's desire or effort, but on God's mercy.... One of you will say to me: 'Then why does God still blame us? For who resists his will?' But who are you, O man, to talk back to God? (Romans 9:14–20)

The cosmos is God's and not the creature's, and thus, as a result of humanity's disobedience, "within the created world man is confronted by innumerable great and small factors in face of the autonomy of which he must bow for good or evil."[41]

7. Finally, Barth drives home this point by assigning the title of 'falsehood' to all protestations of this picture of God. The mistake of the friends of Job is that they sought to speak for God, their own construction of God, and in the process they sought to defend their own theology. By not looking to the *Deus absconditus* and there alone for the understanding of the persecutions of

---

[38] Ibid. pp. 424-425.

[39] In grieving over the loss of his son, Nicholas Wolterstorff struggles over the place and role of God, "I cannot fit it all together by saying, 'He did it', but neither can I do so by saying, 'There was nothing He could do about it'. I cannot fit it together at all. I can only, with Job, endure." (Wolterstorff, *Lament for a Son*, (Grand Rapids: William Eerdmans Publishing Co., 1987), p. 67)

[40] C.D. IV/3.1, p. 431.

[41] Ibid. p. 432.

Job, they represent the falsehood of humanity. Barth's closing statements are critical to this whole line of thought and we will quote him in full,

> [But] the discrepancy between Job and his friends could not have been greater or sharper. For them there was a meaningful system of good and evil, of salvation and judgement, of failure and restitution. This existed from the very first. God was active merely as its Architect, Guarantor and Executor. Man was occupied merely with filling up the different columns of a questionnaire put to him... Job on the other hand, saw a living, active and speaking God uniquely confronting a living man in his unique existence and responsibility... For Job, everything was open, active and in motion... In the speeches of the friends we simply have the repetition of well-worn formulae and sacred clichés. In those of Job we have something original, new knowledge, the truth itself breaking through in all its virgin freshness. It is little wonder that no understanding or even conversation is possible between him and his friends... For when men think and speak from this divine standpoint and therefore non-historically and within the framework of this orderly structure, there is no place in their utterances for two factors, namely, the free God and the man freed by and for Him. Yahweh as the free God of the free man Job, and Job as the free man of this free God, together in their divine and human freedom enter into the crisis in which God becomes so incomprehensible to Job even though He will not let him go, and Job becomes so angry against God even though he will not let Him go. It is in the sphere and exercise of this freedom that there takes place what does take place, the severity of God and the misery of Job, the silence of God and the crying of Job, and finally the self-revelation of Yahweh as the divine decision which closes the case, and the knowledge of Job.[42]

It is in the context of relationship, freedom and movement that we are to pose the theodicy question with regards to seemingly intolerable human suffering. Hauerwas reminds us that suffering, like creation, cannot be explained, "yet both remind us that our existence makes sense only insofar as we are able to place it in a narrative."[43] Likewise, what is clear to Barth is that these categories are large enough not for an understanding, but for the proper response to evil, even the evil of an Auschwitz or Hiroshima. We have here in a sense a vestige of Hick's 'vale of soul making' in this idea that all crises involve a process of movement and growth; Barth would have us add that if we cling to God in the face of these crises, the growth will be positive, if we look

---

[42] Ibid. pp. 459-460.

[43] Hauerwas, *Naming the Silences, op. cit.,* p. 79.

elsewhere, to static theological constructs or to Satan or to fate or to ourselves, we will suffer the isolation which is the true suffering of suffering.[44]

Therefore, while we agree with H.M. Schulweis when he says, "For Barth, the need for theodicy is itself a symptom of man's enslavement to moral and logical criteria and norms irrelevant to the conduct of the divinely unique One"[45], we do find in Barth a desire to bring the discussion back to the place where all theodicy questions must begin and end. Thus Barth does indeed provide a theodicy, but it is characteristically defined by its Subject and not the other way around. In this way, Barth's theodicy is transformed into an anthropodicy, where it is humanity and not God which is in need of justification, and which receives its justification only in its relationship with *this* God. Kenneth Surin made the point, "it is certainly no exaggeration to say that virtually every contemporary discussion of the theodicy-question is premised, implicitly or explicitly, on an understanding of 'God' overwhelmingly constrained by the principles of 17th and 18th century philosophical theism."[46]

To the extent that Barth was able to break out of this constraint and discuss evil in a wholly Christocentric frame, his doctrine of evil is a great contribution to the Church. For Barth's most polemic point is that we have no independent status from which to ask the theodicy question, neither in the ashes of Job's lament, from the academic classroom of Hume's *Dialogues*, from the bitterness of Ivan Karamazov's protest, nor even, ultimately, from the crematoria of Auschwitz. It is instead God who asks the anthropodicy question, and in the face of this question, humanity, in its sinfulness and as the *imago Dei*, must respond by cleaving to the One in whom it receives its preservation and hopes for its future.[47] We remember Barth's comment on Dostoyevski's 'Grand Inquisitor'

---

[44] This position surely confronts the 'theodicy of protest' put forth by Moltmann and Roth among others. For in them, although we are there, too, thrown back to God, it is to a less than sovereign, rather pathetic God who cannot do any better and to whom we must protest against His own ineptitude. This is certainly not what Barth has in mind. For the real crisis in the Christian experience of evil is the unequivocal dilemma of the reality both the evil and the absolute omnipotence of God. Thus there is in Barth's theodicy a real sense of protest, but it is a protest which seeks not some real accusatory position vis-à-vis God, but a protest which seeks after the hard-won faith of Job rather than the escape to the explanations of his friends. It is also a protest which takes seriously the ultimate justification of suffering at the hands of God; a position which can only be taken when God's sovereignty is not compromised, and as such it is the far more acceptable position than the empty and somewhat despairing position of modern 'protest theodicy'.

[45] H.M. Schulweis, 'Karl Barth's Job', *op. cit.,* p. 157.

[46] Surin, *Theology and the Problem of Evil*, (Oxford: Basil Blackwell, 1986), p. 4.

[47] We must quote from one of our most favourite hymns in *The Church Hymnary* of the Church of Scotland where the inspired words of George Matheson catch, in two verses, the understanding of God's triumph of evil, the seriousness of suffering, the promise of God and the hope of the future. He also demonstrates a Barth-like understanding of faith as a flight from God to God when he writes,

'O joy, that seekest me through pain,

who had made violent accusations against Jesus in the setting of 16th century Spain. Jesus listened to the accusations and charges which echo so closely so many modern day theodicy questions, and, in reserved response, Dostoyevski says, "But he [Jesus] suddenly approached the old man and kissed him gently on his bloodless, aged lips. That was all his answer."[48] Barth seized on this incredible moment and commented,

> *Und eben diese einzige, diese ganze Antwort ist die Hoffnung der Kirche: das schlechthin unableitbare, grundlose, nur in Gott selbst begründete ewige Erbarmen, das alles Denken übersteigt.* [49]

We will end this discussion of Barth's theodicy with three of his most poignant statements which, in the most succinct and perspicacious way, provide a fitting summary to our topic. In 1916 Barth drew his methodological line in the sand with regards to the Subject of theology, and for the next 50+ years he dared anyone who would cross it. From this unequivocal position Barth developed his theology and, in the process, his doctrine of evil.

We see the laying of the groundwork for all we have said in this book concerning Barth's doctrine of evil and theodicy in Barth's view of Scripture when he says,

> There are blind alleys of a thousand types, out of which the way to the kingdom of heaven can at first lead only backwards. And it is certain that the Bible, if we read it carefully, makes straight for the point where *one must decide to accept or reject the sovereignty of God.* [50]

I cannot close my eyes to thee:
I trace the rainbow through the rain,
And feel the promise is not vain, that morn shall tearless be.

O Cross that liftest up my head,
I dare not ask to fly from thee:
I lay in dust life's glory dead,
And from the ground there blossoms red, Life that shall endless be.

(*The Church Hymnary,* Third Edition, (Oxford: Oxford University Press, 1973), p. 242)

[48] Dostoyevski, *The Brothers Karamazov, op. cit.,* p. 308.

[49] Barth, *Der Römerbrief, op. cit.,* p. 378. "It is just this answer, alone and in its entirety which is the hope of the Church: the eternal mercy of God, absolutely unswerving, without foundation except in God Himself, this mercy rises above all thinking."

[50] Barth, 'The Strange New World in the Bible', *op. cit.,* p. 41. (emphasis mine)

For Barth, the decision on the sovereignty of God is the basis for one's entire theology.[51] This is then carried further by the second statement which comes from his famous §50 'God and Nothingness'. Here, at the outset, Barth sets the context of the entire discussion of evil within his understanding of this one sovereign Subject by opening with the words, "Under the control of God...(*Unter Gottes Verfügung*)"[52] Everything which is to follow in the 79 pages of discussion, and indeed everything we find in the *Church Dogmatics* concerning his doctrine of evil as we have traced them in this study must be seen to flow from this *a priori* understanding of God's sovereignty. Finally, in view of the highly complex and at times wholly enigmatic theme of evil in Barth's theology, the final statement is perhaps Barth at his most honest when, in struggling again with the proper description of evil and its relationship to God, he simply concludes, "Whatever evil is, God is its Lord."[53]

Suffering and Barth's Theodicy

As we conclude our study of Barth's doctrine of evil we will take a final look at the five categories of suffering which we have developed throughout this thesis. Much of the applicability of any theodicy is dependent upon understanding suffering in these distinct ways instead of viewing it as a single subject.

Three points must be kept in mind in these concluding comments: 1) we have rejected the idea of a *Schattenseite* of creation and therefore all suffering is a result of the fallen state of creation, 2) all suffering must be therefore attributed either directly or indirectly to sin, and 3) God is either active (positive will) or passive (by permission) in all suffering in the world.

Suffering as a Result of Sin

Barth insisted that the decisive and ultimate 'No' of God's all-consuming judgement on Calvary means that although we will continue to suffer as a result of our sin (because of the patience of God), that suffering can never have the annihilating effect which was borne for us. Thus Barth has called this type of suffering *Ankündigungen und um die Nachwehen der Wirklichkeit des göttlichen*

---

51 Moltmann says of this sovereignty in Barth, "*Vielmehr wird hier Gott jenseits der weltanschaulichen Alternative von Gegenständlichkeit und Ungegenständlichkeit durch sich selbst offenbar. Allein sein Wort beweist seine Wirklichkeit. Es knüpft beim Menschen durch sich selbst, d.h. in dr Kraft des Heiligen Geistes, an. Gottes Souveränität muß darum bis in den Erkenntnis - und Verstehensvorgang hinein theologisch durchgehalten werden.* " (Moltmann, '*Gottesoffenbarung und Wahrheitsfrage*', *op. cit.*, p. 159) Moltmann is correct in his contention that 'God's sovereignty must be maintained right into the process of recognition and theological understanding'.

52 CD III/3, p. 289 and KD III/3, p. 327.

53 CD IV/1, p. 408.

Gerichte (announcements and echoes of the reality of the divine judgement), yet they are real sufferings nonetheless. Also Barth can maintain the close tie between sin and suffering according to humanity's responsibility for the *homo lapsus*. Because Barth is able to exonerate God of the charge of the Author of sin, the responsibility for sin and the consequences of suffering are solely upon the shoulders of humanity.

This category responds to the 'theoretical theodicy' we have described. The key feature here is the 'impossibility-inevitability' tension which, in the end, is dissolved in the work of Jesus Christ which assumes it and overcomes it providing the final justification for humanity and God in Himself. This is the essence of what Barth means by election when he says "from all eternity He sees us in His Son as sinners to whom He is gracious."[54] That we suffer because of our sin is a fact of our creaturely reality; that our sufferings in this respect are both assumed in and overcome by God in Christ, and that our future is one in which sin and its consequential sufferings will cease, this is the *Wirklichkeit* of our union with Christ. It is this two-fold state as expressed in Barth's intense realism which can and must be apprehended only in faith.

Suffering as Chastisement and Correction from God

This is the least used category in Barth's theology, yet Barth is not hesitant to show that God was the *causa prima* of evils and sufferings in the Old Testament.[55] In his use of the 'right and left hand of God' motif, Barth has developed a view of God in relationship to evil which allows for His use of evil both by permission and pro-actively to serve His purposes. Yet even in His use of evil in this 'positive' way, in one sense humanity shares the responsibility for it since the entrance of evil into creation came about through the sin of humanity. In this way, it is seldom possible to determine whether suffering is actually from God for the purpose of correction, or whether God is using the suffering we bring on ourselves from our sin (our first category) to bring about a positive result.

Barth would certainly tend toward this second understanding and he has developed his doctrine of evil with a strong sense of God's turning evil into good. This, in addition to his seeming rejection of the idea that God sends evil upon us in his interpretation of the *Heidelberg Catechism*, makes this the better understanding of how Barth would view our suffering to be 'from' God for correction and chastisement.[56] The idea that God manipulates evil and suffering

---

[54] CD II/2, p. 124.

[55] See CD II/1, p. 419-420, for example.

[56] We remember how in his commentary on the *Heidelberg Catechism* Barth rewords the phrase from Question 26, "Moreover, the evils he sends upon me in this troubled life he will turn for good," into "He governs also over evil which, though it does not come from Him, has the dangerous being of non-being." As we have said, here Barth seems to sidestep the direct implications of the original wording of the catechism. (*The Heidelberg Catechism for Today, op. cit.,* pp. 59-61)

to bring about good is more palatable for Barth than God's direct sending of evil (and this is seen in his discussion of Job, where even in its most direct form, God is still the Permittor rather than the Initiator of the persecution), an idea which is surely too Schleiermachian for Barth.

For the theodicy question, in this category of suffering God can be seen to be working in and through the suffering which our sin brings upon us, always seeking to turn evil into good. This view holds whether God is seen to be permitting or even directly sending suffering, since the heart of the Father in bringing about good in his children is always the issue. In this way we find a vestige of the 'vale of soul-making' where the price to be paid for the correction brought about through suffering is small indeed compared to the importance of the positive movement of the human side of the covenantal relationship.

Suffering for the Sake of Testing and Strengthening Faith

The remaining categories consider suffering which is not a direct result of personal sin, but which occur within the context of a sinful and fallen world. There is one element in Barth's exposition of Job that certainly fits here. God has forced Job to consider Him his God even in this alien form of enemy. Within the larger picture of the importance of this 'flight from God to God' Barth is also keen to develop the dynamic characteristics of the God-Job relationship, especially as it develops through the crisis, and in distinct comparison with the static theism of Job's friends. It is in the midst of this intense struggle that Job, "moves through temptation to this goal and ends in a new offering of himself... he will make this forward step."[57]

What God is seeking in Job is suffering obedience, "A partial action in the history in which the relationship between God and Job takes place is the change wherein God executes this change of form in free decision and Job must follow the divine decision with an equally free human decision, i.e., to render suffering obedience to Him."[58] The result is that through this suffering, Job "shows himself to be the witness of Yahweh, taking the new steps forwards with God."[59] In the end, this forward movement, this growth, testing and strengthening of faith is the what is at issue in the entire book of Job, and this forward step is finally taken in that "God spoke to Job and Job heard Him."[60]

The permission of evil for this growth is, for Barth, justification in and of itself for the evil. God is justified in using evil to bring about this good, which means that far from a balance between evil and joy, the benefits of growth and positive movement in our relationship with God is of the highest importance, even to the point of God's allowance and use of the severest forms of sufferings to bring it about. Surely this is what James meant when he said, "Consider it

---

[57] C.D. IV/3.1, p. 388.
[58] Ibid. p. 405.
[59] Ibid. p. 422.
[60] Ibid. pp. 434-435.

pure joy, my brothers, whenever you face trials of many kinds, because you know that the testing of your faith develops perseverance. Perseverance must finish its work so that you may be mature and complete, not lacking in anything." (James 1:2–4) And also Paul, "Not only so, but we also rejoice in our sufferings, because we know that suffering produces perseverance, perseverance character; and character, hope." (Romans 5:3–4)

It is in this way that Barth saw the use of evil shift from permission under the left hand of God, to the positive-willed good which results from the right hand of God. It must be said that if we can accept and acknowledge God's permission of evil in this most excessive of forms as we have demonstrated in Job as the reduction of a person to the barest minimum of human existence, then we are better equipped to see the positive will and work of God in every form of evil and suffering which we may experience in our walk with God.

The underlying requirement for such an understanding and acknowledgement is faith, and thus faith emerges once again as the final foundation for Barth's theodicy. In the face of such suffering, Barth would direct us each time away from the trials themselves and directly to God who is at work in and through them. This means we must reject the attempts to exonerate God of responsibility for evil and suffering (this was the falsehood of the friends of Job!) and instead to walk with Him in faith through the trials. In every crisis we must, with Job, 'flee from God to God'.[61]

Suffering as a Result of our Faith and Faithful Obedience

Now if we are children, then we are heirs–heirs of God and co-heirs with Christ, if indeed we share in his sufferings in order that we may also share in his glory. (Romans 8:17)

Despite the victorious and completed work of Christ on Calvary and the Father's verdict announced in the resurrection, the world remains a sinful world and the Church and Christians must live in it as witnesses to the ontic reality of the reconciliation which has been won for it but which is yet to be universally revealed. This is the basis for these last two categories of suffering. Clearly the great weakness in Barth's 'noetic eschatology' motif makes dealing with suffering under these categories most difficult. If we hold to our emphasis on a more eschatological understanding of the defeat of evil, then we can consider

---

[61] Here we disagree with Hebblethwaite who, in speaking of God's permission of suffering for the sake of trying our faith, concludes, "in relation to such disasters as earthquakes and floods or to human wickedness on the scale of Auschwitz, it seems quite immoral to speak of trial or discipline." (*Evil, Suffering and Religion, op. cit.,* p. 50) From such conclusions Hebblethwaite would have us flee from God to the future of a world in which God's own future is at risk. By denying God's sovereignty and the role of faith, Hebblethwaite can only turn to the shallowness of process theology as an answer to evil.

what it means to suffer as witnesses in a still sinful world. Short of this major modification, this category of suffering remains problematic for Barth.

Barth's realism is critical here in tying together the one great suffering of Christ with our own sufferings as tokens, echoes and shadows. This is possible because of the union of our suffering with Christ's sufferings. As we have said previously, this is seen clearly in Barth's view of an "inner, essential connexion between the one passion of the Son of God and the many sufferings which we see afflicting Israel, the Church, the world and ourselves."[62] Here he follows a very important line of reasoning in his dealing with the reality of the divine intervention for sinful humanity which has taken place in Jesus Christ. This real intervention becomes effective for us only as we are taken up to participate in His life, through our union in Christ. If we are truly to participate in this life, if we are really united with Christ for this purpose, does this not presuppose that we too will see, feel and experience the suffering of the judgement of God[63] even though they are only *Ankündigungen und um die Nachwehen der Wirklichkeit des göttlichen Gerichte?*[64] It is part of taking up our cross where our cross, our sufferings and even our death are alongside His. Because we live under the shadow of the cross, it is a judgement we must bear and one we must accept as a matter of faith. We remember Barth's important statement,

> We do not believe if we do not live in the neighborhood of Golgotha. And we cannot live in the neighborhood of Golgotha without being affected by the shadow of divine judgement, without allowing this shadow to fall on us. In this shadow Israel suffered. In this shadow the Church suffers. That it suffers in this way is the Church's answer to the world on the question of a 'theodicy'–the question of the justice of God in the sufferings inflicted on us in the world.[65]

In this way, in a combination of his realism and his dialectic style Barth is able to affirm a rich understanding of our ability to participate in the sufferings of Christ, and to see through the unreality of our present trials to the One reality

---

[62] CD II/1, p. 405.

[63] In bearing our own cross our suffering "involves hardship, anguish, grief, pain and finally death." (CD IV/2, p. 602), and thus the suffering Christian "exists only in the echo of His sentence, the shadow of His judgement, the after-pains of His rejection. In their cross they have only a small subsequent taste of what the world and they themselves deserved at the hand of God." (CD IV/2, p. 604)

[64] KD II/1, p. 456. "We are not only permitted but commanded to regard all human suffering which we have only briefly sketched as a suffering with Him, in His fellowship, and therefore to understand the irruption of this suffering into the life of the Christian as the sign of this fellowship, and thus *the manifestation of the supreme dignity of the Christian...* we must think of the suffering which... arises in all its terror from the fact that the Christian too, in spite of what he already is, still stands under the law of sin and is still afflicted with the burden of the flesh." (CD IV/2, pp. 611-612)

[65] CD II/1, p. 406.

to which they point and into which they are ingrafted.[66] He does all of this without either denying the reality of the evil we experience or giving to it too lofty a status as a true *Wirklichkeit*.[67] If this time can indeed be justified within a doctrine of evil, then the theodicy which it affirms is surely found in this union of our sufferings with those of Christ. This idea of representative suffering is consistent with our call to be witnesses of the light in a world of darkness. However, without this justification for the time *post-Christum*, no

---

[66] We must trace here Barth's discussion of this type of affliction suffered by the Christian which he provides in CD IV/3.1, §71, Section 5. He gives three answers to the question of "how the Christian comes into the specific affliction which falls on him particularly as a Christian." (CD IV/3.1, p. 619) The first is that this affliction derives "in some sense inevitably from the situation and manner of the world to which he belongs as a man but over against which he is set as a Christian and in his ministry of witness." (p. 620) In this confrontation with the world, as the witness of the light amidst the darkness, the Christian will suffer affliction. Secondly, "We are forced to say that his affliction has an inner cause and is conditioned by himself." (p. 626) By this Barth means that the very nature of the Christian as witness will put him in the unavoidable situation where he is met with persecution and affliction. In this way it is not only an aspect of the milieu of the Christian, but of his make-up as well. Finally, Barth answers, "his affliction is not grounded in the manner or perversion of the world which confronts him, nor his own constitution as a Christian man, but in the affliction of Jesus Christ Himself in which it is impossible for the one who is called, for the man in whom Jesus lives and he in Him, not to participate." (p. 634) In the end, Barth returns everything under the control of God and the all-embracing suffering of Christ. Thus Barth can conclude, "The suffering of his is suffering in reflection of and analogy to the suffering of the one man of Gethsemane and Golgatha. It is suffering under the shadow of His cross. And in this secondary form appropriate to His follower and disciple, it is suffering in real fellowship with Him and with His suffering." (p. 637)

[67] Returning to our three points above (footnote 66), Barth discusses the characteristics of this suffering. He makes the following six points: 1) Christian affliction "is not an evil but a good, for all the unmistakable difficulties, to become and to be a Christian in affliction" (CD IV/3.1, p. 641), 2) it is unequivocal that "it is first and last Jesus Christ Himself who brings the Christian into affliction" (p. 641), 3) this affliction is not a static state, but since it is in fellowship with Christ's sufferings, it is for the Christian "an ecstatic forward movement beyond himself to that horizon and goal" (p. 642), 4) yet the future is not an empty hope, but "that future already determines and shapes the present of the Christian in his affliction" (p. 643), 5) the fruits which arise from affliction are not an end and goal in themselves, for the determination of the Christian in affliction "simply consists in the fact that the Christian in affliction is a man who is absolutely secured by the goal appointed for him in Christ" (p. 645), and finally, 6) Barth drives home the force of the imperative behind and as a result of this dynamic indicative, "The being of the Christian in this sovereignty is demonstrated in his exercise of it. He is hidden in God as he does what he who is hidden in God has to do, and does not do what such an one cannot do" (p. 646). In this way, Barth gives final and clear definition of what he means by the suffering of the Christian the afflictions of the fellowship with Christ.

theodicy is possible, and this realisation hangs as a dark cloud over Barth's doctrine of evil.

'Innocent Suffering' as a Result of the Sinful State of the World

We must begin by stating that the very term 'innocent suffering' is an example of the 'falsehood of man' which Barth has rejected. To expect that some people are innocent to the point of meriting only blessings from God is the abhorrent error of the friends of Job. Barth's point is two-fold, 1) no-one is 'innocent' in this sense, and, more importantly, 2) the focus is not to be put upon our 'innocence' or 'guilt' but upon God who is the Sender and Permitter of good and evil. The entirety of human affliction must look first to the cross as the ultimate justification of God to all suffering, and then to God revealed in Jesus Christ who, within the covenant relationship, will from both His right hand and His left, ultimately bring about the growth and maturation of His children.

There is another tension here which must be finally acknowledged. On the one side, all evil and the resultant suffering of humanity must be traced back to sin whether personal (categories 1 and 2) or corporate (categories 3, 4 and 5), and therefore all suffering is the responsibility of sinful and rebellious humanity. On the other side, and in a more profound way, all suffering must be traced back directly to God, according to His divine and sovereign providence. As we have shown, this is the final interpretation which Barth gives to the story of Job. Our analysis of that interpretation in the previous section are the basis for the conclusions we draw here. Simply put, there is no suffering which is 'innocent'; for there is no suffering for which humanity is not responsible, and there is no suffering which God has not taken on Himself and for which He has not assumed the ultimate responsibility. Even the suffering from natural disasters and the suffering of children must fall into these two unequivocal positions.

Barth's theodicy is first and foremost the product of the 'necessary antithesis' from which God's decision to create brought with it this assumption of human frailty and the resultant evil and suffering it would experience. Yet it must also be developed within the understanding that all forms of dualism are to be rejected. Evil must be affirmed to be both distinct from God and yet never separate from Him; both inimical to Him and yet never out from under His ultimate control. Under the motif of the 'right and left hand of God' evil may be permitted by God, and even sent by Him, but it never acts other than within this final and all-encompassing control. Yet even in its manifestations in the world, in the depth of its horribleness, it is never anything but the defeated enemy of God which faces its sure annihilation at the sound of the last trumpet (according to Barth's 'noetic eschatology'). Thus, without reducing the existential evilness of evil, we agree with Helmut Gollwitzer that for Barth, "justice is done to the resurrection of Christ, the triumph of grace, only when the triumph of God is believed and evil is not therefore taken with final seriousness."[68]

All this, Barth's entire doctrine of evil, hangs ultimately upon one thread which is summed up in his 'revelatory positivism' motif as faith. It is faith which believes and sees the ontic reality of the defeat of evil, and the future annihilation of evil, behind the current noetic manifestation of evil in the world. It is faith which rejects the dualistic picture of the cosmic war between God and evil as two detached and warring enemies and which understands instead the promises that 'all things work together for good', even in the midst of our existential crises and sufferings. Thus "The relationship with Jesus Christ in which we must suffer is sufficient to overrule our suffering and the gift of the whole of our life for good (Romans 8:28)."[69] Finally, it is and must be faith which refuses to look to any other but to God Himself for the final justification of evil, and as the One to whom all questions and protestations must be posed. It is in faith that we must time and again 'flee from God to God' in our search for what is and always must be the open-ended question of theodicy.

Theodicy and the Work of the Church

> Dogmatics and preaching are related in the same way as service at headquarters and at the front. Headquarters has to be there if anything essential is to be done at the front. *Dogmatics has to serve the church.*[70]

Christian Preaching

In view of the pervasiveness of suffering in the world, the subject of the relationship of God to evil and the role of prayer and trust must surely be taken up in the pulpit. As the minister attempts to take on this important and thorny issue, Barth's view of evil in relationship to God and creation can provide some very practical guidance. This guidance conforms to Barth's overwhelming concern that Christian preaching on the subject must conform to the Subject of all theology and Christian praxis. In this way, all Christian preaching and praxis must be that of witness to the Subject of the Christian faith. As the minister attempts to wrestle with this issue from the pulpit, the following points from this study of evil in Barth's theology offer practcal help.

1. Always preach Christ victorious and never preach 'on' evil or Satan. This is not to avoid the issue, but to ensure that all preaching on this subject flows from the indicative of *Christus Victor* to the imperatives of the Christian life.

---

[68]   Helmut Gollwitzer, *Karl Barth's Church Dogmatics*, translated by G.W. Bromiley, (Edinburgh: T & T Clark, 1961), p. 134.

[69]   CD II/1, p. 421.

[70]   Barth, *The Göttingen Dogmatics, op. cit.,* p. 276.

2. Focus preaching on God's sovereignty and goodness and move from there to consider the more difficult areas of evil and suffering. To reverse the direction, from human experience or the 'reality' of evil to an understanding of God will always yield and anthropocentric or overtly existential theology. If God is to be found in suffering, or known from human suffering, He can be so only if the suffering we begin with is that of Jesus Christ *for us*. It is only from this single proper epistemological vantage point that we can then look to our suffering in its relation to that of Jesus Christ. Thus to preach on human suffering is to preach on Christ's ultimate and all-inclusive, once-for-all suffering and see our own trials only in relationship to it and not in isolation from it.

3. This Christocentric focus will also mean we will preach on the importance of our participation in Christ and the challenges we face as witnesses in the midst of darkness. Here the categories of suffering become helful as does the focus on victory through suffering. For that reason, all preaching on suffering must be preaching that focuses on God's working of good through all suffering and evil and His promises that nothing is outside of Him or His providential care. This is to affirm both the omnipotence of God and His benevolence, and to locate whatever we can say of the justification of all suffering in the hope we have in the second coming based upon the historical work of Christ and the continuing work of the Holy Spirit.

4. Ultimately, this means that we must preach the Father, the Son and the Spirit, and not evil, Satan and nothingness. The focus must remain on God and not on us nor our experience of suffering. The God we preach when we preach on suffering must be the God we find solely in a Christocentric epistemology; solely the Father, revealed to us by the Son in the power of the Holy Spirit. We are called to preach this God boldly and courageously, trusting that the Holy Spirirt through us and always in a miraculous way will lead our congregation to the ultimate answer to all theodicy–faith in a God who is *for us*, and who in Jesus Christ is the hope of the deliverance of all God's people both now and in the age to come.

Christian Counseling

It is in the minister's office where the theodicy question is perhaps posed in its most direct and inscrutable form. This book began with the question as to whether there is, in Barth's theology, a practical help for the minister, and indeed for the laity as it struggles to deal with evil and suffering in this world reconciled to God. We will offer a few suggestions with regard to Christian counseling based upon our conclusions.

1. The pastor must help people focus on God in their suffering and not to look away from Him. He is their help and salvation even as He may also be seen to have permitted the evil they have suffered. The God we know, although revealed in hiddenness, is also fully revealed in Jesus Christ, and there, at the cross, we see His heart and purpose and will for us in our relationship with Him.

We must cling to that hope and faith in the very face of trials, rather than attempt to either explain them away or to seek another cause for them.

2. Similarly, we must counsel people away from the sometimes tempting position of dualism which exonerates God by blaming Satan, but which also undermines the sovereignty of God and leads inevitably towards despair. With the rise of books such a *This Present Darkness* [71] among numerous others, a dualistic stance is becoming more and more popular. The story of Job in which Satan is hardly mentioned after the first chapter is striking evidence for the need to look to God and Him alone as we struggle with evil and suffering in our lives.

3. We can put to use here also the categories of suffering by helping people to understand that suffering comes for different reasons, as a result of both our personal sin and the sinful state of our world in which we participate and contribute. Suffering can be allowed to accomplish that for which it was sent or permitted by God (according to categories 2 and 3), or it can be better understood as part and parcel of being a Christian and living in the fallen creation prior to the final *parousia*. And yet, suffering must always be understood, in all categories, to be that which has already been borne for us in its totality. There lies true Christian hope in faith according to the work of Christ.

4. Perhaps the picture which must be stressed here, which is implicit in Barth but which we should articulate more overtly, has to do with the relationship between the time of the community and eternity. In essence, Barth is saying that even in God's use of suffering to the extent which it was experienced by Job, the growth in faith and trust which resulted was more valuable to Job that all it may have cost him. This is an acknowledgement that the eternal benefits of our Christian growth in Christ will far outweigh the temporal sufferings which we may experience. If this is so for Job, how can our sufferings not be so as well! Therefore we must take seriously Paul's statement of faith, "I consider that our present sufferings are not worth comparing with the glory that will be revealed to us." (Romans 8:18) If this world is in one sense the 'vale of soul-making', then we are able to understand better how the temporal state of all of our earthly experiences compare to the eternal rewards of obedience and faith. Perhaps then no price is too great to pay for growth in our spiritual lives, and in God's perfect wisdom, suffering may be employed in such a lofty enterprise to His glory and praise.

5. In the end, Christian counseling will be called upon to change the emphasis from the 'why?' of suffering to the 'who?' of Christian faith. Barth's description of God in Christ is of One who "still bears this burden in all of its reality and is thus with us when we have to carry our burdens and experience our sorrows." [72] Thus while we suffer, we do not do so alone, for "God Himself

---

[71] Frank Peretti, *This Present Darkness*, (Westchester: Crossway Books, 1986). This is a classic fictionalization of a look inside a stark dualistic fight between good and evil. It is compelling reading but devastating theology!

[72] CD IV/3.1, p. 395.

suffers with us as He suffers."[73] It was this *theopaschitism* which stirred Studdart Kennedy to write;

> Father, if He, the Christ, were Thy Revealer,
> Truly the First Begotten of the Lord,
> Then must Thou be a Suff'rer and a Healer,
> Pierced to the heart by the sorrow of the sword.
>
> Then must it mean, not only that Thy sorrow,
> Smote Thee that once upon the lonely tree,
> But that to-day, to-night, and on the morrow,
> Still it will come, O Gallant God, to Thee.[74]

Our suffering becomes a co-suffering and in this way it is transformed into the *'supreme dignity of the Christian'*. [75] We are called as witnesses to be like John the Baptist in Grünewald's painting who,

> can only point–and here everything is bolder and more abrupt, because here all indication of the revelation of the Godhead is lacking–point to a wretched, crucified, dead man. This is the place of Christology. It faces the mystery. It does not stand within the mystery. It can and must adore with Mary and point with the Baptist. It cannot and must not do more than this. But it can and must do this.[76]

By focusing not on justifications but upon promises and certainties in the revelation of the love of Christ, and in faith and hope to the future of all creation, suffering can be set in its proper context, and the theodicy question can be converted into a step on a journey of faith leading to spiritual growth and maturity.

This humble list gives some indications that Barth's doctrine of evil and its resultant theodicy can be used in practical ways in helping us deal with the actualities of suffering and evil which we will all surely experience in some form.

---

[73] Ibid. 397.

[74] Studdert Kennedy, 'The Suffering God', in *The Unutterable Beauty*, (London: Hodder and Stoughton, 1927), p. 3.

[75] "We are not only permitted but commanded to regard all human suffering which we have only briefly sketched as a suffering with Him, in His fellowship, and therefore to understand the irruption of this suffering into the life of the Christian as the sign of this fellowship, and thus *the manifestation of the supreme dignity of the Christian.*" (CD IV/2, pp. 611-612)

[76] CD I/2, p. 125.

Christian Ethics

We will conclude with a look at Christian ethics and offer a brief response to the question, "How then should we live our life?" What does Barth's doctrine of evil and theodicy say about the ethics of the Christian life in a secular world?

1. We will begin with a look at Barth's own life. Barth lived during several great catastrophes in human history and his theology emerged and developed during a time of the trench wars of World War I, the devastation of the Great Depression, the realities of Auschwitz and Buchenwald, the horrors of Hiroshima and Nagasaki, and the new realisation that humanity had entered the atomic era and as such now had the capacity to end its own existence. In all of this Barth did not live aloof from the controversy nor the bitterness of these events. Barth's pastoral heart, his love of people and 'all things human', and his political concerns which flowed from his theology continually pressed him into the centre of controversy amidst the turmoil of Europe in the lead up to and through the entirety of World War II. During the war Barth even served as a part-time soldier, "my bedroom now contained a helmet, a complete uniform, a rifle and bayonet, etc., so that I would be able to go out at any hour of the day or night to decide the issue."[77] Hans Frei has thus described him as "a loyal, but very critically loyal, Swiss Reformed Churchman all his life, and as such he became a dedicated citizen of the universal church of Jesus Christ within a world he saw as one in its suffering and promise."[78] His outspoken stance during World War II was certainly not without cost,

> his courageous stand and his refusal to take the oath of unconditional allegiance to the Führer cost him his chair in Bonn in 1935. He was deposed and deported back to Switzerland. Later on, in 1939, he was stripped of his doctorate by the University of Münster.[79]

His prison ministry and work with unions offer additional proof of Barth's extensive activity in the affairs of suffering humanity.

In the face of this, Barth displayed a rigour, humour and vitality that was evidence of his personal ethic based upon his understanding of the sovereignty of God and the existence of the world under the banner–Jesus is Victor! His life served as a testimony to an overwhelming sense of trust in the providence of God and a hope in the future revelation of the reconciliation of the world. This was manifest in no greater place than his life-long love of Mozart. Torrance comments

> His whole attitude to life, and even to theology, was expressed in his passionate love for the care-free, light-hearted music of Mozart, in which the profoundest questions are put to the eternal and the creaturely

---

[77] Busch, *Karl Barth, op. cit.,* p. 305.
[78] Frei, *Types of Christian Theology, op. cit.,* p. 151.
[79] Torrance, *Karl Barth, op. cit.,* p. 9.

alike without the dogmatic presumption to any final answer or last word, and it was to the accompaniment of Mozart's music that his engagement of the hard work of dogmatics became sheer enjoyment of the majesty and beauty of God.[80]

With regard to evil, Barth most admired Mozart's disinterest with the demonic. In his lecture entitled 'Mozart's Freedom', Barth commented, "he plays and does not cease to play... [with a] great and free matter-of-factness" displaying "the absence of all demons: with him the subjective element never becomes a theme."[81]

Barth's life may best be described as a joyous struggle which attempted to embrace the seriousness of the depth of human suffering without ever losing sight of the one incontestable fact that over and above all struggle is the victory of God in Christ. Yet we wonder how much we see Barth's personality coming through in his doctrine of evil? By that we mean that Barth was a man driven by an overwhelming faith and conviction to the point that he seems never to have been attacked by doubts about faith or the existence and presence of God. In addition, Barth never really suffered any great personal tragedy in life, and so his understanding of suffering came from his interaction with others rather than his own experience.

Perhaps this helps us understand how Barth seized life in such a way that he venerates Mozart to the point of suggesting that the theodicy problem brought about by the Lisbon earthquake was answered in Mozart's music. From this we could conclude that the most common criticism of Barth's doctrine of evil–that he fails to take evil and suffering with sufficient seriousness–is perhaps a result of his unswerving faith which could not but set God over evil and evil forever in the service of God.

Both the positive force of Barth's faith and his unequivocal stance of God's sovereignty are summed up by Torrance,

> Barth engaged in his gigantic task of dogmatics with the consciousness that the angels were looking over his shoulder, reminding him that all theology is human thinking, and that even when the theologian has done his utmost in faithfulness to what is given him, all he can do is to point beyond and above to the transcendent truth and beauty of God, thereby acknowledging the inadequacy of his thought in response to God's Word, but nevertheless engaging in it joyfully, in gratitude to God who is pleased to let himself be served in this way by human thinking and to bless it in his grace.[82]

This view of theology in the presence of angels is brought into final relief by Barth's own quip, "I love angels, but have no taste for demons, not out of

---

[80] Ibid. p. 12.
[81] Busch, *Karl Barth, op. cit.,* p. 410.
[82] Torrance, *Karl Barth, op. cit.,* p. 13.

any desire for demythologizing but because they are not worth it."[83] It is this dismissal of the demonic in the face of the transcendent truth and beauty of God which characterizes Barth's own life and constitutes the heart of his theodicy.

2. This ethic is developed in more detail by Barth's view of the Christian's response to sickness. The question which comes to mind immediately is how one should respond to illness and disease in a world so controlled (evil and all) by God's gracious sovereignty? Is our attitude to be one of passive submission, praise or protest? Barth supplies an important answer in his ethics of creation. Barth's point is an extension of his view that death which must be seen in part as the merited judgement of God on human sin in which humanity became subjected to the power of nothingness. Since sickness is a 'forerunner and messenger' of this sense of death, "from this standpoint, sickness like death itself is unnatural and disorderly. It is an element in the rebellion of chaos against God's creation."[84] Our only obedient response must be one of 'final resistance' where we join with God in battle against the 'No' of His left hand which He has conquered but which still has a sense of superiority over us manifested in sickness and death.[85] Barth produces an ethic which lays hold of both sides of the human situation; the reality of our union with the victorious Christ and the continuing work of His already defeated enemy. Thus sickness must be resisted with full force as a form of the nothingness from which we have been saved and which for us can be only past. The fact that God can and does work good through sickness (see our discussion on the categories of suffering, especially numbers 2 and 3), does not deny the fact that it remains allied with nothingness and must be defied.

Therefore, while the Christian can and must see the gracious hand of God at work in all human suffering, he or she must also reject and resist all forms of sickness and seek after health and wholeness. This defiance takes the form of faith and prayer, "if the conflict enjoined upon man in this matter is to be meaningful, faith in Him and prayer to Him must never be lost sight of as its *conditio sine qua non*, but continually realised as the true power of the will required of man in this affair."[86]

3. A Christian ethic must embrace the full fact that we are called to live within the tension of the ontic reality of our existence and the existential reality of all that seems to contradict it. Our response must not only be one of faith, but there is in Barth's theodicy a call to Christian praxis. The vocation of the

---

[83] Busch, *Karl Barth, op. cit.,* p. 365.

[84] CD III/4, p. 366.

[85] In saying that our actions must be oriented on Christ 'without murmuring or surrender' Barth calls God, "the One who as the Creator of life primarily espouses this as His own cause, and fights and has *already conquered for us* in the whole glory of His mercy and omnipotence." Yet he goes on to say that without God, "all human willing and doing can only be futile and impotent in relation to *the superiority of evil which opposes us* also in the form of sickness." (CD III/4, p. 369, emphasis mine) Here we see again the dilemma of Barth's eschatology where we must view evil as wholly defeated and yet as the empowered and continuing enemy.

[86] CD III/4, p. 368.

Christian has 'a distinctive ethos' which understands the term 'calling' to mean being given a task. Christianity means to 'do' and not simply to 'be'. This calling to this task "consists in the fact that with their whole being, action, inaction and conduct, and then by word and speech, they have to make a definite declaration to other men. The essence of their vocation is that God makes them His witnesses."[87]

The world outside of faith does not see who it is nor whose it is, and thus the Christian is called to announce with great force the reality of this world. This witness involves the self-giving of the Christian to Christ and the result is a life of 'service' and 'ministry'. And ministry brings with it a necessary and unavoidable affliction, "As the action in which, called by God, he must intercede for the world is one of ministry, so his passion or suffering under the affliction caused by the world must be one of ministry."[88] We cannot escape the fact that we, as Christians, are called to suffer with those who suffer. By seeing the world in its reality, by fleeing only to God in our times of trial, by clinging to faith and hope in the resurrected Christ, we can empty ourselves and take on the role of servants for which we have been called. Yet this affliction must not lead us to despair over the world's condition which brings this suffering on us. Even in the face of seemingly senseless and 'innocent suffering', the Christian is called to be a witness to the God of providence and grace.

> The thought of God's royal lordship and fatherly providence overruling even worldy-occurrence must be the first and decisive step of all Christian thinking about world-occurrence, the positive sign before the bracket of whatever else may have to be considered, the point to which the community of Jesus Christ will always have good reason to return.[89]

Our state as Christians is one then of embracing the discontinuity and paradox of the 'already' and the 'not yet' of the reconciliation of the world; the fluidity of the human condition as *simul iustus et peccator*; the state of the world which displays the *hominum confusione* even under the *providentia Dei*. Barth's ethics, under the rubric of his doctrine of evil, points only and always in one direction, the rejection of the *hominum confusione* as the 'inner-truth of world-occurrence'. In this way the Christian must reject all tolerance of evil as the norm in the world and he or she must seek to empower people through the gospel to break through barriers whether ethnic, racial, economic or whatever. If *Christus Victor* is the reality of the world, then we must trust that through us in carrying out our vocation as the people of God, the Holy Spirit will enable people to experience this victory in every dimension of their own lives. Where the world finds no God, or an absent God in the face of the overwhelming questions of theodicy, the Christian must not fall into such despair, "as though

---

[87] CD IV/3.2, p. 575.

[88] Ibid. 615.

[89] Ibid. p. 688.

we really had to reckon with a bedevilment which would necessarily have as its presupposition a withdrawal of the Creator in the face of the confusion of His creation brought about by man," but instead, with a call to faith alone, the Christian must affirm that "there are no forms, events or relationships in world-occurrence unmistakably confused by man in which the goodness of what God has created is not also effective and visible, the only question being how this is so."[90]

This 'how' question is faith, and in this faith, the two-fold state of the human situation is irrevocably changed. For the dichotomy between present and future is collapsed where the Christian community "does not see in Jesus only what might be, or ought to be, or one day will be; it sees what is, what has come into being in Him and by Him."[91] As a result, "the twofold form of world history loses its appearance of autonomy and finality, the character of an irreconcilable contradiction and antithesis, which it always seems to have at first glance" and therefore, "the twofold view loses its sting."[92] The only restriction that remains is noetic, and this is the ministry and vocation to which we are called.[93] Therefore as we serve, as we minister, as we face affliction and as we suffer, we do so fearlessly. For the Christian sees, through the eyes of faith and with all finality, that Jesus is Victor, for "in His self-offering for men the power of nothingness and the confusion of men are just as unequivocally and definitely set aside."[94] In this faith, the Christian lives and works and trusts.

4. Such a position can only lead to the final aspect of a Christian ethic which is that of hope. There is hope in the victorious Lordship of Christ even in the midst of human suffering and even in an acknowledgement of the conflict in which every Christian struggles. If we ask the question how can we be a true and effective witness in the midst of the confusion of humanity, Barth answers, "the only legitimate and meaningful answer to the question–and it really is legitimate and convincing–is that he [the Christian] has the freedom to hope even in this conflict."[95] His and her hope is based on not just He who is to come, but on He who *has* come and is to come. The hope of the future lies not in the conditions of the present but in the certainty of the past. In the past evil is defeated and in the future will be the universal unveiling of that unequivocal fact. "If the Christian has hope of this future, how can the corruptible and mortal be for him a sphere of hopelessness which he can only abandon as a temporary station to be vacated as quickly as possible and with the most vociferous exclamations of horror?"[96]

---

[90] Ibid. p. 698.

[91] Ibid. p. 713.

[92] Ibid. p. 713.

[93] All this is possible, we must remember, only if such adjustments are made in Barth's 'noetic eschatology' to make possible the justification for this time of ministry and vocation by the Christian community.

[94] CD IV/3.2, p. 718.

[95] Ibid. p. 919.

[96] Ibid. p. 937.

This hope is genuine and sure and it constitutes the final and perhaps supreme characteristic of the Christian as one who understands that the relationship of God, evil and creation is reconciled only in Christ, and who believes that the question of theodicy is answered only in the final *parousia* when creation, along with its Creator will be justified. Of this hope, we will let Barth have the final word,

> The genuineness of this Christian hope for the ultimate in the penultimate will be shown first by the fact that it is not bound to either the lighter or darker side which existence may alternatively display, let alone to the optimistic or pessimistic view which the Christian may have of a given situation of his own personal position. Even in relation to aspects which are absolutely black and desperate from the human standpoint, he may still dare to hope for indications of the ultimate. Nor is this true only of those aspects of their future which seem to threaten death and destruction. It is no less true of apparently or relatively more kindly aspects which in contrast to so much menacing gloom invite him here and now to see a feeble light and in the reflection of it to think of the great light. The provisional hope of the Christian is one which is free in face of both possibilities. In this freedom it may confidently expect signs of salvation both in that which is pleasant and that which is unpleasant. As such it is genuine hope.[97]

---

[97] Ibid. p. 938.

BIBLIOGRAPHY

Aboagye-Mensah, Robert. "Karl Barth's Attitude to War in the Context of World War II." *Evangelical Quarterly*, Volume 60, January 1988, pp. 43-59.

Akeroyd, Richard H. *The Spiritual Quest of Albert Camus*. Tuscaloosa: Portals Press, 1976.

Allen, Diogenes. *Philosophy for Understanding Theology*. Atlanta: John Knox Press, 1985.

Aquinas, Thomas. *Summa Theologia* . Volumes II and VIII. London: Blackfriars, 1963 and 1967.

Athanasius. *The Incarnation of the Word of God*. New York: MacMillan Company, 1961.

Augustine. *The City of God*. London: J.M. Dent & Sons, 1945.

_____. *The Confessions of St. Augustine*. Oxford: Parker and Rivington, 1838.

_____. *The Confessions of St. Augustine and Enchiridion*. *Library of Christian Classics*. London: SCM Press, 1955.

Aulén, Gustaf. *Christus Victor*. London: SPCK, 1970.

Barth, Karl. *Action in Waiting: On Christoph Blumhardt*. Rifton, New York: Plough Publishing House, 1969.

_____. *Against the Stream, Shorter Post-War Writings 1946-1952*. London: SCM Press, 1954.

_____. *Anselm: Fides Quaerens Intellectum*. London: SCM Press, 1930.

_____. *A Shorter Commentary on Romans*. London: SCM Press, 1956.

_____. *Call for God*. London: SCM Press, 1967.

_____. *Church Dogmatics*. Edited by G.W. Bromiley and T.F. Torrance. Edinburgh: T & T Clark, 1936 - 1969.

I/1. *The Doctrine of the Word of God.* Prolegomena, Part 1. Translated by G.T. Thomson, 1936.

I/2. *The Doctrine of the Word of God.* Prolegomena, Part 2. Translated by G.T. Thomson and H. Knight, 1956.

II/1. *The Doctrine of God.* Part 1. Translated by T.H.L. Parker, W.B. Johnston, H. Knight, J.L.M. Haire, 1957.

II/2. *The Doctrine of God.* Part 2. Translated by G.W. Bromiley, J.C. Campbell, Iain Wilson, J. Strathearn McNab, H. Knight, R.A. Stewart, 1957.

III/1 *The Doctrine of Creation.* Part 1. Translated by J.W. Edwards, O. Bussey, Harold Knight, 1958.

III/2. *The Doctrine of Creation.* Part 2. Translated by H. Knight, G.W. Bromiley, J.K.S. Reid, R.H. Fuller, 1960.

III/3. *The Doctrine of Creation.* Part 3. Translated by G.W. Bromiley, R.L. Ehrlich, 1960.

III/4. *The Doctrine of Creation.* Part 4. Translated by A.T. Mackay, T.H.L. Parker, H. Knight, H.A. Kennedy, J. Marks, 1961.

IV/1. *The Doctrine of Reconciliation.* Part 1. Translated by G.W. Bromiley, 1956.

IV/2. *The Doctrine of Reconciliation.* Part 2. Translated by G.W. Bromiley, 1958.

IV/3. *The Doctrine of Reconciliation.* Part 3/1. Translated by G. W. Bromiley, 1961.

IV/3. *The Doctrine of Reconciliation.* Part 3/2. Translated by G. W. Bromiley, 1962.

IV/4. *The Doctrine of Reconciliation.* Part 4. Translated by G.W. Bromiley, 1969.

_____. "Christ and Adam in Romans 5." *Scottish Journal of Theology Occasional Papers.* London: Oliver and Boyd, 1957.

_____. *Community, State and Church.* Gloucester: Peter Smith, 1968.

_____. *Credo.* London: Hodder and Stoughton, 1936.

_____. *Deliverance to the Captives.* London: SCM Press, 1961.

_____. *Dogmatics in Outline.* London: SCM Press, 1949.

_____. *Ethics.* Edinburgh: T & T Clark, 1981.

_____ "Evangelical Theology in the 19th Century," in *The Humanity of God.* London: Collins Fontana, 1967.

_____. *Fragments Grave and Gay.* London: Collins Fontana, 1971.

_____. *Göttingen Dogmatics.* Grand Rapids: W.B. Eerdman's, 1990.

_____. *God in Action.* Edinburgh: T & T Clark, 1936.

_____. "Karl Barth's Table Talk." *Scottish Journal of Theology Occasional Papers.* London: Oliver and Boyd, 1963.

_____. *Kirkliche Domatik.* Volumes I/1, II/1, II/1, III/1, III/2, III/3, III/4, IV/1, IV/2, IV/3.1, IV/3.2. Zürich: Evangelischer Verlar A.G. Zollikon, 1942-1959.

_____. *Letters 1961 - 1968.* Grand Rapids: W.B. Eerdmans Publishing Co., 1981.

_____. *Prologomena zur Christlichen Dogmatik. Die Lehre vom Worte Gottes.* München: Christian Kaiser Verlag, 1927.

_____. *Protestant Theology in the Nineteenth Century.* London: SCM Press, 1972.

_____. "*Rechtfertigung und Recht.*" *Theologishe Studien* , Volume 1, Number 3, 1938.

_____. *Revolutionary Theology in the Making: Barth - Thurneysen Correspondence, 1914 - 1925.* London: The Epworth Press, 1964.

_____. *The Christian Life.* Edinburgh: T & T Clark, 1981.

_____. *The Epistle to the Philippians.* London: SCM Press, 1962.

_____. *The Epistle to the Romans.* Oxford: Oxford University Press, 1933.

_____. *The Faith of the Church.* London: Collins Fontana, 1960.

_____. "The Gift of Freedom," in *The Humanity of God*. London: Collins Fontana, 1967.

_____. *The Heidelberg Catechism for Today*. Richmond: John Knox Press, 1964.

_____. *The Humanity of God*. London: Collins Fontana, 1967.

_____. *The Knowledge of God and the Service of God According to the Teaching of the Reformation: The Gifford Lectures of 1937 and 1938*. London: Hodder and Stoughton, 1938.

_____. *Theological Existence To-day*. London: Hodder and Stoughton, 1933.

_____. *Theology and Church*. London: SCM Press, 1928.

_____. *The Resurrection of the Dead*. London: Hodder and Stoughton, 1933.

_____. *Unterricht in der Christlichen Religion* . Volumes I and II. Zürich: Theologischer Verlag, 1985.

_____. *Witness to the Word: A Commentary on John 1*. Grand Rapids: W.B. Eerdmans Publishing Co., 1986.

_____. "The World's Disorder and God's Design." *Scottish Journal of Theology*, Volume 4, Number 3, 1951, pp. 241-256.

_____. *The Word of God and the Word of Man*. London: Hodder and Stoughton, 1928.

Bauckham, Richard. *Moltmann: Messianic Theology in the Making*. Hants: Marshall Pickering, 1987.

_____. "Theodicy from Ivan Karamazov to Jürgen Moltmann." *Modern Theology*, Volume 4, October 1987, pp. 83-97.

Beker, J.C. *Suffering and Hope*. Philadelphia: Fortress Press, 1987.

_____. *Paul's Apocalyptic Gospel*. Philadelphia: Fortress Press, 1982.

Berdyaev, Nicolai A. *Freedom and the Spirit*. London: The Centenary Press, 1927.

_____. *The Destiny of Man*. London: The Centenary Press, 1931.

_____. *The Divine and the Human.* London: The Centenary Press, 1947.

Berkhof, H. *Christian Faith.* Grand Rapids: W.B. Eerdmans Publishing Co., 1979.

Berkouwer, G.C. *Divine Election.* Grand Rapids: W.B. Eerdmans Publishing Co., 1960.

_____. *Faith and Justification.* Grand Rapids: W.B. Eerdmans Publishing Co., 1954.

_____. *General Revelation.* Grand Rapids: W.B. Eerdmans Publishing Co., 1955.

_____ *The Providence of God.* Grand Rapids: W.B. Eerdmans Publishing Co., 1952.

_____. *The Triumph of Grace in the Theology of Karl Barth.* London: Paternoster Press, 1956.

_____. *Sin.* Grand Rapids: W.B. Eerdmans Publishing Co., 1971

_____ *The Return of Christ.* Grand Rapids: W.B. Eerdmans Publishing Co., 1972.

Bettis, J.D. "Is Karl Barth a Universalist?" *Scottish Journal of Theology*, Volume 20, December 1967, pp. 423-426.

Blake, Buchanan. *The Book of Job and the Problem of Suffering.* London: Hodder & Stoughton, 1911.

Blocker, Henri. "Christian Thought and the Problem of Evil." *Churchman: Journal of Anglican Theology.* Translated by D.E. Anderson, G. Bray, and R.T. Beckwith. Volume 99, 1985, Number 1, pp. 6-24; Number 2, pp. 101-130; Number 3, pp. 197-215.

Boers, H.W. "Apocalyptic Eschatology in 1 Corinthians 15." *Interpretation,* Volume 21, January 1967, pp. 50-65.

Bonhoeffer, Dietrich. *Christ the Center.* New York: Harper and Row, 1960.

_____. *Creation and Fall, Temptation.* New York: MacMillan Publishing Co., 1966.

Bowker, John. *Problems of Suffering in Religions of the World.* Cambridge: Cambridge University Press, 1970.

Bromiley, Geoffrey W. *Introduction to the Theology of Karl Barth.* Edinburgh: T&T Clark, 1979.

Brown, Robert M. *Elie Wiesel: Messenger to All Humanity.* Notre Dame: University of Notre Dame Press, 1983.

Brown, R. "On the Necessary Imperfection of Creation: Irenaeus." *Scottish Journal of Theology*, Volume 28, Number 1, 1975, pp. 17-25.

_____. "On God's Ontic and Noetic Absoluteness: A Critique of Karl Barth." *Scottish Journal of Theology*, Volume 33, Number 6, 1980, pp. 533-549.

Brueggemann, Walter. "Genesis," in *Interpretation: A Bible Commentary for Teaching and Preaching.* Atlanta: John Knox Press, 1982.

Bryner, Erich. "*Die Bedeutung Dostojewskis für die Anfänge der dialektischen Theologie.*" *Theologische Zeitschrift*, Volume 38, May-June 1982, pp. 147-167.

Calvin, John. *Institutes of the Christian Religion.* Translated by Ford Lewis Battles. Philadelphia: Westminster Press, 1960.

Camus, Albert. *The Fall.* Translated by Justin O'Brien. New York: Random House, 1957.

_____. *The Plague.* Translated by Stuart Gilbert. New York: Random House, 1948.

_____. *The Rebel.* Translated by Anthony Bower. New York: Random House, 1951.

Carson, D.A. *How Long, Oh Lord?* Leicester: Inter-Varsity Press, 1990.

Cone, James H. *God of the Opressed.* London: SPCK, 1975.

Crenshaw, James L., ed. *Theodicy in the Old Testament,* in *Issues in Religion and Theology 4.* London: SPCK, 1983.

Croxall, T.H. *Kierkegaard Studies.* London: Lutterworth Press, 1948.

Cullman, Oscar. *The Christology of the New Testament.* Philadelphia: Westminster Press, 1959.

de Boer, Martinus C. *The Defeat of Death*, in *Journal for the Study of the New Testament Supplement Series*, Number 22. Sheffield: JSOT, 1988.

Davis, Stephen T., ed. *Encountering Evil: Live Options in Theodicy*. Atlanta: John Knox Press, 1981.

Döring, H. "*Dimensionen Der Abwesenheit Gottes*." *Catholica*, Volume 31, Number 2, 1977, pp. 81-101.

Dostoyevski, Fyodor. *The Brothers Karamazov*. London: Penguin Books, 1958.

Dunaway, L.P. *Evil and God's Own Problem: A Study of the Theodicies of Karl Barth and E.S. Brightman*. Unpublished Dissertation, Baylor University, 1986.

Ferré, Nels. *Evil and the Christian Faith*. Freeport: Books for Libraries Press, 1947.

Fiddes, Paul S. *The Creative Suffering of God*. Oxford: Clarendon Press, 1988.

Ford, David. *Barth and God's Story*. Franfurt Am Main: Verlag Peter Lang, 1985.

Forsyth, P.T. *The Justification of God*. Blackwood, Australia: New Creation Publications, 1988.

_____. *The Person and Place of Jesus Christ*. London: Independent Press, 1909.

Frei, Hans. *Types of Christian Theology*. New Haven: Yale University Press, 1992.

Frend, W.H.C. *The Rise of Christianity*. Philadelphia: Fortress Press, 1984.

Garrison, Jim. *The Darkness of God: Theology After Hiroshima*. London: SCM Press, 1982.

Gaskin, J.C.A. *Hume's Philosophy of Religion*. London: MacMillan Press, 1988.

Gibson, Edgar C.S. *The Book of Job*. Minneapolis: Klock and Klock Publishers, 1899.

Goetz, Ron. 'In Pursuit of the Illusively Enigmatic: The Theodicy of Karl Barth.' Paper given to the Karl Barth Society of North America, June 1992.

Gollwitzer, Helmut. *Karl Barth's Church Dogmatics.* Translated and Edited by G.W. Bromiley. Edinburgh: T & T Clark, 1961.

Gottschalk, Stephen. "Theodicy After Auschwitz and the Reality of God." *Union Seminary Quarterly Review*, Volume 41, 1987, Part 3-4.

Graham, Gordon. "Mystery and Mumbo-Jumbo." *Philosophical Investigations,* Volume 7, 1984, pp. 281-294.

Gregory of Nazianzus. *The Theological Orations. Library of Christian Classics.* London: SCM Press, 1954.

Gulley, N.R. *The Eschatology of Karl Barth.* Unpublished Doctoral Dissertation, University of Edinburgh, 1970-1971.

Gunton, C.E. 'The triune God and the freedom of the creature', in S.W. Sykes, ed. *Karl Barth: Centenary Essays.* Cambridge: Cambridge University Press, 1989.

Gutierrez, G. *A Theology of Liberation.* London: SCM Press, 1981.

Guy, H.A. *The New Testament Doctrine of the 'Last Things'.* Oxford: Oxford University   Press, 1948.

Hartwell, Herbert. *The Theology of Karl Barth: An Introduction.* London: Gerald Duckworth & Co., 1964.

Hauerwas, Stanley. *Naming the Silences.* Grand Rapids: W.B. Eerdmans Publishing Co., 1990.

Hebblethwaite, Brian. *Evil, Suffering and Religion.* London: Sheldon Press, 1976.

Hendry, George S. "Freedom of God in the Theology of Karl Barth." *Scottish Journal of Theology,* Volume 31, Number 3, 1978, pp. 229-244.

_____. "Nothing." *Theology Today*, Volume 39, October 1982, pp. 274-289.

Heppe, Heinrich. *Reformed Dogmatics.* London: George Allen & Unwind Ltd, 1950.

Hick, John. *Evil and the God of Love.* New York: Harper and Row, 1966.

Hume, David. *Dialogues Concerning Natural Religion.* New York: Bobbs-Merrill Co., 1970.

Hunsinger, George. *How to Read Karl Barth.* Oxford: Oxford University Press, 1991.

Joad, C.E.M. *God and Evil.* London: Faber and Faber, 1918.

Jones, G.V. "God and Negation." *Scottish Journal of Theology*, Volume 7, September 1954, pp. 233-244.

Journet, C. *The Meaning of Evil.* London, 1963.

Jüngel, Eberhard. *Death: The Riddle and the Mystery.* Philadelphia: Westminster Press, 1974.

_____. *Karl Barth: A Theological Legacy.* Philadelphia: Westminster Press, 1986.

_____. *"Die Offenbarung der Verborgenheit Gottes ,"* in *Wertlose Wahreit .* München: Christian Kaiser Verlag, 1990.

Kant, Immanuel. *Religion Within the Limits of Reason Alone.* New York: Harper & Bros., 1934.

_____. *Critique of Pure Reason.* London: J.M. Dent & Sons, 1934.

Kennedy, Studdert. *The New Man in Christ.* London: Hodder and Stoughton, 1932.

Kierkegaard, Søren. *Christian Discources.* London: Oxford University Press, 1939.

_____. *Either/Or.* London: Oxford University Press, 1944

_____ *Sickness Unto Death.* London: Oxford University Press, 1941.

Kitamori, Kazoh. *Theology of the Pain of God.* London: SCM Press, 1946.

König, Adrio. *The Eclipse of Christ in Eschatology.* Grand Rapids: W.B. Eerdmans Publishing Co., 1989.

Küng, Hans. *On Being a Christian.* New York: Doubleday and Co., 1966.

Kuske, Martin. *The Old Testament as the Book of Christ.* Philadelphia: Westminster Press, 1976.

Laing, B.M. *David Hume*. London: Ernest Benn, 1932.

Leahy, Frederick S. *Satan Cast Out*. Edinburgh: Banner of Truth Trust, 1975.

Leibniz, G.W. *Theodicy: Essays on the Goodness of God, the Freedom of Man and the Origin of Evil*. London: Routledge & Kegan Paul Ltd., 1951.

Lewis, C.S. *The Problem of Pain*. London: Collins, 1940.

_____. *The Great Divorce*. Grand Rapids: Baker Book House, 1969.

Link, Christian. "*Fides quaerens intellectum: Die Bewegung der Theologie Karl Barths* ." *Theologische Zeitschrift*, Volume 38, May-June 1982, pp. 279-297.

Loades, A.L. "Kant's Concern with Theodicy." *Journal of Theological Studies*, Volume 26, October 1975, pp. 361-376.

Lowe, Walter. "Barth as a Critic of Dualism: Re-reading the *Römerbrief* ." *Scottish Journal of Theology*, Volume 41, Number 3, 1988, pp. 377-398.

Lowrie, Donald A. *Christian Existentialism: A Berdyaev Anthology*. London: George Allen and Unwin Ltd., 1964.

Luther, Martin. *Commentary on the Epistle to the Romans*. Grand Rapids: Zondervan, 1960.

_____. *Luther's Small Catechism*. St. Loius: Concordia Publishing House, 1943.

_____. *Luther's Works*. General eds. Jaroslov Pelikan and Helmut T. Lehmann. Volumes 25 and 42. Philadelphia: Fortress Press, 1969 and 1972.

_____. *Table Talk*. Translated and Edited by W. Hazlitt. London: H.G. Bonn, 1857.

Luthi, Kurt. *Gott und das Böse: Eine biblischthelogische und systematische These zur Lehre vom Bösen, entworfen in Auseinandersetzung mit Schelling und Karl Barth.*. Zürich: Zwingli Verlag, 1961.

MacQuarrie, John. *Twentieth Century Religious Thought*. London: SCM Press, 1963.

_____. *Principles of Christian Theology*. London: SCM Press, 1966.

Marshall, I. Howard. "Does the New Testament Teach Universal Salvation?", in *Christ in Our Place*. Exeter: Paternoster Press, 1991.

McCormack, Bruce. *A Scholastic of a Higher Order: The Development of Karl Barth's Theology, 1921-1931*. Dissertation, Princeton Theological Seminary, 1989

_____. Book review of Simon Fischer, '*Revelatory Positivism?* ', in *Scottish Journal of Theology*, Volume 43, Number 4, 1990, pp. 504-508.

McFayden, John E. *The Problem of Pain: A Study in the Book of Job*. London: James Clarke & Co.

McGill, Arthur C. *Suffering: A Test of Theological Method*. Philadelphia: Westminster Press, 1982.

McGrath, Alister. *The Making of Modern German Christology*. Oxford: Blackwell, 1986.

_____. "'The Righteousness of God' from Augustine to Luther." *Studia Theologica* , Volume 36, 1982, pp. 63-78.

_____. *Luther's Theology of the Cross*. Oxford: Blackwell, 1985.

_____. *The Enigma of the Cross*. London: Hodder and Stroughton, 1987.

McWilliams, W. "Divine Suffering in Contemporary Theology." *Scottish Journal of Theology*, Volume 33, Number 1, 1980, pp. 35-53.

Midgley, Mary. *Wickedness: A Philosophical Essay*. London: Routhedge & Kegan Paul, 1984.

Mill, J.S. "Three Essays on Religion," in *Essays on Ethics, Religion and Society*. Edited by J.M. Robson. Toronto: University of Toronto Press, 1969.

Molnar, Paul D. "The Function of the Immanent Trinity in the Theology of Karl Barth." *Scottish Journal of Theology*, Volume 42, Number 3, 1989, pp. 367-399.

Moltmann, Jürgen. *Creating a Just Future*. London: SCM Press, 1989.

_____. *God in Creation*. London: SCM Press, 1983.

_____. "*Gottesoffenbarung und Wahrheitsfrage* ," in *Parrhesia*. Zürich: EVZ-Verlag, 1966.

_____. *Hope and Planning.* London: SCM Press, 1971.

_____. *The Church in the Power of the Spirit.* New York: Harper and Row, 1975.

_____. *The Crucified God.* London: SCM Press, 1974.

_____. *The Future of Creation.* London: SCM Press, 1979.

_____. *Theology and Joy.* London: SCM Fress, 1971.

_____. *Theology of Hope.* New York: Harper and Row, 1965.

_____. *The Trinity and the Kingdom of God.* London: SCM Press, 1980.

_____. *The Way of Jesus Christ.* London: SCM Press, 1985.

Morgan, G. Campbell. *The Answers of Jesus to Job.* London: Marshall, Morgan and Scott.

Muller, R.A. "Incarnation, Immutability and the Case for Classical Theism." *Westminster Theological Journal,* Volume 45, Number 1, Spring 1983, pp. 22-40.

Oblau, Gotthard. *Gotteszeit und Menschenzeit : Eschatologie in der Kirchlichen Dogmatik von Karl Barth.* Düsseldorf: Neukirchener Verlag, 1988.

Orchard, W.E. *Modern Theories of Sin.* London: James Clarke & Co., 1910.

Ott, Heinrich. *Reality and Faith: The Theological Legacy of Dietrich Bonhoeffer.* Philadelphia: Fortress Press, 1966.

Owen, John. *The Death of Death.* Edinburgh: Banner of Truth Trust, 1959.

Pannenberg, Wolfhart. *Jesus - God and Man.* London: SCM Press, 1968.

Panikkar, Raymond. "Creation and Nothingness." *Theologische Zeitschrift ,* Volume 33, 1977, pp. 346-372.

Plantinga, Alvin C. *God, Freedom and Evil.* Grand Rapids: W.B. Eerdmans Publishing Co., 1974.

_____. *The Nature of Necessity.* Oxford: The Clarendon Press, 1974.

Plotinus. *The Enneads.* Translated by Stephen MacKenna. London: Faber and Faber, 1956.

Polanyi, Michael. *Personal Knowledge: Towards a Post-Critical Philosophy.* New York: Harper and Row, 1958.

Ramm, Bernard. *Offense to Reason: The Theology of Sin.* San Francisco: Harper and Row, 1985.

Reist, J.S. "Commencement, Continuation and Consummation: Karl Barth's Theology of Hope." *Evangelical Quarterly,* Volume 59, July 1987, pp. 195-214.

Ricoeur, Paul. "Evil, A Challenge to Philosophy and Theology." *Journal of the American Academy of Religion,* Volume 53, Number 4, December 1985, pp. 635-648.

_____. *The Conflict of Interpretation.* Evanston: Northwestern University Press, 1974.

Roberts, Richard. *A Theology on its Way?* Edinburgh: T & T Clark, 1991.

Robinson, James M. *The Beginnings of Dialectical Theology.* Atlanta: John Knox Press, 1968.

Ruether, Rosemary R. "The Left Hand of God in the Theology of Karl Barth; Karl Barth as a Mythopoeic Theologian." *Journal of Religious Thought,* Volume 25, Number 1, 1968-1969, pp. 3-26.

Russell, Bertrand. "Why I am Not a Christian," in *The Basic Writings of Bertrand Russell.* Edited by R.E. Egner and L.E. Denonn. London: George Allen and Unwin, 1961.

Russell, J.M. "Impassibility and Pathos in Barth's Idea of God." *Anglican Theological Review,* Volume 70, July 1988, pp. 221-232.

Sanford, John A. *Evil: The Shadow Side of Reality.* New York: Crossroads, 1981.

Schillebeeckx, O.P. *God The Future of Man.* New York: Sheed and Ward, 1968.

Schleiermacher, F.D.E. *The Christian Faith.* Edinburgh: T & T Clark, 1956.

Schmitt, K.R. *Death and After-Life in the Theologies of Karl Barth and John Hick.* Amsterdam: Rodopi, 1985.

Schulweis, H.M. "Karl Barth's Job: Morality and Theodicy." *Jewish Quarterly Review,* Volume 65, January 1975, pp. 156-167.

Scott, Mark A. *Theodicy: Failure and Promise within the Thought of Karl Barth, David Griffen and Jürgen Moltmann.* Unpublished Dissertation, Southern Baptist Theological Seminary, 1987.

Shippey, Robert C. *The Suffering of God in Karl Barth's Doctrine of Election and Reconciliation.* Unpublished Dissertation, Southern Baptist Theological Seminary, 1991.

Slater, R.H.L. *God and Human Suffering.* London: Epworth Press, 1941.

Soelle, Dorothee. *Suffering.* Philadelphia: Fortress Press, 1975.

Suchocki, M. H. *The End of Evil.* New York: State University of New York Press, 1988.

Surin, Kenneth. *Theology and the Problem of Evil.* Oxford: Basil Blackwell, 1986.

Sutcliffe, E.F. *Providence and Suffering in the Old and New Testaments.* London: Nelson Publishing Co., 1953.

Sykes, S.W., ed. *Karl Barth: Centenary Essays.* Cambridge: Cambride University Press, 1989.

Taubes, Jacob. "Theodicy and Theology: A Philosophical Analysis of Karl Barth's Dialectical Theology." *Journal of Religion,* Volume 34, October 1954, pp. 231-243.

Teilhard de Chardin, Pierre. *Le Milieu Divin* . London: Collins Fontana, 1927.

_____. *The Phenomenon of Man.* London: Collins, 1959.

Thompson, John. *Christ in Perspective in the Theology of Karl Barth.* Edinburgh: St. Andrew's Press, 1978.

Tilley, T. "Hume on God and Evil." *Journal of the American Academy of Religion,* Volume 56, Winter 1988, pp. 703-726.

Tillich, Paul. *Systematic Theology.* Volumes I and II. Chicago: University of Chicago Press, 1951.

Torrance, Alan. "Does God Suffer?", in *Christ in Our Place.* Exeter: Paternoster Press, 1991.

Torrance, T.F. *Karl Barth: An Introduction to His Early Theology 1910 - 1931.* London: SCM Press, 1962.

_____. *Karl Barth.* Edinburgh: T & T Clark, 1990.

Ulrich, Simon. *A Theology of Auschwitz.* London: SPCK, 1978.

Van de Beek, A. *Why?- On Suffering, Guilt, and God.* Grand Rapids: W.B. Eerdmans Publishing Co., 1990.

von Balthasar, Hans Urs. *The Theology of Karl Barth.* New York: Holt, Rinehart & Winston, 1971.

von Loewenich, W. *Luther's Theology of the Cross.* Belfast: Christian Journals, 1976.

von Rad, Gerhard. *Genesis: A Commentary.* London: SCM Press, 1956.

_____. *Old Testament Theology.* London: SCM Press, 1957.

Van Til, Cornelius. *The New Modernism: An Appraisal of the Theology of Barth and Brunner.* London: James Clarke & Co., 1946.

Ward, Keith. *Rational Theology and the Creativity of God.* Oxford: Basil Blackwell, 1982.

Watson, G. "Karl Barth and St. Anselm's Theological Programme." *Scottish Journal of Theology*, Volume 30, Number 1, 1977, pp. 31-45.

Weatherhead, Leslie D. *Salute to a Sufferer.* London: Epworth Press, 1962.

_____. *Why Do Men Suffer?* London: Student Christian Movement Press, 1935.

Webster, John B. "The Firmest Grasp of the Real: Barth on Original Sin." *Toronto Journal of Theology*, Volume 4, Spring 1988, pp. 19-29.

Wenham, John W. *The Enigma of Evil.* Leicester: Inter-Varsity Press, 1985.

Westermann, Claus. *Genesis.* Edinburgh: T & T Clark, 1987.

Whale, J.S. *The Problem of Evil.* London: SCM Press, 1936.

Whitehouse, W.A. *The Authority of Grace: Essays in Response to Karl Barth.* Edinburgh: T & T Clark, 1981.

Whitla, W.J. "Sin and Redemption in Whitehead and Teilhard de Chardin." *Anglican Theological Review*, Volume 47, January 1965, pp. 81-95.

Whyte, Adam G. *The Natural History of Evil.* London: Watts & Co., 1920.

Wiesel, Elie. *Night.* Translated by S. Rodway. London: MacGibbon and Kee, 1960.

Williams, N.P. *The Ideas of the Fall and of Original Sin.* London: Longman's, Green and Co., 1927.

Willis, Robert E. "Bonhoeffer and Barth on Jewish Suffering: Reflections on the Relationship between Theology and Moral Sensibility." *Journal of Ecumenical Studies*, Volume 24, Fall 1987, pp. 598-615.

Wright, N.G. *A Study of the Relationships Between Karl Barth and the Evangelical Tradition, with Particular Reference to the Concept of Nothingness.* Unpublished Doctoral Dissertation, University of Glasgow, 1987.

Young, E.J. "Interpretation of Genesis 1:2." *Westminster Theological Journal,* Volume 23, May 1961, pp. 151-178.

Young, F.M. "Insight or Incoherence? The Greek Fathers on God and Evil." *Journal of Ecclesiastical History,* Volume 24, April 1973, pp. 113-126.

Zizioulas, John D. *Being as Communion.* Crestwood: St Vladimir's Seminary Press, 1985.